Y0-ASQ-592

Early identification of skill needs in Europe

Susanne Liane Schmidt,
Klaus Schomann,
Manfred Tessaring (eds.)

Cedefop Reference series; 40
Luxembourg: Office for Official Publications of the European Communities, 2003

A great deal of additional information on the European Union is available on
the Internet. It can be accessed through the Europa server (http://europa.eu.int).

Cataloguing data can be found at the end of this publication.

Luxembourg:
Office for Official Publications of the European Communities, 2003

ISBN 92-896-0202-3
ISSN 1680-7089

© European Centre for the Development of Vocational Training, 2003
All rights reserved.

Designed by Colibri Ltd. – Greece
Printed in Belgium

The **European Centre for the Development of Vocational Training** (Cedefop) is the European Union's reference centre for vocational education and training. We provide information on and analyses of vocational education and training systems, policies, research and practice. Cedefop was established in 1975 by Council Regulation (EEC) No. 337/75.

Europe 123
GR-570 01 Thessaloniki (Pylea)

Postal address: PO Box 22427
GR-551 02 Thessaloniki

Tel (30) 23 10 49 01 11, Fax (30) 23 10 49 00 20
E-mail: info@cedefop.eu.int
Homepage: www.cedefop.eu.int
Interactive website: www.trainingvillage.gr

Edited by: **Cedefop**
Manfred Tessaring, *Project manager*

Published under the responsibility of:
Johan van Rens, *Director*
Stavros Stavrou, *Deputy Director*

Table of contents

- *Susanne Liane Schmidt, Klaus Schömann, Manfred Tessaring*
  Introduction. Early recognition of skill needs in Europe — 3

- *Manfred Kremer*
  Welcome and opening of the European conference
  'Early recognition of skill requirements in Europe',
  30 May 2002, Social Science Research Center Berlin — 11

- *Stavros Stavrou*
  Early recognition of skill requirements in Europe — 18

PART I   Initiatives and research on 'Early identification of skill needs' in Europe at national level

- *Susanne Liane Schmidt*
  Early identification of qualification needs in Germany –
  the FreQueNz research network — 24

- *Mike Coles*
  Qualifications for the future — 42

- *Jordi Planas*
  Developing prospective tools for the observation
  of skill requirements in Spain — 56

- *Mario Gatti*
  Network of national surveys on skill needs in Italy — 63

- *Frank Cörvers*
  Labour market forecasting in the Netherlands: a top-down approach — 72

PART II   Initiatives at sectoral level

- *Jean-Louis Kirsch*
  Industrial maintenance in France: new and traditional
  skill requirements — 88

- *Tom Leney*
  Identifying future qualification needs in the transport sector in the
  United Kingdom: has the scenarios methodology a role? — 108

- *Martin Curley*
  Addressing the ICT skills shortage in Europe — 122

- *Kathrin Schnalzer, Gerd Gidion, Miriam Thum, Helmut Kuwan*
  New skill requirements in logistics — 128

- *Gert Alaby*
  Skill requirements in the care of the elderly – the Swedish example   142

- *Norbert Bromberger, Helen Diedrich-Fuhs*
  Information system for early recognition of sectoral trends –
  results obtained for the construction industry   151

PART III Initiatives for specific target groups and SMEs

- *Gerard Hughes, Jerry J. Sexton*
  Forecasting female shares of employment by occupation in Ireland   164

- *Beate Zeller*
  Services in complex structures – trends in the way skills
  are developing in low skilled work   178

- *Peter Wordelmann*
  Early recognition of international qualifications for SMEs   189

- *Lothar Abicht, Rainer Werner*
  New qualifications in SMEs for societal and technological change –
  skilling of IT users   207

PART IV Initiatives at regional level and in countries in transition

- *Ferran Mañé, Josep Oliver*
  A note on the evolution of labour
  supply in Spain and its implications at regional level   230

- *Olga Strietska-Ilina*
  Qualitative versus quantitative methods of anticipating skill needs:
  perspective of a country in transition   242

- *Pal Tamas*
  Skill markets in a learning society: transformation
  and vocational reforms in Hungary   264

- *Lewis Kerr*
  A demand-side analysis of SME skills needs
  in regions of five candidate countries   286

Résumé and perspectives
- *Manfred Tessaring*
  Identification of future skill requirements. Activities and approaches
  for European cooperation   306

Annex
- List of authors   328
- Abbreviations   331

Introduction
Early recognition of skill needs in Europe
European Conference, Berlin, 30/31 May 2002

Increasing globalisation and internationalisation of labour markets and the ensuing changes in education and training systems represent a challenge for the countries of Europe. The Lisbon European Council set an ambitious goal in 2000: *'The Union has today set itself a new strategic goal for the next decade: to become the most competitive and dynamic knowledge-based economy in the world, capable of sustainable economic growth with more and better jobs and greater social cohesion.'* [1] This goal was subsequently made more specific, especially in terms of establishing lifelong learning as a basic principle governing education and training systems.

The questions that now come to the foreground are what form sustainable skills could take and how education and training systems need to be structured, in order to master these new challenges and achieve these goals.

To explore these questions, the German Federal Ministry of Education and Research (BMBF) and the European Centre for the Development of Vocational Training (Cedefop) jointly held a two-day conference in May 2002 involving experts from various European countries. The conference, which was held at the *Wissenschaftszentrum* in Berlin (Social Science Research Center Berlin), focused on the early identification of skills needs and on intensifying international cooperation in this area.

A total of 45 experts from Germany and other countries attended the conference. Representatives of political institutions and research institutes in EU Member States (Germany, France, Greece, UK, Ireland, Italy, the Netherlands, Spain and Sweden) were joined by experts from candidate countries (Estonia, Lithuania, Slovenia, the Czech Republic and Hungary). Cedefop and the European Training Foundation (ETF) represented the EU level, while business was represented by a speaker from Intel on behalf of Career Space, a consortium of major ICT companies.

Key aspects of the topic, presentations of results and other conference objectives, were discussed in the context of creating a single European

---

[1] These and other European Council conclusions can be downloaded in various languages from http://ue.eu.int/presid/conclusions.htm.

education and labour market. The emphasis was on research aimed at the recognition and early identification of skills needs. The field of early identification of skills needs is becoming increasingly important: in a world of work that is experiencing turbulent times, political and business players are having to respond ever faster to change. To do this they depend on reliable information. As the countries of the European Union grow closer, and with the accession of candidate countries on the horizon, it is becoming ever more important to exchange information in order to make it possible for players to identify in good time the way in which skills are developing. The early identification of skills can greatly help training systems become more future-oriented and prevent or lessen future skills mismatches on the labour market.

As the conference showed, what is needed to achieve this is, first of all, an exchange of good practices on the early identification of skills needs and the available methods. The conference was also intended to lay the foundations for future joint procedures and for developing a European network.

Conference: Early recognition of skill requirements in Europe
Berlin 30-31 May 2002, Social Science Research Center Berlin

Thursday, 30 May

Opening
Welcome: Federal Ministry of Education and Research, *Manfred Kremer*
Speech of the Cedefop Deputy Director, *Stavros Stavrou*

I. Initiatives on 'Early recognition of skill requirements' and research projects in Europe
Moderation: *Manfred Tessaring*
Short presentations and discussion of initiatives in Member States
Introduction: *Klaus Schömann, Susanne Liane Schmidt*
United Kingdom: *Mike Coles*
Spain: *Jordi Planas*
Italy: *Mario Gatti*
Summary: *Frank Córvers*

II. Initiatives on 'Early recognition': best practice examples for different sectors
Moderation: *Klaus Schömann*
Short presentations and discussion
Industrial maintenance, Jean-Louis Kirsch
Transport sector, *Tom Leney*
ICT sector, *Martin Curley*
Logistics, *Kathrin Schnalzer, Miriam Thum*
Healthcare, *Gert Alaby*
Construction industry, *Norbert Bromberger*

Friday, 31 May

III. Initiatives on 'Early recognition': best practice examples for specific target groups and SMEs
Moderation: *Susanne Liane Schmidt*
Short presentations and discussion
Gender, *Gerry Hughes*
Disadvantaged/low skilled, *Beate Zeller*
Early recognition of international qualifications, *Peter Wordelmann*
New qualifications in SMEs, *Lothar Abicht*

IV. Initiatives on 'Early recognition': best practice examples at regional and European level
Moderation: *Manfred Tessaring*
Skill shortages in Spain, *Ferran Mañé*
EU and candidate countries, *Olga Strietska-Ilina*
Qualification systems at the turning point of societal modernisation, *Pal Tamas*
Regional initiatives in five candidate countries, *Lewis Kerr*

V. Final discussion
Moderation: *Klaus Schömann*

VI. Preparation of an international congress early 2003
Moderation: *Manfred Tessaring*
Discussion: Objectives, agenda, networking, cooperation

Main conference topics and conference proceedings

The main elements of the conference were presentations of national initiatives and regional, sectoral and target-group-oriented activities designed to achieve early identification of skills needs. Various levels were considered, namely the micro, intermediate and macro levels. It also became clear that a wide range of approaches were involved, from 'traditional' quantitative projections to more qualitative approaches such as scenarios and case studies. In the conference proceedings presented here, individual contributions follow the order of the conference programme.

The papers are presented under four subject headings (echoing conference sections):
- Initiatives on early identification of skills needs in Europe at national level
- Initiatives on early identification of skills needs in various sectors
- Initiatives on early identification of skills needs for specific target groups and SMEs
- Initiatives on early identification of skills needs at regional level and in countries in transition.

Initiatives on 'Early identification of skill needs' in Europe at national level

Under this subject heading, several individual national initiatives are presented by way of example. The introductory presentation *(S.L. Schmidt)* provides an overview of the early identification initiative of the German Federal Ministry of Education and Research and the existing research network. The British contribution *(M. Coles)* focuses on the problem of the reliability of data sources and of forecasts of, and scenarios for, future skills needs. The Spanish contribution *(J. Planas)* addresses the development of forecasting tools and the development of a "skills observatory" that will collect and evaluate skills needs. The next contribution *(M. Gatti)* presents the Italian survey network for new skills needs. The last contribution under this heading *(F. Cörvers)* considers methods and results of quantitative labour market and skills projections in the Netherlands.

This Part gives readers a good insight into established networks and activities related to the early identification of skills, which have adopted a variety of approaches and methods. The fundamental problems have proved to be very similar in many countries. This applies, for example, to the networking of different vocational training research players and hence the collation of different data sources and analytical procedures, as well as to the long-term reliability of quantitative skills forecasts.

Initiatives on 'Early identification of skill needs' at sectoral level

This Part focuses on contributions investigating future skills needs in various sectors: industrial maintenance, the automotive and transport sector, information and communications, logistics, health care and construction.

The French presentation *(J.-L. Kirsch)* on industrial maintenance shows that owing to organisational and technological innovations enterprises will be seeking new skills in the future. The contribution from the automotive and transport sector *(T. Leney)* outlines the scenario method of identifying future skills needs in the UK transport sector. A contribution from Intel *(M. Curley)*, representing the Career Space Consortium, discusses the broad area of the information and communications sector and in particular the skills gaps apparent within it. The contribution on logistics *(K. Schnalzer et al.)* concentrates on in-company skills development by means of qualitative and quantitative analysis. The Swedish contribution *(G. Alaby)* on the health care sector identifies the ageing of society as a factor triggering new skills needs. The last contribution in this Part *(N. Bromberger and H. Diedrich-Fuhs)* addresses the early identification of company skills trends in the construction sector in Germany.

These contributions illustrate the variety of approaches to specific subject areas in the early identification of skills needs. Job monitoring, company case studies, expert discussions and networks of specialists are all used to answer specific questions about skills trends, as are scenario-based methods and statistical evaluations. However, it is not possible immediately to transfer individual results to other European countries, although parallel trends can be identified.

Initiatives on 'Early identification of skill needs' for particular target groups and SMEs

Skills trends have specific implications for different target groups, and these are brought out in the first two contributions in this Part. The presentation on forecasting the proportion of women in employment in Ireland *(G. Hughes and J.J. Sexton)* analyses data on occupations and investigates future areas of activity in which female employment in particular will increase. The forecast makes it possible to assess future employment opportunities and to develop measures supporting the women's participation in employment. The next contribution *(B. Zeller)* outlines the specific situation of low-skilled people. Despite the forecast reduction in simple jobs, work requirements in this area are changing. This paper from the German early recognition initiative shows, by way of example, how enterprise changes affect the performance of simple jobs and the skills required of employees.

The last two contributions in this Part concentrate on skills trends that are posing particular challenges, above all for SMEs (small and medium enterprises). The development of international skills is also becoming increasingly relevant to smaller enterprises: the rapid globalisation of the economy means that ever more jobs involve internationally oriented tasks, as shown in the paper on early recognition of international skills *(P. Wordelmann)*. However, changes in society and technology are also necessitating the development of new skills, as required, for example, by the use of particular IT applications. These problems are described in the contribution from the German early recognition initiative on new skills in SMEs, with particular emphasis on training IT users *(L. Abicht and R. Werner)*.

The targeted approach adopted makes it clear that experience acquired at sectoral level can be incorporated into various other fields of application in order to achieve positive effects on employment for specific target groups.

Initiatives on 'Early identification of skill needs' at regional level and in countries in transition

The first paper under this heading *(F. Mane)* looks at skills gaps and worker shortages in Spain. It focuses on the characteristics of demographic change and the results of two forecasts, one for Spain as a whole and one for the region of Catalonia.

The next three contributions address the specific problems of countries that are candidates for accession to the EU. First comes the Czech contribution *(O. Strietska-Ilina)*, which offers an insight into the prospects for a country in transition and discusses qualitative and quantitative methods of forecasting skills needs. Next, the Hungarian paper *(P. Tamas)* outlines the pressure on skills systems to change as a result of the modernisation of society. Finally the representative of the European Training Foundation *(L. Kerr)* presents initiatives for forecasting skills needs by discussing the goals, methods and results of a demand-based skills survey carried out in selected regions of five candidate countries.

The contributions under this heading show that systems for the early identification of skills display area-specific characteristics. Their design and method of implementation must therefore take into account the features of the sector, region and country.

Conference results

The conference aimed to initiate cooperation throughout Europe, to increase the exchange of information on approaches, methods and results in respect of early identification of skills needs, and to instigate the formation of a transregional and transnational network. Such a network was not intended to be restricted to the research sphere, but to include the relevant stakeholders in all fields – policy, practice, social partners, etc.

All participants unanimously confirmed the necessity of these objectives, not least because (as shown by the papers brought together in this volume) a very wide range of methods and approaches are being used by different countries and experts, and as yet these activities are insufficiently transparent. Some countries have already made a lot of progress, while others are still in the early stages, either owing to a lack of appropriate experience and competence or because the relevant organisational and statistical infrastructure or political support is as yet inadequate. However, it is often difficult to gain access to this information (not least for language reasons). So far there has not been much cooperation across national borders, despite some recent progress.

In the plenary session that closed the conference, it was argued that EU-level research into early identification should not be restricted to a discussion of methodological and theoretical aspects and results. Possible courses of action should also be developed in support of policy, practice and the social partners, with emphasis on the sectoral and regional levels. It was also argued that a further objective should be to develop 'early recognition or identification standards', which could help to match skills needs and skills profiles. This could also make it easier to compare national methods and results. Countries still in the early stages of researching early identification or currently developing or planning the relevant infrastructure (including candidate countries) should be more closely involved in this.

Against this background, the conference presented in this publication not only offers an inventory of activities in various European countries but also represents a starting point for intensive future cooperation, both between experts and research institutes in different countries and between research, policy and practice. This exchange is aimed at accelerating the continued development of methods and approaches and of mutual learning via transnational cooperation in research. Furthermore, it is essential for policy-makers and practitioners (including the social partners) to be involved from the outset. In this way, all those responsible are made aware that it is necessary for education and training to be sustainably designed on the basis of specific information and recommendations, and they are encouraged to provide staffing, financial and organisational support for the efforts involved.

These are some ways in which cooperation and transparency could be promoted:

- Establishment of a transnational *network*, for which an organisational framework needs to be created, equipped with the necessary staff and resources.
- Creation of a *website* or *Extranet* as a discussion platform for network members. Appropriate infrastructures are already available and could be linked with one another, such as the website of the German FreQueNz Early Recognition Initiative and Cedefop's electronic communication platforms (Electronic Training Village, Cedefop Research Arena and European Research Overview).
- A mutual *exchange* of methods, approaches, projects and results as regards the early identification of skills needs, via regular documented expert conferences or seminars involving researchers, policy-makers and practitioners in various countries.
- Specific *cooperation* between research institutes in various countries on particular projects, including expert visits and exchange.
- Preparation and continued updating of an '*early identification handbook*' and a '*European report on skills development*', which should also be made available on the Internet.
- Development of an *information and documentation database*, involving all members of the network and giving access to external sources.

The final paper in these conference proceedings *(M. Tessaring)* summarises the early identification activities and discusses the prospects for European-level cooperation.

Other planned activities

The proceedings of the European conference on early identification are being published in both English and German. Cedefop is publishing the English version, while the German version forms part of the FreQueNz series. [2]

The contributions and findings of the European conference held in May 2002 are also being used in preparing and orienting an international conference on early identification of skills needs. This conference will be held at Cedefop's headquarters in Thessaloniki in May 2003, on the occasion of the Greek Presidency of the EU.

Susanne Liane Schmidt,
Klaus Schömann,
Manfred Tessaring

---

[2] Schmidt, S.L.; Schömann, K.; Tessaring, M., eds. Früherkennung von Qualifikationserfordernissen in Europa. Qualifikationen erkennen – Berufe gestalten. H.-J. Bullinger, ed. Bielefeld: Bertelsmann, 2003.

Welcome and opening of the European conference
'Early recognition of skill requirements in Europe'
30 May 2002, Social Science Research Center Berlin [1]

Manfred Kremer, Federal Ministry of Education and Research (BMBF), Bonn, Germany

Ladies and Gentlemen,

It is a great pleasure to welcome you to the *Wissenschaftszentrum* here in Berlin today.

Early recognition of skill requirements is an important instrument in the context of a preventive employment and training policy and therefore also an important element with a view to achieving the goal set by the European Council in Lisbon, namely to make Europe the most dynamic and competitive knowledge-based economy in the world.

Allow me to mention just two aspects which highlight the importance of an effective early recognition system. In Germany, there are currently almost four million persons registered as unemployed. But at the same time almost one out of every ten German companies reports job vacancies which they are unable to fill. The number of job vacancies has risen for the third time in the course of this year, and currently stands at some 520 000. This contradictory situation – high unemployment on the one hand and unfilled job vacancies on the other – is largely the result of a frequent mismatch between skill supply and skill demand. Although an effective early recognition system providing timely and appropriate conclusions for employment and skilling policy could perhaps not entirely solve this problem, it could at least partly alleviate the situation.

The second aspect which highlights the importance of a training und skilling policy oriented towards developments in the employment system in very general terms is the demographic development with which we are

---

[1] *Wissenschaftszentrum Berlin (WZB).*

confronted not only here in Germany but also in most other European countries. In the Federal Republic, the number of young recruits will continually fall from 2010 onwards. Whereas almost two-thirds of the population was still under 50 in 2000, this age-bracket will account for only a good half of the population by the year 2030, with a corresponding increase in the proportion of the over 50s. These developments may trigger an exacerbation of existing allocation problems in the training and job market. Whereas certain sectors and regions show a dearth of specialised workers and training places, other regions and future-oriented sectors of the economy find it impossible to fill the existing supply of jobs and training places. And this is true not only of future-oriented sectors of the economy, but indeed also of many traditional areas in which skill requirements are also rapidly changing. In this context, early recognition of skill requirements has two principal tasks. On the one hand, it has the task of guiding the adaptation of the structure and content of training supply to changes in the employment system with the shortest possible time lag. On the other hand, in view of demographic factors, it will no longer be possible – as was often the case in the past – to largely cover new skill requirements by freshly trained young recruits; it will in addition be necessary to invest more in the targeted continuing training of those already in the workplace. This is particularly true of senior members of the workforce, often premature drop outs from working life due to failure to continually develop their qualifications and thereby their employability.

In general, all the forecasts indicate that the main trends can be expected to continue, i.e.
- a shift in economic structures away from the manufacturing industries into the services sector;
- broader, and frequently also higher, skill requirements in a considerable number of workplaces.

In Germany, we intend to cater for this demand for high- and top-level skills not only by means of our higher education system, but also via our differentiated system of initial and continuing vocational training. However at the same time current forecasts indicate that fields of activity involving less complex requirements are by no means expected to disappear completely but will in fact always account for a substantial proportion of job supply. But since skill requirements will also tend to rise at this level, skilling is also necessary at this level.

We have therefore initiated a whole series of reforms in recent years and considerably increased federal government investment in education and training since 1998. Measures to promote university students have been substantially improved and paved the way for the introduction of new course structures, e.g. the introduction of the Bachelor and Master degrees reflecting customary international practice. The service regulations for academic staff have been reformed to substantially improve the incentives for high-quality research and teaching and to attract top-level talent. Moreover, in the framework of our alliance for employment, training and competitiveness, we have also laid substantial foundations for a root-and-branch reform of our initial and continuing vocational training system with the social partners and the Federal States (*Länder*) over the last three years. Within the alliance for employment, the federal government, economic associations and trade unions, with the participation of the *Länder*, have agreed on common guidelines, objectives and concrete steps for the development of all key areas of vocational educational and training policy which we are now rolling out step by step. Moreover, a substantial modernisation of our vocational training system has been initiated in recent years. A considerable number of training occupations have been modernised and new occupations have been created in key areas of industry and employment, particularly in growth sectors such as information technology (IT) and the media. In a similar vein, we are in the process of adapting our system of further training occupations – i.e. state recognised continuing training programmes which can be completed following vocational training and a certain degree of occupational experience – to the new developments, IT and media occupations being a good example.

In the second half of the 1990s, we developed a whole raft of new training occupations for IT and the media which in the opinion of the sector largely cover the skill requirements in this field. Whereas there were a total of some 14 000 trainees in this field in 1998, today's figure stands at over 70 000, clearly ahead of the target of 60 000 training places by the end of 2003 set in our alliance for employment with the employers.

Following on from this initiative, we have created a modern IT continuing training system in collaboration with the trade unions and employers' associations.

The regulation on the introduction of these State recognised continuing training occupations entered into force just recently. The programmes in question provide continuing training opportunities for those having completed the new IT training occupations, as well as for the many 'lateral entrants' in this occupational field: as many some 80% of the 1.6 million IT experts have no relevant vocational or university qualifications. The new further training occupations present an opportunity for this target group to certify their qualifications and make them transferable in the labour market. The three-tier system leads to qualifications for activities currently frequently carried out by university graduates. With the support of the Federal Institute for Vocational Training (BIBB), the social partners and the federal government have thus created instruments with which the sector can effectively combat the dearth of specialists in the IT field.

Since these further training occupations lead to qualifications for activities hitherto frequently carried out by university graduates – and incidentally this is also true of many of our recognised continuing vocational training certificates – we wish to use this as a step towards the recognition of the equivalence of vocational and academic education and the combination of vocational training and a further course of higher education. This is a field in which we have made only cautious progress in Germany compared to other European countries – so much so that in the opinion of the federal government and the social partners, we are wasting essential opportunities to tap the full skilling potential. We will attempt to underpin this initiative by a ECTS-compatible assessment of IT certificates based on performance points, to be transferable not only nationally, but also transnationally, in accordance with the decisions of the Barcelona Council.

Developments in our employment system – and here globalisation, internationalisation and the rapid pace of technological change in particular come to mind – imply constantly changing skill requirements of the both the workforce and the up and coming generation. Lifelong learning is the strategy by means of which all our countries and indeed also the European Union intend to confront this challenge. You are all familiar with the reports, memoranda and decisions at EU level which have made an essential contribution to reinforcing relevant developments in Europe, both at the level of in each individual Member State and at the European level itself.

In the Federal Republic, we have launched a large-scale action programme entitled 'Lifelong learning', for which a budget of EUR 250 m has been allocated over the coming years. It is an extremely broadly-based action programme involving all the major players in the vocational training field. The various lines of action range from the development of new initial and continuing training strategies for so-called disadvantaged groups of society and the lesser skilled, development and demonstration projects to promote regional cooperation and the networking of the players in the field, the development of concepts for the systematic use of informal learning in the working process and assessment and certification of informally acquired knowledge to the development of essential elements of quality assurance for continuing vocational training. We see our initiatives in a European context and commensurate with the resolutions of Lisbon, Stockholm, Barcelona and the recently initiated Bruges initiative of the Directors-General for Vocational

Training. We wish to play a more active role, in particular as far as implementation of the Bruges initiative is concerned, and make a more targeted contribution of our know how to the development of practice and labour market-oriented initial and continuing training. Our main focus in this context is quality assurance in vocational training in the EU, transparency and transnational transferability of qualifications and certificates and joint development of training programmes.

I believe that the general conditions I have outlined clearly illustrate that in the context of international competition, the production factor 'knowledge', hand in hand with a quality- and future-oriented initial and continuing training system, constitute a key factor to safeguard the individual Member States and the European Union as a whole as attractive locations for industry. New employment trends and early recognition of emerging changes in employment and occupational fields must be observed as far as possible to prevent a mismatch between skill supply and demand resulting in a dearth of skilled labour and to ensure that training does not lag behind labour market trends. It is also necessary to foster a broadly-based development of learning in the labour process. Because one thing is clear: lifelong learning cannot be achieved by means of formal continuing training programmes and courses alone. On the contrary, lifelong learning above all implies targeted utilisation of learning opportunities in the workplace and the social environment and validation of the results of informal learning.

For this reason, we need sufficiently reliable and substantiated information on emerging trends. In Germany, early recognition is on the one hand an information base which enables the social partners to adapt initial and continuing vocational training to the specific processes of change in the labour market; on the other hand, it serves individuals as a basis to assess their own specific training needs and independently understand and implement lifelong learning as an active means of shaping their own working and training careers.

The decision on the early recognition of new skill requirements was consequently one of the very first reforms adopted by the alliance for employment, training and competitiveness which I mentioned earlier. This decision is the basis for development of the initiative on the early recognition von skill requirements sponsored by the Federal Ministry of Education and Research.

This initiative, which will be presented to you in detail in the course of our conference and in the conference proceedings, comprises a package of inter-related projects implemented by the social partners, the Federal Institute for Vocational Training (BIBB) and other scientific institutions.

The objectives of these initiatives are as follows:
1. ongoing qualitative identification of those fields of activity in which changes are observed;
2. definition of specific skills and qualifications which will be required in these fields of activity in the future;
3. identification of current related skill supply as well as deficits and gaps in supply; and
4. testing a whole range of different early recognition methods.

A number of these projects have now been underway for almost three years and a whole array of results have already been presented.

A further step is to analyse the results to date and to reflect and follow up new impetus.

In this context it is necessary:
1. to test the methods used to determine skill requirements for their efficiency and implementability and to find ways and means of implementing these efficient methods of analysis in the training arena;
2. to intensify cooperation and exchange of information in existing information networks. The initiation of an ongoing exchange of information and experience on examples of 'best practice' in the identification of skill requirements and the creation of greater transparency on new skill requirements could give fresh momentum to the vocational training reform process;
3. to feed the skill requirements identified in the various fields of activity, sectors, branches and certain target groups into the training policy debate.

In the case of Germany, this means that the results must be made available to the social partners as a basis not only to modernise and promote new developments within the vocational training system but also as the basis for a new learning culture in industry.

Regardless of the experience already acquired in this field, it is also important for us to look beyond our own borders. We wish to contribute our experience to date to the European training area. We wish to ascertain what experience has been acquired by other countries and what we can learn from such experience.

For all these reasons, it was and is only logical for us to organise this European conference along with the European Centre for the Development of Vocational Training, Cedefop.

The conference and its proceedings will focus on an exchange of information on early recognition initiatives and the results of selected examples from various European countries. We also wish to have an exchange of views on the preparation of a conference to be organised by Cedefop in 2003.

Such a conference could not least decide to set up a European network for the early recognition of skill requirements. Because many of the general conditions and developments I have described are also to be found in other European countries, albeit in different forms and against the background of different national education/training systems and specific forms of labour organisation. This is why we must continue to learn from each other within the European Union, seeking examples of best practice and examining and implementing such models against the background of the appropriate specific national conditions. We regard support of this transfer of know how as one of our most important tasks. As I mentioned at the outset, we wish to draw benefit from this exchange with other EU states in the context of our own vocational training reforms. But we also wish to make a more active contribution of our profile and our know-how to labour market and practice-oriented vocational training in Europe.

I am therefore very pleased that we have managed to organise this conference and I look forward to intensive discussions and positive results.

Early recognition of skill requirements in Europe

Stavros Stavrou, European Centre for the Development of Vocational Training (Cedefop), Thessaloniki, Greece

Ladies and Gentlemen,

People, whether as individuals or in formal or informal groupings, have always longed to be able to see what the future held and have devised and used a whole range of organisations and instruments for doing so - for political purposes, in times of war, or to satisfy other public or private interests. Among the examples that immediately spring to mind are the oracles at Delphi and Dodona in ancient Greece, the medicine men of the North American Indians, astrology, and the reading of palms and coffee-grounds - some of them still popular today. It is strange that people often do not seem to realise how little scope for initiative life would hold and how boring it would be if there were no longer any surprises in store.

While the seriousness behind these various means of fortune-telling leaves room for doubt, the same cannot be said of the many attempts made to predict future trends for purposes of educational planning and labour market research, particularly since the end of the Second World War. Research institutes, scientists, and other experts of repute have invested a great deal of time, money and thought in such projects and come up with very sophisticated models and tools. I need only remind you of the OECD's Mediterranean Regional Project in of the 1960s. Even so, with hindsight most of these attempts proved unrealistic for various reasons when the results were compared with actual trends and figures.

Without wanting to appear pernickety, the last two words of the title of this conference - 'in Europe' - look to me rather over-ambitious. It might have been more correct to talk of 'skill requirements in a number of European countries' and keep the present title with its more demanding subject-matter to be tackled at some future date when many of the trends as regards content and organisation of work and technology on the one hand and occupations or occupational groups on the other look likely to converge beyond national frontiers, making the exchange of experience and knowledge and the pursuit of synergy in Europe and wider afield even more necessary.

It would, for instance, be desirable for existing national networks to be linked together without selfishness and rivalry to give a European coverage. In doing so one would have to be careful to distinguish and separate the various purposes and objectives, such as monitoring and reporting or analysis and research.

During this conference - the first multinational working meeting of its kind - we should try to discuss and learn from one another about such matters as:
- methodologies and approaches;
- the choice of sectors and relevant occupations or occupational groups;
- national and/or regional trends;
- possibilities for action on the part of the political powers and other stakeholders.

We will probably find that in some areas such as computer science, transport, the environment and the caring professions the trends are very similar and even converging. Slowly but surely we are witnessing the emergence not just of a European labour market, but one that sooner or later will be supplemented by a European education and training market. Competition will then increasingly make itself felt. Common standards and benchmarks for occupational profiles as well as training quality indicators and a process of quality assurance will then be indispensable. A kind of Bologna process for vocational training is already beginning to show itself after the Bruges initiative. The sovereignty of national governments in matters of education and training policy that is underpinned by treaty means that any discussions and agreements must be voluntary. This is no disadvantage - on the contrary - persuasion has in the longer term always proved more effective than diktats from above, or from outside.

Turning to the relationship of training to the world of work, the training one receives need not inevitably determine the job one actually does. Sometimes people with different educational and training backgrounds may be - and indeed are - employed in the same type of work. The scope and flexibility which this affords is more than welcome so far as politicians are concerned because it widens the field of choice when deciding what measures are most appropriate in any given case.

It is my impression that we have all learned from the past and have become more careful in our attitude to forecasts. And very rightly so. This is noticeable even in our choice of words - the fact that we now tend to talk of 'early recognition, identification or anticipation' rather than 'predictions' or 'projections' suggests a degree of caution. And the fact that we look for alternative options is a sign of progress compared with the previous tendency to regard forecasts as definitive and sound. This testifies to a more scientific approach that is not far removed from political reality but remains closely linked to it, and seems to be leading to a fruitful dialectic.

Faced with the question of whether we should in future give methodological problems equal weighting with those of subject-matter, or whether we should give either aspect preference, my answer would spontaneously be that we should give priority to subjects or sectors and the corresponding occupations but without leaving the methodologies and methods, which are necessary, uncritically to lead their own life. We should concentrate on the practical feasibility of our early recognition efforts, since otherwise we would risk finding ourselves in an academic ivory tower. The practical demands are easily discernible and even force themselves upon us. Public funds are increasingly in short supply at all levels, cost-benefit analyses with their various benchmarks are being carried out more frequently before projects are approved, and individuals are more often being asked to meet the cost for themselves. As a result everyone – individuals, government authorities or sponsors – want to see some concrete and useful result, even if only in the narrow material sense. Our work should be aimed first and foremost at giving a greater and deeper meaning to political action. This is particularly necessary at a time when politicians' credibility and the esteem in which they are held has reached a low, even in Europe.

To be somewhat more specific, I should like to draw attention to a matter deserving of the highest political priority at all levels, namely combating unemployment with consistent, effective measures designed to bring long-term success. NAPs – the national employment action plans – have for some time now been produced annually by all EU countries and as far as possible implemented and evaluated. Here political wishful thinking or window-dressing are definitely on the way out. One cannot pull the wool over the eyes of either neutral (by which I mean European) bodies nor the citizens of Europe in the long run. The vast payments made, for example, by the European structural funds, the Leonardo da Vinci programme and other sources of finance for education and training have to be very well justified, even if the cause-and-effect relationship is sometimes very difficult or even impossible to demonstrate. Here our work can and must produce results in the form of probable and plausible trends that have been thoroughly discussed, are soundly based and serve to guide and instruct politicians and practitioners in their action.

On the other hand, methods used for early recognition cannot simply be taken for granted as reliable or undisputed. They need to be put to debate and scrutinised carefully before being made available to anyone interested in the form, say, of a Manual for the Early Recognition of Qualification Requirements. Even countries or regions that have already made good progress in this respect can still learn from the experience and best practices of others. But it would be particularly useful for those who still have a great deal of catching up to do and need considerable help and support. Merely providing them with a blueprint in the form of an uncritical transfer of know-how would not be appropriate because this method has failed in the past. Instead the recipient countries or regions need to study the experience of other countries critically against the background of their overall context of origin and assess it before trying to apply it, suitably adapted, to their own particular case.

If our conference is to be successful and we are to have taken not just one but several steps forward by tomorrow afternoon, a follow-up meeting in Thessaloniki in the spring of next year, perhaps to coincide with the Greek presidency, could then look like a real possibility.

PART I
Initiatives and research on 'Early identification of skill needs' in Europe at national level

Under this subject heading, several individual national initiatives are presented by way of example. They give readers a valuable insight into established networks and activities related to the early identification of skills, which have adopted a variety of approaches and methods.

The fundamental problems have proved to be very similar in many countries. This applies, for example, to the networking of different vocational training research players and hence the collation of different data sources and analytical procedures, as well as to the long-term reliability of quantitative skills forecasts.

Articles in Part I

Susanne Liane Schmidt (D)
Early identification of qualification needs in Germany – the FreQueNz research network

Mike Coles (UK)
Qualifications for the future

Jordi Planas (E)
Developing prospective tools for the observation of skill requirements in Spain

Mario Gatti (I)
Network of national surveys on skill needs in Italy

Frank Cörvers (NL)
Labour market forecasting in the Netherlands: a top-down approach

Early identification of qualification needs in Germany – the FreQueNz research network

Susanne Liane Schmidt, *Fraunhofer Institute for Industrial Engineering (FhIAO), Stuttgart, Germany*

When the German Federal Ministry of Education and Research launched its project on early identification of qualification needs, it brought into being a research network to deal with questions of future skills development. The project focuses on identifying future skill requirements at an early stage and assessing results in terms of the development and relevance of skills. Individual research activities have been grouped together under the umbrella of FreQueNz (an acronym made up of the German for 'Network of Early identification of qualification needs') and the resulting information made generally accessible. The purpose of the independent FreQueNz network project is to combine findings and coordinate research activities by means of organised events such as joint workshops and presentations and through publications. By promoting and accommodating the early identification initiative, the Federal Ministry of Education and Research seeks to assist the forward-looking design of the vocational training system in Germany.

Processed results are communicated via the www.frequenz.net website which interested users can access to obtain information about the various research activities and gather relevant data. This platform also has links to other bodies and early identification projects.

Research results are additionally published in printed form. There are now eight volumes in the FreQueNz series of book publications and others are planned. Short articles on recent findings are published in a newsletter. Both books and newsletter can be ordered via the website or from the author of this paper directly.

1. Introduction

Recognising trends in skill requirements at an early stage represents a challenge to government, industry and academic bodies, since shortcomings in vocational training and the development of skills impair firms' competitiveness and individuals' career opportunities. It is therefore important that we view skills as vital for sustainable development and for coping with changes in the world of work.

Figure 1. **Early recognition of qualification needs is a specialised and forward-looking area of vocational training research**

The vital role of qualification in coping with change

- The world of work is changing and employees are confronted with changing qualification requirements.
- Qualification research enables firms and their employees to cope with structural, organisational and technical change.
- Early recognition of qualification requirements gives an early warning of changes in occupations and identifies new occupational trends.
- Acquiring qualifications appropriate to requirements enhances individuals' employability. Firms need skilled employees to ensure competitiveness.
- **Early recognition of qualification requirements permits advance planning of initial and continuing training and is a means of coping with technological, economic and demographic change.**

By means of its 'Early identification of qualification needs' initiative the German Federal Ministry of Education and Research helps to provide answers to questions concerning skill and qualification trends and to ensure the future effectiveness of the initial and continuing vocational training system. The project partners in the initiative study emerging skill requirements and assess their likely further development, conscious that a sound basis of education and skills is increasingly important for individuals' chances of finding and keeping employment and for economy and the employment system.

2. The research network: project partners, methodology and objectives

The purpose of the FreQueNz network is to generate results useful for an innovative design of the vocational training system and to enable it to react promptly to changes taking place in the world of work. It seeks to recognise skill requirements at an early stage and to make the findings available together with proposals for possible action at the level of initial and continuing vocational training.

It focuses principally on the following questions:
- Which specific occupations or occupational groups will be affected by changes in working practices?
- Which specific skills will be needed in future and what training is available to meet the need?
- Which skills will be needed when?
- How can skills be constantly developed to keep pace with changing requirements?

In order to identify skill requirements and take action at an early stage it is important to combine a substantial volume of information from different sources in the field of educational and vocational training research with appropriately processed statistical information, such as labour market data. This is achieved thanks to the collaboration of a number of project partners within the FreQueNz research network.

2.1. Project partners

The Federal Ministry's early identification initiative links eight separate bodies in the FreQueNz research network. These are the Vocational Training Research Department of the Bavarian Employers' Associations (bfz), the Federal Institute for Vocational Training (BIBB), the Fraunhofer Institute for Industrial Engineering (FhIAO), Infratest Sozialforschung (Social Research), the Institute of Structural Policies and Economic Development Halle-Leipzig e.V. (isw), the Social Science Research Center Berlin (WZB), and the German Employers' Organisation for Vocational Training (KWB) in collaboration with the Research Institute for Vocational Education and Training in the Crafts Sector at the University of Cologne (FBH).

An important feature of the FreQueNz network is that it is interactive. Networking enables the results obtained by the different research projects to be combined and made available to different user groups (see Figure 2). Empirically confirmed information concerning changes in skilled labour requirements provide hooks on which to hang an appropriate design for initial and continuing vocational training and constitutes a useful future-oriented tool for the decisions and actions of policy-makers and training practitioners, as well as of individuals.

Figure 2. **FreQueNz combines partners' project results and makes them available to the general public**

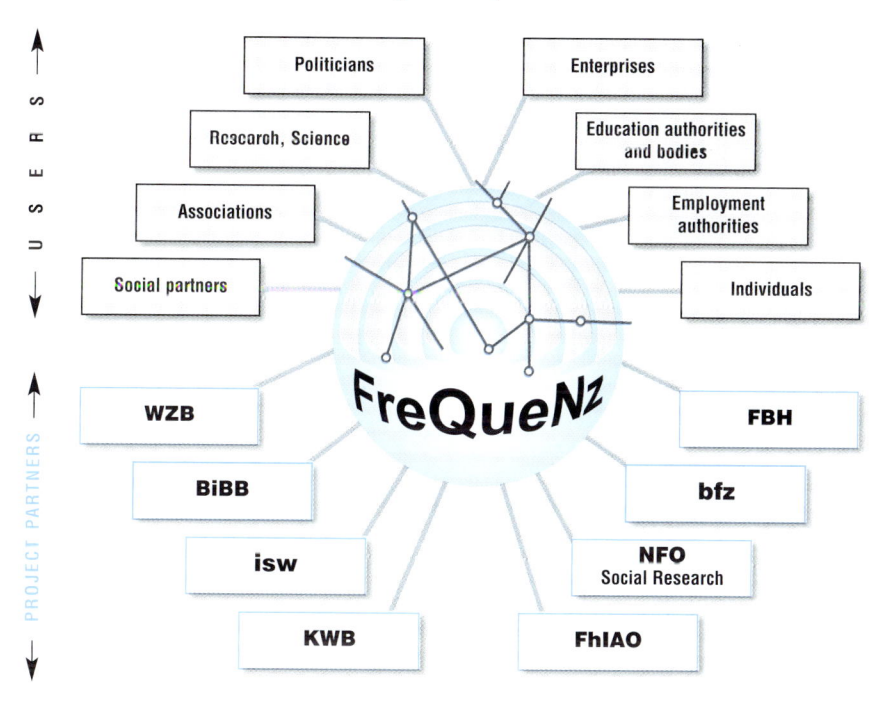

USERS

Politicians
Enterprises
Research, Science
Education authorities and bodies
Associations
Employment authorities
Social partners
Individuals

FreQueNz

PROJECT PARTNERS

WZB
FBH
BiBB
bfz
isw
NFO Social Research
KWB
FhIAO

The research institutes involved in the project adopt a variety of approaches and procedures in order to find answers to the many questions arising. Each project has its own focus and selects the particular methods most suitable for its purpose. This may be monitoring skill trends, prompt identification of critical changes (such as technological innovations), observing trends in competitor countries, signalling the need for action on behalf of specific occupational groups, occupations or sectors of industry and preparing practice-related recommendations for action (see Figure 3).

Combining the various projects in a network from the outset makes it possible to obtain an overview of the broad range of skill trends from different standpoints. The function of the FreQueNz network project is to bring together the various research findings and resulting possible courses of action. Networking simplifies the task of early identification.

Figure 3. **The project utilises different methods for monitoring different areas and linking the results obtained**

Different levels of analysis by means of different methods and approaches are characteristics of the network, making it possible to attain a complementary picture of future qualification needs

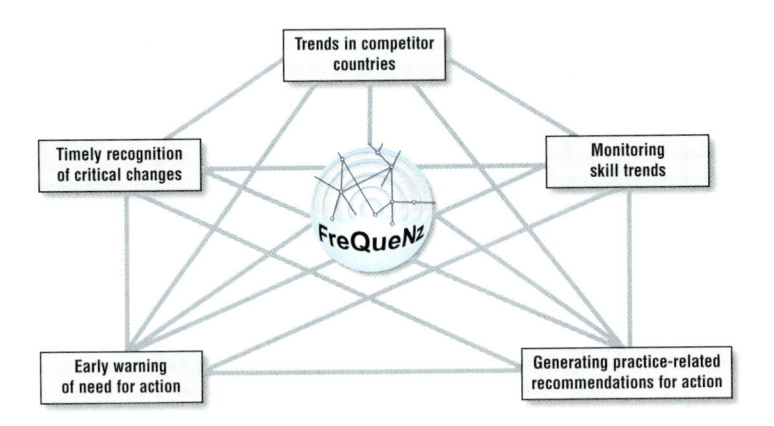

- Trends in competitor countries
- Timely recognition of critical changes
- Monitoring skill trends
- Early warning of need for action
- Generating practice-related recommendations for action

FreQueNz

2.2. Methodology

Research into early identification of qualification needs is concerned with monitoring and assessing critical factors that lead to change. Studies, observations and analyses are directed to predicting future trends in employers' skill requirements in order to avoid any underskilling of people currently in employment or future jobseekers. By selecting suitable methods and levels of investigation it is possible to make predictions for specific occupations, branches of industry and occupational fields (Figure 4). An important aspect is the combination of qualitative and quantitative analysis for the early identification of training needs, future qualification and skill requirements and the assessment of developments in numerical terms. Early identification of future qualification needs benefits not just employees and employers but all those concerned with continuing training in training centres and with vocational training policy.

The projects of the partner institutes and other bodies within the research network cover a broad spectrum ranging from direct monitoring of changes at the workplace to international comparisons of early recognition in competitor countries. The breadth of research coverage and the variety of levels at which it is conducted is designed to answer questions of major significance for the future design of education and training research.

Figure 4. **A feature of the research network is its plurality of scientific approaches. The overall picture is made up of a multiplicity of individual project results obtained at different levels of occupational research using a variety of methods which complement one another**

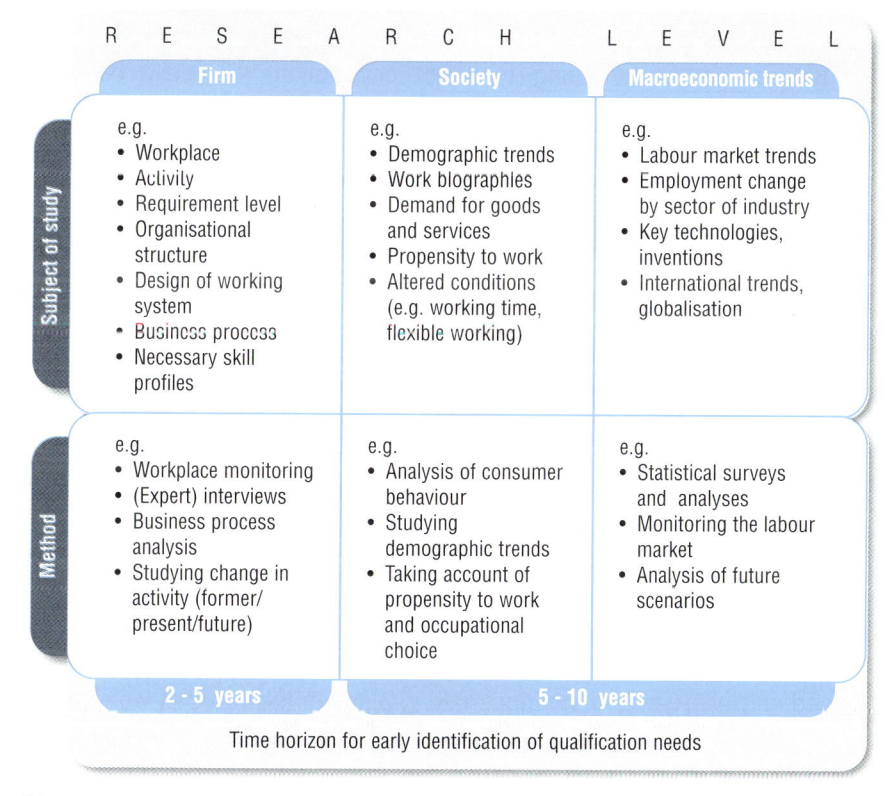

	Firm	Society	Macroeconomic trends
Subject of study	e.g. • Workplace • Activity • Requirement level • Organisational structure • Design of working system • Business process • Necessary skill profiles	e.g. • Demographic trends • Work biographies • Demand for goods and services • Propensity to work • Altered conditions (e.g. working time, flexible working)	e.g. • Labour market trends • Employment change by sector of industry • Key technologies, inventions • International trends, globalisation
Method	e.g. • Workplace monitoring • (Expert) interviews • Business process analysis • Studying change in activity (former/present/future)	e.g. • Analysis of consumer behaviour • Studying demographic trends • Taking account of propensity to work and occupational choice	e.g. • Statistical surveys and analyses • Monitoring the labour market • Analysis of future scenarios
	2 - 5 years	5 - 10 years	

Time horizon for early identification of qualification needs

Changes at a macroeconomic level indicate developments that are driven mainly by market forces and competition. Growing internationalisation and globalisation also mean that developments in other countries become of growing significance since technological innovation or trends observed in neighbouring countries can influence national and regional labour markets.

By looking at society as a whole for purposes of early qualification identification one can include factors such as demographic structure - an ageing population, for example - and other social factors such as consumer behaviour.

Another level of research is the firm, where new occupations can be observed for the first time in practice. Observation is, of course, only possible when the new occupation already exists, but since occupations rarely alter in a short time to such an extent that every gesture and all the logical connections are entirely new, process and workplace monitoring make it possible to include in the analysis and assessment changes and innovations that are already foreseeable. To make sure of obtaining information concerning new skill requirements as early as possible, firms in the forefront of innovation and using cutting-edge technology are frequently chosen for study. When analysing occupational changes within a firm, comparisons between firms can often help to judge whether emerging types of occupation will really become so widespread as to call for training measures or whether they are merely special cases resulting from the circumstances of a particular firm.

Already at the conceptional stage of the project, the partners consider their integration into the network. This contributes to a more complete and balanced overall picture of skill trends than would be gained if individual results were to be looked at in isolation. The fact that the project partners exchange information, the different research methods used and the combining of results also helps to give a more complete view of future trends, making findings as to trends observed and predictions made more reliable and minimising the risk of incorrect forecasting. Using a network to combine findings from various sources obtained at different levels and by different methods thus provides a varied view of newly emerging skill requirements from several standpoints.

2.3. Objectives

A strategic aim common to all the partners in the project is to identify future skill requirements at an early stage and to make recommendations for action based on observation of changes taking place in the world of work.

(a) *Observation of social, structural, technical and organisational drivers for occupational change, structuring principal indicators and combining results as to future skill trends.*

The chief drivers for new skill requirements stem from technological, work organisation or demographic change and the growing importance of information technology and the knowledge society. They bring with them new kinds of jobs with new skill profiles due to product innovation, the introduction of major new technologies, business developments and market changes. Also very important in this respect is the introduction of new production processes that may fuse activities that were formerly separate, as happens, for instance, when skilled IT occupations are restructured. Changes in demand, too - such as the increased demand for health and wellness services - mean new services calling for people with the necessary skills.

(b) *Cooperation within the research network to enhance current research transparency*

The idea underlying networking for the early identification project is not only to link together the project partners and other research collaborators but also to reach out to other bodies and interested individuals. By combining the results of research it is hoped to simplify the process of making recommendations for action to help shape a viable future vocational training system. The central node in the network is the communications centre which promotes research efficiency by avoiding duplication of work and enhancing transparency. Unlike isolated individual projects, networked research allows the partners to work together while adopting different standpoints.

(c) *Strategic aim: to design a viable early identification system for the future*

The various early identification projects with their results gained in different fields together contribute to the creation of a dynamic future-oriented forecasting system (see Figure 5). The FreQueNz research network aims with its results to assist in creating an innovative vocational training system by signalling future trends and possible forms of action. Those involved in the vocational training field will be provided here and now with significant pointers to the likely skill requirements for tomorrow which they can take account of in their planning. The results of the project have a time horizon of between one and five years.

Early information concerning future skill requirements can help to prepare industry for market ups and downs in certain sectors or occupations making it possible to react rapidly to changes as they occur. The research derives its dynamism from the fact that the individual projects ask their questions concerning future skill requirements from different standpoints and process the results obtained at the different levels for use in the initial and continuing vocational training system.

Results of research help to answer the following questions:
- Which specific occupations or occupational groups will be affected by changes in working practices?
- Which specific skills will be needed in future?
- Which skills will be needed when?
- Which specific available training is suitable for meeting the need?
- How can skills be constantly developed to keep pace with changing requirements?

Figure 5. **The networked combination of project partners' results creates a dynamic and future-oriented early identification system**

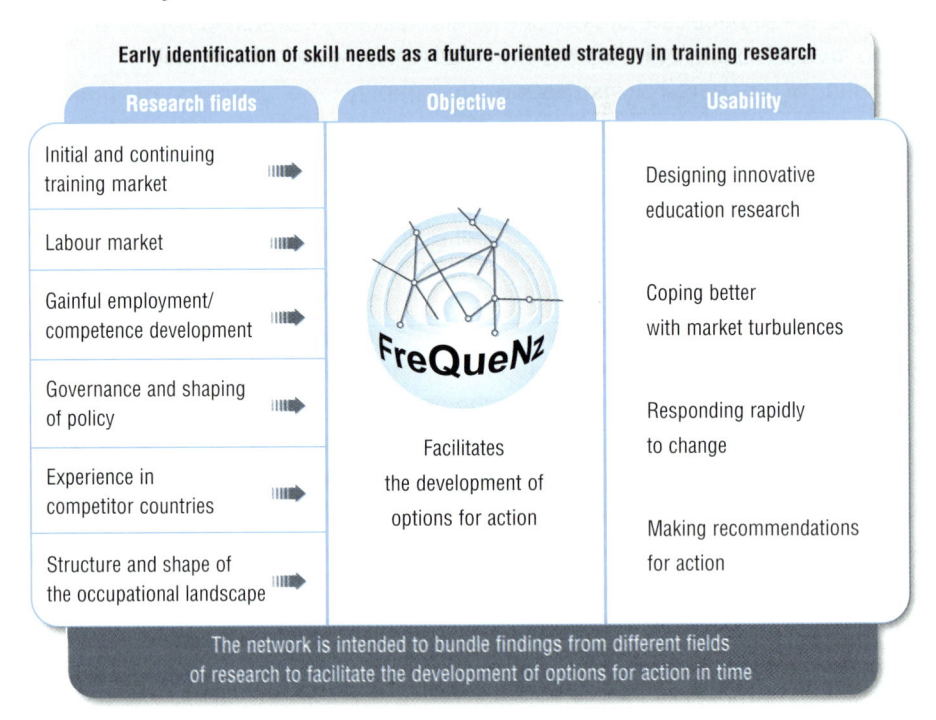

Early identification of skill needs as a future-oriented strategy in training research

Research fields	Objective	Usability
Initial and continuing training market		Designing innovative education research
Labour market		
Gainful employment/ competence development	**FreQueNz**	Coping better with market turbulences
Governance and shaping of policy		Responding rapidly to change
Experience in competitor countries	Facilitates the development of options for action	
Structure and shape of the occupational landscape		Making recommendations for action

The network is intended to bundle findings from different fields of research to facilitate the development of options for action in time

(d) *Data transfer: Using different techniques and media for maximum dissemination*

The results so far obtained by the individual projects present a varied picture of differing occupational scenarios showing that skill requirements are in the process of rapid change thus calling for innovative strategies in initial and continuing vocational training.

Processed results are communicated via the www.frequenz.net website which interested users can access to obtain information about the various research activities and gather relevant data. This platform also has links to other bodies and early identification projects.

Research results are also regularly published in the form of newsletters and in the 'Qualifikationen erkennen - Berufe gestalten' (Recognising skills - shaping occupations) book series which now includes eight volumes.

Figure 6. **Research results are made available on the FreQueNz website as well as in printed form**

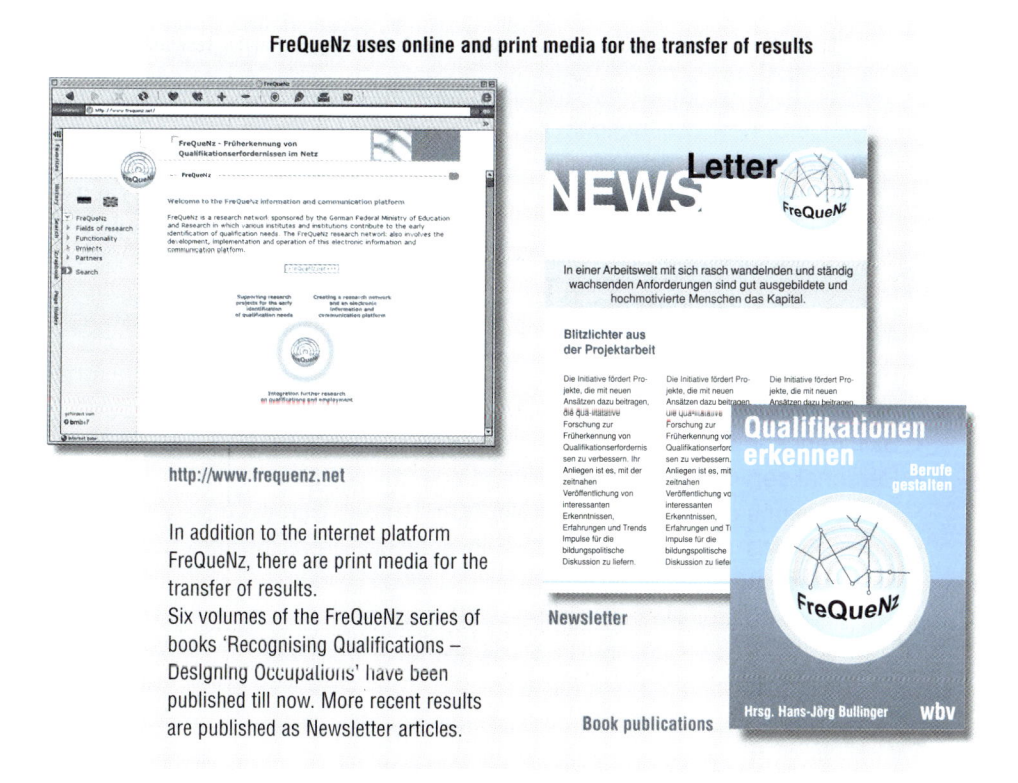

FreQueNz uses online and print media for the transfer of results

http://www.frequenz.net

In addition to the internet platform FreQueNz, there are print media for the transfer of results.
Six volumes of the FreQueNz series of books 'Recognising Qualifications – Designing Occupations' have been published till now. More recent results are published as Newsletter articles.

Newsletter

Book publications

FreQueNz organises conferences and workshops in order to make known its findings and to contact selected user groups. In June 2001, for example, a major conference under the title 'Qualification offensive: Early identification of qualification needs for future-oriented action' with information stands was organised to present and discuss research findings. This was attended by over 400 people from the world of politics and industry, professional and trade associations, and training organisations.

FreQueNz results are also presented at industrial fairs and similar events such as the Education Fair held in Cologne in 2002 ([2]).

([2]) This is the largest German exhibition and information event concerned with schools, teaching, teaching aids and continuing training.

3. Results from the research network

Changes in work are triggered by a variety of factors, among which are the development of new products and services, new production processes, the introduction of more efficient information and communication systems, market turbulence or social trends. Many of these factors lead to the emergence of new occupational fields that call for particular skills.

The FreQueNz project partners have already looked at a great many different factors and their impact and produced findings in a number of fields covering a broad spectrum of skill trends. Results on the following subjects are currently available:
- Changes in skill requirements for the low-skilled
- An analysis of job advertisements in printed and on-line media
- Recording firms' skill requirements in various sectors and occupational fields. Examples from the car industry and retail trade
- Skill trends in the logistics sector
- Personal services in health, wellness and teaching
- Comparisons of best practice in OECD countries with examples
- Case studies drawn from practice in selected areas of activity (facilities management, call centres and technical office work)
- The shortage of skilled personnel in IT occupations
- New occupational skills in ICT occupations
- Changing skills in the retail trade
- New skill requirements in the multimedia sector
- Analysis of continuing training provision
- Reporting systems: early identification of skill trends, skills report, skill structure report and the 'QUO' on-line skills development system.

Results are currently available on the research website (www.frequenz.net). We shall now look at six examples taken from projects concerned with the above subjects.

3.1. Early identification of qualification needs for disadvantaged groups

The 'Early identification of qualification needs for disadvantaged groups' project of the Vocational Training Research Department of the Bavarian Employers' Associations (bfz) looks at new skill requirements for the low-skilled. While market demand for skilled manpower is steadily growing, the next few years still will see many jobs occupied by people with so-called lower skills (some 12-16% of all jobs in 2010). These are mainly semi-skilled occupations which do not require any special initial training. Studies carried out among smaller firms under the research project have shown that skills demanded are no longer determined by the job itself and the various tasks involved, but increasingly by the surrounding working system. Even simpler jobs are now regarded as skilled occupations that are part of the operating working system and no longer performed in isolation from more complex processes. The emergence of new skill requirements in the occupational areas looked at was triggered by changes in work organisation (see Figure 7).

The results of this research shed a new light on low-skilled occupations as, contrary to previous practice, such workers now require some form of qualification.

Figure 7. **New skill requirements for the low-skilled result from changes in work organisation in which individual activities become integrated into the overall operating environment**

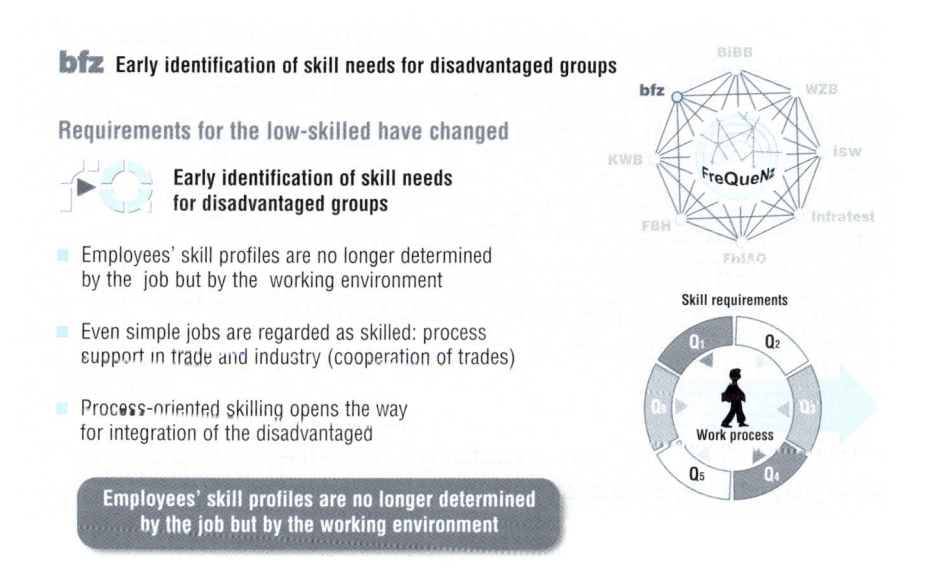

bfz Early identification of skill needs for disadvantaged groups

Requirements for the low-skilled have changed

Early identification of skill needs for disadvantaged groups

- Employees' skill profiles are no longer determined by the job but by the working environment

- Even simple jobs are regarded as skilled: process support in trade and industry (cooperation of trades)

- Process-oriented skilling opens the way for integration of the disadvantaged

Employees' skill profiles are no longer determined by the job but by the working environment

Analysis of IT job advertisements in printed and on-line media

In its 'Analysis of job advertisements in printed and on-line media' the Federal Institute for Vocational Training (BIBB) monitors and analyses advertisements in a range of newspapers and the Internet, concentrating on selected types of occupations in the IT occupations such as those in information technology with a view to obtaining information on qualifications and skills that are desirable or a *sine qua non* for the jobs concerned. The jobs looked at were either core occupations in the IT sector such as programmer, network specialist or the like or new types of job without as yet a fixed designation (see Figure 8).

Apart from recording the numbers of such advertisements, an important aspect of the project was the subsequent questioning of advertisers. In this second step employers were asked whether they had found a suitable candidate for the job and which of the qualifications and skills listed in the advertisement were absolutely necessary. The results obtained showed *inter alia* that in some 50% of cases a university qualification was not absolutely necessary, although asked for in the advertisement.

The analysis of job advertisements yielded useful information regarding the structure of the jobs concerned as well as the actual qualifications or skills needed for the position offered. The method used by the Federal Institute for Vocational Training has been employed for other occupational fields.

Figure 8. **An analysis of job advertisements yields useful information concerning the skills and qualifications actually needed**

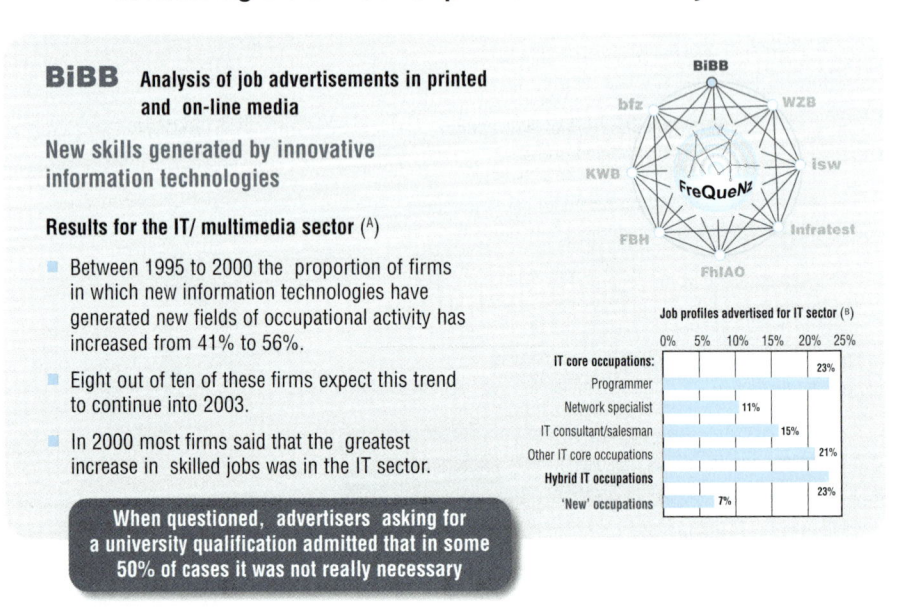

BiBB Analysis of job advertisements in printed and on-line media

New skills generated by innovative information technologies

Results for the IT/ multimedia sector ([A])

- Between 1995 to 2000 the proportion of firms in which new information technologies have generated new fields of occupational activity has increased from 41% to 56%.
- Eight out of ten of these firms expect this trend to continue into 2003.
- In 2000 most firms said that the greatest increase in skilled jobs was in the IT sector.

When questioned, advertisers asking for a university qualification admitted that in some 50% of cases it was not really necessary

Job profiles advertised for IT sector ([B])

IT core occupations:	
Programmer	23%
Network specialist	11%
IT consultant/salesman	15%
Other IT core occupations	21%
Hybrid IT occupations	23%
'New' occupations	7%

([A]) Reference enterprise system 2000, n=876
([B]) Job ads. analysis 2000 (n=2420); IT-core occupations acc. to BA classification: data processing specialists (7740-7749); hybrid IT occupations, non-core IT occupations, new IT occupations: no official BA coding, mostly across occupational classification.

3.3. System for regularly monitoring firms' skill requirements

The German Employers' Committee on Vocational Training (KWB) in collaboration with the Research Institute for Vocational Education and Training in the Crafts Sector at the University of Cologne (FBH) carried out a survey of firms' skill requirements in which 1 545 firms were questioned.

Evaluation of the responses yielded a large number of indicators for new skill requirements. In all, 45% of comments referred to specialist skills, with data-processing and computer literacy mentioned most often. The greatest number of comments (55%) related to general skills such as customer-orientation, the ability to communicate, independence, team-work ability, flexibility, mobility and willingness to learn and work hard, quality-consciousness and decisiveness. This showed that in addition to sound technical training, more informal skills were becoming increasingly important for the firms concerned, and are now referred to more often than specialist skills.

The results of the survey provided useful information for the updating of skilled occupation categories, the need to create new ones, additional skills needed and the subject-matter that should be included in continuing vocational training and school curricula.

Figure 9. **A survey of firms showed that demand for general skills is exceeding that for specialist skills**

KWB / FBH
System for regular observation of firms' skill requirements

Results of enterprise surveys
A total of 1 545 firms representing a varied mix of sectors were questioned as to their qualification requirements

Most frequently mentioned were:
Technical qualifications: specialist DP/IT for various applications

Key qualifications: Customer-orientation, ability to communicate, independence, cost consciousness, team-working, flexibility, mobility, willingness to learn/to perform, quality-consciousness, decision-making ability

Ways mentioned for meeting these requirements:
- Updating existing training occupation profiles
- Creating new skilled occupations
- Developing additional skills
- Continuing training and instruction

45% 55%
Technical qualifications   Key qualifications

Source: KWB, ed.: Dauerbeobachtungssystem der betrieblichen Qualifikationsentwicklung (System for permanent observation of industrial qualification developments), final report. Bonn 2001 (see also: www.frequenz.net).

45% of skills mentioned were technical qualifications and 55% key qualifications

3.4. Regular monitoring of skill trends for early recognition of changes at the workplace

The ADeBar project is concerned with the regular monitoring of skill trends in various sectors of activity with a view to early identification of changes at the workplace. Monitoring is both quantitative and qualitative and is carried out jointly with the Fraunhofer Institute for Industrial Engineering (FhIAO) and Infratest Sozialforschung (Social Research). The qualitative evaluation of case studies is performed initially by the Fraunhofer Institute with Infratest using the results as the basis for quantitative analysis.

The example given here concerns the skills required by warehouse employees in the logistics sector. Workplace studies and subsequent quantitative surveys using questionnaires sent out to firms show that the traditional activities of specialist warehouse employees such as moving goods, allocating storage space and handling incoming and outgoing goods documentation, are changing and giving way to new tasks characterised by a reduction in physical work, the use of information and communications technology, an increase in activities requiring specialist knowledge, and commercial tasks. A new skilled occupation profile is emerging, namely that of 'warehouse process controller', involving new skills such as the ability to use special computer programmes alongside others drawn from more traditional occupations such as warehouseman, packer, industrial clerk etc. (see Figure 10).

3.5. Identifying emerging qualifications for the early recognition of skill trends

In its 'Identifying emerging qualifications for the early recognition of skill trends' project the Institute of Structural Policies and Economic Development Halle-Leipzig (isw) has studied the expansion of activity in the wellness sector in response to the heavy demand for such services due to an ageing population and older people's greater concern for health.

The findings show that the increased number of jobs is leading to the emergence of new occupations that develop into independent skilled occupations. The project came to the conclusion that the new qualifications and skills in the wellness field tend to be complex and multivalent (see Figure 11). They include aspects of personality and character such as enjoying working with people, a sound basic anatomical and medical knowledge, counselling skill and commercial/business acumen. Specialising, for instance, to become a skilled relaxation therapist also calls for knowledge and skills in massage and hydrotherapy and in such specialist fields as Shiatsu and Feldenkrais therapy.

Early identification of qualification needs in Germany – the FreQueNz research network | 39

Figure 10. **Workplace studies and quantitative surveys by questionnaire show demand for new types of warehousing skills**

FhIAO
Institut Arbeitswirtschaft und Organisation

NFO
Infratest Sozialforschung

A|DeBar

Regular close-to-the-job monitoring of skill requirements for early identification of changes at the workplace and within enterprises

New skills for warehouse employees in the logistics sector

Traditional activities of skilled warehousemen:
- Moving goods
- Allocation of storage place
- Handling incoming and outgoing goods documentation

New activities:
- Less physical work
- Use of ICT
- More knowledge-intensive sub-activities
- More commercial tasks

▶ Merchandise information and distribution

▶ Planning, organisation, calculation

▶ Shipment handling and merchandise movements

▶ Item flow, auditing of accounts, controlling

A new qualification profile emerges, e.g. of a warehouse process controller

Requirements are:
- New skills include ability to use special computer programmes and to handle databases
- Skills originating from various other job profiles such as: warehouse management specialist, skilled packer, industrial clerk, clerk in wholesale and export trade, dispatcher

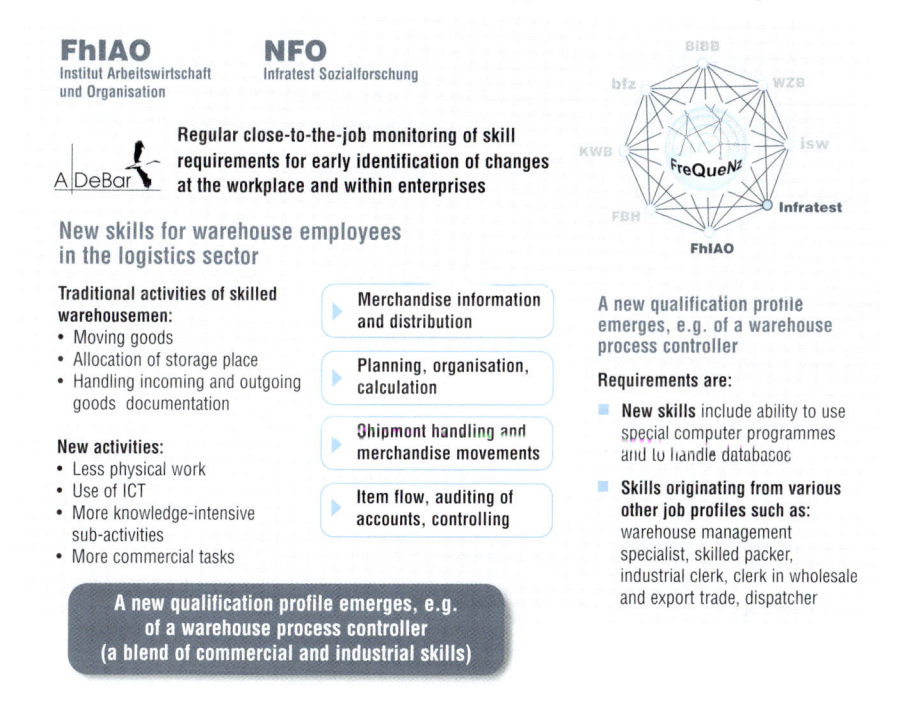

A new qualification profile emerges, e.g. of a warehouse process controller (a blend of commercial and industrial skills)

Figure 11. **The expanding wellness sector is generating considerable demand for persons with core skills as the basis for further specialisation in different types of therapy**

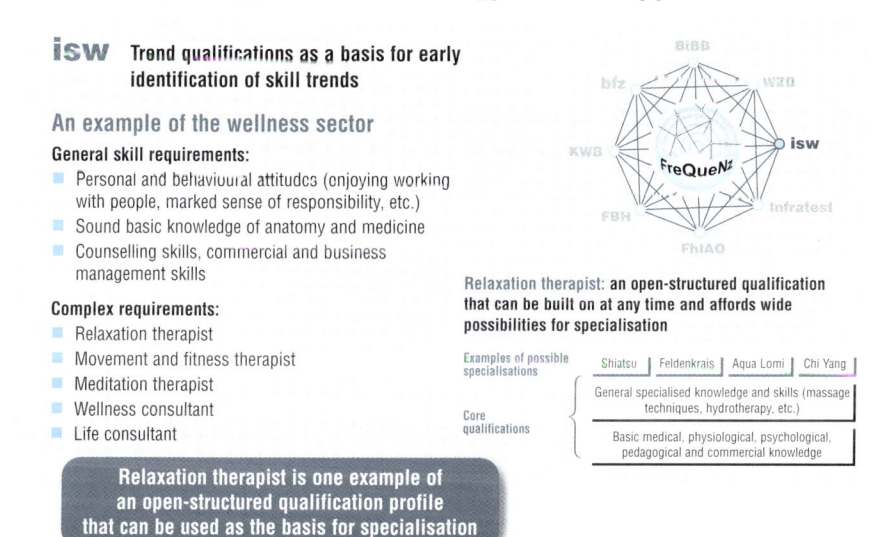

isw Trend qualifications as a basis for early identification of skill trends

An example of the wellness sector

General skill requirements:
- Personal and behavioural attitudes (enjoying working with people, marked sense of responsibility, etc.)
- Sound basic knowledge of anatomy and medicine
- Counselling skills, commercial and business management skills

Complex requirements:
- Relaxation therapist
- Movement and fitness therapist
- Meditation therapist
- Wellness consultant
- Life consultant

Relaxation therapist: an open-structured qualification that can be built on at any time and affords wide possibilities for specialisation

Examples of possible specialisations: | Shiatsu | Feldenkrais | Aqua Lomi | Chi Yang |

Core qualifications:
- General specialised knowledge and skills (massage techniques, hydrotherapy, etc.)
- Basic medical, physiological, psychological, pedagogical and commercial knowledge

Relaxation therapist is one example of an open-structured qualification profile that can be used as the basis for specialisation

When studying the skill requirements for a relaxation therapist it was found that the most appropriate qualification was open-structured so that those acquiring the necessary basic knowledge and general skills could then go on to extend their scope with specialist skills.

3.6. Skill requirements in OECD countries - identification, analysis and realisation

Internationalisation, globalisation and common markets ensure that developments in other OECD member countries also have an impact in Germany. The project of the Berlin Social Science Research Center's (WZB) 'Study of skill requirements in OECD countries' project looks into developments there so as to gain information concerning skill trends in Germany and the possibilities for adopting best practice from other countries.

Figure 12. **International comparisons help to foresee future trends and enable best practice to be learnt from other countries**

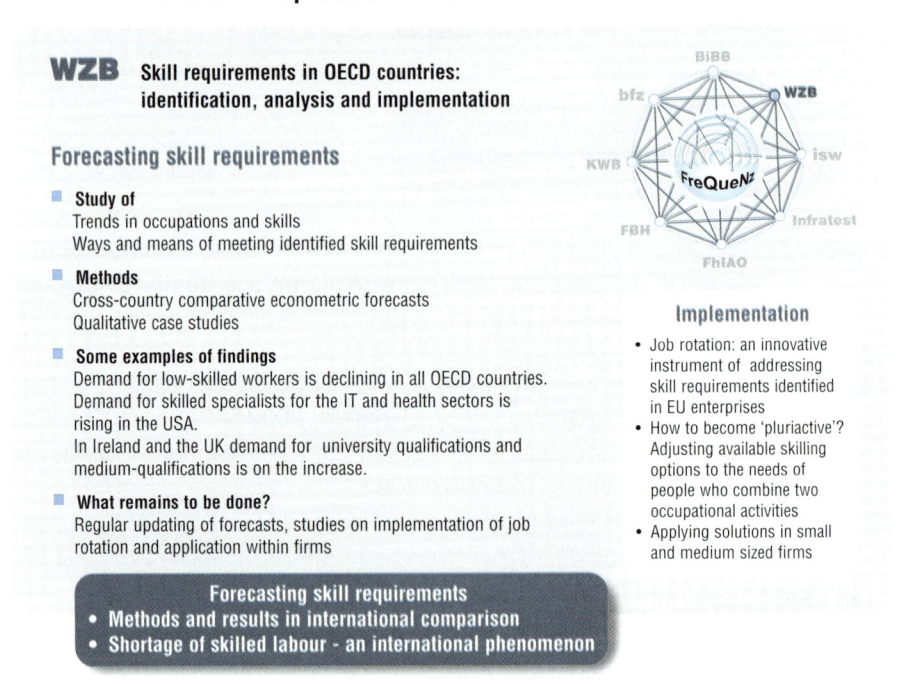

WZB Skill requirements in OECD countries: identification, analysis and implementation

Forecasting skill requirements

- **Study of**
  Trends in occupations and skills
  Ways and means of meeting identified skill requirements
- **Methods**
  Cross-country comparative econometric forecasts
  Qualitative case studies
- **Some examples of findings**
  Demand for low-skilled workers is declining in all OECD countries.
  Demand for skilled specialists for the IT and health sectors is rising in the USA.
  In Ireland and the UK demand for university qualifications and medium-qualifications is on the increase.
- **What remains to be done?**
  Regular updating of forecasts, studies on implementation of job rotation and application within firms

Implementation
- Job rotation: an innovative instrument of addressing skill requirements identified in EU enterprises
- How to become 'pluriactive'? Adjusting available skilling options to the needs of people who combine two occupational activities
- Applying solutions in small and medium sized firms

Forecasting skill requirements
- Methods and results in international comparison
- Shortage of skilled labour - an international phenomenon

The study covers occupational and skill trends and ways and means of meeting skill requirements. The methods used include comparative econometric forecasting and quality case studies.

The results obtained show that demand for low-skilled labour is declining in almost all OECD countries. Demand for skilled manpower was found to be on the increase in the United States, particularly in the IT and health sectors (see Figure 12). In addition to skill forecasting, which shows, for example, that the shortage of skilled labour in small and medium-sized enterprises is an international phenomenon, consideration of ways and means of meeting skill requirements plays an important role in the project. This includes such aspects as job rotation and possibilities that may be utilised by smaller firms.

The examples quoted here and other project findings are set out in detail in the publications listed below and on the www.frequenz.net website.

Bibliography

Bärwald, H.; Meifort, B. *Gesundheit, Wellness, Wohlbefinden - Personenbezogene Dienstleistungen im Fokus der Qualifikationsentwicklung.* Bullinger, H.-J., ed. FreQueNz Vol. 4, Bielefeld, 2001.

Bullinger, H.-J., ed. *Qualifikationen erkennen - Berufe gestalten.* FreQueNz Vol. 1, Bielefeld, 2000.

Bullinger, H.-J., ed. *Qualifizierungsoffensive: Bedarf frühzeitig erkennen - zukunftsorientiert handeln.* Conference proceedings, Stuttgart, 2001.

Bullinger, H.-J., ed. *Qualifizierungsoffensive: Bedarf frühzeitig erkennen - zukunftsorientiert handeln.* FreQueNz Vol. 6, Bielefeld, 2001.

Bullinger, H.-J.; Schömann, Klaus, eds. *Qualifikationen von morgen - ein deutsch-französischer Dialog.* FreQueNz Vol. 5, Bielefeld, 2001.

Gidion, G.; Kuwan, H.; Schnalzer, K.; Waschbüsch, E. *Spurensuche in der Arbeit - ein Verfahren zur Erkundung künftiger Qualifikationserfordernisse.* Bullinger, H.-J., ed. FreQueNz Vol. 2, Bielefeld, 2000.

Gülker, S.; Hilbert, C.; Schömann, K. *Lernen von den Nachbarn.* Bullinger, H.-J., ed. FreQueNz Vol. 3, Bielefeld, 2000.

Schmidt, S.L. Früherkennung als zukunftsorientierte Strategie der Bildungsforschung. BWP-Berufsbildung in Wissenschaft und Praxis, Vol. 1, 2002, p. 22-24.

Qualifications for the future

Mike Coles, The Qualification and Curriculum Authority (QCA), London, United Kingdom

Early recognition of qualification needs has been a problem for the UK for many years. Barriers include such things as poor labour market data supply, long gestation times for the development of qualifications and weak methods for collecting and analysing information about future qualifications needs. This paper concentrates on the early stages of the development of a new methodology, based on scenario planning, for maintaining an up-to-date set of qualifications that serve individuals, employers and the economy well.

The research described in this paper involves using skills needs analysis to develop a qualification or certificate that will act as a proxy for these skills. In other words, the development of a modern national qualification is the goal of the research and not just the recognition of future skills.

1. Introduction

Early recognition of qualification needs has been a problem for the UK for many years. There are barriers to building qualifications that recognise skills that are needed in the workplace now and in the not-too-distant future. These barriers include such things as poor labour market data supply, long gestation times for the development of qualifications and weak methods for collecting and analysing information about future qualifications needs. This paper concentrates on the early stages of the development of a new methodology, based on scenario planning, for maintaining an up-to-date set of qualifications that serve individuals, employers and the economy well.

Most readers will appreciate the dangers of using words such as 'qualification' in a European context. In this paper 'qualification' is used in the sense of a certificated outcome of the assessment of learning. In the UK a qualification certificate does not necessarily show that a person can do a particular job. However, in the context of this paper use of the word 'qualification' will be restricted to certificates in the occupational area and it is reasonable to assume that a person gaining a certificate has shown the capacity to perform certain tasks. The research described in this paper involves using skills needs analysis to develop a certificate that will act as a proxy for these skills. In other words the development of a modern national qualification is the goal of the research and not just the recognition of future skills.

It is widely appreciated (Leney and Coles, 2001) that major benefits for individuals, employment and the economy can flow from a qualification system that is clear, helpful and efficient. A qualification needs analysis process is essentially a modernising process – a way of making sure that users of qualifications - and the framework of qualifications – feel confident about the content and structure of qualifications and the relationship between them. The logic then continues ... if qualifications recognise the right skills, and people are inclined to achieve the qualifications, then a positive effect on the career of the individual, skills supply to the economy, the economy of the sector and international competitiveness will follow.

2. The UK approach to qualification needs

The UK qualification system is based on certain well-established and well-defined qualifications. These have been developed and managed within universities and the professions and it is probably true that even accepting recent government activities to regulate the qualifications system, the UK has a qualifications system that is devolved and voluntarist. Government action has been aimed at rationalising the system; maintaining the demand of assessments and creating a recognition system for those who have poor access to qualifications, such as unemployed youth. Recently the government has been attempting to arrest the rapid decline in the use of apprenticeship as training and qualification.

Within the EU, the methods (Sellin, 2001) for early recognition of skills needs include:
- examination of job specific qualification needs;
- examination of individual occupations;
- comparative qualifications analysis (cutting across occupations);
- qualification analysis at the level of society as a whole.

The UK engages in all of these methods to some degree. There is an infrastructure of organisations including the Learning and Skills Councils, National Training Organisations (now Sector Skills Councils) that work with specific occupational groups to ascertain skills needs. The work of these bodies is supplemented with analyses from specialist researchers in universities and other expert centres. The UK government commissions work on how occupations might change in the future and conducts research into qualification types. Periodically the government conducts a national review of qualifications, recently we have engaged in debate over the qualifications needs of 16-18 year olds and those in higher education. We are about to have a debate of the qualifications needed for upper secondary education in England.

Experts charged with carrying out reviews on qualifications are invariably asked to look to the future; the importance of developing highly skilled people to guarantee the future productivity of the UK nations is usually emphasised. However, as we shall see later, the practice of producing future-oriented qualifications is highly problematic.

How are qualifications modernised in the UK?
There is no generic needs analysis process that is applied to all qualifications across the systems in the UK. Until recently the 'refreshment' of qualifications varied according to the type of qualification. The major school qualifications were required to shift in response to political intent (e.g. for the main qualification taken at the mid-point of upper secondary education the General Certificate of Secondary Education to be a more inclusive qualification than its predecessor qualifications). There is great inertia in the general qualifications system; this may stem from the need to maintain public confidence in standards, it is also the case that UK higher education generally prefers a narrowly specialised preparation for a three-year degree course. Change to the system therefore tends to be incremental. Occupational qualifications have, for many years, been continuously developed to better meet the needs of users and the market for qualifications has been the main force for change. However in the late 1980's wholesale rationalisation followed a review of occupational qualifications (Department of Education and Science and the Manpower Services Commission, 1986). This review was needed because qualifications had developed in diverse ways and the qualifications system became very complex. Today occupational qualifications are developed sector by sector. The Qualification and Curriculum Authority's (QCA) accreditation ([1]) regime, coupled with the establishment of an explicit National Qualifications Framework (NQF), has begun to establish a common system and timescale to revisions of all types of qualifications.

([1]) QCA is a government agency that regulates qualifications by scrutinising them against criteria. If a qualification meets QCA's criteria it is accredited and is admitted to the National Qualifications Framework.

The system of developing occupational qualifications begins with the development of National Occupational Standards (NOS). These industry standards are produced by analysing occupations in the sector; currently over 90% of the UK workforce is covered by NOS. This is then generally followed by functional analysis that defines the competence that needs to be demonstrated in each job type within the occupation. These competencies form the standards that are used to build qualifications. National Vocational Qualifications (NVQs) use them as building blocks, other vocational qualifications need to have demonstrable links with the standards if they are to be accredited by QCA and admitted to the NQF. There are currently about 750 NVQs and nearly 2000 other vocational qualifications.

3. The future is a problem

Looking back for official mention of building qualifications for the future comes in a 1995 statement from National Council for Vocational Qualifications (NCVQ, 1995):

> The analysis should go beyond simple reflection of existing practice. It should address and incorporate predicted future occupational needs and practices so as to permit the skills base of the UK workforce to be updated and upgraded.

A major review carried out by NCVQ/SCOTVEC in 1996 did not address the future skilling issue. This is surprising since one of the characteristics of NOS is:

> Ensure that the competence is broad enough to give flexibility in employment and be capable of adaptation to meet new and emerging occupational patterns.

It was not until a statement from QCA (1999) that NOS were explicitly required to 'take account of the future needs of the sector', through:

- taking account of technology currently used within the sector;
- encouraging the consideration of the sector's anticipated needs;
- using innovative ways of capturing the views and needs of the sector.

However methods of achieving this were not specified.

A research report produced for QCA (Green and Hartley, 1999) concludes:

> In order for future needs to be seen as a priority and to become embedded into the process and outcomes from the development of National Occupational Standards, QCA needs to:
>
> - ensure that preferred tools, methods and processes are clearly identified, have been tested and shown to work, be valuable across a variety of sectors and become part of the funding criteria for the acceptance of tender documents and outcomes from standards and qualification development projects;

- develop guidance notes to accompany the tools, methods and processes;
- market the value of capturing future requirements to industry bodies, especially in demonstrating how future needs of the sector when captured can be reflected in National Occupational Standards that people currently working in the sector can use.

More evidence of the difficulty of identifying future qualifications needs emerged from a recent QCA commissioned pilot study (Green and Hartley, 2000) that investigated the range of techniques used by consultants to identify qualification needs in different occupations. The results were generally disappointing for those who expected to see forward-looking analyses. Many projects only seemed to pay lip service to future-proofing qualifications. Evidence showed that a variety of techniques (see Annex 1) were used to determine the competencies to be included in the NOS and that there was little consistency in the use of these techniques.

The government has recognised that accurately identifying future skills and qualifications needs is fraught with methodological problems. For example a recently convened expert group, the National Skills Task Force (Department for Education and Employment, 1999) [2], was asked to provide advice on such things as:
- the likely changes in the longer term skill needs of the economy and the extent to which these needs will be met on the basis of existing trends;
- how best to ensure that the education and training system responds effectively to needs identified.

Recent research carried out by Wilson (2001) on behalf of Cedefop states that whilst there has been a revival in interest in future skills forecasting the methods used have focused on issues for employers and often do not attempt to collect quantitative data on future skill requirements. In the UK there are many agencies that collate and disseminate information about skills and qualifications needs, however all this effort at data gathering and processing still leaves a data problem. The Skills Task Force (Department for Education and Employment, 1999) extensively reviewed labour market and skills information available in the UK. It found:

> Despite the extraordinary volume of data, there was an almost unanimous opinion from those we consulted that there was too much data overall, that what there was found to be inconsistent and incoherent, and that it was primarily backward looking, and of little use in helping either individuals or providers make sound judgements on future labour market opportunities and demand.

---

[2] National Skills Task Force, 1999, chapter 7 'Informing the market – gaps in our current approach' P87 section 7.35.

This situation has been reported widely elsewhere. Focusing on the issue of future skills, Haskel and Holt (1999) cite the lack of consistent quantitative information about past skills patterns as a reason why accurate forecasts cannot now be made at this level.

4. Researching improvements

There are changes in the UK that might lead to improvements in processes for identifying future skills and qualifications needs. Currently the UK is a restructuring the sectoral bodies that play a major role in identifying skills needs and qualification needs. At the same time a relatively new organisation called the Learning and Skills Council is establishing its role (nationally and regionally) in identification of skills needs and funding training schemes to meet these needs. Recently the area of developing background or underpinning knowledge has received attention. QCA has been consulting on the idea of a Technical Certificate that covers this knowledge and can be taught off-the-job. These Technical Certificates have now been developed by industry experts and, interestingly; some consultants have found it easier to build in future-oriented requirements into these certificates that into the National Occupational Standards.

Within QCA procedures are being developed for encouraging a systematic identification of the need for a qualification and there is growing interest in the application of scenario methodology to qualifications needs analysis. Scenario methodology was first developed by businesses. Its use can be traced to the early seventies in the large oil companies when they were recoiling from the shock of the doubling of the price of crude oil (Shell, 2000) – the planning methods in use at the time had failed to take account of such dynamic variables [3]. The methodology involves the development of plausible scenarios for 10 or 20 years hence and the testing of strategies for achieving objectives in the context of these scenarios. The scenarios can be seen as a kind of lens or 'wind tunnel' through which to explore the potential and detail of different strategies. The methodology does not create a convergent tool that provides a best guess for a single, inevitable future, nor does it provide a 'best possible strategic approach', nor is it a derivative of forecasting. It is fundamentally different to other strategic tools and is best used alongside them. The distinctiveness of scenarios lies in the way it

---

[3] For the latest developments in this area see Buchan and Roberts (Financial Times, 21 Jan 2002).

tackles uncertainty, the richness of the data it generates for discussion and its capacity to facilitate 'out of the box' thinking.

Several applications of scenario methodology have been reported recently. These include the United Nations (1998), the European Commission (Bertrand, Gilles et al., 1999) and the Organisation for Economic Cooperation and Development (OECD, 1999). Some countries have used scenario methodology to look specifically at development of educational systems for example New Zealand (Ministry of Education, 2001). In the UK, the Future Learning Unit (2001) has developed socio-economic scenarios for 2020 which include an education and training dimension. The QCA has completed a joint project with the Institute of Education in London looking the future of vocational education and training in the UK; this was part of a Europe-wide project (van Wieringen et al., 2001) commissioned by Cedefop and the ETF. [4]

Strategic planning based on scenario methodology is now well known and fairly well tested (Schoemaker, 1995). A brief general description of application of the methodology is provided in Annex 2 for readers who are unfamiliar with its structure.

5. Application of scenarios methods to qualification needs analysis

QCA's Research Team has been working on the use of scenario methods to qualification needs analysis for the last two years. The first application was in the financial services sector where an element of scenario planning was added to a sector-led project that aimed to produce a map of qualifications needed by the financial industries in 10 years time. The second application is in the transport sector and is a more substantial application of the methodology than the first. Development work is underway in three transport industries to produce a series of models for qualifications frameworks for 10 years hence. The project is also optimising the ways scenarios might be used with industry stakeholders.

The financial services and transport sectors are two of the most volatile sectors in terms of industry changes and emerging skills needs. The financial services sector has undergone massive restructuring, has been

---

[4] Cedefop: European Centre for the Development of Vocational Training, Thessaloniki, Greece, see: www.trainingvillage.gr, under 'Scenarios and Strategies'; ETF: European Training Foundation, Turin, Italy, see: www.etf.eu.int

spearheading the use of new technologies and whereas some businesses in the sector are increasingly customer-facing others are truly global in nature. The transport sector was selected for this study because:
- it has skills shortages (e.g. in local authorities, rail middle managers);
- it has new national and EU regulatory requirements;
- it is influenced by international developments and some parts operate internationally;
- it has occupations that are regarded as safety critical or safety significant - thus placing considerable importance on the achievement of defined levels of competence;
- licensing is a requirement in a number of key occupations;
- changes in the business environment have led to a high dependency on outsourced services and a consequential need for means to provide assurance about consistency of competency standards.

These features make forecasting qualifications needs in the sectors particularly difficult and in such circumstances scenarios methods can be particularly helpful. In a separate paper ([5]) presented in this publication more detail is provided of the transport project.

Three problems – is scenario methodology an answer?
There seem to be three main problems associated with modernisation of qualifications. The first is the difficulty of obtaining unambiguous, dependable and detailed evidence for the need for change and the second is the resistance or inertia to change within the stakeholder groups. A third is the difficulty of managing an evolution from one qualifications model to another. How might scenario methods help with these problems?

6. Obtaining good quality evidence

The problem of evidence arises because forecast data gets less dependable as the period of the forecast is extended. Uncertainties grow and consequentially decisions are not easy to make with confidence. The production of scenarios that have at their centre the pivot of uncertainty can extend the value of forecasts and increase confidence in a limited range of outcomes. Scenarios also accommodate main areas of agreement amongst

---

[5] See Tom Leney's paper in this volume on the application of the methodology to three industries in the UK transport sector.

experts about what is likely to happen and what is not. This serves to raise the plausibility of the different futures.

In their work on transport scenarios for the UK in 2012, Leney and Mackinnon (2002) have also developed quantitative descriptions of futures to complement qualitative ones. This provides a richness of data types which helps to provide a more secure common understanding of what each scenario means. This welding together of quantitative and qualitative data is another major strength of scenario method.

In summary, data generated through scenario building and the testing of strategies seems to help overcome some significant data problems. However the need for good data sets describing current labour markets and work practices remains key.

7. Generating momentum for modernising qualifications

The process of developing the scenarios requires the involvement of key experts at several stages and serves as an early warning system for change and predisposes some experts to the need to look carefully at options for modernisation. The building of scenarios can lower resistance to change amongst stakeholder groups because it involves these groups in early stages of the development process. However, the method goes further as a consultation and dissemination tool - the testing of new qualifications and qualifications frameworks against scenarios is proving to be a particularly powerful method for building consensus. It is the fact that the method generates models to which people can react that is important. Each scenario is a focus of attention that provides a language which stakeholders can share.

There is one aspect of scenario building work that is potentially helpful with this second problem – that of identifying the precise nature of the 'drivers' of specific proposals for change. There is no shortage of experts who are willing to express an opinion on how a qualification *should* develop, but few express opinions about how it *will* evolve. One reason for this might be people worry about as yet uncertain influences, such as technological developments. Another is the difficulty people seem to face in weighing up which influences will dominate others in years to come. Some of these influences reinforce one another; others are in tension. Drivers of change do not exist in isolation. Lobby groups, public 'champions', legal instruments, financial backing, communication infrastructures may all be part of the driver anatomy. It is essential to consider the nature of these powerful influences on the qualification system in an attempt to help experts decide which changes are likely to happen and which ones are not. Experience of the application of scenario methodology in several projects has shown that defining, as far as possible, the nature of drivers for change is a very important and useful process.

Scenario method seems to have the potential to lower resistance of groups with a tendency to look for small, incremental, change processes and to lengthen the period over which modernisation is discussed.

8. Getting from here to there

The third problem is how to manage the transition from an existing qualification system to a new one. This remains a particularly difficult issue. It would be easy to put too much store on the consultative power of scenario method and conclude that it is likely to help with managing transitions. However experience to date shows that this is not likely to be the case. People do not easily understand scenario methodology until they have used it. It takes time to fully appreciate the strengths and weaknesses of the method and often managers do not have the time required. In QCA we have decided that the current scenario activity should lie outside our formal accreditation schedules until it is clear that the method can be applied easily, efficiently and adds value to the modernisation process. When this is the case we will produce guidance for awarding bodies and industry bodies on how to use scenarios method in combination with other methods.

9. Conclusions

Experience to date of using scenario methodology in the toolbox of methods for identifying future qualifications needs is promising. However it is too early to be sure that the method is practical, efficient and effective when used in the mainstream of methods. We need to test the reactions of stakeholders coming 'cold' to this new and challenging way of looking at the future.

The issue of welding scenarios method to other processes needs to be addressed. There is little research evidence that suggests particular combinations of methods are best suited to particular contexts. There is also a particular problem with engaging managers in the process of integrating the method into current strategic approaches.

The initiation of QCA's research on scenario method originated through involvement in Cedefop's pilot work on Scenarios for VET in Europe. Already there have been three additional applications in different educational fields that have yielded useful and previously unobtainable perspectives on the future. QCA is therefore grateful to Cedefop for the opportunity to research and learn in the VET project. It is also important that we continue to share experiences of applying the methodology in different ways that are suited to different contexts. This conference provides an opportunity to do this and again we are very pleased to provide our experiences and to receive commentary from experts from other countries on our research described in this paper.

References

Bertrand, G. et al. Europe 2010: cinq scénarios pour sortir du no future. *Futuribles, Analyse et Prospective.* European Commission. Brussels, 1999.

Buchan, D.; Roberts, A. Energy study sees break-up of global trends. *Financial Times*, 21 Jan 2002, London.

Department of Education and Science; Manpower Services Commission. *Review of Vocational Qualifications.* London, 1986.

Department of Trade and Industry, Future Learning Unit. *Scenarios for 2020.* London, 2001.

Department for Education and Employment. *Delivering skills for all - Second report of the National Skills Task Force.* London, 1999.

Green, L.; Hartley, P. *Developing National Occupational Standards. Report by LMG associates for QCA.* London, 1999.

Green, L.; Hartley, P. *Final report on a pilot study to explore the methods used to identify the content of National Occupational Standards.* QCA, London, 2000.

Haskel, J.; Holt, R. *Skills Task Force research paper on 'Anticipating future skill needs': Can it be done? Does it need to be done?* DfEE. London, 1999.

Leney, T.; Coles, M. *Analysis and synopsis of the outcomes of the scenarios for VET project.* QCA and the Institute of Education. London, 2001.

Leney, T.; Mackinnon, I. *Scenarios for three transport Industries*, QCA, London, 2002.

Ministry of Education. *Scenarios for NZ curriculum 2020.* Wellington, New Zealand, 2001 (http://www.tki.org.nz/r/stocktake/index_e.php).

NCVQ. *Criteria and guidance.* London, 1995.

NCVQ/SCOTVEC. *Review of 100 NVQs/SVQs – a final report.* London, 1996.

OECD. *What schools for the future?* OECD: Paris, 2001.

Shell, *Global scenarios to 2020*, London, 2000.

QCA. *Developing National Occupational Standards for NVQs and SVQs.* London, 1999.

Schoemaker, P. Scenario planning: a tool for strategic thinking. *Sloan Management Review.* London, 1995.

Sellin, B. *Anticipating occupational and qualifications developments.* Cedefop Panorama Series. Cedefop. Thessaloniki, 2001.

United Nations, Population Division of the Department of Economic and Social Affairs at the United Nations Secretariat. *World population projections to 2150.* United Nations. New York, 1998.

Van Wieringen, F.; Sellin, B.; Schmidt, G. *Uncertainties in education: handle with care.* Max Goote, Kenniscentrum. Amsterdam, 2001.

Wilson, R. Forecasting skill requirements at national and company levels. In Descy, P.; Tessaring, M., eds. *Training in Europe. Second report on vocational training research in Europe 2000: background report.* Cedefop Reference series. Vol 2, pp 561 – 609. Luxembourg, 2001.

Annex 1
Techniques used by UK consultants in identifying future qualifications needs

- Workshops with experts – half or day long structured sessions with high levels of interaction between participants and a sharp task focus throughout.
- Focus groups, discussion groups, working groups, sector expert groups, brain storming sessions – shorter sessions which cover specific issues to exploratory discussion
- Delphi methods – iteration of views by a structured method of engaging with experts
- Questionnaires – these can vary in length, depth, openness, mode of contact with the interviewer
- Interviews – taking the form of one to one interviews, small group or telephone interviews. Interviews can be heavily structured, semi structured or open.
- Desk research – looking at reports, statistics, recruitment data and other company documentation.
- Case studies – applying trend analysis to specific work groups to discover implications. This includes work place observations and HR practices.

ICT is playing a growing role in all of these methods. The lack of consistency in the way the techniques are used may signal a methodological problem in this area.

Annex 2
An outline of scenarios methodology

Once an organisation is committed to the need to define longer-term strategic development in a context that is uncertain, the first step is to conduct desk research on published materials to draw up a list of possible future trends in the field of interest. Experts may contribute their views as to which possibilities to look for.

These trends are put to a predefined sample of experts who judge their importance and likelihood of coming about. Trends that most experts consider to be unimportant are removed from the set. Trends still in the frame that most experts consider will come about, and those that provoke a similarly strong feeling that they will not come about, are set aside for use later. The remaining set of future trends is characterised by divided opinion about the likelihood of their coming about. These are used to build the spine of a set of scenarios. By analysing the areas of uncertainty to identify overarching themes and tensions in these trends, the scenario builders can determine dimensions that could flip one way or the other in the future, according to the experts. For example, if a key theme carrying uncertainty is 'participation in education', a dimension that spans from 'the system becomes open to all and participation is encouraged' to 'the system is geared to those who are willing and able to participate' can be developed - in other words a high-low spectrum.

These dimensions are then set against one another and used to generate scenarios that are narratives describing plausible futures. At this stage the future trends that were set aside earlier are reintroduced to all scenarios. An effective set of scenarios is that the scenarios are all plausible, internally consistent, interesting and challenging to those who will use them to assist planning

Scenarios themselves are only the beginning The power of the method is that it allows the testing of strategies. The agency wishing to plan for long-term change identifies strategies that could be adopted. Each strategy is researched in relation to each scenario, usually by face-to-face interview with a fresh sample of key players. These may be experts in the specific field of interest or may be experts in specialisms tangential to the main field. A robust and useful strategy is one that seems to have potential in a range of scenarios. Some strategies will resonate strongly or weakly, with a particular scenario. In addition, the process of testing the strategies reveals data on driving forces, resistant forces, key players and policy instruments needed to make a strategy effective, and so serves the purpose of rounding off strategies to make them more likely to be more effective. The process can also highlight risks and show why any side effects of deploying the strategy might be unhelpful.

In conclusion there is increasing confidence that using scenarios method to complement other methods of carrying out needs analysis brings major advantages in 'future proofing' qualifications. The way that the method requires stakeholders and experts to back from 10 years forward instead of starting from the status quo is a major advance. However the key advance is the generation of strategic conversations amongst stakeholders about the form of a thoroughly modern qualification system for an industry.

Developing prospective tools for the observation of skill requirements in Spain

Jordi Planas, *GRET, ICE-UAB, Autonomous University of Barcelona, Spain*

In the last decades various tools have been developed in Spain to observe skill requirements and to translate these requirements into provision of adequate initial school-based training, occupational training and continuing training. Although the tools developed in Spain were at first oriented to the different types of training, different territories and different methodologies, they all played an essential role in the general orientation and modernisation of vocational education and training in Spain.

This paper describes the tools for identifying skills requirements in Spain and informs on an observatory (OBINCUAL) which is now being set up. This observatory is closely associated with the creation of the National System of Vocational Qualifications. OBINCUAL has been conceived as a 'network of networks' which can function as a nucleus of information and exchange on skill requirements and vocational training between the different vocational training subsystems in Spain.

1. The subsystems of vocational training in Spain

Vocational training in Spain is divided into three main subsystems:
(a) initial/regulated vocational training (regulated by legislation on education) given in secondary education schools and organised in middle-level and higher-level training cycles;
(b) occupational vocational training addressed to the unemployed as part of an active employment policy;
(c) continuing vocational training addressed people in employment.

Logically, the modes of organising the three vocational training subsystems vary in terms of curriculum design and provision of training courses in different parts of the country.

(a) The curricula of the middle-level and higher-level training cycles in initial/regulated vocational training are essentially designed on a centralised basis and grouped into 'occupational families', that is, they are organised nation-wide (even though, as in the whole educational system, a great deal of latitude in shaping the concrete measures is allowed both to the Autonomous Communities and each school). The training courses in the middle-level and higher-level training cycles, on the contrary, are under the responsibility of the governments of the Autonomous Communities and held in the secondary education centres which, in Spain, are run by the governments of the Autonomous Communities.

(b) Occupational training has been decentralised in the Autonomous Communities in the last few years. But, at national level, INEM (National Institute for Employment under the Spanish Ministry of Labour) has, in the last decades, set up a central Directory of Certificates of Occupational Proficiency. However, these Certificates of Occupational Proficiency are not binding for the occupational training courses offered by the Autonomous Communities. The Autonomous Communities are the bodies which plan the provision of occupational training in their territories, so it is not surprising that the outcome of this situation has been a high degree of heterogeneity in the nation-wide contents of training provision as, basically, these courses have to satisfy a large number of needs as heterogeneous as the different territories.

(c) Continuing training resources are administered centrally (for the whole of Spain) by FORCEM (Foundation for Continuing Training) which prepares its curricula and plans its courses mainly on the basis of the requirements of the companies.

2. The diversity of the tools for observation of skill requirements and the programming of training provision

The diversity of the target groups and the specific objectives of this type of training, the degree of decentralisation in the definition of its contents, the diversity of programming mechanisms and financing sources, led to the establishment of specific observation mechanisms for each subsystem. The methodology of the observation mechanisms set up for each of the vocational training subsystems was essentially that of 'functional analysis'.

Other tools for observation at sectoral or local level were also developed, but in a very uneven manner.

Vocational training in Spain, as in other European countries, has to deal with the necessity of creating a common framework of reference for the different vocational training subsystems; this inevitably implies that better integration of the observation tools for skill requirements and training provision is required, as these, up to now, were developed autonomously by the different subsystems and differ from one another even though they contain some elements of coordination.

Up to the present, the measures which have had a major impact in Spain may be grouped as follows:
- Work on the curricula of initial vocational training is undertaken mainly by the Ministry of Education in collaboration with the Autonomous Communities. This work which has the aim of producing the curricula for the middle-level and higher-level training cycles is carried out in conjunction with experts from the companies.
- The observatory set up by INEM (Ministry of Labour), the 'Observatory for Occupations', is structured more in the form of a dynamic network covering the occupational training centres than a traditional observatory. But, as Cachón (2001) says, it is not capable of extending this dynamic development beyond its institutional borders.
- FORCEM (Foundation for Continuing Training which administers the public funds for the financing of continuing training in Spain) has developed observation tools for skill requirements and training needs primarily on a sectoral basis, but this too is not a genuine observatory, and its special interest is only directed to some occupational fields.
- Some Autonomous Communities have developed observatories which mainly observe and identify the specific needs of the territory for which they are responsible. The Basque Country deserves a special mention for its efforts to improve quality, and similar efforts are being undertaken in other Autonomous Communities such as the Canary Islands or Madrid (Cachón, 2001).
- Mention should also be made of a multitude of 'local observatories', often established at municipal level with heterogeneous resources and varying objectives, which are to be found in Spain today. As the municipal administrations are mainly responsible not only for initial training but also for occupational training policies, many of them have created their own tools to help them to identify and provide the vocational training needed in their own territory.

- Lastly, there are other more or less systematic mechanisms for the identification of training needs linked to the 'spontaneous' demand of companies.

All, or almost all, of these tools contain prospective elements for identifying future skills, but they are clearly insufficient to respond effectively to the challenges arising for our economies from the ongoing process of change. Furthermore, the prospective elements developed in the existing mechanisms do not contain a methodology which is appropriate for this type of work.

3. OBINCUAL - a stake, a challenge, some questions

Although it is still in the initial phase - which means that we can only describe and evaluate its intentions but not its achievements - OBINCUAL (Observatory of the Spanish National Institute for Qualifications - INCUAL) is now being set up in Spain. This institute, and its observatory, is under the responsibility of the General Council for Vocational Training (CGFP) and has organic links with the Ministry of Labour.

This observatory is closely associated with the creation - also under the technical responsibility of INCUAL - of the National System of Vocational Qualifications. The aim of this system is to be an '... integrated vocational qualification and training system ... which will provide the tools for a system capable of enabling a global, coordinated, coherent and optimal treatment of the problems of the vocational qualification and training of the different groups of persons, organisations and companies' (CGFP, 2000).

By integration the project means: a) integration of vocational qualifications in order to establish a common framework of reference for skills defined in accordance with the current needs of the production system for all types of vocational training; b) integration of the different means of acquiring vocational skills; c) integration of training provision in vocational education.

The project states: 'Therefore, the National System of Qualifications will serve as a framework of reference and orientation for all actions, and especially the training activities of the different administrations, the social partners, other bodies, companies and persons, thus facilitating the necessary cooperation and consensus, so that all those involved may coordinate their objectives and interests in the system of qualifications in a coherent and structured manner' (CGFP, 2000).

For this purpose, OBINCUAL has been conceived as a 'network of networks' which can function as a nucleus of information and exchange on skill requirements and vocational training between the different vocational training subsystems in Spain.

With regard to the early identification of skill requirements OBINCUAL intends to set up 'expertise' networks whose work will '.... enable the early detection of needs for new qualifications by defining (endogenous) scenarios of the future'.

The purpose of OBINCUAL's prospective activities, according to INCUAL's working documents, will be to analyse the key areas of qualification and the economic activities to which they are linked and thus: firstly determine the components and the variables of the production process in which most changes are taking place, and secondly, collect information on trends and forecasts on the future development of these components.

This will make it possible to provide information on development trends and forecasts for the future of the 'observation fields' in which OBINCUAL will be organised. The 'observation fields' (CIREM, 2002) '... may be considered as sub-aggregates of economic/productive activities which have a certain technological and professional affinity, and are based on the horizontal categorisation of the National Catalogue of Vocational Qualifications'.

In order to carry out these prospective studies OBINCUAL proposes to do the following:
- conduct a preliminary analysis of the observation field and the fields considered to be key areas for its future development;
- select the nuclei of the network of networks which, through their routine activities, will be most suitable to develop the study of each observation field.

The basic methodology used by OBINCUAL will be the Delphi method.

The experts of the OBINCUAL network will be the persons directing the study of each observation field (one of them will be appointed as head of the project) and establishing the subjects and the variables of the Delphi questionnaires.

As INCUAL only initiated this process recently, we will have to wait for some time to collect enough material to evaluate the results of the measures for the early identification of skill requirements. In addition, not enough time has passed to obtain sufficient information for assessing the strong and weak points of its application.

In any case, even though many points relating to the development of OBINCUAL still have to be discussed at length, we can raise some questions today. At least two questions arise in the discussion of methodology:

(1) *What scope does OBINCUAL have to deal with local and sectoral specificities?*

The process of technological and commercial globalisation to which most companies in Spain, and also in other European countries, are now being subjected, has 'upstream' and 'downstream' effects which go beyond the boundaries of the state. In the field of human resources, regional and even local aspects, as several authors indicate (Manuel Castells for example), may be an essential element of competitiveness for companies in a global economy. The question may also be asked from a reverse angle: what scope do national states actually have for the prospective management of skills?

In view of the vital role played today by national states in the establishment of standards for skills management on our labour markets, it seems to be reasonable that the 'national' mechanisms for early identification of skill requirements should also integrate the other two dimensions, the global and the regional, in order to ensure their effectiveness. For example, the skill requirements and training needs of companies in the micro-electronics sector, or even those of a single company, are not the same in Helsinki and in Barcelona.

Another variable (cross-linked with the above) plays an 'inevitable' role in observatories which pursue objectives or targets such as those of OBINCUAL: the sectoral element and its role in the international division of labour in a specific area. Skill requirements for administrative activities in the micro-electronics sector are not the same as those for the hotel/catering sector, not even if they are in the same locality, or if two hotel establishments of different categories and size are involved. Thus, consideration of intersectoral and intrasectoral specificities is required.

(2) *What room will there be for 'the old' and 'the new' in future?*

Early identification of skill requirements presents a dual challenge: we have to include the observation and detection of both 'new' skills and 'old' skills, the latter will continue to exist and/or facilitate the acquisition of new skills.

In the debate on early identification of skill requirements the essential problem may be that we associate 'early identification' only with 'new skills' as an element of the future. In doing this we run the great risk of forgetting the 'old skills' which will continue to be vital in the future. In everyday terms one may say that many of the essential skills needed to cope with the future are skills which, at least in essence even if their form varies, are extremely old. Knowing how to read or express oneself in writing, or regularly reading the daily or weekly press or books, irrespective of whether they are on paper or electronic.

Because of this, even if it seems very paradoxical, one of the principal challenges of the identification of skills which will be required in the future, consists of identifying and recognising those 'old' skills which will continue to exist or will, at least, be the basis for the acquisition of new skills which are only 'identifiable' in the short term. Therefore, one of the challenges of the future is the ability to recognise the old skills which will continue to serve as the basis of the knowledge society. This is a vital aspect which effects, among other aspects, the contents and efficiency of compulsory education. The human capital of a country can be transformed in the short term only if the working population has a basic training which is not vulnerable to the rapid changes in our economies but is so solid that it can respond to and absorb these changes.

What scope for action does OBINCUAL have in this respect, as this is basically essential for the future?

There is no doubt that for the early identification of skills it is essential to take into account the time horizons of the 'students', the companies and the training systems, all of them essentially different (Planas et al., 2001).

References

Cachón, L. *Observatorios de Formación Continua. Estudio Exploratorio.* Dep. de Sociología I. Universidad Complutense de Madrid, 2001.

CGFP (Consejo General de Formación Profesional). *Nuevo programa Nacional de Formación Profesional.* Published by Consejo General de la Formación Profesional, 2000.

CIREM. Annex I *'Campos de Observación'* in: 'Cuestionario Delphi para el Estudio sobre identificación de los factores que inciden en la determinación de las cualificaciones profesionales', 2002

Planas, J. et al. The skills market: dynamics and regulation. *In* Descy, P.; Tessaring, M., eds. *Training in Europe. Second report on vocational training research in Europe 2000: background report.* Cedefop Reference series. Office for Official Publications of the European Communities, Vol. 2, 2001, pp. 313-381.

Network of national surveys on skill needs in Italy

Mario Gatti, *Institute for the Development of Workers' Vocational Training (ISFOL), Rome, Italy*

In Italy vocational training has been managed by the Regions since 1974. The need to attain integrated education and labour policies at the local level had encouraged research aimed at surveying and anticipating training and occupational needs. This research was intended to guide political choices supporting socio-economic development and employment.

At present the government is establishing a network by creating an information system designed to supply information about:
- sectoral scenarios in which occupational needs are expressed;
- lists of occupational titles by sectors representing needs which have been expressed by companies but which are in very short supply on the labour market;
- descriptions of occupational needs stemming from new skill needs;
- occupational forecasts for the short and medium terms (1-5 years).

This paper presents the project – coordinated by ISFOL – to set up a network of national needs surveys in Italy.

1. Introduction

In the past, analyses of skill and training requirements in Italy followed two parallel and separate strands: the local and the national. Local analysis work took root before national analysis work which has gained ground only in the last five years.

The Italian government promoted, between 1997 and 2000, a set of national surveys of skill requirements in various sectors of the economy and is currently preparing an information system networking these surveys with a view to providing information on trends in skill and training requirements in Italy.

In this respect, the Ministry of Labour and Industrial Policy has commissioned ISFOL (Institute for the Development of Workers' Vocational Training) to design this system which, by creating a network of national surveys, gathers and combines qualitative data on skill requirements with quantitative data on occupational trends.

The purpose of this networked system for the permanent monitoring of skill requirements is to facilitate and improve labour market entry and integration, improve and support employability and promote occupational mobility. As such, it has been included by the Ministry of Labour and Industrial Policy in the Operating Plans of the new 2000-06 programme period of the European Social Fund, among systems measures, as part of Objective 3 of Strand C, Measure C1 and in the 'human resources' strand of Objective 1 of the National Operating Plan which is administered by the Ministry of Labour. Measures planned under Objective 3 must be linked to those planned under Objective 1 in order to promote benchmarking.

At local level, it should be borne in mind that the Italian Regions have been responsible for vocational training since 1974. In recent years, a number of institutional reforms have enhanced and extended local authority education and labour market competences. The need to implement local policies that integrate education and work has paved the way for a whole range of surveys intended to detect/anticipate skill and training requirements whose findings could well be used as a starting point for choices of policy to support development and employment in an area.

The autonomy with which the Regions have conducted their research has meant that their results are not at all comparable, making comparative studies of the various local experiments very difficult. In many cases, different objectives have been pursued, using different approaches and methods, and different instruments have been prepared.

Both nationally and locally, there have recently been attempts to place measures on a less sporadic footing and in both cases to work towards a system configuration.

The regional governments are now clearly aware of the need to reorganise and systemise local needs analysis initiatives. All the Regional Operating Plans for the 2000-06 period include this issue, setting out both specific and horizontal measures.

As part of the overhaul of the institutional scenario, a structural link needs to be found, in the areas of vocational training and labour market policy, between national and local needs analysis initiatives, that does not make one subordinate to the other, but does provide a high degree of consistency. A national system necessarily has to take account of the Regions' needs and experiences as they are responsible for training supply design and labour market management and therefore for human resource development policies. Ex post monitoring of the efficiency and effectiveness of the nationally networked system of needs analysis is also important for the purposes of planning regional training policies. Drawing two strands of initiatives which currently have few links into a coordinated framework is extremely important if tasks are to be correctly allocated to central government, which needs to provide a framework within which local authorities have to draw up criteria for the reorganisation of regional initiatives.

Taking a systemic approach, however, the subsystems have to function as parts of a single mechanism for which criteria for and methods of connection and interaction have to be clearly pinpointed.

2. Networked system for the permanent monitoring of skill and training requirements

The surveys included in the national networked system are to be conducted, during the initial pilot stage, by joint organisations, called Bilateral Bodies, made up of entrepreneurs and trade unionists active in and familiar with the labour market, taking an overall approach in which the networked system is managed by the institutions (Ministry of Labour and Industrial Policy) to guarantee neutrality, and information is produced by the social partners in order to ensure its accuracy.

Up to now, two types of survey have been conducted:
1. the first gathering information on employment and recruitment prospects from enterprises;
2. the second, of a qualitative type, gathering information on occupations and competences lacking in the labour market, but needed by enterprises.

The quantitative surveys have explored the whole of the economy, while the qualitative surveys conducted up to now have covered some 25% of economic activities.

At this experimental stage, different methods have been used for the qualitative research, producing results that are difficult to combine.

To resolve this problem, ISFOL's initial initiatives have involved all the partners in the system to try to ensure that the methods being used for surveys under way are as consistent as possible.

The information and data gathered are managed by an Internet platform-based information system which combines four types of data:
1. trends in the economic scenario in which needs are expressed;
2. sectoral registers of the occupations required by enterprises;
3. description of the occupations required;

4. data on current employment and short- and medium-term forecasts.

To describe the scenario, as shown in Figure 1, the information system provides structural data on:
- enterprise characteristics in terms of size, market, number of employees:
- geographical distribution;
- data employment in terms of numbers and types of employees.

Trends are described on the basis of the following variables:
- technological innovation anticipated in the near future;
- organisational innovation (for instance, lean organisation, outsourcing, spin off, etc.);
- product/service innovation.

Figure 1. **Scenario description**

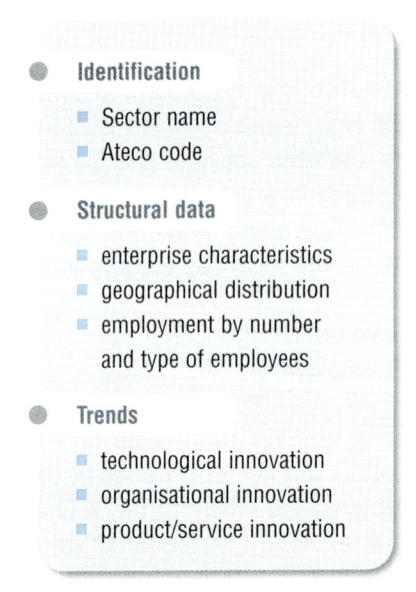

- **Identification**
  - Sector name
  - Ateco code
- **Structural data**
  - enterprise characteristics
  - geographical distribution
  - employment by number and type of employees
- **Trends**
  - technological innovation
  - organisational innovation
  - product/service innovation

The lists of occupations required by enterprises, in each economic sector, are 'processed' by the Bilateral Bodies which then incorporate similar profiles into a single occupational profile and draw up a new list, known as a register, of reference profiles.

These groupings of similar occupational profiles into single broader virtual occupational profiles are felt to be more useful for the design of education and training schemes.

Figure 2 gives an example of a reference profile register for the textile and clothing sector.

Figure 2. **List of virtual occupations** (e.g. clothing and textile sector)

1. administration/finance/auditing technician
2. accountant/bookkeeper
3. human resource management/development technician
4. company information system technician
5. secretarial operator
6. trade services operator
7. product/service-customer assistance technician
8. production planning/logistics technician
9. purchasing/procurement technician
10. warehouse (reception/shipment) worker
11. product designer-textile technician
12. product/process industrialisation technologist
13. quality system technician (process and products)
14. laboratory technician
15. testing technician
16. environment/safety technician
17. maintenance planning and management technician
18. industrial information technician
19. mechanical maintenance operator
20. automation system electric and electronic maintenance operator
21. multi-purpose maintenance operator (mechanic-electric-electronic)
22. plant maintenance operator (thermo-hydraulic, steam, air-conditioning)
23. production technician (department/operational unit management)
24. dying and printing process operator
25. finishing process operator
26. automation system operator
27. production operator

The description of the reference profile, shown in Figure 3, is divided into two sections. The first, identifying the profile, shows:
- the name of the reference profile;
- its link with the ISCO 88 code;
- corresponding occupations in the labour market;
- its link with the Ateco 91 economic activity code in which the occupational requirement is to be found;
- trends in requirements, in the near future, as expressed by a significant sample of enterprises.

Figure 3. **Description of virtual occupations**

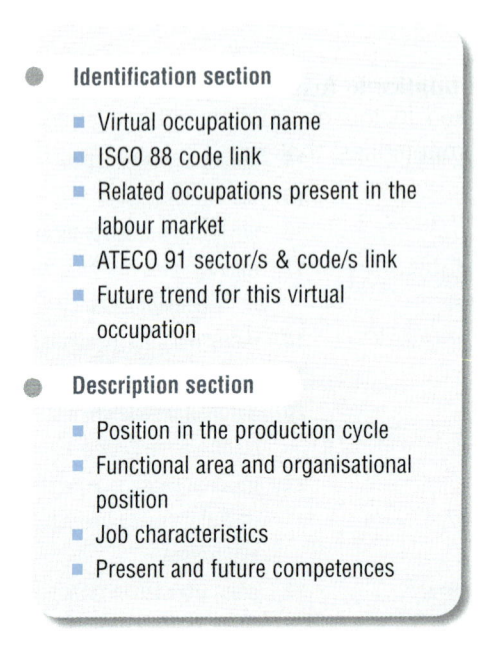

- Identification section
  - Virtual occupation name
  - ISCO 88 code link
  - Related occupations present in the labour market
  - ATECO 91 sector/s & code/s link
  - Future trend for this virtual occupation
- Description section
  - Position in the production cycle
  - Functional area and organisational position
  - Job characteristics
  - Present and future competences

The second is a descriptive section providing information on:
- location of the reference profile in an ideal production cycle;
- functional area and organisational position in which the occupation works;
- work characteristics: mission, activities and tasks;
- present and future skill requirements.

Following on from this, competences, illustrated in Figure 4, are divided into current and future.

Figure 4. **Current and future competences**

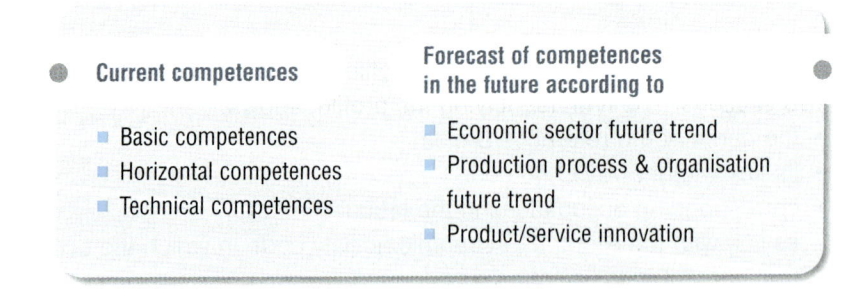

- Current competences
  - Basic competences
  - Horizontal competences
  - Technical competences
- Forecast of competences in the future according to
  - Economic sector future trend
  - Production process & organisation future trend
  - Product/service innovation

Current competences include:
- *basic competences*, i.e. the 'minimum knowledge' essential for employability (for instance language, computing, economic, business management, work research technique competences, etc.);
- *horizontal competences* used in the occupation but not specific to that occupation. These are competences that can be transferred from one occupational context to another (for instance, communication, diagnostic, problem-solving competences, etc.);
- *technical competences* linked specifically to the particular occupation.

In the case of predicted future competences, the aim is to study changes in the competence mix resulting from:
- future trends in the economic sector;
- changes in production and organisation;
- product and/or service innovation.

Information on predicted competences provides significant data on future skill shortages. As well as qualitative findings, the system provides, as summarised in Figure 5, data and information on:
- institutional surveys on the composition and size of the occupation (quarterly labour force surveys conducted by ISTAT);
- data from the Excelsior survey on short-term enterprise recruitment forecasts conducted by Unioncamere (national body of Chambers of Commerce).

Figure 5. **Quantitative data and forecasts**

- Quarterly labour market surveys
- Yearly recruitment forecast
- Macroeconomic studies providing medium-term forecast

In order to improve forecasting, ISFOL is conducting a number of studies based on econometric models applied to sector/occupation grids in order to obtain medium-term employment forecasts (five years).

The overall design of the system is shown in Figure 6. The system provides scenario information and sectoral registers for each sector of economic activity. The system provides information of a qualitative type and on trends for each profile of the register. Each reference profile is linked to an ISCO code which is in turn linked to an ISTAT code. The need for two classification systems is due to the fact that it is easier to classify virtual occupational profile requirements using the ISCO unit and minor group levels for which a description of missions and tasks is available, while the statistical data available in Italy refer to the ISTAT classification of occupations. This ISCO-ISTAT bridge enables qualitative information on occupational needs and competences to be indirectly linked to quantitative information on current and forecast employment.

Figure 6. **Logic diagram of the information system**

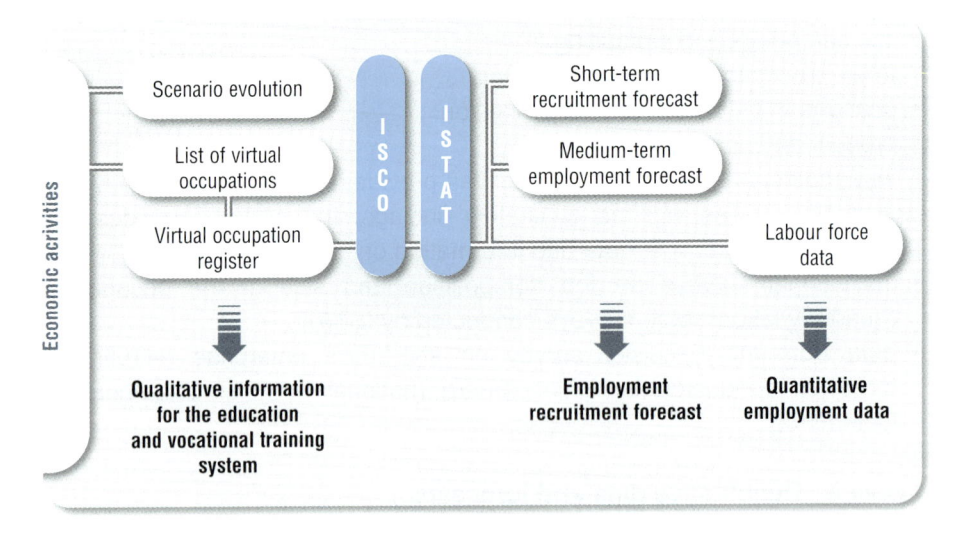

![Logic diagram showing Economic activities feeding into Scenario evolution, List of virtual occupations, Virtual occupation register through ISCO-ISTAT bridge to Short-term recruitment forecast, Medium-term employment forecast, Labour force data, producing Qualitative information for the education and vocational training system, Employment recruitment forecast, and Quantitative employment data]

The mix of information available in the networked system helps to meet the information needs of the education and training system and to support labour market management policies. The findings of the qualitative surveys provide information enabling the education system to design training schemes that are in keeping with the needs expressed by the labour market. From the quantitative point of view, data is provided on employment stocks and flows as well as short- and medium-term forecasts that can be used to design appropriate labour market policies.

3. Conclusions

The first steps have now been made towards the construction of a permanent national system for the analysis of trends in skill and competence requirements, but two problems still need to be resolved:
- how the national level of the needs survey network can be combined with the local/regional level;
- how qualitative information on needs can be made more consistent with quantitative data on employment trends.

As regards the first problem, it should be stressed that although it is necessary to know about national trends in skill needs in order to draw up an overall picture, training and labour market management policies are implemented at local level with the result that specific local aspects of needs have to be properly incorporated into the national framework.

Political agreement needs to be found between the parties, and within this, a technical proposal paving the way for synergy between the systems that are being constructed at local and national level. Unless there is national/local integration, the risk is that information on skill requirements will be available at a national level and therefore difficult to use to draw up local training and employment policies.

It would also be useful to devise a meta-method defining how national skill requirements can be specified at local level. One potential path would be for both levels of government to promote further surveys using coordinated methods in order to obtain results that can be combined.

These methods should from the outset be consistent as regards:
- terminology and concepts;
- classification references;
- IT links.

Finding appropriate ways of linking qualitative information on needs, in particular those relating to current and future competences, with quantitative forecasts of employment trends is the other challenge that this system poses.

The deadline of next autumn for the production of the networked information system prototype will be a turning point in the design of the permanent national system for monitoring skill and training requirements.

There is no doubt, however, that a successful outcome will depend largely on whether the partners involved manage to find and implement consistent choices.

Labour market forecasting in the Netherlands: a top-down approach

Frank Cörvers, Research Centre for Education and the Labour Market (ROA), Maastricht University, The Netherlands

To uphold consistency between aggregated and disaggregated labour market forecasts, it is important to use both a fitting general forecasting model and national databases which distinguish between various occupational groups and types of education. The answer is a top-down approach to labour market forecasting, such as that mainly used by ROA. It can adequately deal with interaction between different labour market segments and substitution processes between occupational groups and types of education. The opposite is the so-called bottom-up approach, in which partial models of labour market forecasting are used, for example for just a selection of sectors or occupational classes, with input from specific (ad hoc) data sources. The bottom-up approach can be complementary to the top-down approach. The paper gives examples of both approaches by reviewing some ROA research.

1. Introduction

The Dutch Research Centre for Education and the Labour Market's (ROA) forecasts aim to increase transparency of the match between education and the labour market. The more transparent a labour market, the better the opportunities and risks resulting from future labour supply and demand developments can be signalled. To anticipate mismatches, suitable labour market forecasts are required. In this paper, it is argued that ROA uses first a top-down approach for making labour market forecasts. In this approach a general - as distinct from partial - forecasting model for the whole labour market and data from national sources are combined to serve two main functions of labour market forecasts: policy and information (see Van Eijs, 1994). The policy function refers to the usefulness of labour market forecasts for government policy-makers, public employment services and employment agencies, employers' organisations, unions and educational organisations. Policy-makers want to be informed of supply and demand developments. By taking account of future employment trends of broadly defined educational classes and occupational groups, they are able to invest correctly in the educational infrastructure. For the Netherlands, ROA biennially publishes the report *The labour market by education and occupation to 200x*, ([1]) which includes analyses of expected labour market developments in the light of particular policy issues. Although the information on which this report is based originally focused mainly on study and career guidance, today the report is aimed more at those involved in policy-making on the match between education and the labour market.

The information function is primarily intended to assist with vocational and educational guidance. This improves the functioning of the labour market, since individuals are better able to adjust their human capital investment decisions to labour market prospects of types of education (see Borghans, 1993). Also, firms may use labour market forecasts as 'early warnings' on future recruitment problems to anticipate human resources policies. The ROA report is based on information providing a detailed insight into the current and future labour market position of 104 types of education, 127 occupational groups and 34 economic sectors ([2]). The information focuses on medium-term labour market forecasts, to give those making choices on further studies, the best possible information on the state of the labour market when they complete their studies. The National Careers Guidance Information Centre (LDC) incorporates ROA's labour market information in various information products for vocational and educational guidance. Besides civil servants from many different ministries (e.g. education, social affairs, economic affairs, agriculture) and public employment services, educational institutes, personnel managers, advisory councils, etc. all use different parts of the information system for their decision-making.

Labour market information serves as vocational and educational guidance, and usually requires much more detail than the information used by policy-makers. Therefore the level of aggregation at which labour market forecasts are disseminated, needs to be higher for the policy than for the information function. The ROA information system covers the whole spectrum of occupational groups and types of education on the labour market, and is designed to meet both functions. To preserve consistency between

---

([1]) See ROA, 1995, 1995a, 2001.
([2]) The forecasts on expansion demand (see the next section) are presented for 13 economic sectors.

aggregated labour market information (e.g. employment trends at sector level, increase in the level of education) and the detailed information, it is important to use both a fitting general forecasting model and national databases which distinguish between the various occupational groups and types of education. The answer is a top-down approach to labour market forecasting, which can adequately deal with interaction between different labour market segments and substitution processes between occupational groups and types of education. The opposite is the so-called bottom-up approach, in which partial models of labour market forecasting are used, for example for just a selection of sectors or broad occupational classes, with input from specific (ad hoc) data sources.

The next section presents the top-down approach of the ROA forecasting model. ([3]) Section 3 discusses the features of the top-down and bottom-up approaches as well as their complementarities. Section 4 concludes the paper.

2. ROA's labour market forecasting model

Figure 1 gives a schematic review of the labour market forecasting model. ([4]) One flow volume important for the demand side of the labour market is expansion demand, which reflects the movement in employment levels in a particular occupational class or for a particular type of education. Forecasts of expansion demand are based on employment level forecasts for economic sectors produced by the Netherlands Bureau for Economic Policy Analysis (CPB). Because particular occupational classes within an economic sector grow more rapidly than others, ROA translates these changes in economic sectors into expansion demand per occupational class. Then the implications of predicted growth in various occupational classes for expansion demand for each type of education are determined. Allowance is made at this point for any shifts occurring in the educational structure of occupational classes. Expansion demand per type of education refers to the number of people with a particular educational background that employers would like to be able to employ. The actual change in employment levels per type of education generally differs with this because changes on the supply side affect relative scarcities and lead to substitution.

([3]) Large parts of this section have been published before in, for example, De Grip, Borghans and Smits, 1998.
([4]) A comprehensive explanation can be found in Cörvers, De Grip and Heijke, 2002. See also Van Eijs et al., 1999, and De Grip, Borghans and Willems, 1995.

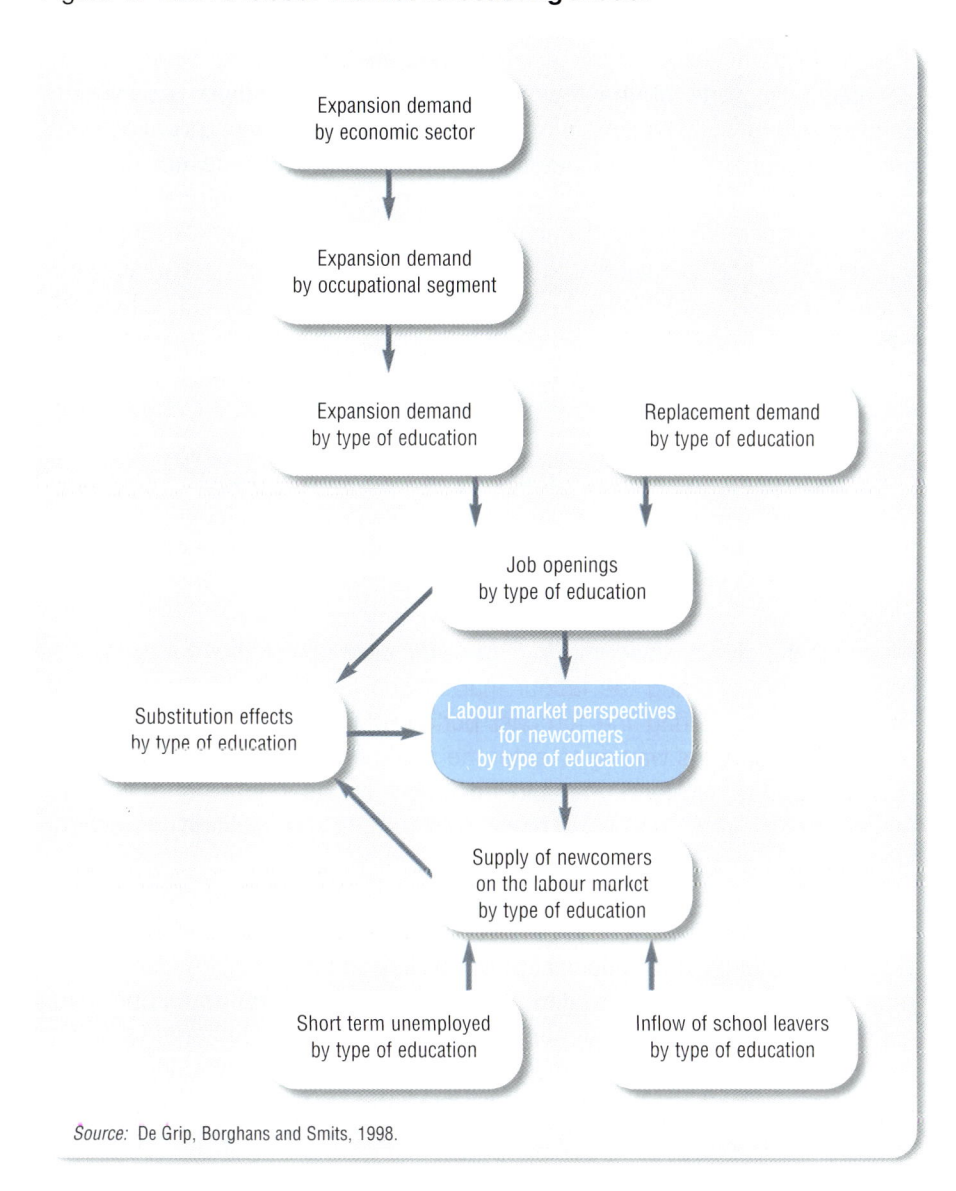

Figure 1. **ROA's labour market forecasting model**

```
Expansion demand
by economic sector
        ↓
Expansion demand
by occupational segment
        ↓
Expansion demand              Replacement demand
by type of education          by type of education
        ↓                             ↓
            Job openings
            by type of education
                    ↓
Substitution effects  →  Labour market perspectives
by type of education        for newcomers
                          by type of education
                                ↓
            Supply of newcomers
            on the labour market
            by type of education
                ↑           ↑
Short term unemployed    Inflow of school leavers
by type of education     by type of education
```

Source: De Grip, Borghans and Smits, 1998.

Labour market demand consists not only of expansion but also of replacement demand, which arises when workers retire, leave the labour force under an early retirement scheme or because of a disability, withdraw from the labour market temporarily, or switch to another occupation, etc. However, replacement demand only arises if the departure of an employee actually leads to a vacancy for a new entrant. If the departure of a worker is taken as an opportunity to cut employment levels, no replacement demand results. These flows out of the labour market are irrelevant for newcomers.

Thus, only parts of the flow leaving the market create replacement demand. There is also an important difference between replacement demand per occupational class and per type of education, because occupational mobility has an influence on replacement demand per occupational class, but not on replacement demand per type of education. Switching occupations has no effect on the educational structure of employment. However, when workers complete part-time studies for a higher level or different qualification, this represents an outflow of workers to another educational category (type of education). In these cases, replacement demand does arise in the educational category under which a worker's previous education was counted.

If employment levels rise, expansion demand and replacement demand together compose the job openings for newcomers to the labour market. If they fall, job openings can only arise because of replacement demand.

To be able to show future labour market prospects for newcomers to the labour market, we have to compare job openings for newcomers with the expected supply of newcomers. The latter consists of the future flow of school-leavers entering the labour market and the outflow from post-initial training courses during the forecast period, plus the supply of short-term unemployed persons waiting to enter the market at the start of this period. It is assumed the long-term unemployed, who have been looking for work for longer than a year, no longer constitute serious competition for school-leavers.

Forecasts of the flows of school-leavers entering the labour market match the *Referentieramingen* (reference forecasts) compiled by the Ministry of Education, Culture and Science for courses in the 'regular' (full-time initial) education system. ROA disaggregates these forecasts by using supplementary data from education matrixes of Statistics Netherlands and its own school-leavers information (see the next section). Supplementary data from Statistics Netherlands are also used to estimate the effects of flows from continuous (vocational) education on the educational makeup of the flows entering the labour market.

An indication of future labour market prospects for newcomers to the labour market is calculated, for each type of education, by comparing the expected flows of demand and supply with each other. This indicator shows any expected discrepancy between demand and supply for each type of education. Excess supply does not necessarily imply the group in question will automatically become unemployed, or a supply shortfall automatically leads to unfilled vacancies. In practice, school-leavers with a type of education for which supply exceeds demand suffer from a worsening of their position. They are more likely to have to accept work below their level, get less favourable contracts, be paid less and more likely to work part-time involuntarily (Wieling and Borghans, 2001). In such situations, employers normally adjust their demands and recruit people with a higher educational background. On the other hand, if there is a supply shortage, school-leavers will not have to accept a job at a lower level, for lower wages, etc.

Because of substitution processes, there are fewer job openings for those suffering from 'crowding-out' with types of education in excess supply. On the other hand, for those with educational backgrounds closely related to types of education in short supply, there will be extra job openings. These passive substitution effects [5] are thus important determinants of labour market prospects for types of education.

3. The top-down versus the bottom-up approach

In general, ROA uses national data sources for the forecasting model discussed in the last section. Both use of national data sources and forecasting with a general - as distinct from partial - model, represent the top-down approach by ROA. Use of national data applies especially to changes in employment in various sectors of industry, which ROA takes from the CPB Netherlands Bureau for Economic Policy Analysis, and to flows from education onto the labour market, which are largely taken from forecasts of the Ministry of Education, Culture and Science. By using these, ROA ensures its labour market forecasts are consistent with authoritative forecasts which provide the basis for policy decisions on important social and economic issues in the Netherlands. ROA makes as much use as possible of regular forecasts on future growth of employment and flows from education onto the labour market. This enables ROA to concentrate on developing its own authoritative expertise within the specialised field of the match between education and the labour market.

Another pillar on which labour market forecasting and the information system are built, is the *Labour force survey (LFS)* of Statistics Netherlands (CBS). The LFS provides information on the number of working people,

---

[5] See Borghans and Heijke, 1996, and De Grip, Borghans and Smits, 1998, for further explanation.

analysed by economic sector, occupation, training, age, sex and working hours. Information from Statistics Netherlands on the number of students in various types of education is also used. Data are used to estimate the models with which developments in the labour market are forecast. Labour market indicators giving a picture of the employment position linked to the choice of a particular occupation or type of education, are also determined based on these data. These indicators concern alternative employment options, competing types of education, and sensitivity to cyclical variations in employment levels.

Existing statistical data from Statistics Netherlands offer only limited information on specific matching problems in the labour market for newcomers (i.e. school-leavers). ROA has put much effort into developing instruments for monitoring the labour market entry of school-leavers regularly and coherently. ROA is coordinating several extensive surveys on the match between initial education and first destinations of school-leavers on the labour market. [6] These include all flows from secondary and tertiary education onto the labour market, using an integrated model, with measurements taken simultaneously and using one list of key questions. This means that representative information is available on graduates across the full range of full-time education. Information on flows from education to the labour market is used as a valuable supplement to disaggregate forecasts made by the Ministry of Education, Culture and Science.

The upper part of Figure 2 shows the role of data sources in a top-down approach. The figure refers to the use of data sources covering all segments of the labour market, consistent with other important national economic developments, e.g. GDP growth, employment growth, demographic trends, which can be consistently differentiated to lower levels of aggregation. These data sources are often available nationally on a regular and coherent basis. This implies data can be used in time series analyses, which is important for forecasting models.

---

[6] On monitoring school-leavers in the Netherlands is the Cheers study of graduates of higher education in 11 EU countries. On behalf of the Netherlands, ROA participates in the project, which is funded by the European Commission in the framework of the TSER programme.

Figure 2. **Use of data sources for labour market forecasting in the top-down and bottom-up approaches**

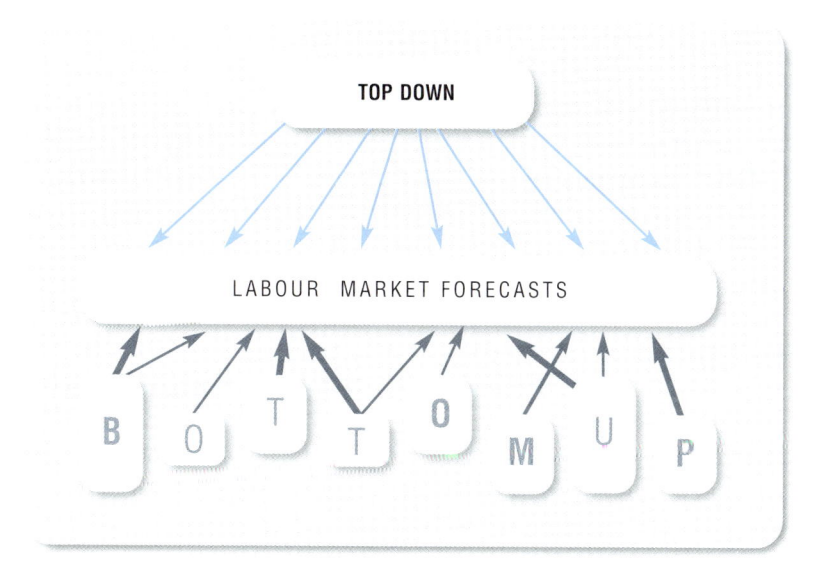

The lower part of Figure 2 points to the bottom-up approach to the use of data sources for labour market forecasting. The various text boxes are different in size and shape. This refers to the features of data sources in the bottom-up approach, which are incompatible with one another and provide partial, often specific but inconsistent and ad hoc information on overlapping labour market segments. Besides, not all data requirements to cover the whole labour market are met, while not all data can be adequately used when sources are too inconsistent with one another. Obviously, it is difficult to integrate data from various sources in one or several consistent and regular data sets. Another disadvantage of the bottom-up approach is using specific data as input for a partial model of the labour market, thereby excluding substitution processes between occupations and types of education.

Nevertheless, partial models of labour market forecasting are useful for a deeper insight into the mechanisms and problems of specific labour market segments, in particular if substitution processes and interactions with other economic sectors are less important (e.g. health care, teachers labour market). Therefore use of partial and ad hoc information may be complementary to the top-down approach. As discussed in Borghans, De Grip and Hoevenberg (1994), partial information of particular labour market segments can be used to differentiate further labour market forecasts generated in the top-down approach. Specific expert knowledge can be used to detect valuable partial data sources, or to judge the plausibility of specific labour market forecasts. In particular, for short-term forecasts it may be useful to incorporate, for example, consensus of judgements of sector experts on particular forecasts (see Batchelor, 2001). However, for medium-term forecasts experts may give too much weight to recent developments on the labour market.

ROA has conducted much research for which the bottom-up was a useful complement to the top-down approach. Below are three examples.

For chemist's assistants in public pharmacies, ROA made forecasts of expected problems (De Grip and Vlasblom, 1999). The problems relate to this rather protected labour market, because of which labour market shortages can hardly be solved in the short term. It is therefore important to have insight of developments of supply and demand at an early stage. Based on administrative sector-specific data on personnel flows and data on destinations of graduates drawn from the above-mentioned school-leaver surveys, a flow model was used to make a long-term forecast. This forecast was complemented by several sensitivity analyses.

For the Science, Research and Development Directorate of the European Commission, ROA developed a model to analyse whether higher education in Member States provides enough science graduates to meet the demand for R&D personnel up to 2002 (see Marey, De Grip and Cörvers, 2001). The model largely follows the forecasting model described in the last section. On the demand side, three sectors are distinguished: business community, public sector, and higher education. The expansion demand per sector per Member State is based on an error correction mechanism that explains the sectoral employment of scientific researchers by sectoral R&D expenses. Data are mostly drawn from Eurostat, although replacement demand is derived from an ad hoc survey of R&D establishments. The model has been used to forecast the supply and demand of scientific researchers by discipline (i.e. natural sciences, technology, agriculture, and medical science) for each Member State. To provide for uncertainties about economic growth and technology and education policies, four scenarios up to 2002 were calculated.

For health care, ROA developed a model in which the flow of workers leaving the sector is explained at institute level (Borghans et al., 1998). The model addresses in particular the effects on this outflow resulting from increasing or decreasing employment levels in an institute. The model was estimated from administrative data from the social insurance organisation for health care. From simulations and scenario analyses of the flow model, it is shown how the sector manages to adapt to changing supply and demand. Although the model does not produce labour market forecasts, it is useful for analysing the impact of future growth and decline (of subsectors) of the health care sector on the flow of workers.

4. Conclusions

ROA uses first a top-down approach for making labour market forecasts. In this approach a general - as distinct from partial - forecasting model for the whole labour market and data from national sources are combined to serve two main functions. The policy function refers to the usefulness of labour market forecasts for policy-makers of government, public employment services and employment agencies, employers' organisations, unions and organisations in education. The information function is primarily intended to assist with vocational and educational guidance. The paper has given a schematic review of the labour market forecasting model used by ROA by discussing three components: expansion demand, replacement demand and the flow of newcomers onto the labour market.

In a top-down approach the data sources cover all segments of the labour market, are consistent with other important national economic developments, e.g. GDP growth, employment growth, demographic trends, and can be consistently differentiated to lower levels of aggregation. These data sources are often available nationally on a regular and coherent basis. In a bottom-up approach the data sources are incompatible with one another and provide partial, often specific but inconsistent and ad hoc information on overlapping labour market segments. Besides, not all data requirements to cover the whole labour market are met, while not all data can be adequately used when sources are too inconsistent with one another.

Nevertheless, partial models of labour market forecasting are useful for a deeper insight into the mechanisms and problems of specific labour market segments, in particular if substitution processes and interactions with other economic sectors are less important (e.g. health care, teachers labour market). Therefore use of partial models and ad hoc information may be complementary to modelling in the top-down approach. ROA has conducted much research for which the bottom-up was a useful complement to the top-down approach.

References

Batchelor, R. How useful are the forecasts of intergovernmental agencies? The IMF and OECD versus the Consensus. *Applied Economics*, 2001, Vol. 33, pp. 225-235.

Borghans, L. *Educational choice and labour market information,* dissertation. University of Limburg, Research Centre for Education and the Labour Market, Maastricht, 1993.

Borghans, L.; Cörvers, F.; Steur M. de; Vlasblom J.D. *Stromen op de arbeidsmarkt in de zorgsector* [Flows on the labour market of the health care sector]. OSA-publicatie, Z 30, OSA, Den Haag, 1998.

Borghans, L.; Grip A. de; Hoevenberg J. *De bruikbaarheid van deelmarktinformatie voor het informatiesysteem onderwijs-arbeidsmarkt* [The usefulness of partial information for the information system education-labour market]. ROA-R-1994/13, Research Centre for Education and the Labour Market, Maastricht, 1994.

Borghans, L.; Heijke H. Forecasting the educational structure of occupations: a manpower requirement approach with substitution. *Labour*, 1996, Vol. 10, pp. 151-192.

Cörvers, F.; Grip A. de; Heijke H. Beyond manpower planning: a labour market model for the Netherlands and its forecasts to 2006. *In* Neugart, M.; Schömann, K., eds. *Forecasting Labour Markets in OECD countries.* Edward Elgar, forthcoming, 2002.

Eijs, P. van. *Manpower forecasting in the western world: the current state of the art.* ROA-RM-1994/1E. Research Centre for Education and the Labour Market, Maastricht, 1994.

Eijs, P. van; Grip, A. de; Diephuis, B.; Jacobs, A.; Marey, P.; Steur, M. de. *Methodiek arbeidsmarktprognoses en -indicatoren, 1999-20040* [Methodology of the ROA information system on occupational groups and types of education, 1999-2004]. ROA-W-1999/4, Research Centre for Education and the Labour Market, Maastricht, 1999.

Grip, A. de; Borghans, L.; Smits, W. Future developments in the job level and domain of high-skilled workers. *In* Heijke, H.; Borghans, L., eds. *Towards a transparent labour market for educational decisions.* Ashgate, Aldershot/Brookfield (USA), Singapore, Sydney, 1998.

Grip, A. de; Borghans, L.; Willems, E. *Methodology of the ROA information system on occupational groups and types of education.* ROA-W-1995/1E, Research Centre for Education and the Labour Market, Maastricht, 1995.

Grip, A. de; Vlasblom, J.D. *Toekomstverkenning arbeidsmarkt apothekersassistenten in de openbare apotheek* [Exploration of the future labour market of chemist's assistants in public pharmacies]. ROA-R-1999/7, Research Centre for Education and the Labour Market, Maastricht, 1999.

Marey, Ph.; Grip, A. de; Cörvers, F. *Forecasting the labour markets for research scientists and engineers in the European Union.* ROA-W-2001/3E, Research Centre for Education and the Labour Market, Maastricht, 2001.

ROA. *The labour market by education and occupation to 2000.* ROA-R-1995/3E, Research Centre for Education and the Labour Market, Maastricht, 1995.

ROA. *The labour market by education and occupation to 2000. Statistical appendix.* ROA-R-1995/3BE, Research Centre for Education and the Labour Market, Maastricht, 1995a.

ROA. *De Arbeidsmarkt naar Opleiding en Beroep tot 2006* [The labour market by education and occupation to 2006]. ROA-R-2001/8. Research Centre for Education and the Labour Market, Maastricht, 2001.

Wieling, M.H.; Borghans, L. Discrepancies between supply and demand and adjustment processes in the labour market. *Labour*, 2001, Vol. 15, pp. 33-56.

PART II
Initiatives at sectoral level

This Part focuses on contributions investigating future skills needs in various sectors: industrial maintenance, the automotive and transport sector, information and communications, logistics, health care and construction.

These contributions illustrate the variety of approaches to specific subject areas in the early identification of skills needs. Job monitoring, company case studies, expert discussions and networks of specialists are all used to answer specific questions about skills trends, as are scenario-based methods and statistical evaluations. However, it is not possible immediately to transfer individual results to other European countries, although parallel trends can be identified.

Articles in Part II

Jean-Louis Kirsch (F)
Industrial maintenance in France: new and traditional skill requirements

Tom Leney (UK)
Identifying future qualification needs in the transport sector in the United Kingdom: has the scenarios methodology a role?

Martin Curley (IRL/Career Space Consortium)
Addressing the ICT skills shortage in Europe

Kathrin Schnalzer, Gerd Gidion, Mirlam Thum, Helmut Kuwan (D)
New skill requirements in logistics

Gert Alaby (S)
Skill requirements in the care of the elderly – the Swedish example

Norbert Bromberger, Helen Diedrich-Fuhs (D)
Information system for early recognition of sectoral trends – results obtained for the construction industry

Industrial maintenance in France: new and traditional skill requirements [1]

Jean-Louis Kirsch, Centre for Research on Education, Training and Employment (Céreq), Marseille, France

The French Ministry of Education periodically commissions a survey of the changes in skill requirements in the major sectors of economic activity. This information helps to define new training profiles for the next five to ten years. Céreq often carries out studies for this survey. Over the years, a tried and tested procedure has been developed, covering different fields, e.g. electronics, trade, building, IT occupations, etc.

This procedure is based on a three-step approach: 1) consultations with experts together with bibliographical and statistical surveys to define the scope of the problematics; 2) in-firm observations using a specific method, namely ETED (Emploi type étudié dans sa dynamique - typical job studied in its dynamics), which analyses the competences involved in different jobs and the various possibilities for skill enhancement; 3) labour-market studies, and more specifically on the conditions of access to jobs.

Industrial maintenance is the most recent field of research and will be presented in this paper. The experts interviewed prior to the in-firm investigations highlighted three major changes likely to modify to a greater or lesser extent the occupations, the structure and the content of activities in the sector: the introduction of predictive methods, the redistribution of activities inside and outside firms, and standardisation and quality certifications. In-firm studies were conducted in twelve firms varying in size and core activity. They measured the real impact of those changes and forecast their consequences for work organisations and skill requirements. Three occupational profiles were drawn up on the basis of observations in the field and accounts from professionals. Skill requirements were therefore identified for the coming years.

---

[1] The following text is largely in the form of extracts from Céreq document 159: "Maintenance industrielle: quels emplois? quelles formations?" [Industrial maintenance: what jobs? what training?], November 2001.

1. Introduction

1.1. The context of the study: a tried and tested method

Since 1980, the French Ministry of Education has been encouraging studies of skill requirements in the main sectors of the French economy in order to obtain an up-to-date picture of these requirements every five years. The aim is to make it easier to adapt the content of vocational training schemes to the needs of the production system. In order to illustrate the outcome of this kind of approach we have taken the case of industrial maintenance, which has just been the subject of such a study. The focus of industrial maintenance, it should be borne in mind, is the production process rather than the finished product.

1.2. Some method details: a three-stage strategy

The first stage was to specify the research area through consultations with experts, together with a summary of bibliographical and statistical data. The experts included consultants, teachers and well-known professional practitioners in this sector.

Studies in enterprise then made it possible to check the hypotheses sketched out at the previous stage. All the people working in the research field, from engineers to operatives, were examined using an original method: ETED (emploi-type étudié dans sa dynamique – typical job studied in its dynamic). This method makes it possible to take account of any variations in the content and scope of the work performed by persons in the job, as well as the various ways in which people performing this work can progress. [2]

In parallel, an analysis of the operation of the labour market, looking chiefly at the employment conditions of the jobs studied, made it possible to specify how the training supply from the education and training system could be geared to enterprise skill requirements.

2. Defining the research area: three main questions

2.1. Technological determinism

Up to the 1950s, the principle of maintenance was one of action following the onset of a malfunction. The key words were therefore 'changing' (i.e. diagnosing, repairing, maintaining) and improving machinery.

---

[2] Nicole Mandon, Emmanuel Sulzer: Analysis of work: describing competences through a dynamic approach to jobs. *Training and Employment,* No 33, Autumn 1998.

There was a shift away from this kind of *corrective maintenance* in the 1960s and 1970s towards *preventive and systematic* maintenance. From then on, the function of maintenance was less to repair machinery than to ensure that it was functioning, thereby reducing plant down times, in view of the following observation: neglecting maintenance cost ten times more if there was a breakdown or production stoppage. The context, nevertheless, was one of a variable geometry production system that had to cope with uncertainty. Maintenance did not escape these constraints. If it had more than ever to 'cope', it also had to ensure that production machinery was maximally available.

This led to the development of *systematic preventive maintenance*, which was felt, however, to have a number of drawbacks. The most frequent objection was the fact that systematic preventive maintenance operations could well disturb the correct operation of machinery. 'Action leading to breakdowns' seemed particularly probable in production processes using old machinery. It was also felt that applying systematic preventive maintenance could run counter to the need to keep operating costs under control. The costs generated by this type of maintenance were recurrent and known because action included, among other things, the systematic replacement of parts (as a function, for instance, of duration of use) during the life cycle of the machinery, in some cases requiring production stoppages.

These constraints go a long way towards explaining why systematic preventive maintenance was gradually 'naturally' supplanted by *preventive conditional maintenance*. This confirmed the role of maintenance in optimising production machinery: from then on, rather than ensuring that equipment was available, the target was to make production machinery as reliable as possible in order to satisfy 'zero deadline, zero defect' policies.

The development and improvement of techniques and technologies and the development of monitoring and diagnostic instruments made it possible to introduce breakdown forecasting techniques and then to move on to the final stage; *forward* (also called *predictive*) *maintenance*. Linked to conditional maintenance, this kind of maintenance is based on a historical analysis of breakdowns, defect symptoms and observed levels of wear from which specific plans of action for each machine can be drawn up following the definition of critical thresholds.

2.2. Integration into production and outsourcing

2.2.1. *Integration into production*

There is no doubt that these trends in maintenance led to a new development in which the maintenance function, particularly 'routine' maintenance, became part of production. The development of preventive maintenance (the systematic linked to the conditional) led, therefore, to the introduction of equipment action, maintenance and monitoring plans. The routine maintenance operations included in these plans were then systematic and prescribed. They included monitoring various components, lubrication, cleaning, adjustment and re-alignment operations and even the replacement of some equipment components or parts. The performance of these tasks was specified in planning sheets. They could be performed by production staff who had been made aware of the importance of their correct performance and had the advantage of an excellent knowledge of the machinery.

At the same time, innovative approaches to maintenance were also being developed: TPM (Total Production Maintenance), MBZ (Maintenance Base Zero), ACP (Production Capacity Assurance). Self-maintenance, where all production personnel played their part in routine maintenance, was a core principle of TPM. MBZ was based on the principle of the utility of an activity for the enterprise and led to the relevance of tasks to be reviewed. As the enterprise's objective was production and not maintenance, the result of MBZ was to shift maintenance tasks into production.

2.2.2. *Outsourcing*

There seems to be a general consensus as regards the outsourcing of maintenance: over the last ten years it has become standard practice and has grown apace in recent times.

Outsourcing takes a number of standard forms:
- subcontracting using 'hired labour': the principal has a labour force for a certain period that he can use as he sees fit;
- 'straight-cost' subcontracting: the principal describes the work in a specification and organises its performance and monitoring;
- 'fixed-price' subcontracting: a set result is laid down and it is up to the subcontractor to organise work in order to achieve this result within previously set deadlines and quality levels;
- *ad hoc* subcontracting based on the principle of performance.

There has undoubtedly been an increase in 'straight-cost' and 'fixed-price' subcontracting although *ad hoc* work continues to be large-scale in small enterprises. How far can outsourcing go?

2.3. Growing standardisation

Standards cover a whole range of fields and concern the maintenance function directly (standard FD X 60000) or less directly (standards on contracts, documentation, quality assurance).

The ISO 9000 standards were drawn up in 1997 and have been constantly revised since then (important dates: 1997 and 2000). Standards 9000 and 9004 are quality system management guides. Standards 9001, 9002 and 9003 are quality reference frameworks.

Enterprises look for ISO 9000 certification for a whole range of reasons. First, enterprises may be committed overall to a total quality policy and any measures that they introduce have to be incorporated into maintenance work. Second, maintenance departments may decide off their own bat separately to apply such a strategy in order internally to improve their work. Third, under pressure (whether by way of encouragement or compulsion) from client enterprises, it may be in the interests of service provider enterprises to be able to demonstrate certification under a particular standard in order to gain the upper hand over their competitors when responding to a call for tenders.

AFNOR has in this case laid down a framework structuring the contractual obligations of principals and contractors (standards X 60-100, 101, 102, 103) covering technical, legal and financial clauses and calls for tender. Bodies certified by the Ministry of Industry attest the conformity of service provider enterprises with the ISO 9000 (quality) and ISO 14000 (quality of the industrial environment) reference frameworks. This rationalises customer-supplier relations, since the former do not need to carry out audits to check the quality of the service provider.

3. Enterprise surveys [3]: maintenance practices

3.1. Different types of maintenance continue to co-exist

Although there is little doubt about the sequence corrective maintenance → systematic preventive maintenance → conditional preventive maintenance → predictive maintenance, it cannot be seen as unequivocal and omnipresent.

Predictive (forward) maintenance is certainly not a panacea. Not all enterprises have as yet reached this advanced stage of maintenance, even though it may be one of their stated objectives. There also seems to be something of a regression, in both discourse and practice, for two reasons:

---

[3] These surveys concerned twelve enterprises of all sizes in different sectors.

technological and financial. Even though conditional preventive maintenance helps to some extent to limit the costs of systematic procedures by triggering maintenance operations in an optimum way, its main drawbacks lie in the major investment it requires in monitoring and analysis instruments and the high labour costs it generates (personnel training costs, costs of a skilled or even highly skilled labour force which has to be permanently employed in the enterprise).

In practice, firms conducting an innovative maintenance policy are attempting less to minimise the internal costs of maintenance work than to make them viable, i.e. to generate a positive cost/efficiency ratio. It may be economically viable in the same enterprise to apply systematic preventive maintenance to a particular production process involving a key product with a high profit margin, whereas curative maintenance may be the only 'economically viable' kind of maintenance for other products. It may be quite rational for the enterprise to give priority largely to curative maintenance and to minimise the proportion of systematic preventive maintenance for reasons connected chiefly, for instance, with the age of the machinery and experience and familiarity in repairing its malfunctions.

It is therefore impossible to sketch out any general, or overall, trends in maintenance in enterprise. The stance that enterprises take on the various types of maintenance is shaped by technical and financial, internal and external, factors (for instance the frequency of cyclical or random breakdowns of machinery, the abilities and competences of maintenance staff and subcontracting services, methods of work organisation, competitive position in the market by product, etc.).

Keeping a maintenance function in the enterprise

There are two conflicting opinions about the future of maintenance outsourcing.

First scenario: outsourcing of the maintenance function will continue. Those factors felt to play a part in encouraging enterprises to subcontract part of their activities have much to do with this: strategic, organisational, budgetary, technical and human factors:
- technologically, outsourcing is, for the enterprise, a gauge of quality and efficiency as maintenance work is performed by professionals and specialists;
- from an organisational point of view, the current trend among enterprises to re-focus on their core function, on what they are able to do, may be reflected by the delegation of anything outside this function. Similarly, the

spread of new methods and organisations such as TPM and MBZ is increasing the propensity to outsource some maintenance fields;
- lastly, from a financial point of view, outsourcing of maintenance minimises maintenance costs. The enterprise pays per 'service' and does not therefore have to bear the costs of a large maintenance division that is permanently on call in the enterprise (to cope with general and/or specialist overhauls). However, there may be human resources problems here, connected with the motivation and integration of staff permanently available in the enterprise but called on only from time to time.

Second scenario: the three above arguments are used to justify the opposite opinion that the growth of maintenance outsourcing will level off or even decline in some cases:
- from a technological and organisational point of view, outsourcing of the maintenance function has grown because it concerned various factors peripheral to the hard core of production, i.e. to the core of the enterprise's trade. When this stage of outsourcing is reached, it cannot continue because it would place the enterprise on too fragile a footing. The counterpart to advanced outsourcing is the loss of a degree of autonomy over the management of the production process, with maintenance operations becoming key stages in the production continuum. The loss, moreover, of a field of competence and knowledge to which outsourcing leads seems to be a process that is difficult (and certainly very costly) to reverse because of ongoing technological development;
- the enterprise is unable to stand back and assess the value of the work: the principal becomes completely unable to assess the quality of work and in particular the pertinence of the costs invoiced. Overall, outsourcing of the maintenance function is a practice that now seems to have come up against some limits.

Although there is little doubt that sector, size, enterprise strategies and national or international competitive situations may shape major divergences from these two stances, it is difficult, at a macroeconomic level, to decide between continuing outsourcing or levelling off or even decline. Some enterprises are pursuing these two strategies (outsourcing/ internalisation) at one and the same time: Renault, for instance, has decided for strategic reasons to outsource line maintenance to service provider companies only during the last two years of a model's life.

3.3. Standardisation: a new form of prescription

In addition to criticisms of the cost of certification and introduction of IT methods, several interviewees stressed their constraining nature. What seems to be the problem is not so much the standards and methods themselves but the practices that are inferred from them. If an enterprise already has a coherent organisation and management methods, certification of compliance with a standard should merely involve the simple formalisation (writing down) of procedures already in place.

However, if the enterprise has not regulated (or has done little to regulate) maintenance in the past, certification may well entail major upheavals. Quality strategies are demanding in various areas, including and in particular the formalisation of procedures: there are heavy constraints in terms of documentation. This may include drawing up a quality manual, updating the various documents, keeping control of quality records through accurate histories of defects, preventive maintenance operations, new work measures, etc.

When enterprises opt for certification, there are a number of effects on maintenance jobs. The most significant trend is the growth of prescriptive action, which is being reflected by an increasing amount of writing up of work. In terms of competences possessed and used, this bears out the trend mentioned above: need for minutiae, meticulous work and respect of rules. Some employees feel that the counterpart to this is a loss of initiative and autonomy and of a standardisation of work. Looked at positively, however, writing up makes it possible to gain a better view of the work actually performed and thus to make the most of the competences that people possess (Campinos-Dubernet and Marquette, 1998). The resultant workload, linked with the requirements of 'traceability' inherent in writing up, may be substantially alleviated by means, for instance, of CAM.

4. Enterprise surveys: structuring of activities and jobs

4.1. Description of standard jobs

Analysis of the interviews conducted in the various sample enterprises allowed us to pinpoint three standard jobs, two at 'maintenance technician' level – a maintenance action technician and a maintenance methods technician – and one at 'maintenance operative' level.

The standard 'maintenance operative' job has largely technical functions which are also covered by the action technician. Similarly, the two standard technician jobs overlap in a number of areas (see Figure). The specific nature of each of these standard jobs is then shaped by the fact that their ultimate objectives differ. [4]

Figure 1. **Standard maintenance jobs**

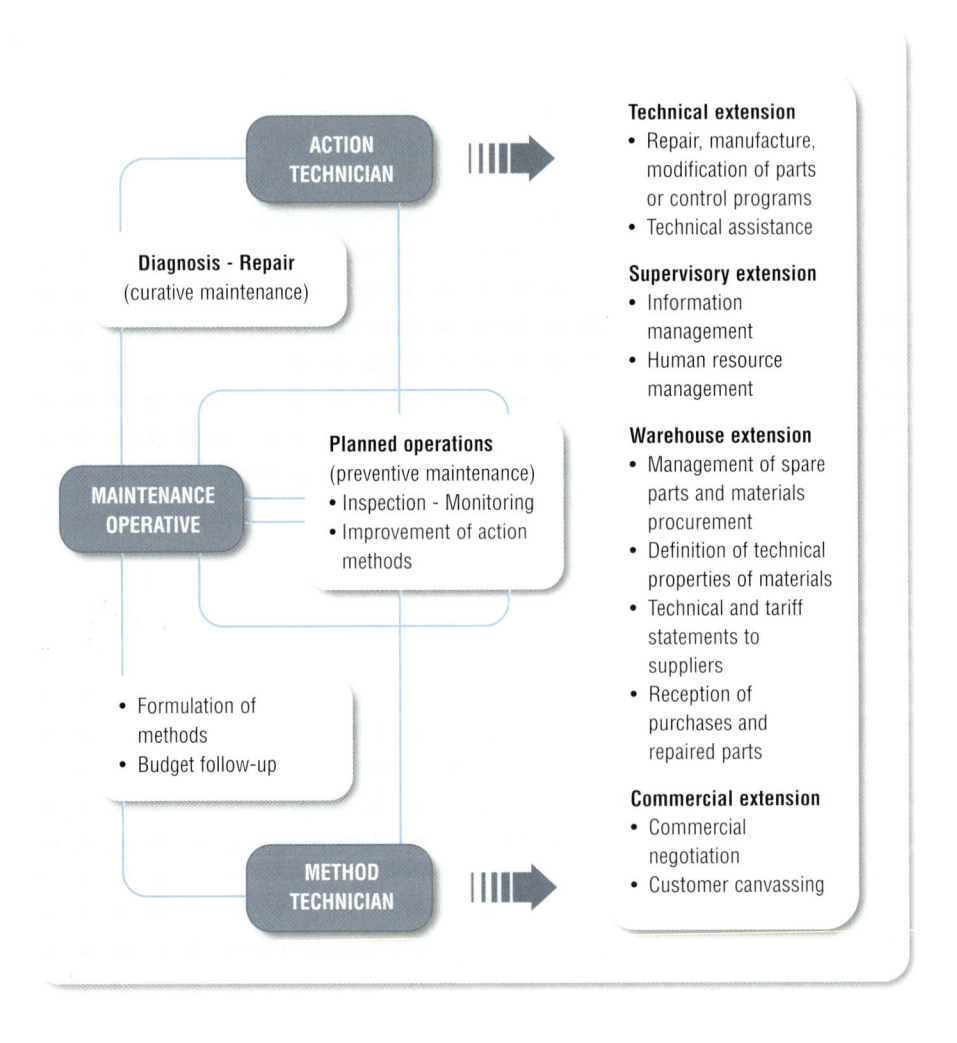

```
                        ACTION              Technical extension
                      TECHNICIAN            • Repair, manufacture,
                                              modification of parts
                                              or control programs
                                            • Technical assistance
     Diagnosis - Repair
     (curative maintenance)                 Supervisory extension
                                            • Information
                                              management
                                            • Human resource
                                              management

                        Planned operations  Warehouse extension
                        (preventive maintenance)
                                            • Management of spare
     MAINTENANCE        • Inspection - Monitoring
                                              parts and materials
     OPERATIVE          • Improvement of action
                                              procurement
                          methods
                                            • Definition of technical
                                              properties of materials
                                            • Technical and tariff
                                              statements to
                                              suppliers
     • Formulation of                       • Reception of
       methods                                purchases and
     • Budget follow-up                       repaired parts

                                            Commercial extension
                                            • Commercial
                        METHOD                negotiation
                      TECHNICIAN            • Customer canvassing
```

---

[4] For each standard job, an Annex contains a detailed description of the activities performed (table of occupational range) and the competences mobilised (table of expertise in action). The Annex can be obtained from the author.

4.2. The maintenance operative

The task of maintenance operatives (i.e. their overall purpose in terms of the ETED method) is to repair an unexpected breakdown or malfunction as rapidly as possible and at any time (corrective maintenance). They may also perform preventive operations to improve the performance of plant.

In the case of corrective maintenance, an operative must be able to identify the causes of the equipment malfunction (location, cause of the problem: mechanical, electrical, etc.), decide on the type of action needed and get the equipment operating again. These successive stages of action must generally have short turnaround times, particularly if they entail a temporary production stoppage.

> Bearing in mind the constraints imposed by its customer delivery deadlines, enterprise R (mail order sales) has set itself the rule that any unforeseen breakdown should be repaired in ten minutes. This time imperative consequently shapes methods of action (number of people to be mobilised, type of operation: temporary or final repair, etc.) with the result that those involved are always under pressure. In enterprise S (iron and steel), the operative we interviewed told us 'we have machines here that give us problems. The buzzword at present is getting tonnage out and the machinery is therefore important ... we have to take action straight away. In some cases it is important for the machine to work, and in other cases it is less critical, but in all cases we need to make it work and we all have our own little solutions. Sometimes what we do is a bit makeshift and sometimes it is a bit more robust. This does not work too badly as long as we can set the train in motion again ... In normal circumstances we have ten minutes to a quarter of an hour to take action and make repairs ...'.

More generally, just-in-time production organisation means that enterprises need to keep a skeleton personnel to take action at any time in case of emergency. Corrective maintenance is, for this reason, very rarely handled by subcontractors, except in cases where the service enterprise is continuously available on the production site, for instance, as a result of a global maintenance contract.

> In enterprise F, the compressed air system is subcontracted. The total outsourcing of nitrogen production and follow-up failed because it needed immediately available local teams. Remote monitoring did not solve the problem of rapid action, which requires personnel *in situ*. The company now works with local maintenance making it possible to deal with problems in short periods of time.

Moreover, although enterprises state that an objective is to move towards a larger number of scheduled operations in order to reduce inconvenient machine stoppages to a minimum, in many cases there are fairly high breakdown levels.

In enterprise M (electronic components) which has a whole range of resources to support a preventive maintenance policy, the head of the maintenance division estimates that corrective operations account for 30% and preventive operations for 70% of work. There are very similar proportions in some sectors of enterprises S and P (cosmetics). The reverse (70% corrective – 30% preventive) seems to be much more the case in enterprises I and F (printing, cosmetics) where a systematic preventive maintenance system is fairly new and is being introduced gradually. In enterprise T (agri-foodstuffs) corrective maintenance continues to be practised more or less exclusively on one very old production line for which, as the profit margin for the product in question is low, there has been no specific investment.

These stages of diagnosis and repair, forming the core of the work of maintenance operatives, require technical skills in an increasing range of disciplines (mechanical engineering, pneumatics, hydraulics, automation, etc): the more complex the production machinery, the more sophisticated the skills.

This range is borne out by what we were told by one of the maintenance operatives in enterprise M. Asked about the technical skills he used, he said: 'in the case of this machine, electronics, with a PC which manages the robot sequences. After that mechanical engineering with anything to do with motors, couplings, robot movement belts, and pneumatics with the valves and jacks...' Another example was provided by a skilled mechanical engineering operative in enterprise S: 'we even have a little to do with electricity and understand something of the reasoning behind the hydraulic parts. As a result of working with them (the electricians), we are able to diagnose minor faults in the same way as they would ...'

The introduction of 'new generation' machinery with large numbers of electronic components seems set substantially to raise the level of the technical competences required for their maintenance (in cases where maintenance does not simply involve the replacement of defective boards).

In the case of preventive maintenance, operatives are required to perform scheduled operations – decided by the technicians – including cleaning, lubrication, changes of parts, etc., but also to detect any anomalies in the machinery via various checks. In some cases, these are chiefly sensory checks (smell, sight), but in other cases action needs to be taken.

'I look round my machinery once a month, I do all the machines and make notes in accordance with the written specification ... we look at a whole range of things, pressure deviations, compressed air, robot offsets, the general condition of the machinery ... if, in the case of a pressure reducer, it needs to be set to three bars of pressure, what I check is whether there has been any pressure variation from one month to the next ... if it is a robot whose settings are going wrong and which is starting to put the baskets sideways in the acid tank or some other problem, we know that we need to schedule work before it breaks down ...'. Maintenance operative, enterprise M.

In contrast to diagnosis and repair operations, which require relatively advanced and varied skills, the performance of preventive operations mobilises fewer technical skills, when, for instance, it involves changing parts or machine settings. This explains why some tasks, considered routine, have been delegated in certain firms to production operatives.

In enterprise F, setting work following a change of format (product packaging), performed in the past by maintenance operatives, has been delegated to production workers. Similarly, in enterprise M, the replacement of electrodes (in an acid tank), scheduled by the maintenance division, is performed by the production worker who has been given the necessary training and electrical authorisations.

These examples bear out the most recent trends in maintenance, i.e. the transfer of routine maintenance tasks from maintenance to production workers. Our field studies tended to show, however, that this development is far from being the case everywhere.

In enterprise R, it even became necessary to take a step backwards. The main work of production workers is to package parcels of various articles, which arrive automatically on conveyor belts. They had been asked to take responsibility for routine maintenance tasks at their own workstation (cleaning, lubrication of the packaging line) but also to take action on the line in the event of minor malfunctions (and had been given a toolkit). The management rapidly met with a refusal by the production workers – mostly women – to go any further in this direction as they felt that this kind of work was not up to them and they did not have the necessary skills. As the work was not in practice being very well done, there were more and more problems. The line was then developed and fitted with a larger number of sensors; when a problem comes up on the control screen, a maintenance operative is immediately dispatched.

We also found that preventive operations are more likely to be outsourced to subcontractor enterprises.

In enterprise S, for instance, where production is continuous, the work of maintenance operatives (working in shift teams) is largely corrective. All the preventive maintenance work has been outsourced to external operators largely for reasons of labour costs. In the unit surveyed, scheduled stoppages may require, on the same day and taking account of the gigantic nature of the production machinery (1 000 metres long), over 100 operations performed by over 200 people. It would obviously be impossible for the enterprise to keep this number of personnel on a permanent basis.

Lastly, maintenance operatives must be able to report on operations and events that have occurred in order to keep their operative or technician colleagues informed both orally and increasingly in writing (in record books, by computer) so as to facilitate and improve methods of action.

In the enterprises surveyed, we noted significant numbers of maintenance operatives in the largest concerns (principals) or service provider enterprises.

They were fewer in number or not to be found at all, however, in the smaller concerns (200 or fewer employees). Here, maintenance work was largely the task of maintenance technicians (action technicians in particular), whose wide-ranging profile covers the necessary requirements (see the beginning of the following paragraph).

4.3. The maintenance technician: one level, two profiles

4.3.1. *The action technician*

As the above diagram shows, one of the specific features of standard jobs in industrial maintenance is that they tend to overlap. The action technician is thus required to perform all the activities of the maintenance operative: diagnosis, repair, conduct of scheduled operations, monitoring, writing up.

In practice, the boundary between operative and technician continues in some cases to be fairly hazy, in some cases justifying the choice to employ solely personnel with technician status.

> The maintenance division of enterprise T has a manager, eight technicians and a project manager (research – new works). Three of these technicians have a CAP (Certificate of Vocational Aptitude) – one in class 185 and 2 in class 190 – two have a MSMA Vocational Baccalaureate (classes 175 and 180) and three have a BTS (Higher Technician's Certificate) in industrial maintenance (class 185). Six of the technicians work eight-hour shifts (rotating between the three shifts) for three weeks and then work 'regular' hours for the following three weeks (08.00h – 17.00h). The other two technicians work only regular hours but are on call at weekends. The geographical division of the factory by production line makes it possible to allocate each technician to a specific area. During regular working weeks, technicians are responsible for preventive maintenance in their area and may also be called at any time by their shift colleagues if they are needed. The shift workers are chiefly responsible for corrective maintenance. They may also be involved in scheduled works. In this example, the organisational choice explains the smoothing of personnel status.

However, the fact that they possess higher technical skills than operatives do works in favour of action technicians.

In enterprise P, the technological development of machinery has led to new maintenance profile needs. In the case of the 'old generation' machines, experience was important. The introduction of programmable robots now requires sophisticated knowledge of industrial automation, with 60 to 70% of operations involving electronics. The profile of the current jobs requires multi-skilling developed from a solid initial grounding. Supervisors go as far as saying that most current technicians, even those with a BTS, have difficulties because they lack basic knowledge.

The line between operative and technician can be fairly clearly drawn when looking at the overall purpose of the latter. Technicians tend in practice to remedy defects in equipment by seeking and implementing appropriate technical solutions but also to improve machinery performance by planning specific measures.

For each problem identified, and making use in particular of the analysis instruments available (analysis of breakdown levels, analysis of vibrations, etc.), action technicians must be able to study appropriate technical solutions and propose a set of preventive measures (cleaning of part of the plant, use of a stronger gasket, change of material, etc.). They prepare, plan and coordinate the performance of these measures. For this purpose, they procure the necessary equipment (spare parts, etc.) directly from suppliers or via the warehouse division, set the dates on which the work is to take place, decide the nature of this work, and decide who is to perform the work (operatives, technicians – including themselves – service providers). They ensure, during all operations, that they are being carried out correctly and comply with safety rules, set deadlines and any written procedures. At the end of each work sequence, they are also responsible for monitoring and approving the operations carried out.

They also have to draw up or amend written procedures (information sheets) for all the operations performed within each type of action on particular equipment.

Action technicians have jobs in 'principal' enterprises and in service provider enterprises.

4.3.2. *The method technician*

As in the case of maintenance operatives and action technicians, there is an overlap between the standard jobs of method technician and action technician (see diagram).

The specific task of the method technician is to draw up, always with a view to improving operating methods, rules for work that take account of technical specifications, deadlines, costs and materials procurement, and to ensure that they are applied by the personnel of their enterprise and/or service providers. They must be able to identify and optimise the costs of maintenance work.

Method technicians are therefore responsible for preparing for maintenance work by drawing up rules for work – whether this involves major or minor maintenance work on a particular machine or a set of machines from an entire production sector, or work in the enterprise or by a service provider. When preparing for maintenance work they draw up specifications for maintenance or new work, write up or amend operating procedures or information sheets and schedule operations following analyses of machine reliability (breakdown levels, etc.). They supervise ongoing operations and ensure that these are being performed correctly and in compliance with existing maintenance procedures (in-house rules or official standards). They also provide expert help with plans to improve equipment or, more widely, with investment plans. They draw up and analyse cost summaries and any gains from the operations conducted.

> In enterprise S, the area technical managers have this profile. They are allocated to each production unit and split between the two maintenance sectors: mechanical and electrical. Under the direct responsibility of the head of the maintenance division (mechanical or electrical), each area technical manager is responsible for part of the machinery. The area technical manager that we interviewed explained that there were three strands to his work: technical, financial and human. Technically, he has to be able to meet the objectives set by his supervisors in terms of equipment operation levels (mechanical sector). For this purpose, he draws up action plans (preventive maintenance) taking account of the annual maintenance plan drawn up jointly by the various sectors of the unit. During scheduled stoppages, he oversees the conditions in which work is being performed (safety, materials used, respect of specifications, deadlines, etc.). Financially, he is responsible for implementing the annual budget that he is allocated, where necessary justifying any overspend to his supervisors. From a human resource point of view, he manages the technicians (setters) under his responsibility allocating each technician's workload, checking their work and managing all aspects of their career advancement (interviews, assessment, etc.).

This same enterprise provides another example, this time concerning a technician (research officer) employed in the electrical division (research office) for general maintenance. His responsibilities include ensuring that the electrical boards located in the blast furnace, coking and charge preparation sectors are working. For this purpose, he draws up, according to a specification devised in cooperation with the sector's technicians, all the maintenance operations (cleaning, changes of components, etc.) to be carried out during scheduled plant stoppages. He puts this specification out to tender and then selects, with his supervisors, the service provider enterprise responsible for carrying out all the maintenance work. He ensures that all operations comply with safety rules, carries out inspections and where necessary provides solutions or technical advice for the personnel of the outside enterprise. He studies every operation report forwarded by the outside enterprise in order to identify any recurring problems so that they can be resolved, or the rate of replacement of some parts changed.

4.3.3. *Activities common to the two technician profiles*

Our initial analyses, as well as individual situations and the initial groupings drawn up (see ETED method in the section on methods), showed that we probably needed to add extensions, representative of four areas of work involving supervisory, commercial, disciplinary, technical and warehouse management competences, to the core activities of the standard jobs of action technician and method technician. These may all be stepping stones for the advancement of both action and method technicians ([5]).

4.3.3.1. Supervision

In a recent study looking, among others, at industrial maintenance trades (see APRODI report), the surveyors drew up a profile for a maintenance supervisor alongside the maintenance technician. Our investigations showed, however, that maintenance divisions tended to be organised in a functional rather than a hierarchical way with the result that very few employees had the status of supervisors responsible solely for overseeing staff. ([6]) We therefore felt it more appropriate to incorporate this kind of work as an extension of the core work of the two standard technician jobs.

Supervisory work chiefly involves information management and human resource management. In the first case, the purpose is to help staff (technicians and operatives as well as production workers) to master all the

---

[5] For each extension, the Annex contains a detailed description of the activities performed (occupational range) and the competences mobilised (expertise in action). The Annex can be obtained from the author.

[6] This comment is borne out by the results of the employment survey (see below).

tasks involved in or instructions for the performance of corrective or preventive operations, in particular by offering them training, and to organise and lead meetings to ensure that organisational, technical and regulatory information is circulated. In the second case, technicians are responsible for allocating the tasks to be performed to staff on the basis of their competences and availability. They may also draw up a chart of the competences available within their team and possibly propose ways in which they can be improved.

There is no doubt that the way in which the maintenance division's work is designed shapes whether or not these tasks are added to the core tasks of the standard method and action technician jobs.

It is only when there is a greater splitting up of the hierarchical line that staff (particularly action technicians) tend to lose these competences.

> This situation arose in enterprise R following a reorganisation of the maintenance division. At the outset, operatives and technicians were answerable to the manager of the maintenance division, the technicians straddling the two technician profiles (action and method). At the time of the reorganisation, a specific methods office was set up and an intermediate hierarchical line occupied by area technical managers, with responsibility for preventive maintenance work and personnel management, was introduced into each of the factory's geographical sectors. These area technical managers were recruited by promoting the existing technicians with the longest service. Technicians who were not promoted doubled up with the operatives on work almost exclusively involving plant repairs. This meant that some technicians therefore lost – in some cases with some resentment – part of their job.

4.3.3.2. Technicians' involvement in the principal-service provider relationship
As already mentioned, the spread of subcontracting practices and changes in their form as well as increased competition in the market are making it necessary to step up service provider enterprises' commercial relations and place them on a more professional footing.

While this is often the work of technical and commercial staff, the task may be taken up by personnel directly involved in maintenance work.

It seemed necessary, therefore, to include a commercial extension, which could be termed 'commercial negotiation', to take account of the competences required in order to obtain a particular service at the best price and by the best deadline. This is work, moreover, in which both technicians employed in 'principal' enterprises and in service provider enterprises are involved.

A second activity involves canvassing for customers in order to maintain or expand the enterprise's activity. Technicians employed in service provider enterprises are more involved here.

These two extensions may pave the way for a shift towards chiefly technical and commercial functions in an enterprise (although this kind of path did not crop up during our interviews).

In enterprise A (service provider), the technician that we interviewed, with an action technician profile, has to approach enterprises in his region. Using the enterprise's literature and brochures, he presents his enterprise's most important achievements to potential customers. After drawing up an estimate for his customer's order, the technician has to present this estimate himself and justify the choices made (suppliers, type of materials, human resources, etc.). Aged 26, this technician has a BTS in mechanical robotics. At the interview, he stressed the multi-skilled nature of his job as he deals with 'business' both upstream (canvassing, estimates, performance) and downstream (invoicing, chasing up 'bad payers').

4.3.3.3. *Disciplinary technical profiles*

Over and above general technical knowledge in the main disciplines (electricity, mechanical engineering, hydraulics), some people in the job have skills in a sophisticated technical area acquired in initial training (electromechanics, electronics, etc.), or specialist skills with certain plant acquired from occupational experience. In both cases the jobholder is then considered to be an expert in a particular field.

The first purpose to which these technical competences are put involves the repair, production or modification of parts or of control programs. This makes it necessary to provide, within set deadlines, the parts or control programmes needed for the correct operation of machinery. The second purpose involves technical assistance and, in this case, technicians help their colleagues (technicians or supervisors) to identify why machinery is malfunctioning and to work out the most appropriate action to take.

One of the technicians interviewed in enterprise S, allocated to the central mechanical workshop (division responsible for supplying the whole of the factory with new or repaired mechanical spare parts) is a specialist in tribology and fractology (methods of analysing component wear from its surface, perceptible friction, etc.). He thus helps his technician colleagues in the sector to locate the cause of the wear of mechanical components whether this involves premature ageing or actual breaks.

4.3.3.4. Warehouse management profiles

The warehouse management work for which maintenance technicians are responsible is in four main areas: managing spare parts and materials procurement, drawing up the technical properties of materials, providing suppliers with technical information and price statements, and receiving purchases and repaired components.

This extension of the maintenance technician profile depends exclusively on the way in which the enterprise is organised. In some cases, personnel attached to the warehouse (whom we did not include among our jobholders) are responsible for all work connected with spare parts and materials management. In other cases, maintenance technicians are responsible for some or all of the four main activities described above.

One of the method technicians of enterprise S is, for instance, responsible for procuring (in the case of new plant) or re-procuring (in the case of plant already in service) spare parts for the factory's electrical equipment, i.e. some 22 000 article codes. For this purpose, he has to draw up a technical sheet (detailed description of the equipment, quantity of parts to be stocked, etc.) and allocate a code number for each new electrical part used in the factory. He studies every new request for new supplies from the area technicians using the IT equipment available (CAM software) and draws up a purchase request which he passes on to the factory's purchase department. He checks the conformity of the equipment ordered when it arrives at the warehouse. He decides, where appropriate, on the quantities of parts to be ordered and gears their delivery deadlines to their frequency of use.

5. Labour market and entry into employment

Training in maintenance is undeniably an asset when looking for a job. People leaving such training are more often in employment than others and these jobs are more often permanent and well paid... albeit outside the maintenance field (see table)! It would seem training of a multidisciplinary nature helped people find jobs offering better working conditions, whether immediately or after a period of employment in maintenance.

In this context, maintenance jobs in the business services sector are a kind of turntable which both offers work to people leaving training and re-allocates them to other tasks:
- from one year to the next, one out of five people leave or enter this sector;
- new recruits are almost equally divided between training leavers, the unemployed and employees working in other sectors;
- slightly under one third of those leaving become jobseekers, and the others enter the other sectors of the economy;
- in this sector, there is a 20 to 30% turnover in numbers in the various maintenance trades.

Table 1. **Breakdown of jobs, at the survey date, held by industrial maintenance training leavers, by training level**

	Level III No	Level III %	Level IV No	Level IV %	Level V No	Level V %
Industrial maintenance operative	57	5	659	15	40	2
Manual setter	0	0	209	5	145	6
Industrial maintenance technician and supervisor	162	13	80	2	21	1
Industrial maintenance manager	0	0	0	0	0	0
Blue-collar/white-collar maintenance worker (other sectors)	47	4	315	7	80	4
Middle maintenance occupation (other sectors)	39	3	54	1	0	0
Maintenance manager (other sectors)	40	3	17	0	0	0
Other manual workers	215	18	1 798	41	1 448	65
Other white-collar workers	178	15	823	19	356	16
Other middle occupations	390	32	391	9	102	5
Other managers	84	7	0	0	42	2
Total	1 212	100	4 346	100	2 234	100

Source: Céreq – Survey '1992 Generation'.

6. Conclusion

Reviewing the situation in France in order in terms of forecasting qualification needs, and in turn to provide a starting point for the definition of training needs, leads us to stress three points:
- it is difficult to project beyond a period of five to ten years if qualitative information on the content of work and the structure of jobs is to be taken into account;
- current work needs to be researched in greater depth as regards the mechanisms by which occupations, the labour market and training pathways are renewed. Much more thought is needed here about the validation of experience and lifelong training;
- the results put forward provide a starting point for decisions by the actors, but in no way constitute ready-made solutions.

Identifying future qualification needs in the transport sector in the United Kingdom: has the scenarios methodology a role?

Tom Leney, Institute of Education, University of London, United Kingdom

> This paper outlines how the scenarios method is being used to help identify future qualification needs in three industries – motor, rail, and road haulage – within the UK's transport sector. It describes the scenarios methodology as a complementary tool to help develop future training needs in the industries concerned. The paper describes a recently developed series of scenarios and the next steps in this ongoing project.

1. Introduction

This paper describes in outline the method that a team of consultants is developing in collaboration with the regulatory authority for qualifications in England (The Qualifications and Curriculum Authority; QCA) in attempting to be more forward-looking in identifying future qualifications needs in three industries within the UK's transport sector.

A recurrent problem in identifying future skills and qualifications needs is that the policy makers in government and in the industries concerned tend to concentrate on immediate needs and past experience, and often fail to capture future needs effectively (Green and Hartley, 2000). Since new qualifications take several years to design, develop and implement, this is a critical issue to tackle, if qualifications are to be fit-for purpose in a fast-changing environment. Conventional forecasting techniques have not proved sufficiently effective, either in identifying longer-term needs in a future characterised in part by uncertainties, or as a way of opening up a strategic conversation among policy makers and stakeholders as to how to make effective provision to meet future training and qualifications needs (Descy and Tessaring, 2000; pages 299-314). The scenarios methodology may offer at least a partial solution to these problems, if it is used alongside more traditional techniques. Mike Coles' paper in this collection deals more fully with these considerations, and should be read in conjunction with this paper.

This paper describes work that is in progress at the time of writing. It identifies why we are attempting to use the scenarios methodology as an additional tool to help develop more rounded consideration of future training needs in the transport industries concerned. The paper outlines the progress made in Phase 1 of the research, in which we developed a series of scenarios for the transport sector in the UK and for the three industries with which we are working in particular. Then the method that we are using for Phase 2 is outlined.

2. Context and issues

The UK government's Qualifications and Curriculum Authority and the author have worked with other UK agencies - together with Cedefop and an international team - to develop a scenario methodology that can be used in education and training planning (Van Wieringen et al., 2001; Leney and Coles, 2001; QCA Research, 2002; Coles, 2002; Coles and Leney, 2002).

In the UK we have recently begun to apply the approach to three industries in the transport sector: rail, road haulage and the motor industry. The work is at quite an early stage, and this paper concentrates on the output of Phase 1 and the methods we have decided to use in Phase 2. At a later stage I hope to be able to report on the outcomes of our work.

3. The task identified

QCA and the Transport Skills Alliance (an umbrella employers' group in the sector) have commissioned an analysis that will use scenarios thinking alongside more traditional tools such as forecasting, functional and occupational analysis. The purpose is to identify the kinds and contents of qualifications that may be needed a decade or so from now in the transport industries.

The aims of the project can be summarised as follows.

Firstly, the project aims to facilitate stakeholders' thinking, particularly in the sectoral and government agencies, about how to modernise qualifications to meet future needs. We are applying the scenarios methodology to provide a language for those involved to look at options for the future, and in a way that research suggests happens little at present. See Mike Coles' paper to this Conference.

Secondly, the project team will reach conclusions and make recommendations on the extent to which current qualifications in the industries concerned are likely to prove fit-for-purpose- in the future. We will use scenarios and more traditional techniques to identify new skills, competences and perhaps kinds of knowledge that may need to be built into qualifications.

Thirdly, we will reflect on the outcome of using the scenarios method alongside other tools, and report our conclusions as to whether (and, if so, how) scenarios methods can be built more routinely into skills and qualifications needs analysis.

4. The project

The project falls into two distinct stages.

The remit for Stage 1 was to develop sets of scenarios for the transport industries specified, focusing on the year 2012, without a particular emphasis on skills or qualifications needs.

Phase 1 is complete. The following are now available.
1. A set of four meta-scenarios for the transport sector in the UK for 2012;
2. A set of four more detailed scenarios for each of the three industries identified in the sector;
3. A quantification (by industry and scenario) of each of the key criteria used to construct the sets of more detailed scenarios.

Phase 1 began with desk research. Working with Iain Mackinnon, an expert in skills needs analysis in the transport sector, we examined much of the published analysis of skills needs for the UK (e.g. National Skills Task Force, 2000; IER, 2001) and, in particular, trends for the different industries in the transport sector (e.g. Department of the Environment, Transport and the Regions, 2001; Mackinnon and Cooper, 2001; Strategic Rail Authority, 2001). Indeed, Iain had undertaken significant amounts of this research. We used the published industry-specific analyses to understand current forecasts of future skills needs (MITC, 2001; RHDTC, 2001; RITC, 2001). We also analysed carefully the transport strategies of the UK government (Department of the Environment, Transport and the Regions, 2000) and a number of large local authorities, as well as the policies of key lobby groups.

We wanted to begin by developing holistic scenarios for the transport sector. Initially, this was made more difficult by the focus of our remit. This included the rail industry (freight, passengers and the infrastructure), road haulage (i.e. goods carrying, but not people or passenger carrying aspects of road transport) and the motor industry (i.e. sales and service). Our specific remit did not include air and maritime transport industries. However, the UK's Department of Trade and Industry (DTI) had established a Foresight Futures Unit, which had developed four scenarios for the future of industry in the UK, and these were made available to us as we were conducting our work

From these we were able to devise four scenarios for the future of transport as a whole in 2012. The titles are:

Scenario 1: World Markets

Scenario 2: National Enterprise

Scenario 3: Global Responsibility

Scenario 4: Local Stewardship

For each, we were able to adapt the DTI scenarios, which had been widely researched, to include criteria for the following 'environments':
- Scenario drivers;
- Economy and sectoral trends;
- Transport;
- Environment and sustainability;
- Energy;
- Employment;
- Education and training.

We conducted a survey of stakeholders in the sector and made use of other survey material that was already available from different sources, in order to establish which trends experts considered likely or unlikely to occur in the three particular industries, and which developments experts disagreed about the likelihood of. We combined the results of this analysis with the broad scenarios for transport, and produced quantified statements under a number of headings for each of the specific industries we were looking at.

From these quantified scenarios we produced scenario statements under each of the four meta-scenarios for transport outlined above, for each of the following industries: the rail industry, road haulage and the motor industry (sales and service).

These scenarios are to be tested out a little further with experts and stakeholders in Phase 2 and adjusted, and used to stimulate an exploration of the skills and qualifications needs that planners should take into account when planning qualifications for the future.

Phase 2, which is now beginning, is intended to establish the extent to which current qualifications contribute to meeting the skills needs identified in

the scenarios for 2012 work and related analysis, and to make recommendations on the requirements for qualifications likely to be needed in a decade's time. The members of the core team for Phase 2 have been chosen to achieve a careful balance of expertise.
- An expert in identifying occupational profiles, skills standards and qualifications needs across different vocational sectors;
- A labour market economist with wide experience in the transport sector;
- A consultant who has been developing the scenarios methodology.

A steering group and a sectoral reference group are being established in order to ensure the close involvement of government agencies and strategic players from the sectoral oganisations concerned.

5. The next steps

Phase 2 is just beginning. The main stages in this phase are shown on the table that follows.

PHASE 2	MAIN ACTIVITIES	
Stage 1 Identification and analysis	Map all existing qualifications for the sector concerned	Desk research using QCA etc databases
	Test the transport scenarios for plausibility and write in implications for skills needs	Expert interviews and meetings
	Apply forecasting techniques to sectoral data and to the scenarios	Team/expert input
	Develop 'framework of usefulness' to link existing standards with future needs	Team
Stage 2 Further analysis	Apply the framework of usefulness to all existing qualifications	Team
	Explore how experts consider skills needs are best met in different scenarios	Expert interviews and meetings
	Identify with organisations how scenario thinking can help identify skills and qualifications strategies	Interviews, meetings. Working with stakeholders and organisations in the field
Stage 3 Conclusions and recommendations	Report on the appropriateness of current qualifications to anticipated future needs for the industries concerned	Team, working with project and steering groups
	Develop recommendations about future qualifications needs and content	
	Make recommendations about the usefulness and problems associated with the scenarios approach when used with other tools	

6. Conclusion: How we're using scenarios to help build the strategic conversation

The hypothesis is that the use of the scenarios methodology can help planners and stakeholders to improve on their analysis and understanding of future skills and qualifications needs in the sector. This should help sectoral organisations and the regulatory body in planning for change in qualifications.

We are developing the scenarios methodology as an additional tool for identifying future needs and developing strategies – not as an alternative to more traditional techniques. We are exploring whether and how key stakeholders could be encouraged to adopt scenario techniques as part of their normal planning processes.

Bibliography

Coles, M. *Creating a language for strategic conversation*. London: QCA, 2002.

Coles, M.; Leney, T. *QCA Scenarios for the school curriculum and assessment in 2011 – Report*. London: QCA, 2002.

Department of the Environment, Transport and the Regions. *Transport 2010: The 10 year plan*. London: DETR, 2000.

Department of the Environment, Transport and the Regions. *Transport trends. 2001 edition*. London: DETR, 2001.

Descy, P.; Tessaring M. *Training and learning for competence. Second report on vocational training research in Europe*. Luxembourg: Office for Official Publications of the European Communities, 2001.

Green, L.; Hartley, P. *Final report on a pilot study to explore the methods used to identify the content of national occupational standards and vocationally related qualifications*. Chesterfield, UK: LMG Associates, 2000.

IER. *Projections of occupations and qualifications 2000/2001*. London: DfES, University of Warwick and Cambridge Econometrics, 2001.

Leney, T.; Coles, M. *Scenarios and strategies for training in the UK*. London: QCA and Institute of Education, University of London, 2001.

Mackinnon, I.; Cooper, C. *An assessment of skill needs in transport*. London: DfEE, 2001.

MITC. *Motor industry workforce development plan 2001*. London: MITC, 2001.

National Skills Task Force. *Skills for all: Research report from the National Skills Task Force*. London: DfEE, 2000.

RHDTC. *Workforce development plan 2001-2004: Making the case for the road haulage & distribution sector.* Milton Keynes, UK: RHDTC, 2001.

RITC. *Workforce development plan for the UK rail industry.* London: RITC, 2001.

Strategic Rail Authority. *Progress report: Delivering the framework for skills in the rail industry.* London: Strategic Rail Authority and DfES, 2001.

QCA Research, 2002. *Five scenarios for schooling in England in 2011.* London: QCA 2002.

Van Wieringen F.; Sellin, B.; Schmidt, G. Uncertainties in education: Handle with care – scenarios and strategies for vocational education and training in Europe. Amsterdam: Max Goote Kenniscentrum, University of Amsterdam, 2001.

ANNEX 1
Scenarios for transport 2012: Meta scenarios (*)

Scenario 1: World markets
People aspire to personal independence, material wealth and mobility to the exclusion of wider social goals. Integrated global markets are thought to be the best way to achieve these goals. Internationally co-ordinated policy sets framework conditions for the efficient functioning of markets. Services are privatised wherever possible and society and the economy operate on the principle of minimal government. Increased mobility of people and goods has created the conditions where high levels of investment in renewed transport infrastructures are possible due to the increase in the volume of road, air and rail traffic.

Scenario 2: National enterprise
People aspire to high levels of wealth and welfare, but balanced by more equally distributed opportunities and a sound environment. Communities with shared values are stronger. Most believe these values are best achieved through active UK public policy, with a degree of international cooperation. Tensions exist between economic and social objectives. Control of markets and people is achieved through a mixture of regulatory and norm-based mechanisms. In transport policy the 'low investment versus high environmental protection' conundrum has proved difficult to resolve.

(*) draft version.

Scenario 3: Global responsibility
People now aspire to high levels of welfare within communities with shared values, more equally distributed opportunities and a sound environment. People believe that these objectives are best achieved through active public policy and international cooperation at European and global level. Social objectives are met through predominantly public provision, increasingly at an international level. Government and international authorities such as the EU ensure that control of markets and people is achieved through a mixture of regulatory and norm-based mechanisms. Environmental concerns are high on the agenda, alongside a determination to establish an eco-friendly, integrated transport system.

Scenario 4: Local stewardship
People have begun to aspire to sustainable levels of welfare and income in networked communities. Markets are subject to social regulation to ensure more equally distributed opportunities and a high quality local environment. Public policy aims to promote small-scale and regional economic activities, and acts to constrain large-scale markets and technologies. In some parts of the UK, local communities are strengthened to ensure people's involvement in governance in a complex world: Wales is steering strongly in this direction. The development of the transport system has slowed down, while innovation now concentrates on using new technologies and ingenuity to provide low cost and environmentally friendly outcomes.

ANNEX 2
Scenarios for transport 2012: Criteria and matrix

CRITERION	MEASUREMENT	CRITERION	MEASUREMENT
1. Sectoral economic and market developments		**4. Management of the environment**	
Growth in UK economy	Average % annual growth in GDP	Who is winning the argument?	Agencies and outcomes
Transport market trends		Energy sources for transport industries	Traditional and innovative sources
Volume	Index: Year 2000 = 100	**5. The labour market for the industry**	
Market share: goods	% share		
Market share: people	% share	The size of the labour force in the industry	Index: Year 2000 = 100
Productivity in the industry	Comment on overall trend	The skills equilibrium: supply	High/patchily high/ medium/low continuum Specify
Motor vehicle licences	Number		
Innovation in the industry			
Technological change	Scale 1-5: opportunities grasped to change inhibited	Demand for skills	Identify professional, technical and low skills demand levels
An integrated transport system?	Scale 1-5: Fast to no development	Flows of people	How do people come into the industry, progress and move on?
Investment	Index: Year 2000 = 100		
2. Organisations in the industry		**6. Education and training**	
Networks		Qualifications of potential entrants	Comment on similarities/differences c.f. 2000
Process management	Comment		
Outsourcing	Scale 1-5: high to low levels	Lifelong learning	Characterise UK approach
Learning organisations?	Extent and emphasis	Attitude to skills acquisition in the industry	Identify the dominant attitude of employers
Flexible or inflexible workforce?	Scale 1-5: Flexible to inflexible Comment		
3. Government and governance of the industry			
Government values and priorities	Characterise		
Light touch / heavy touch regulation	Scale 1-5: light to heavy		
UK and EU frameworks	Who leads; character of frameworks		
Impact of sectoral organisations	Comment		

ANNEX 3
Example: Scenarios for Transport 2012: Motor Industry (*)

Scenario 1 for 2012
- With GDP averaging an increase of 3.5% per year, this is a high growth economy. The volume of traffic on the roads has increased steadily and shows no sign of slowing down. Twenty six million cars are now registered, an increase of three million over a ten year period. New car sales are 30% higher in 2012 than in 2001. Comparable increases have taken place in the sales of lorries, light vans etc.
- Government favours improved and commercially viable motorway and trunk road systems, and the expansion of towns to provide new housing has led to thousands of new miles of road being laid. Driving can be a frustrating experience for road users, but motorists show no sign of wanting to leave their cars at home, let alone convert to two wheels.
- Government regulates car use with a light touch. Congestion charging has only been imposed in seven major cities. Levels of congestion and pollution remain high, and in the main the government relies on road users to use smart in-car technology, rather than impose charges or limitations.
- For the motor industry, however, the regulatory framework is more restrictive, mainly to control safety and emission levels. International conventions have been agreed to ensure that all new vehicles are more economical and environmentally friendly to run. Safety factors are subject to strict regulations, and customers have litigated successfully against garages that failed to spot repairs that needed doing and could be a safely risk. Automotive technology is changing rapidly.
- Among people who live in crowded towns, state of the art micro vehicles have long been fashionable, but the volume of road traffic has meant that cycling, walking, etc never achieved a critical mass that would encroach on volumes of car use.
- Sales networks have changed. Manufacturers no longer dominate either sales or servicing. After a major shakeout UK companies (not manufacturers) dominate the new vehicles business. Showrooms mostly sell used cars. E-commerce carries more than 50% of sales. The numbers of staff involved in selling cars and other vehicles has remained much the

---

(*) draft version.

same for a decade. However, the operations that staff are involved in have changed. The market has developed rapidly in other ways, too. European trading standards have opened up the market internationally, and one in three cars sold or bought in the UK market has to be transported to/from a customer or sales business elsewhere in the EU.
- The business of maintaining cars has also changed. The next generation of 'Quick Fit fitters' carries out a wider range of operations, most of which involve responding to diagnostics carried out on a computer. In the latest models, in car technology does the diagnosis. The culture of repairing bodywork and mechanical parts is almost a thing of the past. Nevertheless, a clear difference exists between the quick fit culture and more traditional workshops that carry out a wide range of repairs and maintenance on a wide range of vehicles. Both kinds of operation are subject to stringent quality control checks for which workshops must be badged. Mechanics are required to have appropriate qualifications and to attend refresher training. The culture of diagnosis and replacement is advanced. Mechanic hours spent per vehicle in servicing operations has reduced by 15% since 2002. Even so, customers expect repairers to anticipate faults and take preventative action. Mechanics need a clear understanding of how to use a computer to identify and rectify faults. Otherwise, the skills demanded have not changed greatly. Turnover of staff is relatively high.
- Sales staff now need a clear understanding of safety and environmental requirements as customers become more discerning and car manufacturers seek an environmentally friendly and safety conscious image. The internationalisation of the sales business requires people with a quite advanced level of general education, and knowledge of languages helps materially. Customer care receives more emphasis on both the sales and servicing side of the industry.
- Government adopts a decentralised approach to lifelong learning and training initiatives are left largely to companies It is difficult for colleges to provide trainees with experience on the kinds of technology that are developing, because of the costs involved. Most continuing training is of short duration, and short-termism is still the order of the day.

Scenario 2 for 2012
- With GDP averaging an increase of 2% per year, the economy shows moderate growth. This is reflected in the index of new car sales – up 25% on the rates of a decade earlier – and the number of cars licensed, now 25 million.
- Individualistic social values continued to dominate in the UK, but people also look for a better quality of life in their communities. Government is expected to give a strong lead. The aspirations to high levels of earnings and consumption have meant that people continue to rely heavily on their cars as the key means of transport. People also look to government for better environmental conditions and less congested cities. In practice, market values have tended to carry greater weight than environmental issues, and management of the environment has remained difficult in the densely populated UK.
- Wherever possible, the government has supported the UK motor sector by making it difficult for companies in other EU countries to establish direct sales arrangements in the UK market, though e-commerce etc have inevitably opened up the market somewhat. Worldwide car manufacturers still franchise sales operations to UK enterprises in the traditional way, though their dominance of the sales operations has weakened somewhat.
- Incremental changes have taken place in the ways that the car sales business operates. 60% or so of cars are still sold by businesses with a forecourt. This has meant that sales people and managers in the sector have had to develop strong ICT skills and the ability to interest customers from a distance. By 2012, the size of the workforce in sales had decreased by 5% compared to levels in 2002. The changes in sales networks and customer liaison meant that 40% of the people involved in sales no longer worked primarily on the forecourt.
- In the repair business, garages and workshops have continued with the same mixture of replacement and repair of parts as prevailed earlier in the decade. 'Quick fit' arrangements had secured a significant part of the market by 2003, but by and large people still prefer to go to traditional outlets for a variety of repairs needing a mechanic's diagnostic skills and experience. A large number of computer led safety checks form a statutory part of each regular service. In other respects, the skills required of mechanics did not change greatly, compared with the skills requirements at the turn of the century. The size of the workforce needed increased by some five per cent over this time.
- In spite of the developing demands of the business, the natural tendency in the sector was for firms to develop slowly. Traditional ways had a strong

hold and, in any case, the large number of small businesses in both sales and servicing found it difficult to make rapid strides to become 'learning organisations'.
- Skills required on entry to both sales and maintenance changed little, except that greater skills with ICT were a requirement. Turnover remained high in parts of the business. Customer care has remained an issue
- With more young people leaving the school systems qualified at levels two and three an element of qualifications drift has been evident in the motor trade, as in other service industries. Seeking reliable employees who have the ability to learn the trade and develop customer skills, employers now tend to think that young people with a general or vocational diploma at level 3 would make the best long-term investment.
- The government has led the introduction of a vocationally driven system of lifelong learning. The quality of on-the-job learning and of outside training providers varies greatly. Over the decade, a variety of apprenticeship models were tried out; in practice, most new entrants to the servicing side of the business are trained at colleges, with 'alternance' training in the workplace. The training outlook of the SMEs in the sector tends to concentrate on immediate, short-term needs, while the run of small and one-person businesses often treat training as a low priority.

Scenario 3 for 2012
- Economic growth has been quite strong over the period, averaging a 2.5% increase in GDP per annum over the ten-year period. The UK took a firm decision to join the Euro and became a 'mainstream' EU country by 2005. The decision was taken to adopt gradually the European social model, which in turn had a strong impact on the motor industry.
- The total annual volume of passengers and goods carried reflected the growth in living standards and increased by 35% over the decade. People still aspire to high levels of welfare, but within communities with shared values and a safe, healthy, pleasant environment. Acquisitiveness has been tempered by a belief in the need for a sound quality of life and more equally distributed opportunities and rewards. Social policies are further up the agenda, and environmental concerns are high on people's public and private priorities. There is a determination to develop an eco-friendly, integrated transport system.
- Government has consistently prioritised the development of rail rather than road transport. The social partners, government and the EU legislators are the main drivers promoting change across the European transport

industries. The instruments are a mixture of regulatory and norm-based mechanisms with an emphasis on innovative and problem-solving strategies that the different policy groups can buy into. Sectoral organisations regrouped in the transport industries when change began and are now key partners in both the change and training agendas. Partnership between different stakeholders has become routine.
- A strong shift has taken place in the market shares of the different transport industries. The key factor is the reduction in market share of road transport for both freight and people. Thus, for example, the dominance of the motorcar began to wane for the first time in 50 years. Twenty four million vehicles were on the road in 2012, an increase of only one million over the figure for 2000. Nevertheless, levels of new car sales were high (25% higher than in 2000) as people went for economic, environmentally friendly vehicles. The market share of road haulage fell from 65% in 2000 to 57% in 2012. This still marks an increase in the volume of goods carried.
- Environmental management and congestion control policies have created a regulatory framework that penalises individuals, firms and garages that breach environmental and safety standards. Smart technology has been introduced into new cars and regional network control centres. Cities are more or less no-go areas for HGVs, and light van systems (some of which have pioneered new forms of electronic power) have proved to be a successful innovation.
- Considerable productivity gains have been made through efficiency, technological advance and some new ways of organising. For example, servicing a vehicle takes on average 80% of the time it had taken in 2002. The industry has an improving skills profile, and this fits well with a regulatory framework in which licence to practice requirements have become more common and more demanding. Both salespeople and mechanics must follow programmes of initial and continuing training, and are expected to meet high standards in technical, interpersonal and IT skills. Skills recognition as well as qualifications are built in.
- The rapid development of mechanical and in-car technology has created a need for mechanics or teams skilled across a range of mechanical, electrical and computerised technologies. Being a mechanic is no longer a default career for young people who left school or initial training with few qualifications. The national debate questioned whether apprenticeship should start at 16 or at 18 after a full general education has been completed; the decision was for the latter to be introduced gradually.
- A partnership approach to lifelong learning has developed – employers and employees have both rights and obligations. Initial training is done through

school-based alternance systems or work-based apprenticeships and continuing training is a requirement for continuing to practice. Sectoral organisations have a strong influence. Although training systems have been developed in consultation and many firms welcome the moves to a high skills profile, some smaller firms feel 'left out in the cold' by the new partnership and training arrangements.

Scenario 4 for 2012
- Economic growth has been slow at an average of 1.25% of GDP per annum. This is partly a result of deliberate policy, when the priorities of government and the values of most people in the community changed. People started to turn their back on the 'massification' that had developed in the 20th century. They were seeking sustainable levels of welfare and income in local, networked communities. Government and regional authorities subjected markets to strong forms of social regulation. The aim was to provide more equally distributed opportunities in local communities and a high quality environment. In parts of the UK the large-scale economy was constrained as local community governance was strengthened and the whole focus of both business and social life were regionalised, with Scotland and Wales drawing apart. There were economic costs to this, but people felt that there were personal and social benefits.
- Strong emphasis was placed on small-scale innovations using new technology to meet local needs. Ingenuity was seen as the key to providing low cost and environmentally friendly outcomes.
- Against the background of these economic and social drivers, the volume of goods and passengers moved on all forms of transport increased by only 5% over the decade. Urban tramways, cycle tracks and even attempts to regenerate marine/water transport began to find their place alongside the road, rail and air networks. Road marginally increased its share of the haulage business (from 65% in 2000 to 66% in 2012), but cars lost out a little (3% market share) to other forms of road and urban transport.
- The scrap and replace mentality of earlier years in the vehicle service industry was superseded by a preference for vehicle parts with a long life and for repairs wherever viable. This meant both that car manufacturers were expected to produce durable components that could be dismantled and fixed, and that mechanics needed advanced skills. Repairing cars took, on average, only 10% less time in 2012 than had been the case in 2000. Interest in renewable fuels, alternative technologies and environmentally friendly modes of transport meant that garages were

handling a wide range of operations and technologies. Mechanics were seen as skilled craftspeople who needed a command of a range of technical and IT skills. Entrants needed prior qualifications at 17 or 18.
- Cars sales had become a different kind of operation. Now only 15% of cars were sold through conventional showrooms as customers made full use of the opportunities provided by e-commercial outlets. In fact, the volume of sales of new vehicles was not as low as might be expected: sales were 15% higher in 2012 than in 2000. A part of this quite buoyant market comprised innovative vehicle engineering powered by non-pollutant energy forms. These were mainly very small vehicles that were exempt from pollution and congestion charges. New forms of small, versatile, hi-tec delivery vans were also a growth market.
- Although SMEs constituted a large proportion of the businesses, many aspired to be learning organisations in which the skills and contribution of employees were valued. The extent varied from region to region. In the most innovative areas, some novel networking arrangements between very different kinds of company in the transport and related sectors produced successful and stable business outcomes.
- Lifelong learning partnerships were defined at the local and regional level and cut across most aspects of the community. They provided socially inclusive education and training services, which employers valued as a way of ensuring that appropriately educated young people would enter the labour market. Colleges and universities had a clear local and regional role in high skills development. Thus, training, research and innovation could be linked through a permanent series of networks. Local skills needs were carefully mapped and pathways were well signposted. However, national standards were more difficult to identify and meet

Addressing the ICT skills shortage in Europe

Martin Curley, Intel Corporation, Leixlip, Co Kildare, Ireland

Information and communication technologies (ICTs) are pivotal tools for advancing EU prosperity. In this context the emergence of the knowledge economy is driving a structural change in skills requirements toward ICTs. This paper discusses how the Careerspace consortium is helping to tackle the ICT skills shortage in Europe. The Careerspace Consortium is led by IBM, Intel, Nokia, BT, Philips, Siemens, Telefonica, Cisco, Thales, Nortel, EICTA and the European Commission.

1. Introduction

We live in an uncertain age, with the shape of society changing from being resource based to being more knowledge based. The well known management guru Peter Drucker says 'In today's economy, the most important resource is no longer labour, capital or land; it is knowledge'. Whilst this is a statement over which one could have much discussion and argument, it is clear that the creation and sharing of knowledge is a key modulator in the progression of an economy and indeed a society.

The information revolution is being driven by Moore's Law, which predicts a doubling of processing capacity every eighteen months with an accompanying cost reduction. This means that more and more computing power in PC's is becoming available at lower cost. Information and communication technologies, used by small minorities just a few years ago, are now offering easily accessible on-line facilities to an incredible number of people.

2. European ICT skills gap

The IDC [1] Summit on Technology, Innovation and Skills Training in March 2000 was a catalyst for popularising the existence of a European ICT skills gap. On IDC broad skills definition, the demand for IT workers was expected to grow to over 13 million in 2003 while the supply was projected to remain a little above 11 million. Whilst the recent high-tech downturn lowered the gap somewhat, the demand for skills centred around the Internet working environment continues to grow (EITO estimated the ICT market grew by 5.1% in 2001 amounting to a value of 643 billion Euro). The main drivers for this demand are the growing importance of Internet technology, telecommunications devices and infrastructure as well as the increasing use of Internet technology as a foundation for business processes. IDC also predicted that the current skills shortage in Western Europe would become more acute unless urgent action is taken.

The main areas of the shortage are:
- Analysts and programmers
- Engineers
- Software engineers
- Managers
- Computer operators
- Consultants

Also in 2000, Datamonitor estimated that Western Europe would lose 100 billion Euro in total wage revenue over the next three years because of Europe's inability to fill vacancies in the ICT sector. With this context the need for the Careerspace consortium came into being and a concerted efforts was made to put in place long-term measures to close the gap.

3. Industry response to the ICT skills gap

It's clear that the depth and breadth of ICT skills penetration across the European Union will be an important factor in future success. This has been recognised and a unique collaboration between the European Commission and private industry, in the shape of the Careerspace Consortium was formed a number of years ago to improve the quality of ICT skills and drive further penetration of ICT skills. The Lisbon European Council of 23 and 24 March 2000 set the European Union a major strategic goal for the next decade 'to

---

[1] International Data Corporation.

become the most competitive and dynamic knowledge based economy in the world, capable of sustainable economic growth with more and better jobs and greater social cohesion'.

The Council recognised that there is a widening skills gap, especially in information technology where increasing numbers of jobs remain unfilled and at the same time acknowledged that 'every citizen must be equipped with the skills needed to live and work in this new information society'.

To attain this strategic objective, the European Council called for Europe's education and training systems to be adapted both to the demands of the knowledge society and to the need for an improved level and quality of employment. The Information and Communications Technology (ICT) industry in Europe, which is acknowledged as the driving force of the new economy supported this call and is playing an active role in partnership with all stakeholders to achieve this strategic objective. The Careerspace Consortium is led by Intel, IBM, Nokia, BT, Philips, Siemens, Telefonica, Cisco, Thales, Nortel, and EICTA, the European Information and Communications Technology Industry Association. It is funded by these companies and the European Commission.

The Careerspace consortium priorities are focussed on increasing studying opportunities in ICTs, encouraging and preparing young people to enter technical education and careers, improving mathematical and science education and technical skills training and increasing the participation of women in technical education. Other measures include rapid adoption of eLearning.

A crucial first phase of the Careerspace program was to better describe the roles essential to achieving e-Europe and the wide range of skills and capabilities these involve. The Career Space core generic skills profiles were offered as a reference point for universities and students alike. The Career Space core profiles represent the most important areas where skills shortages are currently experienced and anticipated in the future.

The next phase was to build on this and work with the education sector to devise curricula guidelines that would equip new ICT graduates for life in the information age. This curricula work has been actively supported by over twenty universities and technical institutions across Europe and CEN/ISSS - the European standardisation body for the information society, Eurel - the convention of national societies of electrical engineers of Europe and *e*-skills NTO - the UK national training organisation for ICT.

Working with these 20 universities across Europe, the Consortium has developed new Information and Communication Technologies curricula, matched to the needs of the 21st century. These new curricula will hopefully become the European benchmark and are providing the basis for evolutionising ICT education across Europe.

An important other strand of the Consortium's work is to attract more people, especially women and people with disabilities, to develop ICT skills. A significant marketing effort, centred on a website (www.careerspace.com) is underway to attract more people, especially women into the ICT industry. As Careerspace moves into it's third phase there is increasing emphasis on vocational ICT training and generation of profiles for users in generic industries.

4. Supply/demand working group findings

Because the ICT industry is dynamic, volatile and highly influenced by the development of related technologies, there is a constant need to monitor the ICT skills shortage and the supply of new graduates into the labour market in Europe. To this end, Careerspace established a supply/demand working group to get better information on supply/demand trends.

The Supply Demand Working Group of the Skills Consortium focused on looking at ways to better understand the skills shortage especially when it is related to the most relevant ICT skills profiles defined in Careerspace phase 1. In order to better capture the ICT skills shortage, a pilot study, based on occupational statistics was conducted in UK by IBM. The ICT jobs (defined according to the 13 Careerspace skills profiles) were matched in a matrix against the official classifications of occupational statistics and thus, the demand for ICT skills could be derived. This method also enabled the utilisation of the national official statistics and moreover, the comparison to the corresponding OECD occupational statistics. The same method with country specific adjustments was used in estimating the demand in other European countries. With this method the consortium found a useful match with the true current skills shortage on the job level.

The main findings of the Supply Demand working group were as follows:
- In 2000 there were about six and a half million ICT workers in Western Europe, accounting for just over four per cent of total employment;
- Over the next four years another two millions will be added to the ICT workforce which by 2004 will account for nearly five and a quarter per cent of all jobs;
- In 2000 the ICT supplier industries accounted for 28.8% of total jobs, 50% of these jobs were with end-users, and the remainder, 21.2% were employed in call centres;

- Analysts and programmers were the largest occupational group, comprising 27% of the total ICT jobs excluding call centres. Growth in demand is growing fastest for these skills together with software engineers.

The group found that direct evidence on the skills gap was difficult to come by. Perhaps the best indicator of this shortfall was that salaries in the software and services industry were rising at nearly twice the rate of national average earnings

5. Consequences and solutions

A consequence of the globalisation and uncertain times is that today's European workforce and researchers face unprecedented challenges and competitive pressures. Researchers and Employees need to learn faster and colleagues often need to collaborate cross-functionally, across offices and borders to create new research, products and achieve operational excellence.

Taking some poetic license with the physics definition of linear momentum, being the product of 'mass by velocity', one could argue that the momentum of an economy is somehow related to the product of the size of the population and the learning velocity (where learning velocity or knowledge velocity is defined as the directional speed with which knowledge is flowing and people are learning). The wide scale adoption of e-learning across Europe will be a key tool for closing the ICT skills gap. eLearning will provide just in time learning to people's PCs whilst enabling mass economies of scale in education.

6. Conclusion

ICT is a major force in the global economy. Societies have the choice of being proactive or reactive in the face of this wave of change. The 2002 edition of the EITO (European Information Technology Observatory) outlined that in 2001 the Internet strongly increased its penetration in Europe. 148 million web users, that is 38% of the total population, had access to the web. EITO expected an increase in the number of web users up to 63% of the population in 2005. Despite the economic slowdown e-business activities continue to grow and traditional industries are increasingly adopting e-business tools to restructure, reduce costs and sustain competitiveness. With this context, Careerspace phase III is shifting it's focus to vocational ICT skills and end user profiles. Only through concerted pan-European effort can the digital divide be transformed into a digital dividend for Europe.

References

Hernaut, K. et al. *New ICT curricula for the 21st century - designing tomorrow's education.* Brussels, 2001.

Lamborghini, B. *European Information Technology Observatory - EITO 2002.* Brussels, 2002.

Manninen, A. *EICTA position on skills shortage in European ICT industry.* Helsinki, 2001.

Niitamo, Veli-Pekka, Telford, Keith. *The level and growth of ICT skills needs in Europe. A pilot study, methodology and initial results.* Helsinki, 2001.

Straub, Richard; Bourke, Thomas. *Internal Careerspace memos and documentation.* Paris, 2001-2002.

New skill requirements in logistics

Kathrin Schnalzer, **Gerd Gidion**, Fraunhofer Institute for Industrial Engineering (FhIAO), Stuttgart, Germany; **Miriam Thum**, Infratest Social Research; **Helmut Kuwan**, Social Research and Consultancy, Munich and Infratest Social Research, Munich, Germany

The ADeBar project aims at making available at an early stage information about changing qualification needs in the workplace and in enterprises. It combines qualitative and quantitative surveys with longitudinal and cross-section analyses. At the core of the early recognition instrument are case studies from the Fraunhofer Institute for Industrial Engineering. These studies analyse complete working tasks within their respective working systems and business processes. The sum of all the case studies gives a picture of general trends and theses, which are subjected to a test for representativeness conducted in each case by Infratest Social Research together with Helmut Kuwan – Social Research and Consultancy Munich. The current focus of the project is the fields of logistics, facility management, commercial office jobs, and the media sector.

The qualification-related and in-house specialisations as well as the new sets of qualifications in logistics, derived from qualitative case studies in businesses, can be summarised in 'process controller', 'IT logistics specialist', 'transport organiser', and 'technical delivery specialist'. Current and future qualification requirements were assessed in a survey of 440 enterprises, about 200 of which are logistics enterprises: customer-focus will continue to be the major qualification requirement for skilled logistics employees. With regard to some Internet and e-commerce qualifications, a considerable increase in significance is expected within the next three years.

1. Basis and methods of the ADeBar project

Along with Infratest Sozialforschung and in cooperation with Helmut Kuwan, Social Research and Consultancy, the Fraunhofer Institute for Industrial Engineering (FhIAO) are carrying out the research project 'Permanent workplace-based observation of skill developments with a view to the early recognition of changes in work and industry - ADeBar', commissioned by the Federal Ministry of Education and Research, the results of which are to be submitted to industry and training policy decision-makers as empirical information for the adaptation and restructuring of initial and continuing vocational training. The project is focused on practice in the workplace as the starting point for skill developments and is designed to provide clear, concrete and empirically weighted information on the development of real working tasks and related future skill requirements which can be recognised at the level of the work process itself.

The research approach consists of a combination of qualitative and quantitative company surveys. The Fraunhofer Institute for Industrial Engineering is responsible for the qualitative part of the case study and the generation of hypotheses. The core of the ADeBar scientific approach is the implementation of specifically prepared two-day intensive company case studies consisting of:

- exploratory, directed observation interviews with approx. seven respondents per company;
- analysis of work tasks, work system and business processes by means of observation and standardised interviews, examination of the working environment and business process-related operations;
- analysis of documentation of specific relevance to the work and company in question.

The case study approach not only offers the researcher the opportunity of 'full immersion' in the specific situation of the company in question, but also provides company respondents with the opportunity to address the questions of the survey from the perspective of their own specific experience. The results of the case studies are also presented to the company partners. The survey is also expected to offer company partners new findings on expected trends in their specific context.

Starting out from the analysis of complete working activities and related work systems and business processes, development trends are determined and hypotheses for the future drawn up. Building on this, representative interviews are conducted in selected companies. This quantitative verification of the hypotheses is the task of Infratest Sozialforschung and Helmut Kuwan

(Social Research and Consultancy, Munich). The main fields of investigation for the project period 1999-2002 are the cross-sectoral field of logistics, industry involved in the field of facility management, new office activities and the value added structure of media design.

A detailed description of the basic principles and methods of the ADeBar project can be found in Gidion et al. (2000). ([1])

2. Empirical qualification bundles derived from case studies

Kathrin Schnalzer, Gerd Gidion

In the first part of the survey involving the case studies, company practice reveals considerable changes in job requirements in the key research field of stock inventory and shipping logistics. New tasks are emerging in the wake of extended technical options (satellite navigation, GPS, electronic transmission) and market-led requirements (client-specific just-in-time delivery, chaotic stockkeeping) on the one hand, and in the light of the logistical maturity and overlapping of previously irrelevant areas (automated shipping systems, automatically controlled transport systems, information and data logistics, global logistics), on the other.

So far however these changing skill requirements have only been addressed from the point of view of vocational training by regulations in courses leading to academic qualifications delivered by institutions ranging from colleges of advanced vocational studies and specialised colleges of higher education to universities. Within the German dual system of training, on the other hand, the basic premise is frequently that of low skill requirements with little need for measures at the level of occupations in the logistics field. However, evaluation of the ADeBar project case studies indicates extended skill requirements for non-academic personnel at middle qualification level in logistic systems, an aspect which should be incorporated into existing initial and continuing training programmes with a view to optimal skilling.

The empirical skill requirements identified can be classified into skill bundles which are to a certain extent based on requirements in existing training occupations (see Figure 1).

([1]) Gidion, G.; Kuwan, H.; Schnalzer, K.; Waschbüsch, E. Spurensuche in der Arbeit – Ein Verfahren zur Erkundung künftiger Qualifikationserfordernisse. In: *Qualifikationen erkennen – Berufe gestalten*, Vol. 2, 2000.

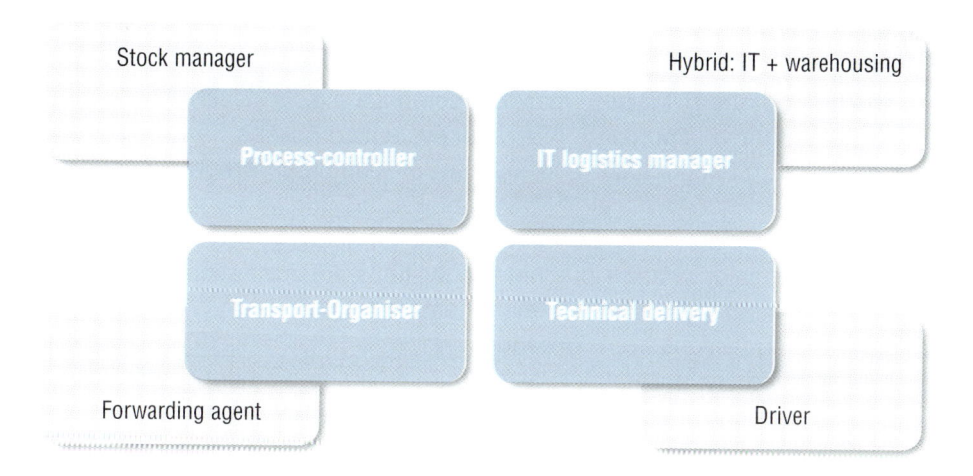

Figure 1. **Empirical skill bundles in logistics**

```
  Stock manager                          Hybrid: IT + warehousing

        ┌─────────────────┐           ┌─────────────────┐
        │ Process-controller│         │ IT logistics manager│
        └─────────────────┘           └─────────────────┘

        ┌─────────────────┐           ┌─────────────────┐
        │ Transport-Organiser│        │ Technical delivery│
        └─────────────────┘           └─────────────────┘

  Forwarding agent                                  Driver
```

In the following, two examples from the workplace serve to demonstrate company-specific solutions and identified skill bundles.

■ *Example 1:* **The IT logistics manager**

A surveyed automotive company showed particularly stringent requirements in terms of quality and reliability in the shipping of automobile components, which can only be guaranteed by optimised quality assurance. The materials are delivered from the points of production and storage locations and scanned into the materials management system in the incoming goods department. Once the materials are consigned, the containers are transferred by a high-lift truck driver into the outgoing goods department. Here each packing station is filled with a computerised image documentation system, comprising figures of over 3 000 different automotive components, designed to guarantee correct packaging of the shipped goods and the loading of the transport containers. This system facilitates the operational tasks of the personnel in identifying and distinguishing the various automotive components. It also means more reliable recognition and removal of defective parts. Quality assurance and error minimisation are among the most important requirements for all shipping department personnel. The ready packed parts are finally conveyed by high-lift truck to the dispatch centre, scanned out of the system, loaded onto containers and shipped to the client by various means of transport (truck, internal navigation, ocean liner, aircraft).

The use of a networked materials management system as well as databases and information systems calls for a hybrid of skills in the surveyed company. These include knowledge of inventory management, IT administration, installation, maintenance and programming.

The tasks of the IT logistics manager comprise e.g.:
- Localisation and appropriate referral of systems problems
- Installation, configuration and update of computer programmes and systems
- Problem solving for computer systems and printers
- Referral of major systems problems to systems administration
- Design of input masks for data management programmes
- Answering questions from colleagues
- The intermediary function between programmers and other personnel
- Training personnel in the use of materials management systems
- Monitoring the shipping process by checking consignment lists
- Monitoring of correct transmissions (interface transmissions)
- Retransmission of non-transmitted data (e.g. data unrecorded by the scanner)
- Forwarding cancellations to programmers.

Skill requirements are expected to rise, especially as far as commercial knowledge and modern office technology are concerned. Necessary characteristics and abilities are logical thinking, coping with stress (induced, among others, by changing requirements) and perseverance in troubleshooting. Process control with planning and organisational activities is expected to gain momentum.

The tasks of the IT logistics manager call for particularly high requirements in terms of a combination of knowledge and skills from materials and inventory management, on the one hand, and computer technology and programming, on the other. Given the use of increasingly automated and networked inventory and materials management systems, skills in a whole range of different working systems are required from an IT logistics manager. The bundle of skills required from the logistics manager is illustrated in Figure 2.

Figure 2. **Skill bundle: IT logistics manager**

Technical requirements
- Knowledge of systems
- Materials management systems
- Programming knowledge

Social requirements
- Intermediary function between programmers and other personnel

Organisational requirements
- Thinking in terms of processes, dispatch monitoring
- Virtual worlds

Specialised requirements
- Installation, configuration and update of computer programmes and systems
- Problem solving in the case of computer systems and equipment, e.g. printers
- Localising of systems problems and referral to fields
- Handling automated ordering systems

- *Example 2: **The process controller***

In a AdeBar partner company in the aeronautics industry, freight build-up on palettes is a core process and the most manpower-intensive unit within the company. The build-up process has numerous interfaces with other functional areas in the logistics centre. Optimisation of paletting is decisive for the fulfilment of corporate targets. A project designed to improve work processes was therefore launched within a project team comprising different functional levels. The goal was to optimise utilisation of resources in the freight build-up process which involves surfaces, materials and personnel. In the planned work system, the foreman is replaced by a process controller whose role is to guarantee information-controlled coordination of freight build-up. In contrast, the freight build-up process has so far operated on the basis of consignment notes from the documentation department. The purpose of this change is to eliminate the previous strict division of labour between different areas and to change the highly physical/industrial orientation of the foreman's activities to a more planning and coordinating activity. A new activity profile had to be introduced to cover these new requirements, the *process controller*. The process controller's field of activity comprises the tasks of the previous foreman, part of the tasks of the documentation department as well as preparatory activities. He plans and controls the entire build-up process. This process of change is accompanied by a greater degree of IT support for the overall work process. A back-office has been set up, comprising staff assuming documentation and detailed research tasks, to compensate for the process controller's increased tasks.

The example of this company illustrates the introduction of the new skill bundle of the process controller, building on existing activity profiles, with the technical, social, organisational and specialised requirements of personnel in logistics occupations illustrated in Figure 3.

Figure 3. **Skill bundle: process controller**

Technical requirements
- Handling communication and information systems
- Controlling SAP materials management systems
- Automatic order systems

Social requirements
- Personnel management

Organisational requirements
- Planning and organisation of processes, calculation
- Overall systems orientation
- An insight into processes, virtual worlds

Specialised requirements
- Goods and sales management
- Shipping management, merchandise movements
- Merchandise control, accounting, cost controlling

Changing labour system and working tasks imply changing manpower skill requirements, as illustrated by the empirical skill bundles observed. These include both new requirements, e.g. handling materials tracking systems, new combinations of requirements, e.g. the combination of materials management and IT skills, and the integration of qualifications from neighbouring activities within the labour system, e.g. the tasks of the process controller.

3. Results from the company survey on the activity field 'logistics'

Miriam Thum, Helmut Kuwan

In the second part of the project, Infratest Sozialforschung carried out face-to-face representative interviews among company experts to determine quantitative results based on the trends observed by the FhIAO. The first wave of the survey examined the fields of activity logistics and facility management.

Face-to-face interviews were conducted in a total of 440 randomly selected companies from the logistics and facility management sectors. The following report relates to the field of logistics in which 197 of the interviews were conducted.

Figure 1. Survey investigation concept of ADeBar main study

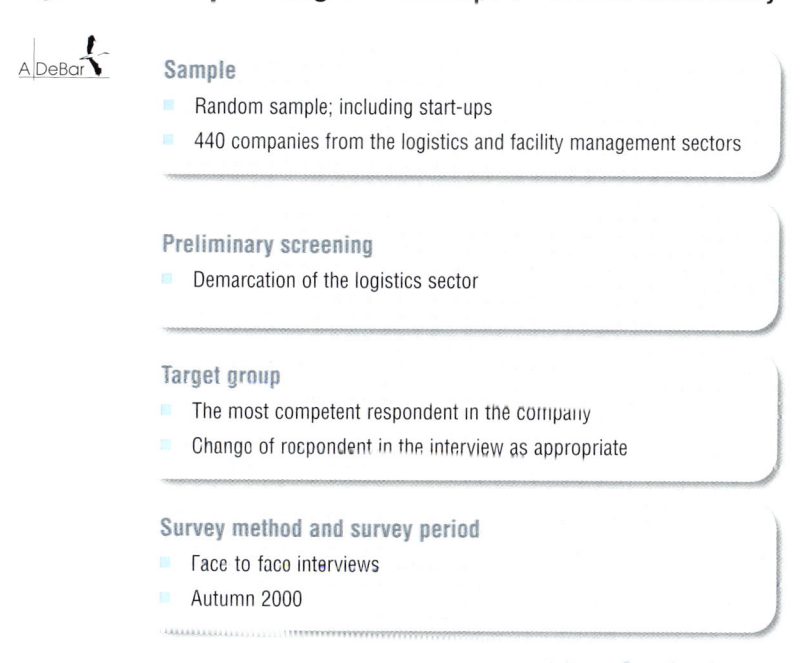

Sample
- Random sample; including start-ups
- 440 companies from the logistics and facility management sectors

Preliminary screening
- Demarcation of the logistics sector

Target group
- The most competent respondent in the company
- Change of respondent in the interview as appropriate

Survey method and survey period
- Face to face interviews
- Autumn 2000

Infratest Sozialforschung

The basis for the selection of the random sample of the companies with the core activity of logistics was the 'workplace master sample' (AMS), developed by Infratest and unique of its kind to the Federal Republic. The AMS comprises 160 000 companies, records business start-ups on a continuous basis and is constantly updated.

Since there is no specific definition of the logistics sector as such, preliminary screening was carried out in those areas of industry in which logistics processes constitute an essential business component. Companies were selected from the manufacturing and construction industries, commerce, transport and services, while sectors which seemed very unlikely to have logistics as a core business were ruled out. The sample was additionally classified into the following three size classes: 10 to 49, 50 to 99, 100+ employees, whereby large-scale enterprises with a headcount of 100+ were given an over-proportionate weighting.

In a preliminary screening process, the interviewer ascertained whether the relevant company's core business involved transport or organisation of the transport of persons, raw materials or goods or organisation of the sale of goods or raw materials. Companies fulfilling this screening criterion were included in the survey while the others were eliminated.

The persons initially allocated to the interviewers as respondents were personnel managers, and, in the case of smaller businesses, managing directors or proprietors. In those cases in which it subsequently transpired that these persons were not in a position to adequately assess the trends in the selected occupational area, an alternative respondent was chosen, i.e. the person with the deepest insight into the field of activity of logistics. This alternative respondent had to be identified by the interviewer on the spot. However in 97% of the interviews there was in fact no change of respondent. The survey was conducted from 12 September to 25 November 2000.

The central themes of the AdeBar representative survey were as follows:
- Initial/continuing training and informal vocational learning in their various forms
- Innovations in the enterprise, R&D
- The status of early recognition in the company
- General skill trends
- Current and future skill requirements
- Specific trends in logistics and facility management.

Logistics as a dynamic industrial sector

Logistics is a dynamic industrial sector. This was demonstrated by the answer to question as to whether one or more organisational changes had taken place in the company in the course of the last three years. One or more of the following changes had occurred in almost all the surveyed enterprises. Measures to improve quality management/quality assurance, applied by 76% of the companies, stood in first position, followed by the introduction of new procurement and sales channels. Most of the companies had carried out a redistribution of tasks, either in the form of a reorganisation of departments, a downward shift in responsibility or outsourcing. The introduction of independent teams and units with their own cost/profit accounting is also to be seen in conjunction with the downward shift in responsibility. Responsibility for costs and entrepreneurship are no longer limited to the graduate level but play an increasingly important role at the level of specialised personnel. As many as one out of every ten firms had introduced a call centre in the course of the last three years. All the changes had been more frequently applied in companies which were economically sound. And changes had been more frequently carried out in innovative than in traditional companies.

Figure 5. **Organisational changes in the course of the last three years** (percentages)

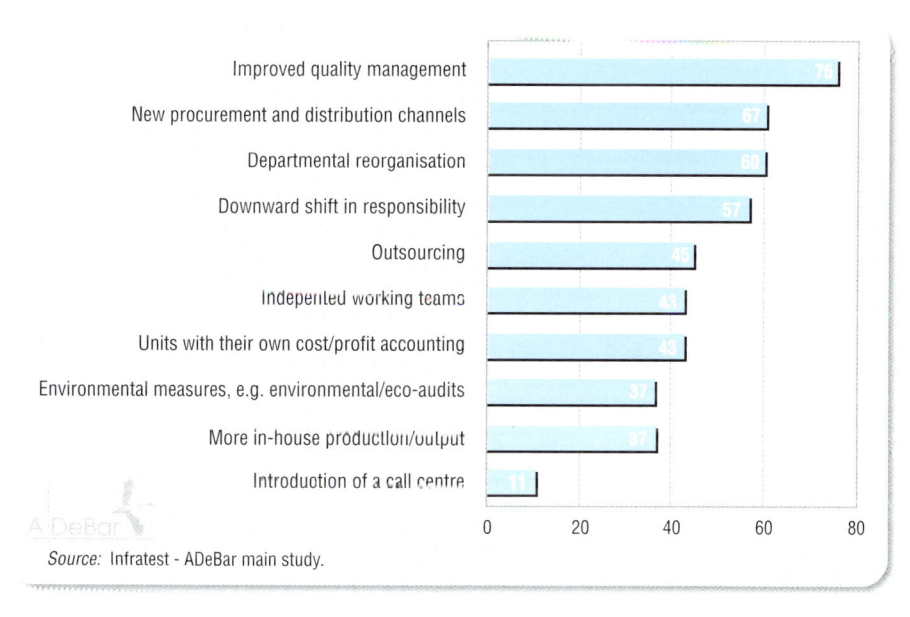

Organisational change	%
Improved quality management	74
New procurement and distribution channels	67
Departmental reorganisation	60
Downward shift in responsibility	57
Outsourcing	45
Independent working teams	43
Units with their own cost/profit accounting	43
Environmental measures, e.g. environmental/eco-audits	37
More in-house production/output	37
Introduction of a call centre	11

Source: Infratest - ADeBar main study.

General skill trends in the field of logistics

What are the general skill trends to be observed for specialised personnel in the field of logistics? The experts were asked to evaluate 20 relatively general statements in the context of the company survey ([2]). The statement describing IT skills as a basic overall skill which is becoming part and parcel of general knowledge met with the greatest degree of approval: 92% of the experts from the field of logistics agreed with this statement.

([2]) Evaluated on a scale of 1 to 4 as follows: 1= 'Absolutely true' to 4 = 'Not at all true'.

A statement referring to a specific facet of customer orientation stood in third position. The trend towards intensive mutual influence and interaction between the commissioning unit and the client in innovations, so-called customer development, was regarded as a requirement for specialised personnel by approx. nine out of ten experts. 79% of the experts moreover confirmed the trend that working in an international context would expand considerably.

The increasing significance of IT is reflected in the evaluation of the statement on the broad expansion of e-commerce and e-business in virtually all company functions. 77% of the experts confirm this trend (7th position).

Figure 6. **Statements on general skill trends in the field of logistics -A-**
Ranking of 20 statements

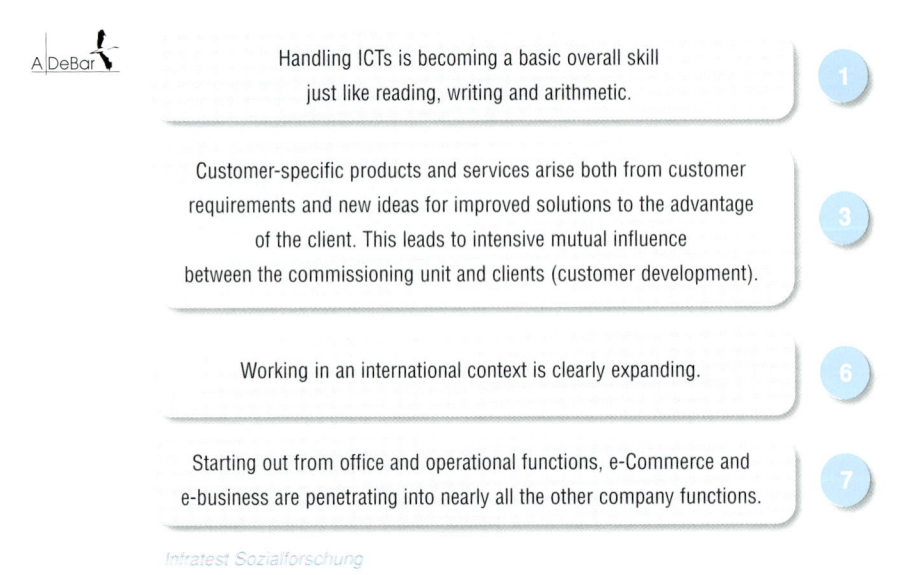

A DeBar

Statement	Rank
Handling ICTs is becoming a basic overall skill just like reading, writing and arithmetic.	1
Customer-specific products and services arise both from customer requirements and new ideas for improved solutions to the advantage of the client. This leads to intensive mutual influence between the commissioning unit and clients (customer development).	3
Working in an international context is clearly expanding.	6
Starting out from office and operational functions, e-Commerce and e-business are penetrating into nearly all the other company functions.	7

Infratest Sozialforschung

The experts were asked to evaluate a number of statements on the importance of specialised vocational knowledge in relation to other requirements. The statement that *the division and organisation of labour is no longer principally oriented towards occupations and functions but rather towards operations and processes in working routine* met with the most approval (8th position). In the opinion of the experts, a more holistic form of organisation and a less strict division of tasks are to be expected in the future (10th position).

A further trend with which the majority of the experts agreed was electronic error documentation on the basis of which errors can be precisely identified.

This is a development which may be of wide-ranging significance for the legal position of employees, in particular from a long-term perspective.

The only statement rejected by a majority of respondents concerns the uncertainty as to whether there is a virtual system or a real colleague is behind a DP interface. It will be interesting to see to what extent this opinion changes over the coming years.

Figure 7 **Statements on general skill trends in the field of logistics -B-**
Ranking of 20 statements

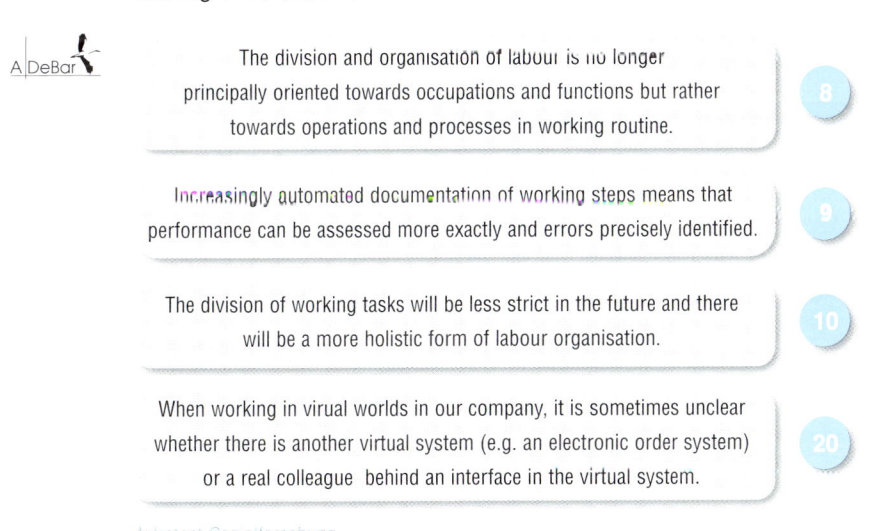

A DeBar

Statement	Rank
The division and organisation of labour is no longer principally oriented towards occupations and functions but rather towards operations and processes in working routine.	8
Increasingly automated documentation of working steps means that performance can be assessed more exactly and errors precisely identified.	9
The division of working tasks will be less strict in the future and there will be a more holistic form of labour organisation.	10
When working in virual worlds in our company, it is sometimes unclear whether there is another virtual system (e.g. an electronic order system) or a real colleague behind an interface in the virtual system.	20

Infratest Sozialforschung

Skill requirements of specialised personnel in the field of logistics

Whereas the previous statements related to general development trends in the field of logistics, the focus in the following statements was on two questions: (1) How high are *current skill requirements* at the level of specialised personnel in the field of logistics? (2) To what extent will these requirements change over the next three years?

A total of 35 skill requirements were presented to the experts for evaluation. The following two graphs summarise the current rating of a number of selected requirements and the expected rise in requirements *over the next three years*.

As far as current requirements are concerned, orientation towards the interests and circumstances of the client very clearly stands in top position (with an average rating of 3.59 on the scale of 1 to 4, see figure 8). Problem solving along with the client was also given a high rating. The experts expect

Figure 8. **Expected changes in skill requirements**

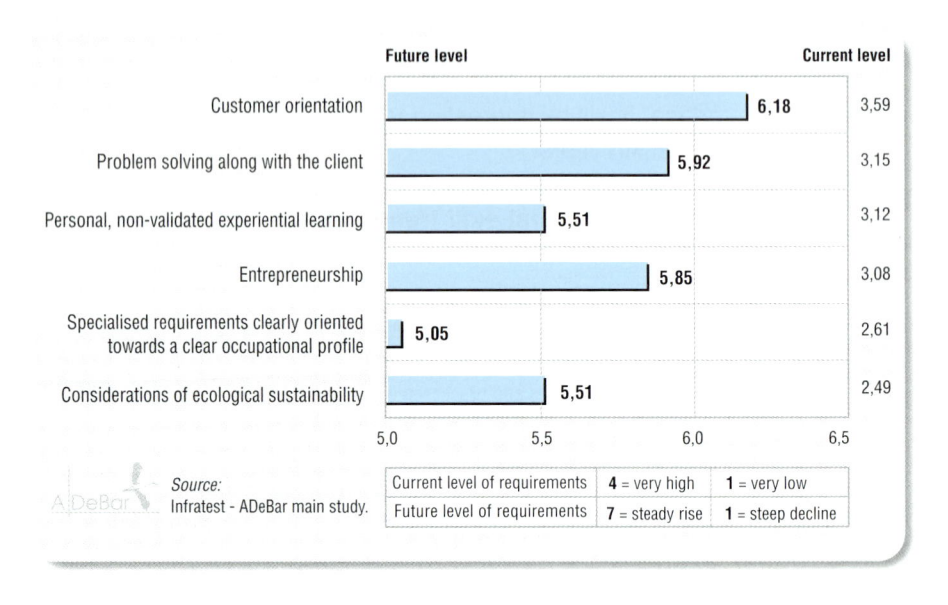

	Future level	Current level
Customer orientation	6,18	3,59
Problem solving along with the client	5,92	3,15
Personal, non-validated experiential learning	5,51	3,12
Entrepreneurship	5,85	3,08
Specialised requirements clearly oriented towards a clear occupational profile	5,05	2,61
Considerations of ecological sustainability	5,51	2,49

Source: Infratest - ADeBar main study.

Current level of requirements: 4 = very high, 1 = very low
Future level of requirements: 7 = steady rise, 1 = steep decline

Figure 9. **Expected changes in skill requirements**
Average changes over the next 3 years - Part B

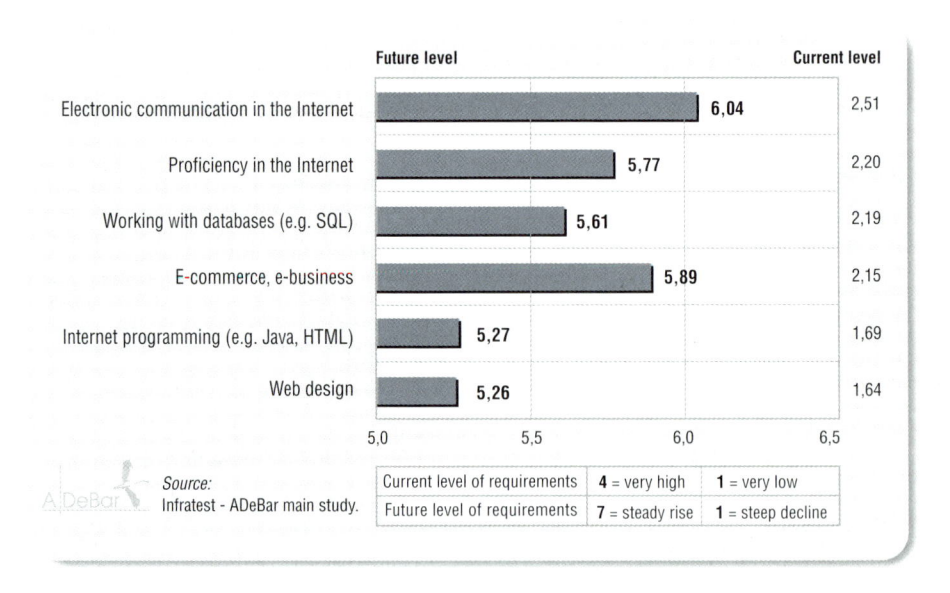

	Future level	Current level
Electronic communication in the Internet	6,04	2,51
Proficiency in the Internet	5,77	2,20
Working with databases (e.g. SQL)	5,61	2,19
E-commerce, e-business	5,89	2,15
Internet programming (e.g. Java, HTML)	5,27	1,69
Web design	5,26	1,64

Source: Infratest - ADeBar main study.

Current level of requirements: 4 = very high, 1 = very low
Future level of requirements: 7 = steady rise, 1 = steep decline

a steep rise in the importance of these skill requirements over the next three years. And entrepreneurship, already in fourth position in the companies' ranking of requirements and of considerable importance today, is also expected to become much more important in the future.

The status of specialised knowledge shows a number of shifts in emphasis within the spectrum of skill requirements. Despite a certain rise in the importance of specialised knowledge, other skills and qualifications show a much greater increase in importance.

Almost all IT skills tend to rank in the bottom third of the current scale of importance for specialised personnel in the field of logistics. However this situation will soon change. The importance of many of these skills will rise considerably over the next three years. This applies both to more general ICT skills, e.g. web-based communication, as well as specific application-oriented competences, e.g. working with databases or e-commerce and e-business. In contrast, the rise in importance is considerably less evident in the case of other IT skills, e.g. knowledge of Internet programming or web design, which will above all become important for a small group of specialised personnel.

4. Conclusion and perspectives

As case studies show, changes in the actual working task and in the surrounding work system lead to new and changing qualification requirements. In this way, for instance, the 'process controller' and 'IT logistics specialist', as new and empirically confirmed sets of qualifications in logistics, include new qualification requirements such as knowledge of business processes, materials tracking systems and people-centred leadership. Furthermore, new combinations of qualification requirements emerge such as the combination of IT skills and knowledge of enterprise resource planning in the case of the 'IT logistics specialist', or the integration of elements from the surrounding work system into the actual working task in the case of the 'process controller'.

The company survey shows that the importance of specialised knowledge is changing. Its significance will still increase but the significance of other qualifications will increase much more markedly. Thus, qualified workers are increasingly expected to have communication skills and a comprehensive understanding of the needs of other business departments and the market. As a result, various skill combinations are required: combinations of specialised and overarching skills; new combinations of industrial/technical and commercial requirements; and a stronger orientation towards in-company processes and operations.

Skill requirements in the care of the elderly – the Swedish example

Gert Alaby, The National Board of Health and Welfare, Stockholm, Sweden

The question as to which professional skills should be required of future staff in healthcare and social services for the elderly should be seen in a wider perspective. This article opens with a section on the global demographic changes and their impact on the scope of future assistance requirements among the elderly. After that, the current situation regarding the supply of skills in Sweden is described, and forecasts of the future demand for labour in the healthcare and social services sector are outlined. In a final section, some conclusions are presented.

1. Introduction

Worldwide, a demographic transition is taking place. This process will accelerate over the next decades. The proportion of older people in the population compared to the number of persons in the labour force is rising, and so is the average life expectancy. Certainly this is a major step forward, still it challenges decision-makers globally.

In Sweden, the workforce in healthcare and social services for the elderly comprises 200 000 persons. Approximately 10% are university graduates. However, 40% of home helpers lack adequate vocational training.

A representative sample of managers within healthcare and social services for the elderly in Swedish municipalities were interviewed in early 2001. The results highlight major difficulties in the recruitment of personnel, especially nurses, occupational therapists and physiotherapists.

Most municipalities do have strategies on how to attract appropriate personnel, but unfortunately they are not effective enough.

The Swedish National Board of Health and Welfare has established skill standards for certified health-care personnel. At present, we are considering if it is possible to do the same for social workers and home helpers.

Without doubt there is a need to define skill requirements and the proper mix of professionals in future healthcare and social services for the elderly. Furthermore, working conditions have to become more attractive.

2. Global demographic trends

In several sectors developments are difficult to predict. Long-term forecasts often prove to be wrong after only a few years. This also applies to healthcare and social services for the elderly, where great uncertainties exist as to future needs and the ensuing demand for labour. However, one important element determining requirements, which has comparatively strong forecasting power and which is also fairly stable, is demographic development. The number of old people is probably the single most important factor for forecasting the future demand for labour in this field.

Currently, a global demographic transition is taking place. The number of old people is growing in most countries, albeit at differing rates. This development has been going on for a long time in several developed countries and is expected to continue and indeed accelerate in a number of OECD member states. But several developing countries, too, are expected to experience considerable demographic change with a growing proportion of elderly citizens. In 2020, 1 000 million people are expected to have reached the age of 65 or older, 700 million of which will be living in developing countries.

Although a major increase in average life expectancy is expected in the developing countries, Europe will maintain its leading position as the 'oldest' continent in 2020. The individual countries that are estimated to have the oldest populations by then will be Japan, Italy, Greece and Switzerland. In the OECD member countries, the proportion of the population aged 65 or above is expected to grow from 146 million to 298 million between 2000 and 2050, i.e. by more than 100%. This is undeniably a dramatic change, which will affect our societies in a number of ways. The changes in the population structure of the OECD countries become clearly apparent in the figure below, in which the situation in 1960 is compared with the development by the year 1995 and with forecasts for the years 2030 and 2050. The changes can be described as a shift from a triangular to a rectangular shape.

Early identification of skill needs in Europe

Figure 1. **OECD: Population estimates and projections**

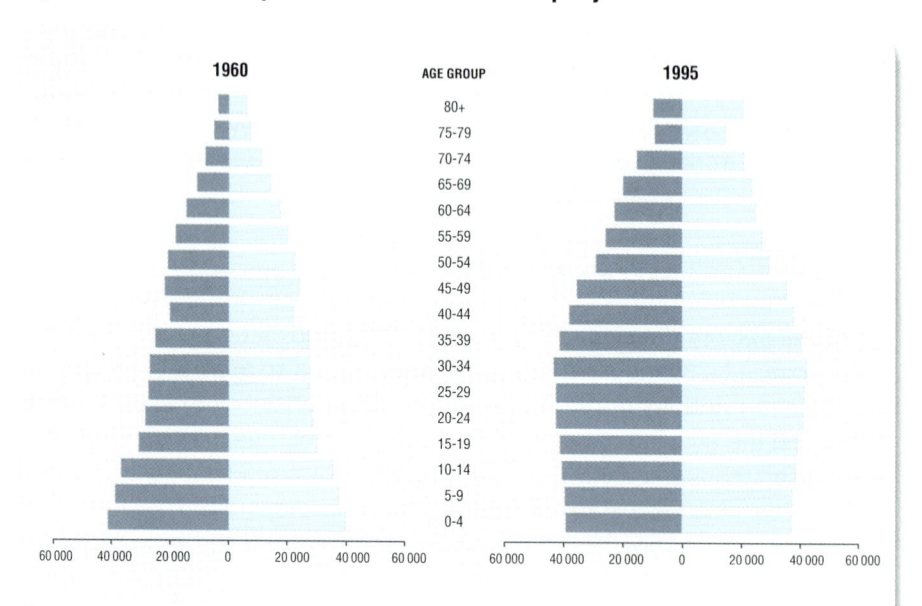

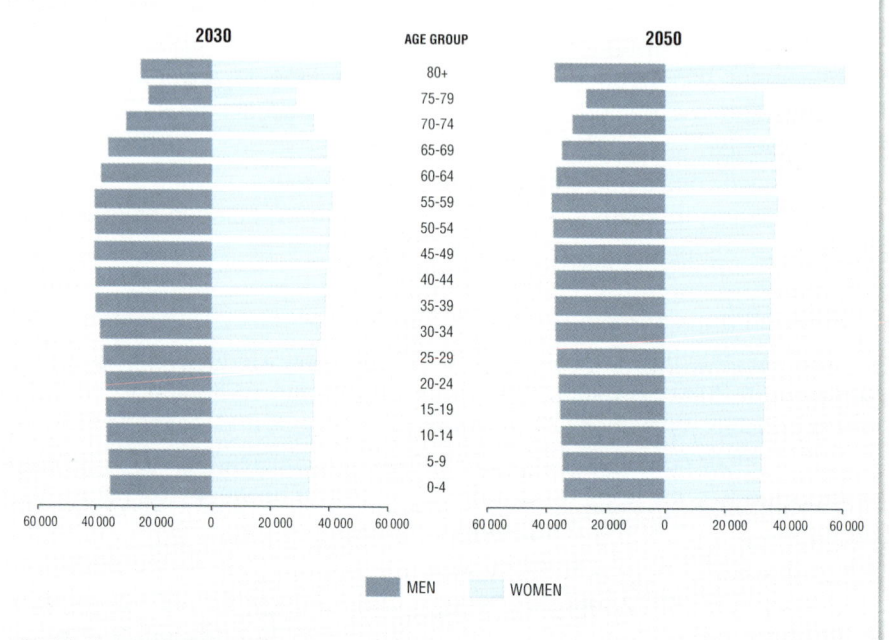

Population by sex and age group in thousands.
Source: United Nations Population Division, 'World Population Prospects: The 1998 Revisions'.

However, it is not only the number of elderly people in the population that is important, but also the development of the ratio between persons in dependent ages – children and the elderly – and those of working age. When the average life expectancy of the population in the developed countries is increasing at the same time as birth rates are falling, an unfavourable development of the dependency rate will ensue in the long run. This development can be illustrated by a few examples from some G7 countries. The figures below show that the dependency rate is expected to undergo an unfavourable development between the years 2015 and 2050 in all the countries described.

Figure 2. **Overall dependency ratios in G7 countries**
Population aged 0-14 plus aged 65 and over as percentage of the population aged 15-64

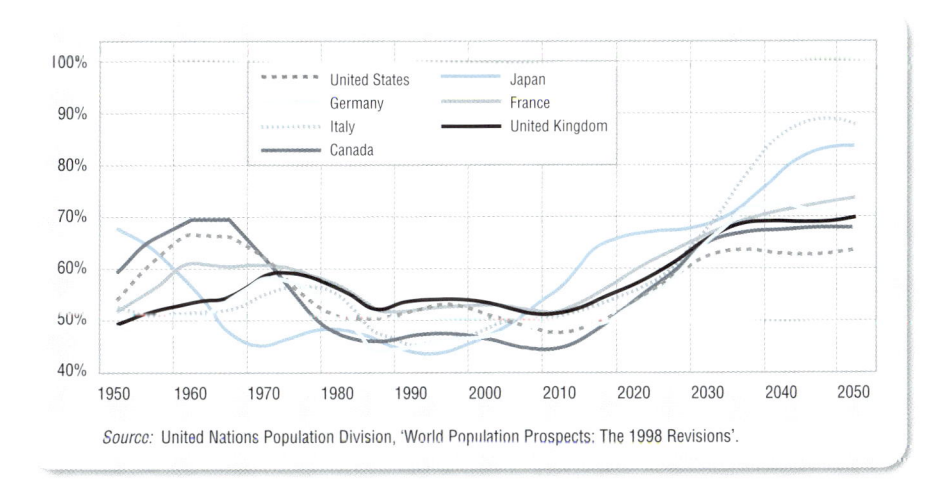

Source: United Nations Population Division, 'World Population Prospects: The 1998 Revisions'.

The scope of the present article does not allow us to elaborate on the significance of these changes for society and the labour market.

If the number of people in different age groups within the population is fundamental for the assessment of the future labour market for healthcare and social services, there are two further topics which are of relevance. The first one refers to changes in morbidity over time and the second one to the balance between the family, the market and the public sector.

As for changes in morbidity and the functional impairments this can lead to, there are various hypotheses regarding the expected development. These can be described as compression of morbidity, expansion of morbidity and postponement of morbidity. There is some data to support the postponement of morbidity hypothesis. For certain groups of illness, however, we can see a trend towards increasing periods of illness-induced functional handicaps. At present, we do not seem to possess sufficiently reliable data to allow us to take a stand on this issue.

The third element in the analysis of the future demand for healthcare and social services directed at the public is how the balance between the responsibility of the family and the market and the public sector's commitment may change. In several European countries, families' – i.e. in practice women's – capacity for taking charge of caring and nursing tasks is decreasing. In Sweden, on the other hand, we have witnessed a certain increase in family responsibility over the past decade as a result of cutbacks in public healthcare and social services. In a European perspective, however, the trend is clear – family responsibility is declining, while that of the public sector is growing.

It is difficult to assess the combined effect of the three elements described. It is clear, however, that demographic change has a very powerful impact. Moreover, it is perhaps dangerous for us to assume that a decline in morbidity would lead to a more substantial reduction in age-standardised assistance needs, i.e. the risk that a person will require help with various tasks at a given age. The possibilities of families to meet this growing demand are likely to be limited in most developed countries.

The conclusion we can draw from this is that both the developed and the developing countries can be expected to be faced with demographic challenges which will pose great demands on various actors to adjust and develop new ways of living and caring relations. In this process, cooperation and exchange between countries are fundamental. Mutual learning on how societies can 'grow old' while retaining their social balance and reaching set welfare targets appears vital in this context.

3. The present situation and future prospects for the supply of skills

Healthcare and social services for the elderly in Sweden were built up following the Second World War. Public responsibility was extended, and the duties of municipalities and county councils were defined. In the 1960s and 1970s, public healthcare and social services underwent an enormous expansion. The 1990s, however, saw sharp cutbacks in the sector.

Currently, approximately 645 000 persons are working in Swedish healthcare and social services, which corresponds to 15% of the labour force. The services provided are to an overwhelming degree financed through taxes and are offered on the basis of universal criteria to all citizens according to need. The costs incurred by these services correspond to approximately 12% of the country's GNP.

In the long-term care of the elderly, the competence level among staff is relatively low. No more than approximately 10% of the employees have a higher education degree; this can be compared with the childcare and emergency healthcare sectors, where the corresponding proportion is between 55 and 60%. Most of the employees are nurse's aides and assistant nurses. Of these, approximately 60% have completed vocationally oriented upper secondary education, which is estimated to be adequate for the tasks performed by the staff in this field. More than half of the nurse's aides and assistant nurses recruited during the second half of the 1990s lacked adequate vocational training, something which has caused the proportion of unskilled and semi-skilled workers to increase among staff.

The National Labour Market Board (*Arbetsmarknadsverket*) has recently published an analysis of the supply of and demand for staff in Swedish healthcare and social services up to the year 2015 (Arbetsmarknadsverket, 2002). Scenario techniques were applied in this study. The results of the projections show an expected annual recruitment need of approximately 12 000 persons with various higher education degrees. The higher education programmes that exist in the field today are designed for approximately 6 500 students per year. This means that the analysis anticipates a considerable shortage of staff with higher education qualifications within healthcare and social services. As for staff with upper secondary education, the shortage of qualified personnel is expected to grow even more. The present educational capacity within youth and adult education corresponds to only about 30% of the predicted recruitment needs for the period up to 2015. These recruitment needs are mainly dependent on large and growing numbers of staff going into retirement, natural departures into other areas of activity and the need for an increased number of employees.

The National Board of Health and Welfare (*Socialstyrelsen*) was commissioned by the Swedish government to carry out a descriptive study on the supply of skills in Swedish municipalities and in companies providing healthcare and social services for the elderly on behalf of the municipalities. A representative nationwide sample of managers within municipalities and companies were interviewed during the winter of 2001.

Some of the results are presented below (Socialstyrelsen, 2001).
- For various staff categories within healthcare and social services for the elderly, between 40 and 75% of the municipalities and companies stated that they had experienced difficulties in recruiting staff. The greatest

difficulties were encountered in the recruitment of nurses, physiotherapists and occupational therapists.
- Increasing recruitment problems were expected for the coming two-year period.
- The strategies considered to be most efficient for securing the supply of skills in the future were changing working hours, encouraging employees to undergo vocational training and improving working conditions.
- Less than a third of the respondents considered it necessary for nurse's aides and assistant nurses to have undergone vocational training, while another third considered this to be desirable.

During the winter of 2002, a follow-up to the above-mentioned study was carried out. The results were on the whole unchanged compared to the situation in 2001 (Socialstyrelsen, 2002).

The National Board of Health and Welfare is commissioned to certify doctors, nurses, occupational therapists, physiotherapists and certain other categories of staff in the healthcare sector. For an individual to be certified, he or she must have met certain skill requirements. For social services staff as well as for assistant nurses and nurse's aides, there are at present no nationally defined skill requirements that need to be met by employees before they may perform certain types of tasks. The National Board of Health and Welfare is currently analysing the possibilities of establishing skill requirements for social services staff. The Board is also considering which professional skills will be needed within healthcare and social services in the future. There are many indications that the proportion of staff with higher education degrees will have to grow. Furthermore, new workplace-based forms of qualifying staff will have to be developed. This will require close cooperation between the persons in charge of healthcare and social services, those in charge of labour market issues and those in charge of education.

Over the past few years, the Swedish government has taken a number of steps to promote the supply of skills in the area. One example of this is the expansion of capacity in higher education programmes for the medical and nursing professions. In addition, municipalities and county councils are – as employers and authorities in charge of healthcare – carrying out extensive developmental work in order to improve working conditions, skills and recruitment procedures. According to the assessment of the National Board of Health and Welfare, the steps taken so far have not been sufficient. Therefore further measures are required from all actors in the area in order to secure the supply of skills – both in the short and the long term.

4. Summary and conclusions

1. Globally, healthcare and social services for the elderly constitute a fast-growing labour market.
2. In order to improve the quality of the services, e.g. increased customisation and user influence, skill requirements for the various staff groups need to be defined.
3. Qualification processes should be established in close cooperation between the education system and those responsible for healthcare and social services. Even greater emphasis needs to be placed on workplace-based learning.
4. The education system must be rapidly adjusted to the growing demand and new skills requirements. Customised, flexible adult education needs to be developed and expanded.
5. Improved working conditions are a prerequisite for attracting a sufficient number of employees. This includes improving terms of remuneration, better leadership, increased self-determination of the staff and better opportunities for skills development at work.
6. International cooperation is needed in order to create beneficial conditions for the mobility of staff who have undergone vocational training or intend to undergo such training. This is also necessary for sharing experience on how the demographic transition may be handled in such a way that the growing demand for healthcare and social services can be met with dignity.

The Scandinavian welfare states have extensive responsibilities within healthcare and social services. Moreover, Sweden has already completed the first phase of the demographic transition that many developed countries are now confronted with. Thus, we have gained valuable experience on how one of society's important commitments can be met – experience that could also be useful for other countries.

References

Arbetsmarknadsverket (National Labour Market Board). *Den framtida personalförsörjningen inom vård och omsorg – Tillgång och rekryteringsbehov till år 2015* [The future supply of personnel in healthcare and social services – supply and recruitment needs up to the year 2015]. Ura 2002:3, Stockholm, 2002.

Socialstyrelsen (National Board of Health and Welfare). *Kompetensförsörjning i vård och omsorg till äldre* [The supply of skills in healthcare and social services for the elderly]. Stockholm, 2001.

Socialstyrelsen (National Board of Health and Welfare), Nationell handlingsplan för äldrepolitiken, slutrapport [National action plan for policies for the elderly, final report]. Stockholm, 2002.

Information system for early recognition of sectoral trends – results obtained for the construction industry

Norbert Brumberger, Research Institute for Vocational Education and Training in the Crafts Sector (FBH) of the University of Cologne, Germany; **Helen Diedrich-Fuhs**, German Employers' Organisation for Vocational Training (KWB), Bonn, Germany

The ability to recognise trends in firms' skill requirements is of vital importance to industry as a whole if it is to remain competitive over the longer term. The procedure described in this paper is designed to make systematic use of industry's wide-ranging networks of experts to improve the available data on skill requirements. The system was developed by the German Employers' Committee on Vocational Training (KWB) in collaboration with the Research Institute for Vocational Education and Training in the Crafts Sector (FBH) of the University of Cologne and has been used for various branches of industry.

This paper describes a method for the regular monitoring and early recognition of qualification trends known as the IDQ©, the results obtained in the specific case of the construction industry and how these can be used in developing initial and continuing training.

1. Introduction

The world of work in the 21st century is notable for the rapid changes taking place in firms and sectors of business and industry. The ability rapidly to adapt initial and continuing training provision to meet new requirements as they arise is vital if firms are to be able to find workers with the skills they need. A situation of growing imbalances on the labour market in which substantial demand for skilled manpower goes hand in hand with high levels of unemployment enhances the importance for policy purposes of access to up-to-date information on trends in firms' skill requirements. As time goes on the ability to recognise changes in skill requirements at an early stage will take on increasing importance by making it possible more rapidly to update existing skilled occupations and create new ones, and to devise additional training and skill qualifications in line with industry's needs.

The membership of professional and trade associations comprises several thousand qualified experts who are in direct contact with the firms in their sector. By using this dense network it is possible at comparatively low cost to maintain a regular contact not just with larger companies but also with small and medium-sized firms. The KWB, as the body coordinating the activities of industrial organisations in all matters connected with the reform of initial and continuing training and the introduction of new skilled occupation categories, works closely with experts in the professional associations, trade organisations, firms and educational establishments. The KWB's own committees of training managers, and the vocational training committees and training centres of the trade and professional associations are another source of expert assistance.

These are the resources which the KWB in collaboration with the University of Cologne's vocational training research institute (FBH) is able to utilise in projects concerned with early recognition of skill requirements sponsored by the German Ministry for Education and Research.

Figure 1. **Industry's vocational training network**

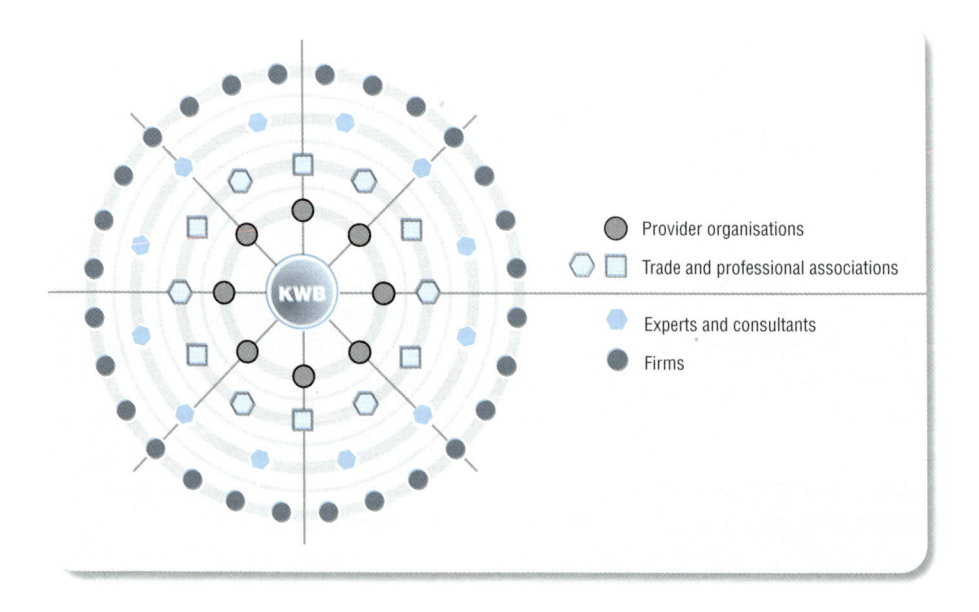

The KWB projects form part of the FreQueNz research sponsored by the German Ministry for Education and Research which is concerned with early recognition of skill requirements.

2. Project design

The project was based on the realisation that firms themselves are largely aware of their skill requirements but that the means for systematically recording this information to allow its prompt exploitation in planning appropriate training do not exist. This calls for an efficient system whereby the information possessed by persons in industrial organisations and other bodies can be centrally recorded and regularly communicated to the authorities responsible for initial and continuing training.

The requirements for an efficient information system are twofold:
1. reliable sources;
2. efficient gathering and processing of information.

Figure 2. **Features of an efficient information system**

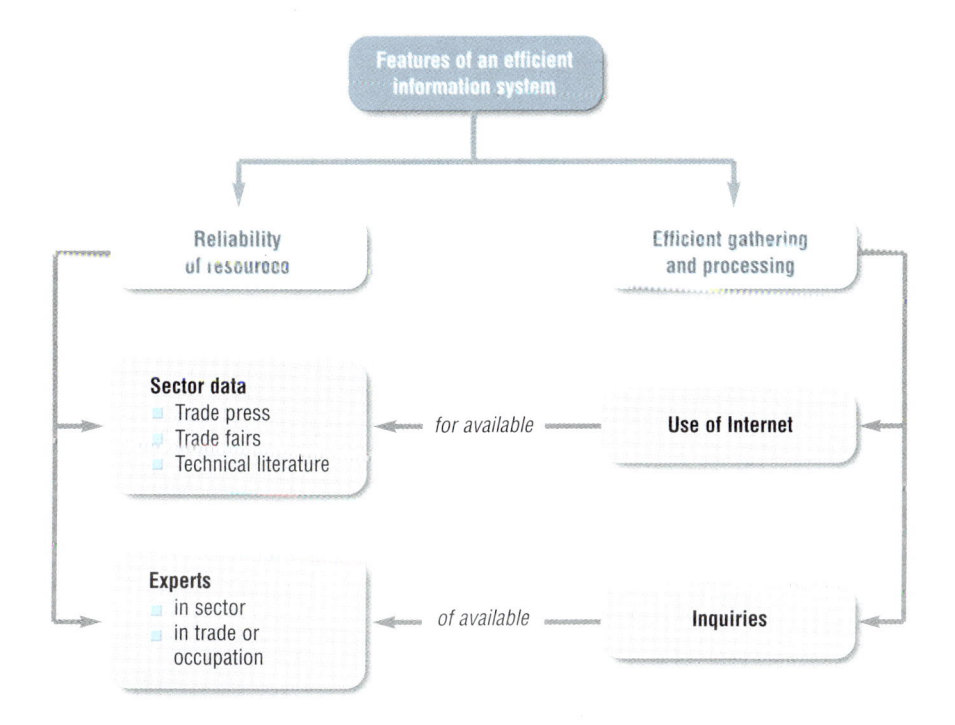

```
                    Features of an efficient
                    information system
              ┌──────────────┴──────────────┐
         Reliability                 Efficient gathering
         of resources                and processing

    Sector data
      · Trade press
      · Trade fairs         ← for available →    Use of Internet
      · Technical literature

    Experts
      · in sector
      · in trade or          ← of available →    Inquiries
        occupation
```

The KWB project utilises the IDQ© system for the regular monitoring of skill trends. This is a multistage information gathering system in which sector experts actively participate. The IDQ© process, which was developed by the KWB with the assistance of its academic support team, may be illustrated graphically as follows:

Figure 3. **The IDQ© process**
Instrument for regulary monitoring skill developments

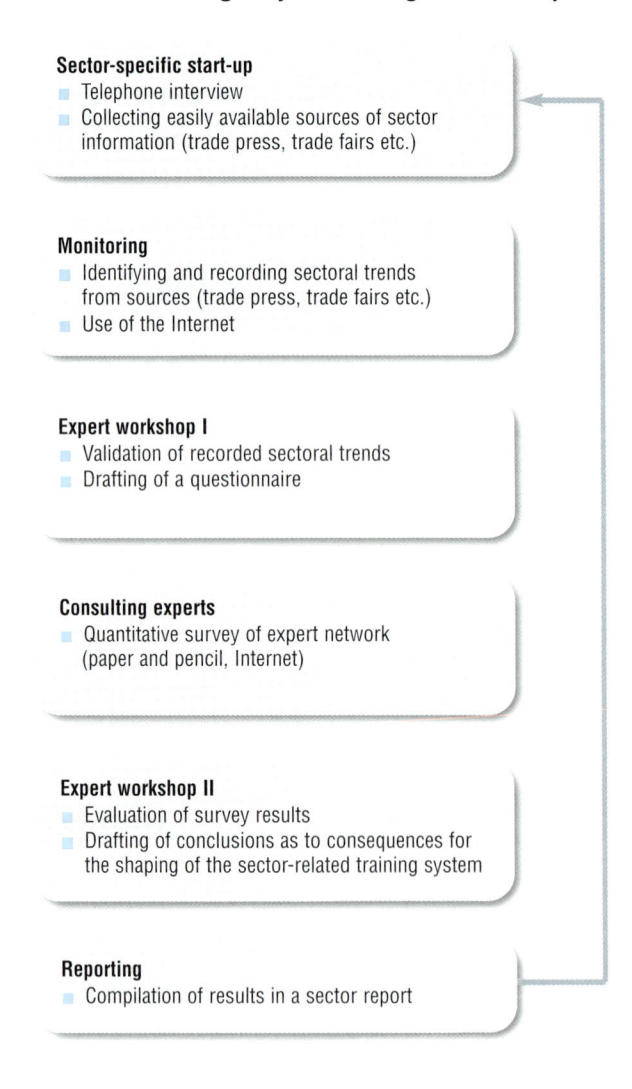

Sector-specific start-up
- Telephone interview
- Collecting easily available sources of sector information (trade press, trade fairs etc.)

Monitoring
- Identifying and recording sectoral trends from sources (trade press, trade fairs etc.)
- Use of the Internet

Expert workshop I
- Validation of recorded sectoral trends
- Drafting of a questionnaire

Consulting experts
- Quantitative survey of expert network (paper and pencil, Internet)

Expert workshop II
- Evaluation of survey results
- Drafting of conclusions as to consequences for the shaping of the sector-related training system

Reporting
- Compilation of results in a sector report

The system operates as follows:

Sector-specific start-up
In order to conduct the search for subjects relating to skill trends in a given sector as efficiently as possible, the project coordinator of the trade association concerned is initially interviewed by telephone, briefed about the project, its objectives and methodology and consulted as to the principal sources of information. The latter are then used as the basis for a search operation by computer-assisted robots – known as 'intelligent agents'. Preferred sources are those easily accessible via the Internet that can be evaluated at relatively low cost (Internet addresses of associations, trade press, trade fairs, publishers' information, etc.). These sources then form the basis for monitoring operations.

Monitoring - gathering sectoral information as basic data
Fundamental to the monitoring process is the assumption that items at the level of softer (informal) forms of continuing training can already be taken as leading indicators. The term 'monitoring' is used here to mean employing intelligent agents to identify and gather information from the Internet. The cost of the process varies according to the type of soft continuing training involved. Thus trade publications, trade fair programmes or recently published technical literature are easily tracked down via the Internet.

During the monitoring process sectoral subject-matter of relevance is extracted from the various sources proposed by the project coordinator at the start-up stage or found through the Internet. The results are then collated and summarised in a monitoring report and processed ready for the first expert workshop.

First expert workshop
Workshop participants are the project coordinator of the relevant trade association and the academic support team, together with two or three specialist representatives of the sector concerned who are nominated by the project coordinator.

The information gathered during the monitoring process is checked for relevance and presented by the academic support team in a form appropriate to the sector. This presentation facilitates processing by the workshop participants who can supplement it with their own expert knowledge. The results are then recorded and converted to questionnaire form.

Consulting the expert network

The purpose of the questionnaire is to reach the maximum number of specialists in the sector who are able to assess the workshop's findings as to skill trends and add to them where necessary.

The questionnaire has so far been sent out by conventional means direct to the experts in the trade and professional associations, the number of whom will depend on the size of the network accessed. It is circulated with the help of the academic support team and the relevant trade and professional associations. The results are evaluated and processed by the academic support team.

Study of questionnaire findings by the second expert workshop and reporting procedure

In a second workshop the experts who took part in the first study the findings obtained with the questionnaire in order to draw conclusions as to the consequences for training in the sector. These are then summarised in a report by the academic support team.

Finally the process is critically reviewed before being repeated.

3. Results

3.1. General results

The survey method described has so far been used for the construction, printing/publishing, retail, electrical/electronics, car and insurance industries. In all, 1 814 useful items of information concerning future training requirements were obtained. The procedure followed allowed comments to be made on more than one type of training under a single heading (see Table 1).

Table 1. **Total comments concerning training in the sectors studied**

Updating or creating new skilled occupations	Additionals kills (during training)	Regulated continuing training (professional association or government regulation)	Non-regulated continuing training	Other informal continuing training	Total
195	186	305	592	536	1 814

- 195 items were put under the heading of 'Updating or creating new skilled occupations', pointing to the need for a central government training regulation.
- 305 items were assigned to 'Regulated continuing training (professional association or government regulation)', similarly indicating a need for continuing training to be regulated by professional association or central government.
- 186 items were assigned to 'Additional skills (during training)' and 592 to 'Non-regulated continuing training'. Thus 778 items concerning initial and continuing training were considered by the experts as not requiring strict legal regulation and suitable for inclusion in a normal training programme.
- 536 items were assigned to 'Other informal continuing training'. These include practices specific to a given firm, technical literature or trade fairs, which are of a less formal nature and focus more on the specific requirements of a training requester that may have to be met at short notice. In the experts' opinion those items do not require regulation by a training body or by law.

3.2. Specific results for the construction industry

Given the overall volume of data obtained we shall present the ten items considered most important by the experts in the case of the construction industry accompanied by references to possible initial or further training measures (Table 2).

Table 2. **Top Ten items for the construction industry with mention of possible training measures**

No	Item	Mean	Standard deviation	Updating or creating new skilled occupations	Additional skills (during training)	Regulated continuing training (professional association or training regulation)	Non-regulated continuing training	Other informal training
1	Customer satisfaction	4.72	0.54				✛	✛
2	Assessment of performance in executing orders	4.64	0.49				✛	✛
3	Rationalisation of construction work	4.64	0.70	✛			✛	✛
4	Personnel management	4.60	0.50	✛			✛	✛
5	CA quotations	4.52	0.59	✛			✛	✛
6	Computerised invoicing	4.52	0.51	✛			✛	✛
7	Computerised order checking	4.52	0.59	✛			✛	✛
8	Assessment of contract settlement	4.52	0.51				✛	✛
9	Compliance with government contract regulations	4.44	0.71				✛	
10	Ensuring liquidity	4.43	0.71	✛			✛	✛

In evaluating the results one sees that none of the comments relating to skills referred to updating or creating a new job category. Although this might at first seem surprising, it is explainable by the fact that the occupations in the construction industry have been thoroughly overhauled and the process was completed shortly before the questionnaire was sent out.

The current revision of the master qualification profile for the construction industry will serve as an additional aid in evaluating results. To this end we compared our results with the items of the process that is still under way. We found that a number of the subjects touched upon are taken into account in the provisional master profile, where reference is made, for example, to environmental considerations and use of information technology.

The comments recorded and evaluated in Table 3 show the importance attributed to the use of computers in executing orders to be high. The experts consider the use of information technology as a relevant aspect of skills since it is used increasingly in preparing work, progress-chasing and subsequent processing. Accordingly employees will need the skills required to cope with the new technology as an additional qualification or acquire it through continuing training.

Table 3. **References to growing computerisation and training requirements**

Item	Mean	Standard deviation	Updating or creating new skilled occupations	Additional skills (during training)	Regulated continuing training (professional association or training regulation)	Non-regulated continuing training	Other informal training
CA price calculation	4.29	0.84		+		+	+
Computerised work preparation	4.19	0.86		+		+	+
Computerised order checking	4.11	1.00		+		+	+
Computerised progress-chasing	3.08	1.03				+	+
Use of Internet for advertising	3.88	0.93				+	+
Computerised site planning	3.80	0.96		+		+	+

References to low-energy and ecological building or recycling of building materials also emphasise the importance given to environmental considerations by the construction industry (Table 4).

Table 4. **Comments indicating growing environment-consciousness and relevance for training purposes**

Item	Mean	Standard deviation	Updating or creating new skilled occupations	Additional skills (during training)	Regulated continuing training (professional association or training regulation)	Non-regulated continuing training	Other informal training
Low-energy building	4.03	0.94				✣	✣
Ecological building	3.63	1.07				✣	✣
Environmental management in executing orders	3.33	0.94				✣	✣
Materials recycling	3.44	1.18				✣	✣

4. Conclusion/Outlook

Project results and experience to date indicate that the IDQ© approach makes for an efficient and comprehensive gathering of data utilisable for early recognition of skill requirements.

Essential for the lasting efficiency of this method is the active involvement of those in the industrial sector concerned, viz:
- gatekeepers who open doors to sector experts for the KWB and its researchers;
- the sector experts who assist in research;
- expert networks committed to active participation in the questionnaire.

The more active the part played by the trade organisations in the KWB project the greater the usefulness for all those taking part. The data assembled can be used not only as an argument for the need for training in certain skills but also, after further processing, for market research or structural organisation purposes.

The use of the IDQ© concept does, however, come up against certain limits when searching out data relevant to skills in newer sectors of industry, which frequently are not associatively structured and thus have no established network of experts who can be consulted on matters of vocational training so as to permit the early recognition of skill requirements.

A follow-on project started in May 2002 is aimed at further developing the information system with the following specific focus for research and testing:
- conducting further sectoral studies (studies of the chemical industry, the banking and financial sector and the food industry are planned for 2002);

- follow-up studies to determine the trend of skills within a single branch of industry;
- expanding the range of tools to include new branches of industry without associative structures by means of surveys in the field;
- Internet-based expansion of the information system for future-oriented uses and a more efficient mode of data gathering;
- developing a questionnaire for identifying skill shortages and incorporating it in the IDQ© process.

A further objective of the project is the comprehensive preparation and evaluation of survey results in collaboration with experts so as to produce recommendations for initial and continuing training.

PART III
Initiatives for specific target groups and SMEs

Skills trends have specific implications for different target groups, and these are brought out in the first two contributions in this Part: on women's employment and on low skilled people. The last two contributions in this Part concentrate on skills trends that are posing particular challenges, above all for small and medium sized enterprises (SMEs).

The targeted approach adopted makes it clear that experience acquired at sectoral level can be incorporated into various other fields of application in order to achieve positive effects on employment for specific target groups and SMEs.

Articles in Part III

Gerard Hughes, Jerry J. Sexton (UK)
Forecasting female shares of employment by occupation in Ireland

Beate Zeller (D)
Services in complex structures – trends in the way skills are developing in low skilled work

Peter Wordelmann (D)
Early recognition of international qualifications for SMEs

Lothar Abicht, Rainer Werner (D)
New qualifications in SMEs for societal and technological change – skilling of IT users

Forecasting female shares of employment by occupation in Ireland

Gerard Hughes and **Jerry J. Sexton**, Economic and Social Research Institute (ESRI), Dublin, Ireland

Sectoral employment forecasts for Ireland are produced using the ESRI medium-term macro-economic model. Past trends and expectations of the likely development of occupations are used to project occupational profiles within each sector. Occupational share coefficients are calculated for each sector. The trends revealed by these shares are analysed and summarised in linear or semi-log trend equations. The projected occupational profiles within sectors are then applied to the employment forecasts for each sector.

A gender-based occupational forecast is obtained by means of a separate sub-model. This involves the projection of past trends for the share of female employment in different occupations. The female shares of employment are made consistent with the female labour force forecasts produced by the ESRI medium-term macro-economic model. The forecasts of female shares of employment by occupation is illustrated with long-term occupational forecasts for 2015.

1. Introduction

The occupations in which most women work differ significantly from those in which men work. This may not be clear when one compares the distribution of male and female employment at the level of the nine major groups used to classify employment by occupation in the European variant of the International Standard Classification of Occupations (ISCO 88 COM). However, it becomes very clear when the comparison is made at the unit group level. Defining 'male' and 'female' occupations as those in which at least 80% of the workers are of one sex, Table 1 shows the top twenty gender dominated occupations at the unit group level in Ireland in 1996.

Men employed in the top ten male-dominated occupations are concentrated in building and construction whereas women employed in the top ten female-dominated occupations are concentrated in medical and personal service sectors. While occupational segregation by sex is very obvious in the case of both the top ten male and female gender-dominated occupations the top ten female occupations are somewhat more integrated than the top ten male occupations. The full list of gender-dominated occupations in 1996 shows that the number of occupations which were male-dominated was six times larger than the number which were female-dominated. In terms of the depth and breadth of occupational segregation by sex the difficulties of access to a wide range of occupations are far greater for women than for men.

Similar concentrations of male and female workers are found in other European countries. For example, in France and West Germany at the beginning of the 1990s over 80% of nurses, typists, housekeeping service workers, and hairdressers and beauticians were women (see Anker, 1998, Table 11.1).

Table 1. **Top twenty gender-dominated occupations at the three digit level in Ireland 1996**

	Male-dominated occupations	% M		Female-dominated occupations	% F
500	Bricklayers and masons	99.7	459	Secretaries, medical, legal, personal assistants, typists and word processor operators	98.2
502	Plasterers	99.6	670	Housekeepers (domestic and non-domestic)	97.1
501	Roofers, slaters, tilers, sheeters and cladders	99.5	460	Receptionists and receptionist-telephonists	96.9
885	Mechanical plant drivers/operatives and crane drivers	99.5	342	Medical radiographers	93.3
570	Carpenters and joiners	99.4	340	Nurses and midwives	92.3
923	Road construction workers etc.	99.4	343	Physiotherapists and chiropodists	91.2
540	Motor mechanics, auto electricians, tyre and exhaust fitters	99.2	652	Educational assistants	90.5
504	Builders and building contractors	99.1	553	Sewing machinists, menders, darners and embroiderers	88.6
895	Pipe layers/pipe jointers and related construction workers	99.1	660	Hairdressers, barbers and beauticians	87.3
922	Rail construction and maintenance workers	99.1	953	Counterhands and catering assistants	86.7

Source: Census of population 1996, Volume 7, Table 8.

Because of the concentration of female employment in particular occupations it is important when making occupational employment forecasts to provide some information on future employment prospects for women. The occupational employment forecasts for Ireland, therefore, provide estimates of the female share of employment by occupational group in the target year. The purpose of this paper is to explain how the forecasts of female shares of employment by occupation are made using data from the occupational employment forecasts for Ireland for 2015 which were published recently.

Figure 1 provides a graphical representation of the structure of the FÁS/ESRI occupational forecasting model. On the left hand side it shows the various steps involved in developing the projections of the number employed in each sector, while on the right it shows the sequence of steps required to produce forecasts of each occupation's share of employment in each sector. In the centre it shows how these two sets of forecasts are linked to provide forecasts of expected employment in each occupational group in the target year.

Figure 1. **FÁS/ESRI occupational forecasting model**

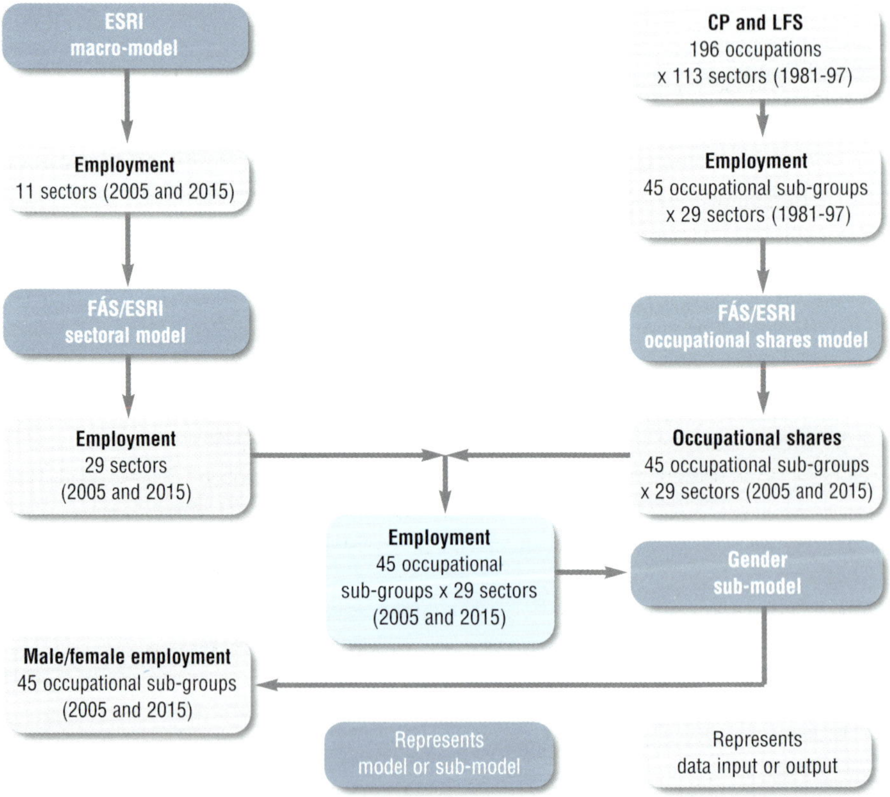

The basic approach adopted involves the use of employment forecasts which are produced for the target year (2015) by the Economic and Social Research Institute (ESRI) macro-economic model. (¹) Employment forecasts are made for 11 major sectors as part of the Institute's regular *Medium-Term Reviews* (MTRs) of the Irish economy. For the purposes of compiling occupational projections, these are disaggregated to provide employment forecasts for a wider range of 29 more detailed sectoral categories. To do this, past relationships between the original MTR sectors and the more disaggregated sub-sectors were analysed over the period 1981-97. These were then used to project the sub-sectoral shares within the eleven aggregate MTR industries, mainly on the basis of linear regressions.

The next step in the process, which takes account both of past trends and expectations as to the likely development of occupations over the forecast period, involves the calculation of projected occupational profiles within the 29 sectors. The basic data used to analyse occupational shares within industries were taken from 1981 and 1986 censuses of population and from the annual labour force surveys carried out between 1989 and 1997. These sources were used to produce detailed and consistent employment data classified simultaneously into 196 occupations and 113 industries for selected years over the period 1981-97. The data were subsequently aggregated to provide matrices showing employment in 29 sectors and 45 occupational sub-groups. Occupational share coefficients for each sector were then calculated for each of these matrices for the selected years and the trends derived from these were used to project within-industry occupational distributions for the target forecast year. These projected occupational profiles were then applied to the employment forecasts for the 29 industries in question in order to derive occupational forecasts for 2015 in absolute terms.

It will be noted that it is an inherent feature of the method used that occupational change is, to a significant degree, influenced by developments in different sectors or industries. This does not imply that the pattern of change for different skills and occupations is not subject to other independent influences, or does not relate to a wider range of factors in society generally. Nonetheless, the approach used does imply that the sectoral pattern of underlying output and employment growth constitutes a primary influence.

The gender-based classifications of the occupational forecasts are obtained by means of the separate sub-model shown in Figure 2. Basically

---

(¹) The description of the FÁS/ESRI occupational forecasting model is taken from the report by Sexton, Hughes and Finn, 2002.

this involves the projection of past trends for the share of female employment in different occupations, taking into account, where relevant, the changing nature of these trends over the period since 1981. For the great majority of the 45 occupational sub-groups involved the initial forecasts for 2015 were obtained on the basis of linear regressions. However, for a few categories semi-log equations were used, as there was either evidence of a fairly longstanding stabilisation in the relevant female employment shares, or the use of the regression approach would have implied unrealistically large such shares in the forecast year. All of the female employment shares as calculated by the above methods were moderated slightly in order to render them consistent with the independently compiled female labour force forecasts for 2015 as derived from the *Medium-Term Review* macroeconomic modelling process.

Figure 2. **FÁS/ESRI gender forecasting model**

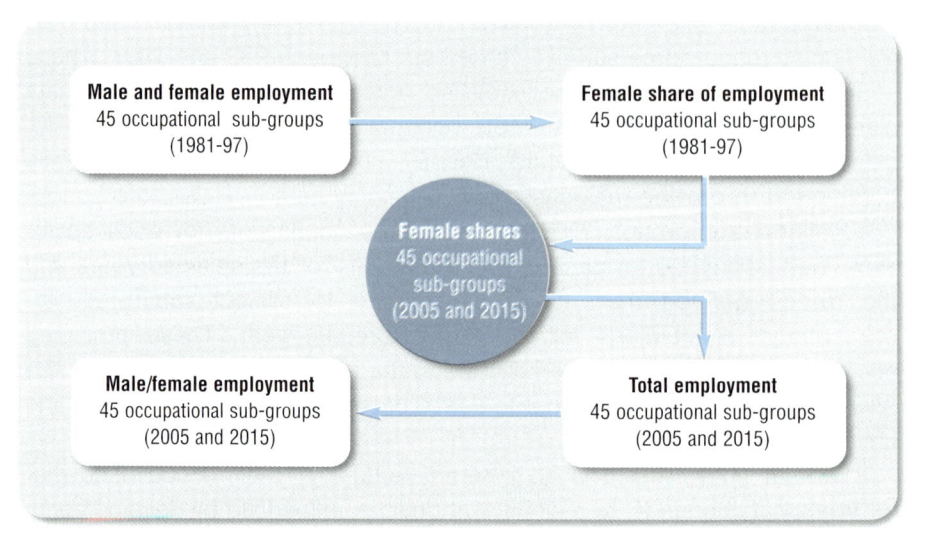

2. The occupational classification

As already indicated, the most detailed occupational classification used involves 45 occupational sub-groups which are, in turn, amalgamated into 14 major groups. The 45 sub-groups were initially formed by combining much larger numbers of occupational codes used in the 1981 census of population (numbering some 200 in total). The 1981 census structure was used to ensure the availability of a consistent trend pattern covering a sufficiently long retrospective period. Census classifications are revised on an ongoing basis, the changes made usually involving more detail. In this regard, for the period over which trends are observed, one is constrained by the level of detail in the census structure for the earliest year. The detailed 1981 census occupational codes are, therefore, basic to the forecasting exercise and the data in detailed occupational tabulations taken from later censuses and labour force surveys were subject to amalgamations in order to render them consistent with the 1981 figures.

Details of the structure adopted are set out in Table 2, which shows the 14 major groupings and the 45 constituent occupational sub-groups. The basic rationale underlying the amalgamation procedures applied to the detailed census codes is to try and achieve occupational groupings which bring together (a) persons exercising similar types of employment-related functions and (b) possessing similar levels of skill and/or qualifications. One might summarise the group structure by saying that the major groups (apart from those which relate to agricultural occupations and self employed persons in services) are generally hierarchical in nature in that they purport to bring together activities requiring the same level of skill. At the sub-group level the objective is to distinguish different types of activity within each major group.

While every effort has been made to establish appropriate relationships between the standard occupational categories and the functions chosen, and, where appropriate, specific skill or qualification levels, the source material clearly limits the extent to which this can be achieved. Nevertheless, it is considered that the occupational categories as finally defined constitute relevant and distinct entities on the basis of the criteria employed. The system as described above is broadly compatible with the ILO International Standard Classification of Occupations (ISCO-88) and the UK Standard Occupational Classification (SOC).

Table 2. **Occupational groups and sub-groups**

GROUPS		SUB-GROUPS	
1.	Agricultural occupations	1.1	Agricultural
2.	Managers	2.1	Higher managers
		2.2	Other managers
3.	Proprietors in services	3.1	Proprietors in services
4.	Professional occupations	4.1	Health professionals
		4.2	Education professionals
		4.3	Engineering and science
		4.4	Business/finance/legal profs.
		4.5	Religious
		4.6	Other professions
5.	Associate professionals	5.1	Health
		5.2	Science and engineering
		5.3	Others
6.	Clerical occupations	6.1	Clerks
		6.2	Typists, telephonists etc.
		6.3	Warehouse/dispatch clerks
7.	Skilled workers (maintenance)	7.1	Electricians, electrical fitters
		7.2	Fitters and mechanics
8.	Other skilled workers	8.1	Metal/engineering workers
		8.2	Woodworkers
		8.3	Clothing/textile workers
		8.4	Printers
		8.5	Skilled building workers
		8.6	Foremen/supervisors
		8.7	Other skilled workers
9.	Production operatives	9.1	Electrical/electronics
		9.2	Metals/engineering
		9.3	Food, drink, tobacco processing
		9.4	Clothing/textiles
		9.5	Other plant and production opers.
		9.6	Packers/bottlers
10.	Transport/communications workers	10.1	Drivers
		10.2	Postmen, couriers
		10.3	Others
11.	Sales workers	11.1	Sales agents
		11.2	Retail sales assistants
		11.3	Others
12.	Security workers	12.1	Army/Gardai (excl. officers)
		12.2	Other security workers
13.	Personal service workers	13.1	Catering occupations
		13.2	Domestic servants and cleaners
		13.3	Other personal service workers
		13.4	Occupation unstated
14.	Labourers	14.1	Agricultural labourers
		14.2	Other labourers

3. Occupational forecasts 2000-15

The main features of the results, showing net employment changes for the fourteen standard occupational groups used, are shown in Table 3 and Figure 3. The MTR forecasts, which underpin the occupational projections, envisage a significant rise in total employment over the period up to 2015, even if this is expected to be at a slower pace than in the economically buoyant years of the 1990s. The total number of persons at work in the economy is predicted to rise by over 25% over the forecast period, from 1 588 000 in 2000 to 1 989 000 in 2015, an aggregate increase of over 400 000, or nearly 27 000 (1.5%) on an annual average basis. While this represents a noticeably slower rate of employment growth than in the ten years from 1990 to 2000 (which was 45 500, or 3.4% per year on average), it is somewhat greater than the pace of expansion which occurred over the longer period between 1981 and 2000, which involved a net increase of 24 000 annually.

Table 3. **Employment by occupation, 1981-2000, with forecasts for 2005 and 2015**

	1981	2000	2005	2015	Change 2000-15	
	000s					%
Agriculture	177.4	121.9	110.8	92.4	-29.4	-24.2
Managers	57.0	115.0	135.3	169.5	54.5	47.4
Proprietors in services	37.6	49.7	44.2	47.7	-2.0	-3.9
Professionals	106.8	192.7	233.2	291.1	98.4	51.1
Associate professionals	49.1	102.7	125.8	157.5	54.8	53.4
Clerical	157.9	208.2	222.8	230.2	22.1	10.6
Skilled workers (maintenance)	54.3	79.7	84.7	93.6	13.9	17.4
Other skilled workers	109.2	150.9	160.7	179.1	28.2	18.7
Production operatives	99.4	129.4	141.3	150.2	20.8	16.1
Transport and communications	50.2	65.6	73.2	77.7	12.1	18.5
Sales workers	74.2	129.0	145.6	178.4	49.5	38.4
Security workers	31.3	42.8	46.0	52.2	9.5	22.1
Personal service	69.3	142.2	168.7	213.8	71.6	50.3
Labourers	64.1	58.4	60.7	55.3	-3.1	-5.3
Total	1 137.8	1 588.1	1753.0	1 989.0	400.9	25.2

Source: Sexton, Hughes and Finn, 2002, Table 3.1.

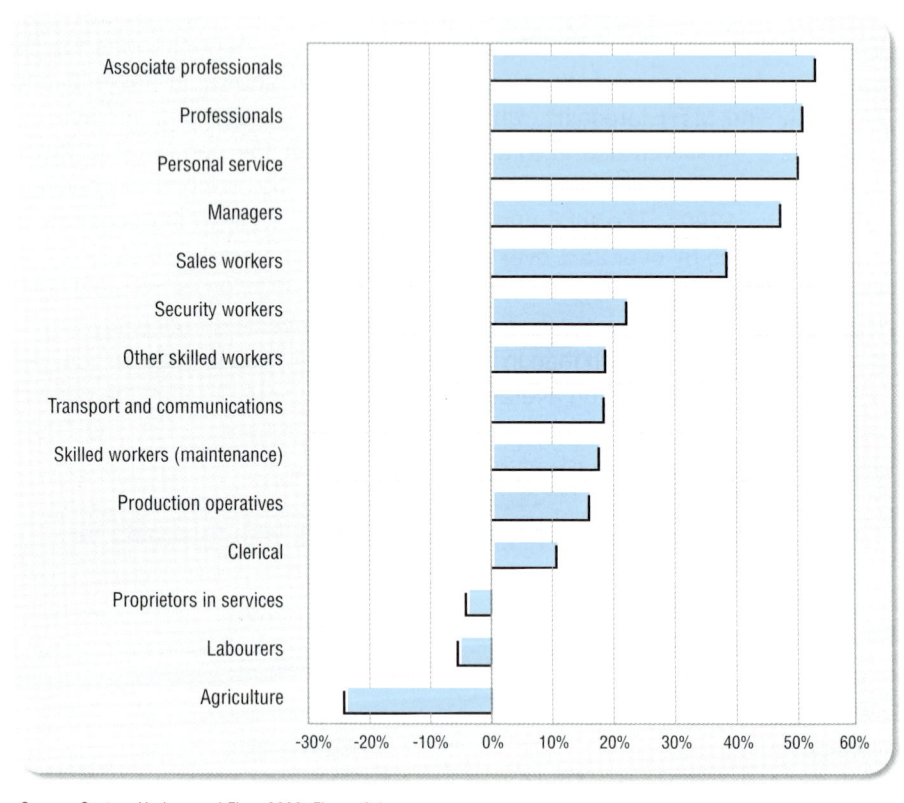

Figure 3. **Change in employment by occupation, 2000-15 (%)**

Occupation	Change
Associate professionals	~52%
Professionals	~50%
Personal service	~50%
Managers	~45%
Sales workers	~38%
Security workers	~22%
Other skilled workers	~19%
Transport and communications	~19%
Skilled workers (maintenance)	~18%
Production operatives	~16%
Clerical	~10%
Proprietors in services	~-3%
Labourers	~-3%
Agriculture	~-23%

Source: Sexton, Hudges and Finn, 2002, Figure 3.1.

Turning to the changes for individual occupations, the numbers engaged in agricultural activities are expected to fall over the forecast period, by nearly 30 000. As a result, the predicted 2015 employment level for this occupation, at just over 92 000, will then represent only some 4.5% of the total number at work in the economy. This compares with just under 8% in 2000 and 14% in 1990. This implies, of course, an even faster rate of growth among non-agricultural occupations than that reflected in the global figures already quoted. The number at work outside of agriculture is forecast to increase by over 430 000 between 2000 and 2015, a relative rise of over 1.7% on average each year. However, within this broad occupational spectrum, while increases are expected for all occupational activities, different rates of expansion will apply to the various sub-categories identified.

The largest employment increases are predicted to occur in the case of professional workers at both degree and diploma (i.e. associate) level and for those engaged in personal services - each with an expected increase in excess of 50%. A significant expansion in employment is also anticipated for managers and sales workers, the relevant increases being 47 and 38% respectively. For security workers, those involved in transport and communications and manual workers generally (both skilled and semi-skilled) the increases are forecast to be much lower (broadly between 15 and 20%) and smaller still for clerical workers at about 10%. In addition to the fall in the numbers in agricultural occupations, decreases in employment (of a smaller order of magnitude) are forecast to occur for unskilled labourers and proprietors in service activities.

4. Forecasts of female employment

The proportion of women in total employment is forecast to increase from just under 40% in 2000 to 44.7% in the year 2015 (see Table 4). This represents a significant increase on the corresponding share which prevailed in the early 1980s – it was less than 30% in 1981.

Table 4. **Female employment shares by occupational group, 1981-2015 (%)**

Occupational group	1981	2000	2005	2015
Agriculture	7.0	9.4	9.8	10.9
Managers	12.6	30.1	33.7	40.9
Proprietors in services	25.1	33.7	35.8	40.7
Professionals	39.2	44.9	44.0	49.6
Associate professionals	65.3	67.6	65.9	65.2
Clerical	65.9	75.6	76.2	73.1
Skilled workers (maintenance)	0.3	3.9	4.9	7.1
Other skilled workers	17.1	12.8	12.4	11.8
Production operatives	24.9	31.7	33.9	35.7
Transport and communications	2.2	6.5	7.1	8.2
Sales workers	40.3	53.8	56.6	62.5
Security workers	3.1	10.9	12.5	15.8
Personal service	66.5	76.3	75.5	75.1
Labourers	1.0	6.9	8.6	12.1
Total	**28.9**	**39.7**	**41.4**	**44.7**

Source: Sexton, Hughes and Finn, 2002, Table 3.5.

When the female share forecasts are translated into estimates of the actual numbers at work they indicate a substantial rise in total female employment over the forecast period – from 630 000 in 2000 to almost 890 000 in 2015, an increase of nearly 41%. The (derived) forecast for male employment also involves a substantial rise (from 957 000 to over 1 100 000), even though in relative terms (at 15%) this is significantly less than that for women.

The data for major occupational groups are best interpreted in graphical terms as given in Figure 4, which shows predicted female shares at the level of broad occupational groups for 2000 and 2015. These indicate that in the year 2000 the highest proportions applied to those engaged in personal services and in clerical activities – some 75% in each case. These are followed by associate professionals (nearly 68%) and sales workers (54%). Agricultural and manual workers generally tend to be positioned at the other end of the share spectrum with quite small female proportions – 15% or less. The lowest female employment share (under 4%) relates to the manual skilled maintenance category.

Observing the forecasts for 2015 the most significant increase in the female employment share is predicted to occur in the managerial category. The relevant proportion was just over 30% in 2000 and is expected to rise by 11 percentage points to 41% by 2015. This feature has emerged as a longstanding and consistent trend. The corresponding proportion among managers was 21% in 1990, and as low as 13% in 1981. Significant increases in the female share over the forecast period are also indicated for sales workers and proprietors in services – both of the order of 8 percentage points. The results also indicate fairly substantial increases (about 5 percentage points) for professional workers, unskilled labourers and those involved in security duties.

The graphical presentation shows that for a number of numerically large occupational groups for which female employment shares are already quite high the proportions of women in employment are anticipated to decrease somewhat in the period up to 2015. This is the case for those engaged in personal services, clerical workers and associate professionals, for which in each case the female shares exceeded 65% in 2000. These trends derive to a significant degree from the need to moderate the rates of change in female employment shares generally in order to maintain consistency with the labour force estimates for women which form an intrinsic part of the underlying *Medium-Term Review* forecasts. The sectors and occupations associated with high levels of female involvement (such as those related to services) are expected to continue to show substantial employment

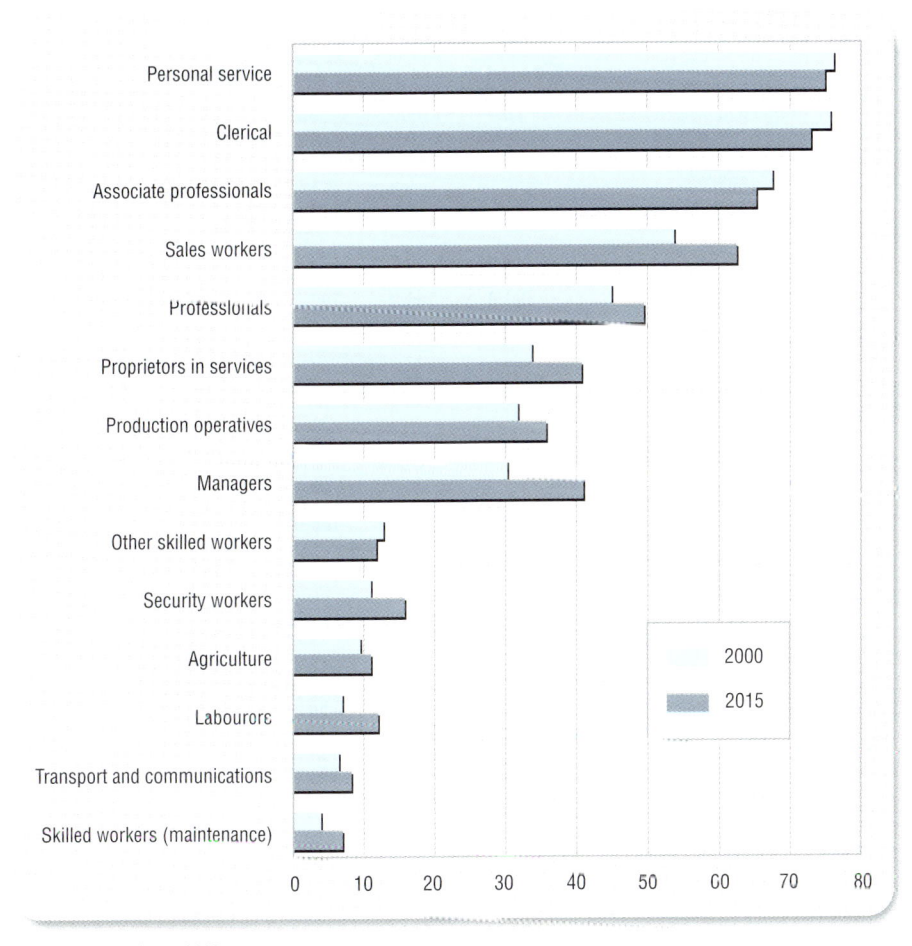

Figure 4. **Female employment shares by occupation, 2000 and 2015 (%)**

Data shorted by shares 2000.
Source: Sexton, Hughes and Finn, 2002, Figure 3.6.

increases in the period up to 2015 – thus ensuring a significant rise in the *actual* number of women at work.

However, during this period female labour force participation rates, though still rising, are expected to increase more slowly, and this, in turn, implies a need for moderation in female employment shares if serious inconsistencies between these two entities are to be avoided (e. g. zero unemployment or negative unemployment rates). [2] This, in effect, means

---
[2] The Irish labour force participation rate in 2000 was 44.1%. In the context of the MTR forecasts this is anticipated to rise to 48.9% in 2005 and (more slowly) to 52.3% in 2015.

Table 5. **Distribution of employment across broad occupational categories, 1981-2015 (%)**

		1981	2000	2005	2015
MALES	Agricultural	20.4	11.5	9.7	7.5
	Managers, professionals	19.8	26.4	28.4	30.0
	Clerical	6.7	5.3	5.2	5.6
	Skilled, unskilled manual	41.1	43.1	42.7	42.0
	Services and sales	12.1	13.7	14.1	14.9
	Total	100.0	100.0	100.0	100.0
FEMALES	Agricultural	3.8	1.8	1.5	1.1
	Managers, professionals	27.5	32.9	34.0	37.8
	Clerical	31.6	25.0	23.4	18.9
	Skilled, unskilled manual	13.8	11.4	11.3	10.6
	Services and sales	23.4	28.9	29.7	31.5
	Total	100.0	100.0	100.0	100.0
MALES & FEMALES	Agricultural	15.6	7.7	6.3	4.6
	Managers, professionals	22.0	29.0	30.7	33.5
	Clerical	13.9	13.1	12.7	11.6
	Skilled, unskilled manual	33.2	30.5	29.7	28.0
	Services and sales	15.4	19.8	20.6	22.3
	Total	100.0	100.0	100.0	100.0

Source: Sexton, Hughes and Finn, 2002, Table 3.6.

that to a limited extent men will substitute for women in some of these employment growth areas.

It is clear from the substantive changes indicated in the preceding analyses, that as well as variations in the female share of employment within occupations, the overall occupational structure of female employment is changing over time. It is best to consider this feature in terms of rather broad occupational categories viewed over a relatively long period. This is done in Table 5 which shows the distribution of employment for men and women over the period from 1981 to 2015 for five broadly defined occupational categories. Concentrating on the figures for total female employment, the most notable change is the expected decrease in the proportion of women clerical workers, down from 32% of total female employment in 1981 to less than 20% in 2015. The proportion associated with manual work (of all levels of skill) is also predicted to fall, even if not to the same degree as for clerical activities.

A significant factor here relates to the ongoing job losses in industries such as clothing and textiles, which have traditionally involved a large element of semi-skilled female labour. In contrast, the shares of female employment related both to managerial and professional work and to sales and services occupations are set to rise substantially. In the case of the former category, the relevant proportions are 28% in 1981, about one-third in 2000 and rising to just under 38% in 2015. An important influence underpinning this trend is the rapidly increasing share of women employed as managers, as previously described.

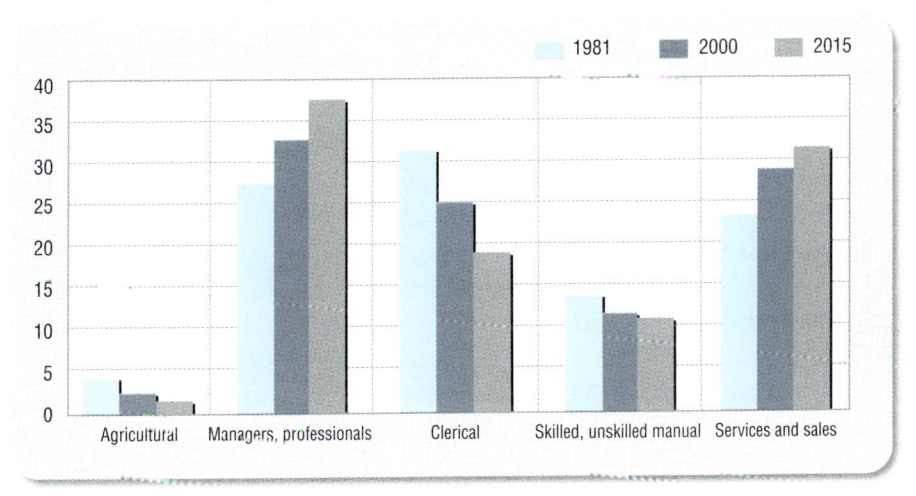

Figure 5. **Female employment shares across broad occupations, 1981-2015 (%)**

Source: Sexton, Hughes and Finn, 2002, Figure 3.7.

References

Anker, R. *Gender and Jobs: Sex Cogregation of Occupations in the World*. Geneva: International Labour Office, 1998.

Sexton, J.J.; Hughes, G.; Finn, C. *Occupational Employment Forecasts 2015*. Economic and Social Research Institute, FÁS/ESRI Manpower Forecasting Studies Report No. 10, Dublin, 2002.

Services in complex structures – trends in the way skills are developing in low skilled work

Beate Zeller, bfz Vocational Training Research Department of the Bavarian Employers' Associations, Nuremberg, Germany

The change in the world of work influences all kinds of employment relationships and imposes new demands on employees and those looking for a job. The present article presents empirical non-quantitative considerations and assessments on the future employment prospects of the working population without professional training, who are already disadvantaged on the labour market. According to available forecasts, in the next decade about 16% of employees will perform 'low skilled work'. To define 'skilled work' in the future and how qualification requirements for this group will develop, the bfz Bildungforschung (bfz Educational Research) has studied trends in the workplace, tapping into the know-how of company experts, in the following fields: 'low skilled' work in the metal-processing industry, aircraft service, and sales assistance in a baker's shop.

1. Introduction

The current changes in the working world are affecting all types of employment relationships and imposing new demands on workers with jobs and jobseekers. There is no doubt that people without a formal vocational qualification are at present at a great disadvantage ([1]) on the labour market. But what does the future hold?

I have no intention of presenting quantitative observations and estimates here. There are already reliable sources for them, and they indicate that even

---

([1]) The term 'disadvantaged group' is used as a generic term in the survey: A disadvantage can originate from economic, educational or social factors. When 'disadvantage' is associated with the criterion of qualification, the groups under observation are those without completed vocational training or with a training which is no longer utilisable on the labour market.

in 10 years, some 16% of all workers will probably continue to perform so-called 'low skilled work' in businesses. (²) But what will 'low skilled work' (³) mean at that time? How will company requirements relating to low skilled work develop? And what demands will then be placed on workers in this field?

In our survey we have tried to identify the trends on the spot in the enterprises making maximum use of the know-how of company experts collaborating with us on this survey. Our survey is divided into four phases and follows a preliminary study. Information on skill trends in selected sectors is first processed in three field phases in two regions. In a fourth field phase the results of the survey of selected target groups is processed with the aim of incorporating the results in the design of measures.

In terms of methodology, the aim is to closely link the survey to the situation in the company as a basis for data collection. Through the concept of the 'cooperative analysis procedure', company experts in moderated control groups are actively involved in the survey process. This procedure gets much of its innovative force from its affinity to practice and the know-how of the experts who, together with the moderating unit in the control groups, plan the steps of the survey, coordinate the implementation of the empirical surveys in the enterprises and evaluate the results.

I would like to invite you to a small virtual tour of some enterprises. Let us take a look at ongoing and anticipated changes and the impact on the skills demanded of the workers.

2. Development of qualifications in selected work activities

2.1 Activity field 'low skilled work' in the metalworking sector

Let us first of all visit *a medium-sized enterprise in the metalworking sector*. This enterprise is highly specialised and manufactures a large number of products needed for measuring and surveying: measuring instruments, as the expert would say. We know some of these instruments from our daily life, e.g. the tape measure consisting of a metal tape which is drawn out of a small case for measuring and then rolls back automatically when a button is pressed.

(²) The IAB/Prognos study expects that in 2010 16% of all jobs (that means 1/6 of all employed people) will still consist of unskilled activities; cf. Dostal and Reinberg, 1999, p. 3.

(³) The term 'low skilled work/activities' is based on an approach used by Prognos; cf. Weidig et al., 1999.

The female production worker whom we see here is, like 90% of her colleagues, a semi-skilled or unskilled worker. For some time she has been working with 11 colleagues in a section which is called the 'Drawing-in Section'.

She certainly cannot complain about the monotony of her job. In her work environment, the different jobs are not only very closely linked to one another, but the workers are also familiar with the skills required at each workplace because they regularly rotate between the different workplaces. In this way, the team is able to react flexibly in the case of sickness or leave and can take over one another's jobs or help one another out if the workload suddenly increases. The work process in the narrow sense of the term, let us call it the *'operative process'*, is anything but 'low skilled work' here because of the work organisation; on the contrary it is a very highly varied and versatile activity. The skills demanded of this worker are also very diverse. She must be able to adjust quickly to a new situation and she has to master a large number of manual activities at different workplaces.

She knows that this rotation and the flexible standing-in for colleagues leads to a better utilisation of capacity for the company because it reduces downtime, and this means that she is also directly involved in the *business process*.

Whichever workplace she is currently working at, the requirements in the 'Drawing-in Section' have undergone a substantial change in the last few years. No foreman or supervisor tells her what to do. She has to deduce that herself from the so-called distribution cards. These are documents generated by the computer setting out what the customer has ordered and what therefore has to be done in the manufacturing process. On the basis of these distribution cards the group decides in advance the sequence in which the customers' orders will be carried out. This has to be coordinated with the departments involved upstream, and care has to be taken that the necessary raw materials, e.g. metal parts, etc. are delivered in time and are ready at hand when they are needed. All the workers are involved in these planning activities; they all have to have a clear picture of the work processes and to anticipate what may be required, otherwise operations cannot proceed smoothly.

As a machine operator, this worker has to take the pre-fabricated steel strips from the machine, sort them and check them for flaws. The *quality* ordered by the customer plays a crucial role and orders vary greatly. The measuring tapes are first cut roughly on a cut-machine and then adjusted by hand to the exact length. The first step entails the programming of the cut-machine according to the instructions on the distribution card. The worker must programme the cut-machine correctly if spoilage or rejections and downtime are to be avoided.

The worker told us that even if the machine stops, she does not have to call a skilled worker straight away. She has learned to make an initial diagnosis of the problem. The machine failure can be due to a programming error, but it can also be due to the pre-fabricated product. The worker identifies the error, programmes the machine anew or removes the defective pre-fabricated parts. While doing this, she follows the instructions for the sorting of waste products and thus ensures an environmentally friendly disposal of waste. She then winds the steel strip to the point from which the machine can run automatically again.

What we see here is certainly far removed from low skilled work in the sense of a simple support activity. But despite the diversity of the requirements, it is not skilled work either. The semi-skilled and unskilled workers cope with the requirements of a work environment which exceed the boundaries of a single workplace.

Figure 1. **Skill profile in the Drawing-in section**

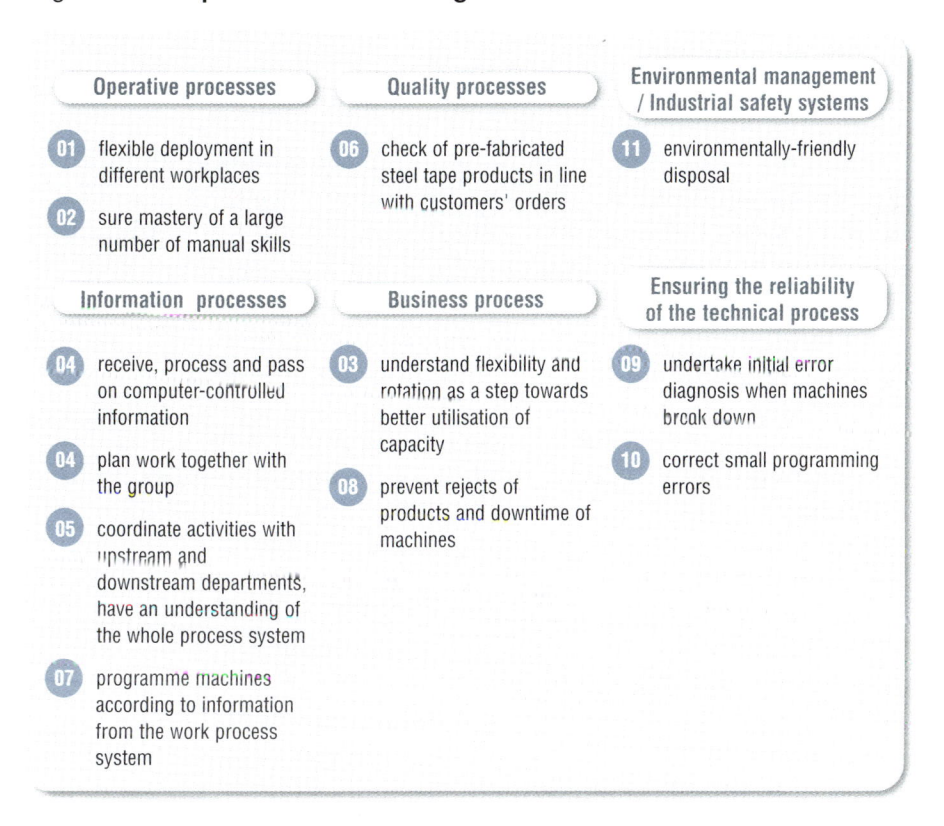

Operative processes

- 01 flexible deployment in different workplaces
- 02 sure mastery of a large number of manual skills

Information processes

- 04 receive, process and pass on computer-controlled information
- 04 plan work together with the group
- 05 coordinate activities with upstream and downstream departments, have an understanding of the whole process system
- 07 programme machines according to information from the work process system

Quality processes

- 06 check of pre-fabricated steel tape products in line with customers' orders

Business process

- 03 understand flexibility and rotation as a step towards better utilisation of capacity
- 08 prevent rejects of products and downtime of machines

Environmental management / Industrial safety systems

- 11 environmentally-friendly disposal

Ensuring the reliability of the technical process

- 09 undertake initial error diagnosis when machines break down
- 10 correct small programming errors

The actual operative processes which used to be characteristic of support activities have now become more differentiated and diverse. In addition, other processes have become more important:
- information must be processed and passed on;
- the technical process must be understood and its smooth operation ensured without unnecessary downtime;
- this means that all employees have to be aware of the importance in economic terms of full utilisation of resources and customer satisfaction, that is they must have a certain understanding of the business process;
- quality must be assured within the process itself; it is not delegated as a separate function to an outside unit but has to be an inherent component in each working step;
- the same applies to industrial safety and environmental protection aspects.

Activity field 'low skilled work' in servicing of aircraft

We first took a look at a production company. What is the situation in a modern services enterprise? Let us now look around a *major airport*.

One sector in which a particularly large number of semi-skilled and unskilled workers are employed is the ground service for aircraft. In addition to passenger check-in, which we all know from our experience as travellers, and the cargo section, we also have the so-called servicing of aircraft. A worker who has been employed in this sector for many years tells us that, basically, this implies the loading and unloading of baggage in and from aircraft, the sorting and transport of baggage and, of course, the cleaning of the interior of the planes. In this context many crucial changes have occurred in the work environment and thus also for the workers who do the low skilled work.

Competition between the airlines is making it increasingly important to shorten the ground time of an aircraft. 'A plane only makes money when it is in the air', the worker explains. Today, modern technical equipment is used by workers everywhere to ensure quick and safe servicing. The *fleet of vehicles* with the baggage carriers, lifting platforms, the self-propelled stairway for passengers, the electrically operated fuelling vehicles, the cleaning vehicles and snow ploughs are all proof of this. Earlier, the low skilled work was performed by a loader who had to have a good physical constitution and the ability to work in shifts. But it is now scarcely possible to obtain such a job without a driving licence and driving practice. And only then do the various courses begin, courses on how to operate the vehicles and the mechanical equipment, some of which have to be repeated every year.

The actual handling of baggage, the loading and unloading of the aircraft, not only has to be done rapidly but certain things always have to be kept in mind and done properly. Because aircraft have three wheels, when they are loaded the weight has to be distributed evenly so that the aircraft do not become unstable. This applies even more to the safe distribution of the loads for the flight. That is why there is a separate stowing plan for each aircraft and for each flight which the workers have to read and follow. Only by adhering to this plan can the right luggage be found at the right place and unloaded during stop-overs. Despite the time pressure, the luggage has to be handled with care, particularly in the case of special containers in which, for example, live animals are sent by air.

The speed at which the work has to be done should not impair *quality* and above all *safety*.

As a reduction in ground time is only possible through an optimised loading system and an intricate interaction of all workers and machines, so *communication* between the workers plays an essential role. Radio equipment is used, head-sets, computers, etc. Although the workers are of many nationalities, there is one firm rule: only German is spoken during work, otherwise communication might not be as smooth. In airports the international language of aviation, English, is playing an increasingly important role even in low skilled work. English technical terms are used in almost all operations and activities.

In addition, activities and requirements are constantly being enlarged. The ground service for aircraft has long assumed the task of guiding the aircraft to its parking position, during which communication with the captain of the plane must be in English via the head-set. Two other colleagues stand ready to place the chocks. After the engines are shut down the aircraft immediately receives electrical energy from an electric truck. The baggage has to be unloaded, the stairway for the passengers has to be placed in position, and all this has to be done at the same time. The workers discuss in the team who does what and when with the responsible 'operator' and their 'ramp agent', because none of them is a specialist who can ignore other operations and cannot assume other functions. All this, obviously, cannot be achieved overnight. A person who starts as a baggage handler is trained further, course by course and unit by unit, and consolidates his knowledge by doing the practical work. Reading the loading plans, knowledge of the different aircraft models, courses on how to operate the diverse technical equipment, etc. – all this is part of the job.

For our contact at the airport, as for many of his colleagues, this was one way of acquiring a vocational qualification. The 'certified aircraft servicing worker' has become a recognised semi-skilled occupation with a certificate from the Chamber of Commerce and Industry.

This shows the direction in which the qualification of low skilled work can develop. Here the concrete requirements for the job were combined to form a package of training modules leading to qualification. In this case, the action was directed to a clearly defined service sector: ground services at an airport. And it was seen here that a modular concept has the advantage of being open: it is capable of absorbing new trends. That will be crucial for the future.

In order to remain competitive, the airport management is thinking of offering all ground services as an integrated package. The fuelling will in future also be done by ground service staff. And as the goal is still to reduce ground time and improvements in technical equipment no longer help to achieve that goal, time saving can only be achieved through better coordination and interlinking of the activities of the staff. This means that the ability for self-organisation in the group under the severe time constraints will have to be developed even further.

Figure 2. **Skill profile in servicing of aircraft**

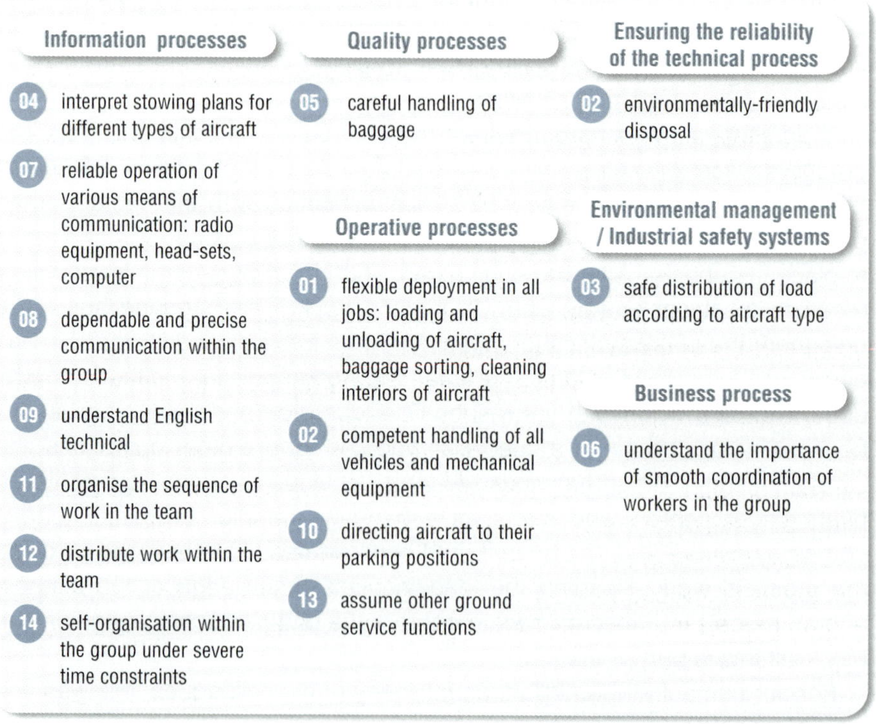

Information processes
- 04 interpret stowing plans for different types of aircraft
- 07 reliable operation of various means of communication: radio equipment, head-sets, computer
- 08 dependable and precise communication within the group
- 09 understand English technical
- 11 organise the sequence of work in the team
- 12 distribute work within the team
- 14 self-organisation within the group under severe time constraints

Quality processes
- 05 careful handling of baggage

Operative processes
- 01 flexible deployment in all jobs: loading and unloading of aircraft, baggage sorting, cleaning interiors of aircraft
- 02 competent handling of all vehicles and mechanical equipment
- 10 directing aircraft to their parking positions
- 13 assume other ground service functions

Ensuring the reliability of the technical process
- 02 environmentally-friendly disposal

Environmental management / Industrial safety systems
- 03 safe distribution of load according to aircraft type

Business process
- 06 understand the importance of smooth coordination of workers in the group

Activity field 'low skilled work' in bakery

After looking at the metalworking sector and the services required at an airport, we will now turn to the changes in a service sector with which we all have frequent contact: the bakery, and in this specific case, the sale of its products. More than half of the employees, and in particular the female employees, in the company we will examine, have no formal skill training. The company is expanding and has some 90 branches where the bakery products are sold.

What trends may be observed here for the way skills are developing in low skilled work?

Today it is no longer enough just to sell rolls, cake and loaves of bread. The staff has to cater to the specific wishes of the customers and to have a certain amount of *product knowledge*. Good knowledge of German and friendly service to customers are not enough; employees must also be able to give people with allergies or health-conscious customers information about the ingredients and substances in the products.

Mental arithmetic is not as important today as it used to be, but the ability to *operate the computerised cash register* calls for specific skills. Every product group is registered separately, which is the basis of the internal information system used to plan production levels and branch deliveries.

One thing is changing above all: the small bakers' shops are turning into small cafés or even bistros. Take-home sales are playing an increasingly important role in these bakers' shops. This means that the low skilled work in the shops now tends to include *production and service activities*. A constant supply of oven-fresh goods has to be ensured by putting pre-baked or par-baked products into the bakery oven. Small snacks, ranging from breakfast to lunch snacks, have to be prepared by the shop employees. This means knowledge of the manufacturing process and the ability to handle the raw material and the technical equipment.

What is more important is *self-organising skills*. Even though every shop has a manager, all staff must ensure the smooth sale of bakery products, a constant supply of freshly-baked products and, at the same time, customer satisfaction with the service and production in the café section of the shop. Many different objectives must be borne in mind and pursued simultaneously.

Quality control in the sale of bakery products means that each employee has to check the goods supplied from outside as well as the items produced in the shop by the individual employees. Even if things get hectic, hygiene cannot be neglected.

Figure 3. Skill profile in bakery chain – branch sales

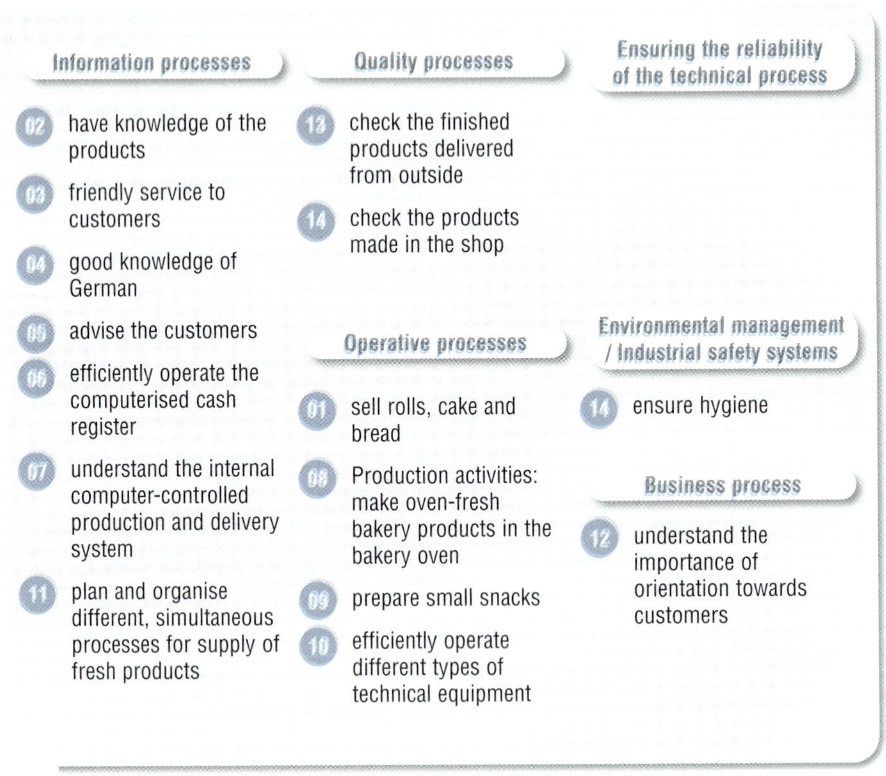

Information processes
- 02 have knowledge of the products
- 03 friendly service to customers
- 04 good knowledge of German
- 05 advise the customers
- 06 efficiently operate the computerised cash register
- 07 understand the internal computer-controlled production and delivery system
- 11 plan and organise different, simultaneous processes for supply of fresh products

Quality processes
- 13 check the finished products delivered from outside
- 14 check the products made in the shop

Operative processes
- 01 sell rolls, cake and bread
- 08 Production activities: make oven-fresh bakery products in the bakery oven
- 09 prepare small snacks
- 10 efficiently operate different types of technical equipment

Ensuring the reliability of the technical process

Environmental management / Industrial safety systems
- 14 ensure hygiene

Business process
- 12 understand the importance of orientation towards customers

2.4. Summary and perspectives

One modest conclusion to be drawn from our brief review of the changes in skill requirements for low skilled work is that the work organisation based on new technologies demands new skills even for low skilled work. We are witnessing the disappearance of niche jobs for support staff in the traditional sense who contribute to the business operation by performing unchanging low skilled activities. This is happening without the so-called low skilled work of semi-skilled and unskilled employees disappearing or becoming superfluous. These employees too are now confronted with new skill requirements; they are no longer just given instructions and told what to do. The possibility – and the point – of direct supervision and guidance no longer exist in complex work situations; instead, goals are set and all employees have to understand them and achieve them by cooperating as a team.

Through this survey, which was conducted in close cooperation with the practitioners in the company, we can identify the trends which determine the changes in the sector of low skilled work. On the basis of the concrete activities – which today are derived less from the individual workplace and more from the overall work environment – different interrelated categories of requirements may be analysed which lead to a configuration of extremely different types and levels of skills: in addition to *operational activities* semi-skilled and unskilled workers also perform tasks which are needed to ensure the reliability of the *technical process* – this implies maintenance and care of machines and equipment including simple machine-setting operations. These workers are now integrated in the *information process* of the company – this implies involvement in information processes of a personnel and technical nature. They participate actively in *quality processes* and the *business process* and assume tasks in the environmental management and industrial safety systems of the company.

Figure 4. **Cross-sectoral skill requirements**

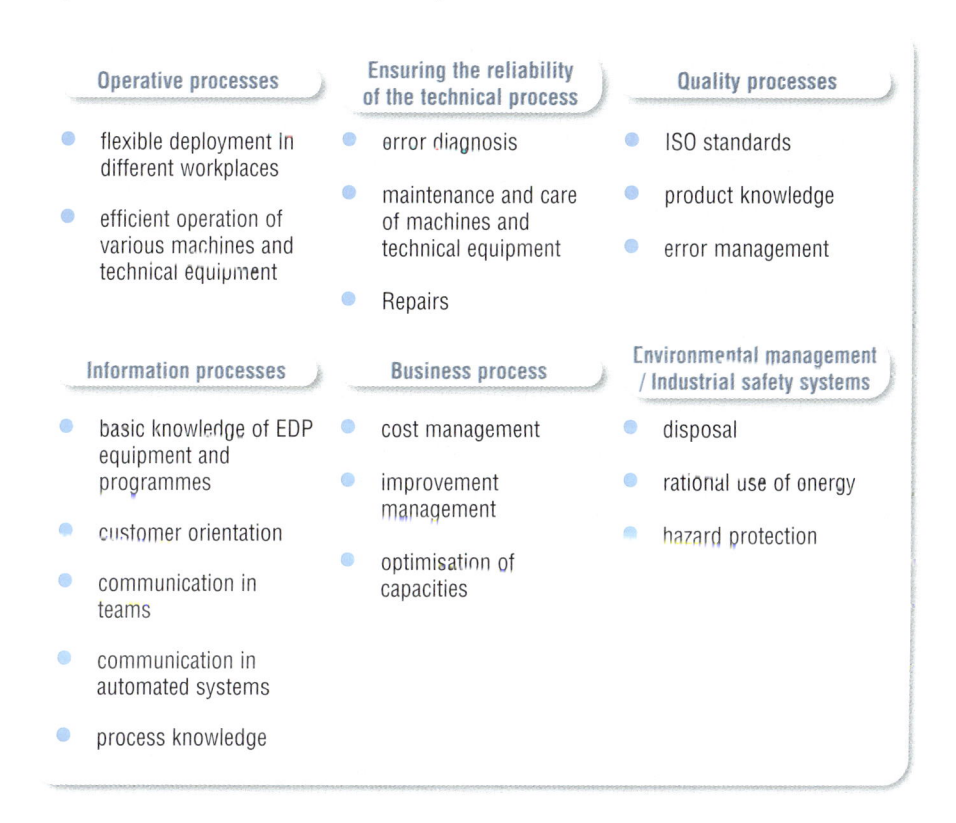

Operative processes
- flexible deployment in different workplaces
- efficient operation of various machines and technical equipment

Ensuring the reliability of the technical process
- error diagnosis
- maintenance and care of machines and technical equipment
- Repairs

Quality processes
- ISO standards
- product knowledge
- error management

Information processes
- basic knowledge of EDP equipment and programmes
- customer orientation
- communication in teams
- communication in automated systems
- process knowledge

Business process
- cost management
- improvement management
- optimisation of capacities

Environmental management / Industrial safety systems
- disposal
- rational use of energy
- hazard protection

Although the activities described in our examples could not be more different, some common denominators for skill requirements may be identified in this cross-section of different sectors. The question which arises here is to what extent these common skill requirements can be used to derive skills and competences which lend themselves to cross-sectional application over different sectors. The description of such cross-sectoral skills for low skilled work would make it possible to design trans-sectoral skill training concepts for low skilled activities. From this set of training concepts, basic skilling packages could be compiled which would make the people concerned employable in a certain sector, e.g. the metalworking industry, technical services or commerce. If in future semi-skilled and unskilled people seeking their livelihoods on the labour market acquire these skills step by step, then they will continue to have a chance in companies.

References

Dostal, W.; Reinberg A. *Arbeitslandschaft 2010 – Teil 2: Ungebrochener Trend in die Wissensgesellschaft.* IAB Kurzbericht 10/1999, also available in: http://www.iab.de/ftproot/kb1099.pdf.

Weidig, I.; Hofer, P.; Wolff, H. *Arbeitslandschaft 2010 nach Tätigkeiten und Tätigkeitsniveau.* Beiträge zur Arbeitsmarkt- und Berufsforschung, vol. 227, Nuremberg, 1999.

Early recognition of international qualifications for SMEs

Peter Wordelmann, Federal Institute for Vocational Training (BIBB), Bonn, Germany

'International qualifications', required to deal with increasing economic activities as a consequence of economic globalisation, include three original dimensions: foreign language skills, intercultural competence and excellent professional competence. In addition, there are two other important aspects: mental and physical robustness as a condition for working abroad, and international qualifications as a corporate and social obligation.

The dissemination of information and communication technologies will have a decisive impact on future trends in international qualifications. To an increasing extent, physical mobility can be replaced by virtual mobility and international contacts can be facilitated from the workplace at home. At the same time international qualifications will have to be extended to include the dimension of 'network competence', which not only encompasses the ability to cope with Internet and Intranet, i.e. to work with networks, but also to work in networks. This includes indirect communication with people from another culture. Network communication, organisation, creativity, safety, learning and training, confidence building, and virtual mobility in the network are new requirements which should also be incorporated in international qualifications.

1. The consequences of the European Single Market

The creation of the European Single Market in 1992 also paved the way for the creation of a European training area comprising some 370 million people, an area which will expand considerably in the future. This European training area across international borders and the increasing globalisation of the economy are lending increasing momentum to the internationalisation of training. More than ever before, training is becoming not only a factor of production, but also a cultural asset in the dichotomy between national identities and international forms of competition and cooperation. [1]

In the absence of a theory on global economies which would provide a basis for an appraisal of its consequences, in an initial approach to this question the dimensions of relevance to training behind the efforts towards economic integration were identified (not only in Europe). These are the dimensions of space, time and competition.

Space, time and competition are in fact very closely correlated. In the field of training policy, these close links are illustrated e.g. by the debate on the dual system within the European area or the relatively late age at which German students finally become available for the labour market – just two examples, the former regarded as a competitive advantage, the latter as a disadvantage.

The forwarding business is a prime example of the relevance of the space, time and competition approach to vocational training policy. It is a sector in which the conditions of space and competition have undergone a considerable short-term transformation in the wake of the Single Market, e.g. in the light of free negotiation of tariffs following the deregulation of road haulage tariffs in January 1994. [2] These transformations have also triggered enormous changes in the relevant occupational profile. Indeed, transport and traffic remain a subject for practice-oriented research approaches even today. [3]

The theoretical approach to the identification of qualifications for the process of internationalisation has been complemented by empirical studies (Busse, Paul-Kohlhoff and Wordelmann, 1997). This led to the identification of the following possible skill elements, from which the concept of international qualifications was subsequently derived.

---

[1] Cf. Wordelmann (1995a) on the following.
[2] Cf. ILSE, 1994. This publication refers to the need to 'gear vocational training towards the objective of holistic action-oriented vocational competence.'
[3] Cf. e.g. Peppinghaus (2001) in the context of BIBB project 4.2013.

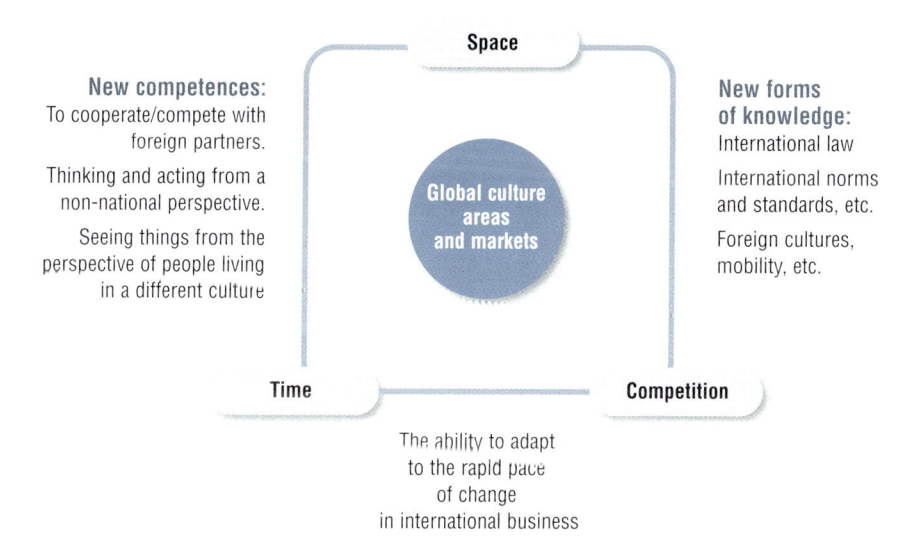

Figure 1. **Elements of the development of international qualifications**

New competences:
To cooperate/compete with foreign partners.
Thinking and acting from a non-national perspective.
Seeing things from the perspective of people living in a different culture

Space

Global culture areas and markets

New forms of knowledge:
International law
International norms and standards, etc.
Foreign cultures, mobility, etc.

Time

Competition

The ability to adapt to the rapid pace of change in international business

2. The concept of 'international qualifications'

Despite the fact that research in the field of internationalisation has been under way for a relatively long period of time, daily practice remains characterised by a confusion of terms: 'Euro-skills' or 'Euro-qualifications', 'fit for Europe', 'ready to meet the challenge of Europe', 'intercultural communication skills/competence', and more recently 'skills for working abroad' and 'international professional skills'.

However the concept of 'international qualifications', developed in 1997, has become widely accepted, at least in specialised circles, both inside and outside Germany. ([4]) This concept includes the three dimensions: foreign language skills, intercultural skills and outstanding specialised knowledge (Busse, Paul-Kohlhoff and Wordelmann, 1997). Moreover, the importance of mental and physical robustness as a condition for a transnational placement has been identified. And, finally, the concept of international qualifications also comprises a mission in the context of both industry and society, to the extent that culturally induced conflicts both inside and outside the firm can be solved by means of learning.

The most important elements are illustrated in the following diagram.

([4] Cf. e.g. Kristensen, 1998.

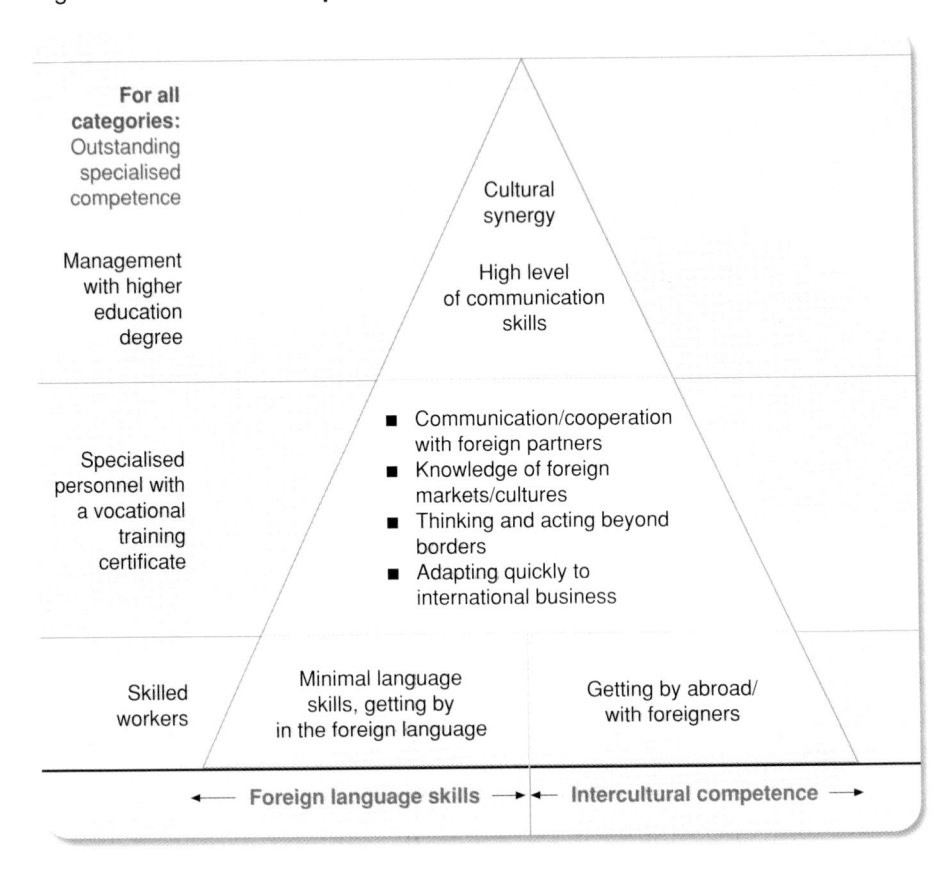

Figure 2. **International qualifications – content and requirements**

	Foreign language skills	Intercultural competence
For all categories: Outstanding specialised competence — Management with higher education degree	Cultural synergy	High level of communication skills
Specialised personnel with a vocational training certificate	■ Communication/cooperation with foreign partners ■ Knowledge of foreign markets/cultures ■ Thinking and acting beyond borders ■ Adapting quickly to international business	
Skilled workers	Minimal language skills, getting by in the foreign language	Getting by abroad/ with foreigners

Outstanding specialised knowledge is above all emphasised from the perspective of the enterprises for which specialised competence is clearly the initial premise for international activities or missions. In practice the other dimensions tend to be neglected in personnel planning.

Foreign language skills ([5]) are required at different levels. At management level, where direct contact with foreign clients/partners will presumably play an increasing role in the future, the requirement is often not only a sound command of business English, but also a knowledge of other languages. It is occasionally pointed out that international activities – including transnational

---

([5]) The call for foreign language skilling in vocational training goes back some time and has been frequently reiterated, among others in the Memorandum on Lifelong Learning, published following the Lisbon European summit. The five 'new' basic skills for all include foreign languages, alongside IT skills, technological culture, entrepreneurship and social skills.

missions – can be carried out with no or with only rudimentary knowledge of a foreign language. However as new technologies bring the internationalisation process to the workplaces of the specialised personnel trained within the dual system in Germany, at least an adequate command of English will be necessary at this level.

The dimension of *intercultural competence* as the third aspect of international qualifications ranges from 'getting by in a foreign country' and 'cultural curiosity' to high negotiating skills in a transnational situation/foreign language. Although an important requirement in daily business routine, it is probably the most neglected in practice

All in all, it is important to note that all these dimensions belong to a comprehensive concept of skilling for international activities and that the requirements can by no means be reduced to foreign language skills alone. The concept itself probably remains largely valid for the majority of SMEs in the process of internationalisation. As an overall concept, it essentially applies to the following occupations (not to be regarded as an exhaustive list):

- forwarding agent
- travel agent
- specialised catering/hotel employee
- specialised employee in system catering
- chef/cook
- wholesale and foreign trade clerk
- industrial clerk
- banking clerk
- specialist in event technology
- mechatronics engineer
- digital and print media designer
- service agent/air traffic
- service agent/rail and road traffic.

International qualifications are ideally acquired in the framework of transnational placements. Against this background, Kristensen in particular has examined the didactic dimension of transnational work placements (Kristensen, 2001). He points out that there is no theory specifically relating to the learning process in the context of transnational work placements. This remains an important task of vocational training research, as transnational placements alone will presumably no longer suffice for the substantiation of mobility projects in the future. The concrete learning potential of transnational placements, their 'European value added', must also been ascertained in order to counter the widely held prejudice that these placements are essentially a form of tourism.

In terms of training policy, it would seem to make sense if those training occupations in which foreign language learning is not compulsory in view of considerations of demand were to introduce a basic intercultural qualification, including a foreign language element, but at a generally lower level. [6] This qualification would have a dual objective:
- with reference to foreign language skills (English): as a means of preventing failure in contacts such as telephone calls, etc.
- with reference to intercultural skills: to learn that many things may be different elsewhere and to facilitate the development of intercultural conflict management potentials.

An approach of this kind would not only correspond to the training policy mission – of primarily vocational schools in this instance – but also the long-term interests of industry which constantly evokes the in-company and societal importance of intercultural skills. And it would generate a certain degree of mobility capacity for individual employees – an aspect which could gain further importance in the future in the light of trends in the domestic labour market.

3. On the demand for international qualifications

Two different approaches have developed in the context of research into the quantitative and qualitative demand for international qualifications. The Cologne Institute for Business Research (IW) conducts company surveys while the Federal Institute for Vocational Training (BIBB) along with the Fraunhofer Institute for Industrial Engineering (FhIAO) surveys a 0.1% sample of the gainfully employed. Both approaches have their drawbacks. [7] As the IW response rate tends to be fairly low, its data cannot be regarded as representative. On the other hand, its results tend to be prospective, pointing to the trends and wishes of in particular multinationals.

Although the results of the BIBB/IAB surveys are representative, they merely reflect the current personal judgement of the gainfully employed in their workplace and only refer to the demand for foreign languages which has so far been rated as an indicator of the 'internationalism' of an enterprise.

In the BIBB/IAB surveys, the gainfully employed are surveyed on the fields in which they require particular knowledge, i.e. not only basic knowledge, and

---

[6] Cf. Busse, Paul-Kohlhoff and Wordelmann (1997), in particular p. 240.
[7] Cf. Commission of the European Communities (1991) for a diagnosis and analysis of foreign language requirements.

on the corresponding need for continuing training. The latest survey dates back to 1998/99 (cf. Dostal, Jansen and Parmentier, eds., 2000). In 1991/92 a survey was conducted among some 34 000 gainfully employed persons (Jansen and Stooss, 1993). Partial data from a similar survey in 1985/86 [8] are also available.

The results of the representative BIBB/IAB surveys among the gainfully employed show a relatively stable picture in the long term. Approximately every tenth person surveyed requires foreign languages in their current jobs. [9] Table 1 shows the results of the 1998/99 surveys broken down according to vocational qualification and field of training.

Table 1. **In what areas do you require special knowledge, i.e. not only basic knowledge, in your present job?**

Foreign languages (data in %)	
Total dependent employees	9
Apprenticeship	
Apprenticeship only	6
Apprenticeship + specialised college of higher education	9
Apprenticeship + specialised college of higher education + university	17
Area of training (last apprenticeship completed)	
Industry	9
Crafts	3
Commerce	8
Public service	7
Other services	8
Vocational education qualifications	
Master craftsman/technology, etc.	12
Specialised college of higher education	18
University	29

Source: BIBB/IAB survey 1999.

---

[8] Cf. Wordelmann (1991) for the results on 'foreign languages'.
[9] The question was worded as follows: 'Let us now turn to the knowledge you require in your present job. Please look through this list and indicate those areas in which you require special knowledge'. One possible response was 'Foreign languages'.

The *demand for continuing training* in foreign languages has risen among the gainfully employed in recent years. In 1991/92, it stood at 5%. Table 2 shows the figures for 1998/99, broken down according to various levels of training. As before, the highest demand for continuing training is still to be observed in those areas showing the greatest need for foreign languages, whereby it is always a question of additional foreign languages in this context.

Table 2. **Please go through this list again. Does it include areas in which you should improve, update or extend your knowledge by means of continuing training? If so, which areas?**

Foreign languages (data in %)	
Total dependent employees	8
Apprenticeship	
Apprenticeship only	5
Apprenticeship+ specialised college of higher education	11
Apprenticeship+ specialised college of higher education + university	15
Area of training (last apprenticeship completed)	
Industry	9
Crafts	4
Commerce	7
Public service	7
Other services	7
Vocational education qualifications	
Master craftsman/technology, etc.	12
Specialised college of higher education	14
University	16

Source: BIBB-IAB survey 1999.

In interpreting these results, it should be borne in mind that the indicated need for foreign languages in the workplace can presumably only up to a certain degree be regarded as an *indicator* of the internationalisation of skill requirements. For some respondents, use of English is no doubt taken so much for granted that it is no longer regarded as out of the ordinary. On the other hand, as workplace automation increases, there are certainly many elements other than the need for foreign languages pointing to internationalisation. From this angle, the results of company surveys presented in the following show higher requirements and are therefore of a more prospective character.

As early as in 1992, a study conducted by the IW showed that 70% of the surveyed enterprises required multilingual members of staff and every fourth respondent frequently needed to use a foreign language (plus 27.5% 'now and again' and only 30% 'never'). And this figure was almost 50% in companies with 100 to 500 employees (Weiss, 1992). However the survey in question was a written company survey which even the authors do not regard as representative in view of the low response rate (12.1%!, a total of 232 cases).

The most recent survey in this field conducted by the IW on the basis of the concept of international qualifications involved some 4 000 companies, surveyed on their international activities and the consequences for the skilling of specialised personnel and trainees. ([10]) The results of this survey show e.g. that 32.4% of specialised personnel regularly use 'international qualifications' in terms of 'job-related foreign language skills', 21.6% in terms of 'international specialised knowledge' and 15.9% in terms of 'other international knowledge and qualifications'. According to the company ratings, the relevance of the individual dimensions was 23.6% for 'foreign language skills', 23.3% for 'international specialised knowledge' and 25.5% for 'intercultural knowledge/planning'. On balance, therefore, the international dimension of skilling is regard as important by approx. one quarter of the surveyed enterprises – whereby it is interesting to note that the intercultural dimension is rated as the most important element, although it is the most difficult to define and is the least firmly rooted in vocational training.

4. International qualifications and the development of information and communication technologies

The combination of globalisation and the rapid development of information and communication technologies triggered a further development of the concept of international qualifications in the late 1990s. Although not all the developments predicted by the wave of internet hype occurred – and particularly not as quickly as predicted (cf. e.g. Pförtsch, 2000) – information

---

([10]) Cf. Lenske and Werner, 2000. However the response rate was only 19%.

and communication technologies have undoubtedly become a decisive factor in job requirements and lent new dynamism to the interaction of space, time and competition.

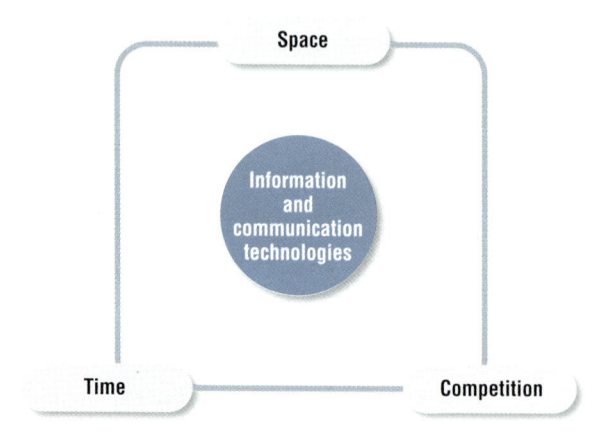

Figure 3. **Technologies in the context of internationalization**

[Diagram: Information and communication technologies at the center, with Space, Time, and Competition at the corners.]

In the form of hypotheses, this dynamism implies the following consequences for skills and qualifications:
- Virtualisation of job requirements is advancing at great speed and increasingly impacting on SMEs.
- It tends to effect all jobs.
- The individual no longer has the choice whether or not to work in an international context or decide on the modern tools s/he wishes to use.
- Physical mobility can be increasingly substituted by virtual mobility.
- Those equipped with the necessary qualifications – both individually and institutionally – have a competitive advantage whereas those lacking the necessary qualifications encounter problems in the management of their future.

A principal reason for the growing process of internationalisation within the employment system is the continuing advance of modern information and communication technologies. This process transcends borders in principle: it brings international requirements to domestic workplaces, a consequence not so much of the mobility of labour as the mobility of capital. This implies higher and to a certain extent different international qualification requirements (virtually mobility (Wordelmann, 2000a), digital culture) in the future.

In order to develop the concept of international qualifications a step further, the term *'network competences'* was therefore introduced (Wordelmann, 2001). This concept combines internationality, i.e. occupational activity can in principle be transnational, and the use of ICT media which can also in principle be transnational. As this integration occurs, the original importance of the internationality aspect diminishes and is increasingly taken for granted in the occupational context. Network competences are not only a basic qualification for the international division of labour but also for the future-oriented design of in-company organisation.

The strategic key qualification 'network competences' ([11]) is not merely a question of the technical ability to work with the internet/intranet, i.e. to work with networks. It has in principle no borders and therefore requires the ability to work successfully in networks, by means of either personal or 'only' technical contact. The ability to decide which forms of contact are selected is in itself part of this comprehensive competence. The general skilling objective is 'to think and act in networks' and therefore acquire occupational capacity of action in the process of 'internationalisation '. A basic precondition is the technical ability to handle networks. Over and above this, a whole series of vocational skilling elements appear in a different or a new light. In brief summary, these are as follows (Wordelmann, 2000b):

- *Specialised competence in networks:*
  Consulting, purchasing, sales, marketing, maintenance, etc. in networks require appropriate skills and qualifications.
- *Communication in networks:*
  Real and virtual networks require different communicative competences – not least in view of their asynchronicity. Language is only a vehicle. Foreign language skills (in particular English; other languages may be very important in certain cases) must also be differentiated, ranging from basic computer and network literacy to higher-level negotiating skills in the case of real contacts.
- *Cooperation and competition in networks:*
  The dictate of networking and worldwide cooperation implies a new relationship between cooperation and competition. Competitors may quickly become cooperation partners and vice versa.
- *Intercultural competence in networks:*
  In virtual transnational contacts, the importance of intercultural competence is not the same as in real contacts but it is nevertheless not superfluous. It is also important for the national and regional presentation and design of bids in the global network.

([11]) The term 'media competence' which is often used in this context is too narrow in our opinion; moreover it cannot be differentiated from the ability to work with 'public media'. Cf. e.g. Hüther, Schorb and Brehm-Klotz, 1997; Schiersmann, Busse and Krause, 2002.

- *Confidence-building in networks:*
  Those in a position to swiftly and securely build confidence in a networked economy enjoy a competitive advantage. This applies in a special way to cooperation between persons from different cultural backgrounds.
- *Organisation in networks:*
  Networked and virtual forms of work call for new organisational forms and related competences. Although team and project forms of organisation may generate synergies, they may also imply considerable competitive disadvantages in the case of failure.
- *Mobility in networks:*
  Workers must be able to handle the various instruments of virtual mobility, in particular with reference to the relevant tasks and objectives. When is personal contact required, when will a phone call, an e-mail or a videoconference suffice?
- *Creativity in networks:*
  The internet evidently requires new forms not only of design and presentation, but also of creativity.
- *Networked learning:*
  Networks offer the necessary forum to link up work and learning and therefore provide the conditions for lifelong learning. The future prospects of both individuals and firms will become increasingly dependent on their ability to use network-based learning applications and therefore implement dynamic skill development.
- *Network security:*
  Network and open systems are incident-prone and the impact of incidents may be considerable. For this reason, new criteria and standards of particularly technical, but also organisational security are applicable in network applications. Network security must be systematically and permanently guaranteed for all jobs as a fundamental element of working activity in the new economy.
- *Networking risks:*
  On the other hand, it is necessary to differentiate between the macro and micro economic risks of networking. In general, a greater readiness to assume risks seems to be required in the new economy where speed competes with substantiated planning. Individuals too must be in a position to reappraise their vocational and personal risks.
- *Space and time in networks:*
  The worldwide availability of space and globalised time require thinking and action which is in principle characterised by openness.

- *Network boundaries:*
  Insofar as they exist all, network boundaries are fluid because networks are dynamic. But they also manifest themselves as the boundaries of power.

The individual elements cannot be imparted in isolation, but are in themselves intertwined within a networked relationship (see Figure 4). For example, intercultural competence and confidence-building represent new requirements resulting from indirect contact with people from other cultures. This means that manifestations of ethnic culture may in the future be superimposed by a new 'digital' culture which may – perhaps – open up opportunities for new forms of transcultural communication.

Figure 4. **Network competences as a strategic key competence of internationalisation**

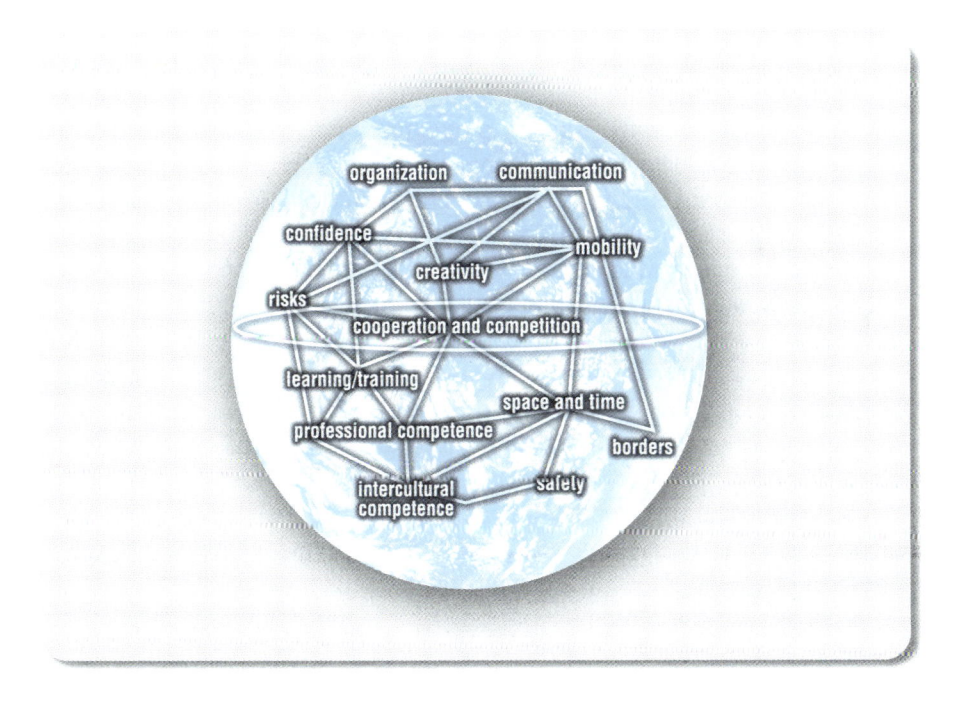

5. International qualifications in SMEs

Since the level of specialised personnel with vocational training qualifications is particularly impacted by international qualification requirements in the workplace in the context of SMEs, BIBB project 1.2005 examined relevant deficits and requirements which were placed in the context of internationalisation strategies (Hering, Pförtsch and Wordelmann, 2001). In general terms, three different types of SME were identified as far as the *planning of internationalisation* is concerned:
- marketing-oriented
- customer-oriented
- visionary and intuitive, notably the specific case of a company which applies a training-based internationalisation strategy.

The specific case in question is interesting in the present context, because form the point of view of training policy it includes the ideal approach to an *international training culture*.

'A company included in the survey has for some time been implementing an internationally oriented training programme. For example, all company trainees receive additional foreign language tuition and complete placements in partner companies abroad in the course of their training. The reason behind this approach was the vision of the entrepreneur that with a view to the Single European Market, an international form of training would provide his company with manpower who would be "fit for Europe". Over the course of time, an international training culture has therefore developed, which is part and parcel of corporate identity and serves to sustainably support the company's internationalisation strategy. However the company is also a good example to illustrate that a change of paradigm towards "web savvy" is currently taking place. For example, new ICT media are used in the form of videoconferencing by company trainees to introduce themselves to potential placement firms abroad.' (op. cit., p. 9) And the company has now begun to organise long-term transnational placements for its trainers.

In contrast to the aforementioned types of internationalisation planning, there are two strategic variants in the *implementation and organisation* of the process which are very much dependent on company size. Whereas in the case of SMEs, the internationalisation process is often organised and implemented from head office, large-scale enterprises generally have other means at their disposal.

For the transnationally-oriented process, it is necessary to differentiate between personnel working in the national and the transnational context.

Table 3 gives an overview of the necessary skill potential.

Table 3. Manpower skills within different internationalisation processes

Skill	Head office orientation	Transnational orientation MS in the national context	Transnational orientation MS in the transnational context
Strategic competence			
Understanding and taking decisions on complex facts and circumstances	++	+	0
Market skills	++	+	0
Development skills	+	+	++
Competitive skills	++	0	+
Specialised competence			
Product/service skills	+	0	++
Implementing skills (client requirements in technology)	+	0	++
Marketing skills	++	0	+
ICT competence			
Network competence	+	++	+
Management and controlling tools	+	++	+
Methodological competence			
Project management	+	0	++
Problem solving/decision-making skills	++	0	++
Cost accounting/controlling	+	0	++
Financial management	+	0	++
Social competence			
Presentation	++	+	++
Communication	++	+	+
Team work	+	+	++
Leadership, delegation of tasks	++	0	++
Intercultural competence			
Religious and social values	+	0	++
Manners	+	0	++
General language skills	+	+	++
English	++	++	++
2nd/3rd language	+	0	++
National language	+	0	++

The skills were classified as follows:
++: very high requirements, +: high requirements, 0: low requirements. MS = member of staff

Source: Hering, Pförtsch and Wordelmann, 2001, p. 11.

6. Early recognition and implementation of skill requirements

To a certain extent, the results presented above draw on earlier studies and were therefore 'recognised early' at the time. Moreover, the more recent research results, in particular those on 'network competences', are of a prospective character.

Although the concept of 'international qualifications' is valid for most enterprises in the medium term, it is not the customary standard in either training practice or in formal regulations (Borch and Wordelmann, 2001).

The deficit in the implementation of new skill requirements is particularly problematic, as concrete effects of innovative approaches in VET require a substantial lead-time. It therefore seems necessary for those involved in early recognition research to attach greater importance to the actual implementation of their findings.

Bibliography

Baur, R.; Wolff, H.; Wordelmann, P. *Herausforderungen des europäischen Binnenmarktes für das Bildungssystem der Bundesrepublik Deutschland.* Federal Ministry of Education and Science, Bonn 1991.

Borch, H.; Wordelmann, P. Internationalisierung des Dualen Systems. Strategien und Forderungen. *Berufsbildung in Wissenschaft und Praxis*, 2001, Vol. 4, p.5ff.

Busse, G.; Paul-Kohlhoff, A.; Wordelmann, P. *Fremdsprachen und mehr. Internationale Qualifikationen aus der Sicht von Betrieben und Beschäftigten. Eine empirische Studie über Zukunftsqualifikationen.* Federal Institute for Vocational Training, Bielefeld 1997.

Commission of the European Communities /Task Force Human Resources. *Eine Untersuchung der bei der Diagnose und Analyse von Fremdsprachenbedarf in Handel und Industrie verwendeten Techniken*, Luxembourg 1991.

Dostal, W.; Jansen, R.; Parmentier, K., eds. *Wandel der Erwerbsarbeit: Arbeitssituation, Informatisierung, berufliche Mobilität und Weiterbildung.* Beiträge zur Arbeitsmarkt- und Berufsforschung 231, Nuremberg 2000.

Hering, E.; Pförtsch, W.; Wordelmann, P. *Internationalisierung des Mittelstandes. Strategien zur internationalen Qualifizierung in kleinen und mittleren Unternehmen.* Federal Institute for Vocational Training (BIBB), Bielefeld 2001.

Hüther, J.; Schorb, B.; Brehm-Klotz, C., eds. *Grundbegriffe Medienpädagogik*, Munich, 1997.

ILSE, F. Speditionskaufmann/Speditionskauffrau. Neue Anforderungen durch Europa. *Informationen für die Beratungs- und Vermittlungsdienste der Bundesanstalt für Arbeit*, 1994, No 43, 26.10.94, p. 3431

Jansen, R.; Stooss, F., eds. *Qualifikation und Erwerbssituation im geeinten Deutschland.* Federal Institute for Vocational Training (BIBB), Berlin/Bonn 1993.

Kristensen, S. Transnational mobility in the context of vocational education and training in Europe. *In* Cedefop, ed. *Vocational education and training – the European research field. Background report 1998.* Cedefop Reference Document. Luxembourg 1998, Volume II, pp. 273-295.

Kristensen, S. *Developing transnational placements as a didactic tool.* Cedefop, Thessaloniki 2001.

Lenske, W.; Werner, D. *Globalisierung und internationale Berufskompetenz*, Cologne 2000.

Peppinghaus, B. Berufsausbildung im europäischen Verkehrssektor - eine „Probebohrung'. *Zur Internationalisierung der beruflichen Bildung, Ergebnisse, Veröffentlichungen und Materialien aus dem BIBB.* January 2002, p. 57 ff.

Pförtsch, W. *Mit Strategie ins Internet. Qualifizierung als Chance für Unternehmen.* Nuremberg 2000.

Schiersmann, C.; Busse, J.; Krause, D. *Medienkopetenz - Kompetenz für neue Medien. Studie und Workshop.* Materialien des Forum Bildung 12, Bonn 2002.

Weiß, R. Fremdsprachen in der Wirtschaft: Bedarf und Qualifizierung. *In* Kramer, W.; Weiß, R., eds. *Fremdsprachen in der Wirtschaft.* Cologne 1992, pp.77 ff.

Wordelmann, P. Fremdsprachen in Ausbildung und Beruf. *Gewerkschaftliche Bildungspolitik*, 1991, Vol. 2.

Wordelmann, P., ed. *Internationale Qualifikationen. Inhalte, Bedarf und Vermittlung.* Federal Institute for Vocational Training (BIBB), Bielefeld 1995a.

Wordelmann, P.; Matthes, C.-Y. *Fachkräfte, Fremdsprachen und Mobilität.* Federal Institute for Vocational Training (BIBB), Bielefeld 1995b.

Wordelmann, P. Qualification development of internationally skilled workers - from mobility of labour to 'virtual mobility'. *In* Cedefop, ed. *Internationalising vocational education and training in Europe. Prelude to an overdue debate.* Thessaloniki 2000a, pp.71 ff.

Wordelmann, P. Internetionalisierung und Netzkompetenz. Neue qualifikatorische Herausforderungen durch Globalisierung und Internet. *Berufsbildung in Wissenschaft und Praxis*, 2000b, Vol., p. 25ff.

Wordelmann, P. Globalisierung, Qualifikation und Migration. *In* Gümrüksü, H., ed. *Globalisierung.* ITES-Jahrbuch, Hamburg 2001, p.71ff.

New qualifications in SMEs for societal and technological change - skilling of IT users

Lothar Abicht, *Rainer Werner*, Institute of Structural Policies and Economic Development Halle-Leipzig e.V. (isw), Germany

Particularly in small and medium sized enterprises (SMEs) there are qualification needs for applying information and communication technologies (ICTs). Thus, the employment services of Saxony-Anhalt-Thuringia and the Ministry of Labour, Women, Health and Welfare of Saxony-Anhalt cooperated with the Institute of Structural Policies and Economic Development (Institut für Strukturpolitik und Wirtschaftsförderung Halle-Leipzig eV) (isw) to establish the *Telekompetenz* initiative. Translating the initiative into action, seven educational service providers and about 130 SMEs took part in a pilot series of e-learning-based continuing training projects consisting of two five-month courses. In the first period with the respective educational service provider, unemployed persons from various occupational backgrounds underwent ICT training during which a learning project for each participant was defined. The learning project included developing and implementing a company-specific ICT application during the second period of on-the-job training. An Internet database linked participants to one another as well as to their teletutors and in-company advisers. Evaluation of the pilot series of projects shows that increased adjustment of the qualification process to the needs of SMEs leads to more practical results for this kind of enterprise. This is evident from adjusting qualifications to real labour market conditions, an increase in orders, increased use of ICT applications, and creating new jobs. Half the participants found new gainful employment immediately after completing the continuing training measure. Most of them would not have found jobs without the *Telekompetenz* pilot projects. The blend of previous vocational and new ICT qualifications was the decisive factor for taking on participants. The initiative continues with a second series of projects.

1. Identification of qualification requirements in sectors with forecasting problems

The methods normally used for the early identification of skill requirements either follow the 'top-down' or 'bottom-up' approach. In the case of top-down models success depends on substantiated data at the macro-economic level which is taken as the basis for calculations of the different scenarios. Bottom-up models, on the other hand, rely on interviews with the different players involved who provide the data for the subsequent aggregation operations. The second method in particular is an effective means of obtaining detailed qualitative information on the occupations and skills required in specific sectors, provided the people covered by the surveys are in a position to recognise and describe their own needs. These conditions are mostly to be found in sectors with conventional occupational profiles and players who have enough competence in the field of vocational training. The situation becomes more difficult when, as a result of scientific and technological change, new skills which do not yet exist in this form are needed and when, at the same time, the issues of skilling are still a peripheral problem for practitioners. In this case, interviews in the traditional sense of the term do not produce the desired results because the respondents themselves have no clear perception of the situation. This leads to a hazy scenario where the usual forecasting methods cannot clarify the situation or can do only inadequately.

It was precisely this hazy situation which existed at the beginning of the *'Telekompetenz'* (tele-competence) project presented below. The aim of this project was to give unemployed people qualifications which would enable them to develop different kinds of information technology (IT) applications in small and medium-sized enterprises and to implement, maintain and operate these applications. In this project the aim was not only to conduct analyses of skill requirements but to use these analyses as tools which would enable unemployed people, by means of innovative training schemes, to acquire skills geared to the concrete requirements of the enterprises. In this project, the hazy situation prevailing at the beginning not only required identification of the skills needed in the enterprises, but the majority of the small and medium-sized enterprises to be integrated in the project were themselves uncertain which information technology (IT) applications would actually be needed in the foreseeable future, i.e. what training would be required for the staff responsible for the maintenance and operation of these applications.

Thus, the aim of this project was to detect these concealed needs and to disclose the potential opportunities which would then emerge for the enterprises.

Here it should not be forgotten that the project was launched in the German federal state of Saxony-Anhalt, a region in which enterprises with up to 50 employees predominate and over 30% ([1]) of people employed in the manufacturing sector work in firms with a maximum of 19 employees. The prevailing situation in these enterprises with regard to the application of IT may be summarised as follows:
- they lag behind in the use of modern IT as a means of optimising the company's business functions;
- deficits and problems in the identification and description of the need for IT applications;
- difficulties in financing specific (IT) solutions;
- problems of acceptance by management and employees.

The enterprises have a latent need for complex IT applications but if these needs are to be identified and gradually satisfied, the overall conditions conducive to this process have to be created.

The situation required for the identification and implementation of IT applications is closely related with the staff and skill requirements of the enterprise. If the employees do not possess the basic skills in this area, very hazy notions exist of which IT applications are most suited to promote the development of the enterprise under its specific internal conditions. Furthermore, the small size of the enterprises makes it difficult to employ full-time staff for IT applications, firstly for financial reasons and secondly, because there will not be enough tasks for a full-time post. There are also considerable differences in the contents of the various IT applications which will probably be needed (latent need), so that a very heterogeneous picture of the probable skills emerges when these needs are translated into skill requirements. While the basic skills in question present relatively uniform characteristics, the specialised knowledge required is a part of this uniform picture. The same applies to the necessity of showing specialised staff for IT applications in small and medium sized enterprises (SMEs) how to interlink IT knowledge and knowledge of work processes in SMEs.

Given this general situation, a hypothetical approach was developed for the *'Telekompetenz'* project where the following assumptions were combined to create the necessary conditions.

([1]) *Source:* Bundesanstalt für Arbeit: „Zahl der Betriebe und ihrer Beschäftigten" (as of 30.06.00).

- Unemployed people with basic knowledge can assist enterprises to identify their (latent) need for IT applications.
- Within the framework of skilling projects these unemployed people can develop specific IT applications in this SME after its goals have been approximately described at the beginning of the process.
- The enterprises or the decision-makers in the firm will accept the relevance of these IT applications for the optimisation of in-company operations and will, through practical demonstration, show that they have overcome their reluctance to introduce the new technologies.
- The enterprises will run IT applications on a permanent basis and thus create new jobs for the further development and operation of these applications.
- Unemployed people will be sufficiently trained for this task in the enterprise through a combination of traditional learning and work-process-integrated learning.
- In the course of this work-process-integrated learning the unemployed people will demonstrate their suitability for employment in this firm and thus get a chance to be recruited for the new jobs created through their activities.
- Unemployed people will be recruited to fill the new jobs and will now have the requisite skills for a job which did not exist at the start of the process and could only be defined in very vague terms. Through the competence acquired in the course of their training to undertake and consolidate self-directed learning and apply it at the workplace, the former unemployed people will ensure the ongoing relevance of the newly created IT applications and thus secure their jobs.

2. The goals of the Telekompetenz project

The following goals were defined for the networked *Telekompetenz* project:
- Provide unemployed people with IT-related qualifications as an opportunity for re-entry into the profession;
- make available specially trained staff for SMEs (the predominant type of enterprise in Saxony-Anhalt) who are able to design and operate IT applications for companies in cooperation with specialists;
- enable work-process-integrated learning in order to adapt vocational skills more closely to the actual requirements of the workplace;
- implement modern IT solutions in SMEs as a form of innovation transfer for the small and medium-sized enterprises of Saxony-Anhalt;

- train and inform in-company instructors and other company employees so that they are aware of modern IC solutions and the possibilities of implementing them in the company as a means of transferring up-to-date IT-related knowledge to SMEs in the classical sectors who, by using IT and the new media, wish to increase their competitiveness;
- test possibilities of creating new high-value jobs in the participating companies who, at the same time, visibly increase their competitiveness through the use of e-commerce solutions. In this context, the project not only had the aim of generating new IT-related jobs, but also stabilising the other jobs in the company and thus contributing to the creation of classical jobs through company expansion;
- enhance the importance of the educational establishments as skill providers in the context of IT-supported continuing vocational training in Saxony-Anhalt;
- create a state-wide network of educational establishments, experts and other supporting institutions – generate synergy effects for the promotion of this new learning.

3. Project design

3.1. The basic structure of the *Telekompetenz* model project

The *Telekompetenz* project had a duration of 12 months, oriented to the sequence of the seven networked training schemes for jobseekers conducted within the framework of the overall project. This aim of this measure was to formulate objectives and contents which, on the one hand, created various possibilities of using IT applications and which, on the other, were geared to local skill requirements and human resource potential.

Seven educational establishments and six labour offices in Saxony-Anhalt participated in the project. The training measures were characterised by a new and innovative structure which was based on the principles of *'work-process-integrated learning'* ([2]) or *'work-process-oriented continuing training'* (cf. Rohs, 2002). A decisive component of this structure was the equally important share of classroom phases in the educational establishment and the in-company learning phases in the partner firms from the SME sector in the course of which the participants worked on one or more specific learning projects on the spot.

([2]) Cf. S.n. Perspektiven..., 2001.

Figure 1. **Basic structure of the training measures in the project**

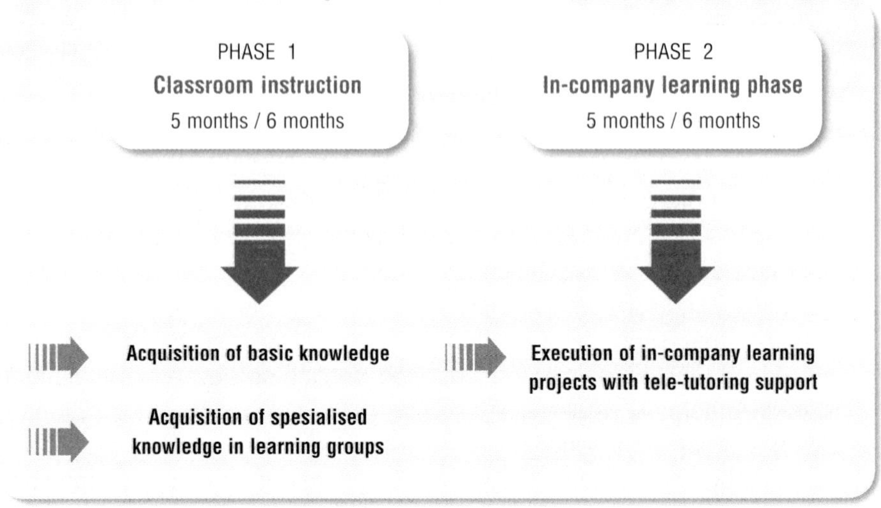

```
   PHASE 1                              PHASE 2
Classroom instruction              In-company learning phase
  5 months / 6 months                 5 months / 6 months
         ↓                                    ↓

▶ Acquisition of basic knowledge    ▶ Execution of in-company learning
                                       projects with tele-tutoring support
▶ Acquisition of spesialised
  knowledge in learning groups
```

In this form of work-process-integrated learning another decisive component proved to be indispensable: *tele-tutoring support* (cf. Freikamp, 2002) for the practical, project-related learning process in the firms. It was a novelty as, at present in the whole of Germany, tele-tutoring is used almost exclusively to support and guide learners only in the IT-assisted systematic acquisition of theoretical knowledge (cf. Hohenstein and Wilbers, 2002). But, IT-assisted support of the learner in the solution of practical problems in a company environment which, as a rule, places more diverse and much more complex demands on the tutor, is hardly practised.

Another important feature of the project was the *mutual networking of the participants*. In order to facilitate, coordinate and provide scientific backing for the networked implementation of the whole package of the innovative continuing training measures mentioned here, the *Telekompetenz* Project Office, funded by the federal state of Saxony-Anhalt and the European Union, was set up. It assists the regional educational establishments in the preparation, implementation and evaluation of the training measures.

3.1.1. *Role and design of classroom teaching*

The implementation of the *'work-process-integrated learning'* (cf. Bergleiter, 2002) principle not only implies that new and – in comparison to the conventional continuing vocational training measures – much higher demands are placed on the didactic and organisational set-up in the in-company learning phase. It also necessitates an integral approach to the overall design of the *entire* continuing training measure, an approach which, in advance, takes due account of both the general requirements and inherent contents of the training objective and the relevant contents and specific requirements of the in-company learning phase.

Given the high degree of complexity of the demands placed on the participants of the scheme, much attention had to be paid to the selection of suitable people (cf. Abicht and Bärwald, 2002). It was to be kept in mind that the motivation of the participants (cf. Zimbardo, 1992, p. 374 ff.) is crucial for the success of the entire measure including the tele-tutoring provided in the in-company learning phase. It was important to ensure that participants were prepared to adapt themselves flexibly to new elements. This also included a high level of readiness to develop autonomous activities to close gaps in knowledge. It was necessary for the participants to be aware of the fact that they could eventually create their own jobs in the companies or institutions in which they attended the in-company learning phase as part of the skilling measure. This meant that the teachers and tele-tutors/project managers required a great deal of didactic competence for the selection, motivation and preparation of participants for the in-company learning phase; they also needed the ability to effectively assess the individual starting conditions and the expectations of each participant.

When constituting the groups of participants for the training measures, it was seen as a rule that, even if the starting conditions in terms of the learners' formal qualifications were *relatively uniform*, the individual bias in terms of different competences, interests and aptitudes was highly varied. This applied for instance to different areas of knowledge and experience such as commercial, business and economic knowledge, and engineering and management know-how. But it also applied to different aptitudes e.g. with regard to technical/organisational and creative tasks. It was necessary to turn this into a productive element for the effective design of the measure and in particular for the contents of the learning projects. This meant that the teachers and tele-tutors had to consciously set up different interest groups from the total aggregate of participants, because it would be easier for these groups to identify themselves with the differing specific requirements of the individual project tasks and it would – keeping the requirements of the in-company learning phase in mind – facilitate the transmission of specific group-oriented and task-oriented knowledge.

The *classroom phase* of instruction, which was undertaken in the educational establishment, had to be designed in such a way that a certain degree of differentiation of knowledge acquisition was possible depending on the requirements to be expected from the learning projects in the companies.

Thus, the training process had to be designed as a homogeneous process for the transmission of basic knowledge, project-related knowledge and personalised special knowledge. Above all, the participants' starting level – especially in the area of EDP proficiency – had to be equalised taking their existing knowledge and skills into account. Together with the acquisition of basic knowledge as laid down in the training objective, it was intended – somewhat later – to impart differentiated project-related knowledge depending on the needs of the learning group. This was an important prerequisite so that the participants could, through the training measure, acquire the technical and methodological competence to execute the learning tasks in the enterprises and to continuously acquire further proficiency on their own. Thus, in addition to the trans-sectoral contents imparted to all participants, specialised knowledge had to be introduced step by step which could then be used as project-related input in contacts with the potential training firms. This meant that 'project groups' had to be formed. Their main function was to enable the participants to acquire the skills basically needed for action-oriented vocational competence in addition to technical and methodological competence. The specific features of the different sections of the classroom phase of the training are presented in the phase model for contents/methods design of the training measure.

Figure 2. **Phase model**
Model for the contents/methods design of knowledge transmission in training measures with tele-tutoring back-up in the company learning phase

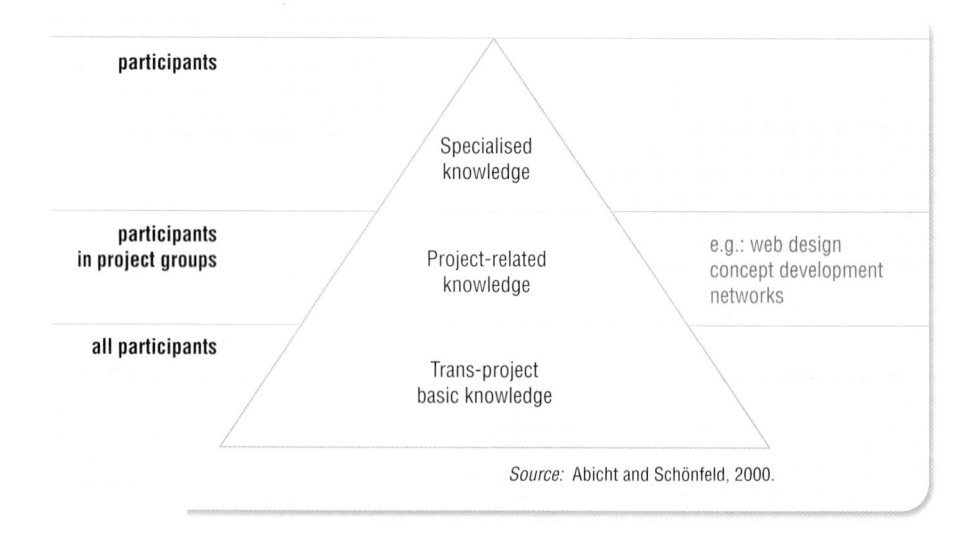

participants		
	Specialised knowledge	
participants in project groups	Project-related knowledge	e.g.: web design concept development networks
all participants	Trans-project basic knowledge	

Source: Abicht and Schönfeld, 2000.

In the different sections of the classroom phase the teachers not only had to cope with new requirements relating to the flexibility and differentiation of knowledge transmission, but also had to deal with specific requirements which emerged for the work of the project manager (who, as a rule, also assumed the tele-tutoring of the learners later).

3.1.2. *Role and design of the in-company learning phase*
The decisive requirements for the design of the in-company learning phase in the project arose from the decision to design work-process-integrated learning as a process for the execution of an *in-company learning project.* In doing this, the designers drew on the experience and theoretical findings gained in the application of this project method as formulated by, among others, Kerres (1998). According to him a learning project is '... a practical project, as close as possible to life, in which the learner to a large extent is involved in the setting of objectives, the implementation and the assessment or evaluation. In other words, he does not train or exercise just one isolated manual skill but also cognitive (e.g. planning) skills, social/communicative competence (e.g. coordinating the segmented tasks in the group) and affective competence (e.g. coping with setbacks). It is the *holism* of the manufacturing process, e.g. making a product, and the *self-organisation* or *cooperative* coordination of the learning and working process which is important for the success of learning progress. However, the learning environment must also support these self-organised or group-organised learning activities.' (Kerres, 1998, p. 73 ff.)

The in-company *learning projects* implemented in *Telekompetenz* take the knowledge conveyed in the classroom phases and use it for a practical task set in the company (knowledge transfer). While executing the learning project the participant is forced to make practical use of his knowledge in the company context and to fill the knowledge gaps which emerge during this process either by himself or with the help of his tele-tutor. In this case the learning projects are not a simulation of possible practical problems and processes, but genuine events occurring in the daily work of the company; by doing this, the learning aspect does not lose its significance and the participant is not at a loss because of lack of experience or knowledge.

The desired quality of the in-company learning projects could only be achieved if they had already been prepared in detail by the project manager/tele-tutor during the classroom learning phase in the educational establishment. This preparation of learning projects which is an inherent part of the first phase of the training measure includes:

- early search for suitable companies and contractual agreements with them;
- definition of the learning projects with the components:
  - objective from the angle of the company;
  - learning objectives;
  - in-company instructors;
  - time plan for execution;
  - presentation of results; and
  - monitoring of results;
- identification of specialised knowledge which has to be imparted during the classroom phase to small groups;
- imparting this specialised knowledge;
- early establishment of contacts between the participant and the company, and precise definition of the learning project with the cooperation of the participant.

Already in the preparatory phase of in-company project work but in particular in the participants' learning phase in the work process, the staff of the company was involved in the learning process. This primarily applies to company instructors. The educational institutions and the tele-tutors included them from the beginning in the knowledge transfer process and they were given targeted information on the concrete possibilities and limitations of IT applications in the company. In particular, the IT specialist in the educational establishments helped them to assess what concrete benefits could be attained for the company through the targeted use of information and communication technologies.

3.2. Tele-tutoring support and back-up

The individual support and back-up given to the participants during the work-process-integrated learning phase by a *tele-tutor* (Freikamp, 2001) played a key role in the *Telekompetenz* project.

The tele-tutor had the job of guiding and monitoring the personalised learning process by combining computer technology and telephony. Thus, the tele-tutoring of the participants implied that the training firms had to have the required technical facilities (ISDN connection, etc.).

The tele-tutoring was also to ensure that all participants would be integrated equally in the IT-assisted communication process and would assimilate the necessary working techniques. After all, these are a decisive feature of the 'added benefit' which job-seekers and companies obtain from training with tele-tutoring as compared to the classical forms of training.

Figure 3. **Central position of the Tele-tutor**
Support given to the participants in the in-company learning phase

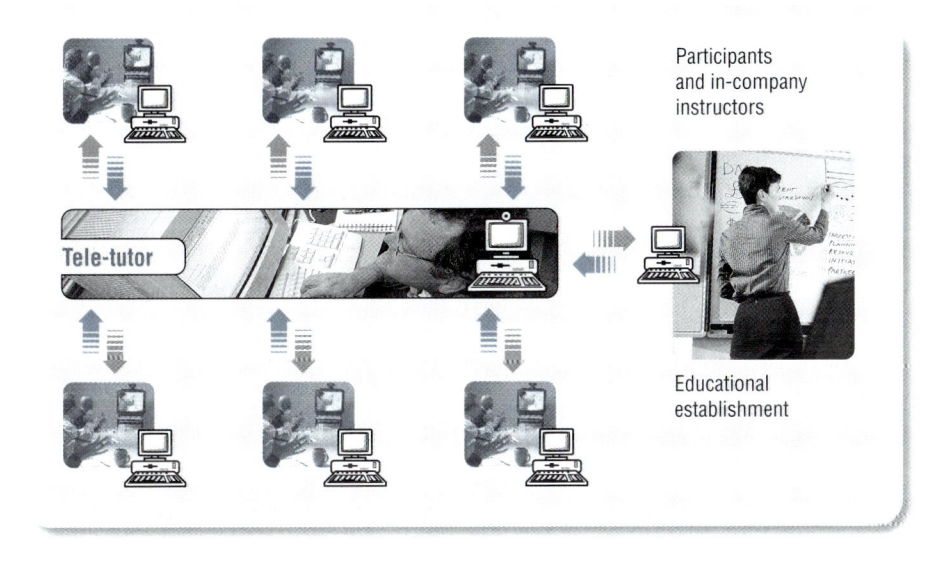

3.3. Networking the project partners with the inclusion of external experts

Given the innovative nature of the *Telekompetenz* project, the *interconnection* of all project partners in a learning-promoting network was indispensable. Only on this basis was it possible to create the essential preconditions which would enable all partners to fulfil all the requirements for the implementation of the skilling measure and make them skilled practitioners in the field of IT-assisted learning.

This requirement was the outcome of experience gained previously in other experiments with tele-tutoring as part of the work-process-integrated learning method. In the case of tele-tutoring for theoretical learning processes one could assume that the tele-tutor not only had the specific methodological competence but also the full range of technical competence for all the questions to be clarified, but in the case of in-company projects as a tool for work-process-integrated learning, this was no longer possible. Given the complexity and the wide range of questions requiring problem solving and the new problems arising in the practical process, more competent partners were needed whom the tele-tutor could approach for assistance and who would help him to give satisfactory information to the learners within a reasonable period of time. These partners were generally the specialised teachers in the educational establishment but also experts in specific technical fields who could be contracted to provide assistance when it was required.

4. The implementation of the *Telekompetenz* project

The following factors facilitated the successful implementation of the project and the creation of new jobs through the course participants themselves:
- The in-company learning phase of the project made it possible for the companies to at long last fulfil a wish they had had for many years but had not been able to undertake for lack of time and competence – namely, the introduction of certain IT applications (web presence, shop, Intranet solution, etc.). In this connection the lack of technical know-how was not the determining factor as an outside firm could have easily supplied this. What was crucial was the possibility of establishing what is possible and useful for this firm, what inputs would be required for such a solution, how the specific features of company business or production could be taken into account, what resources would be required to maintain the IT application, etc.
- The cooperation between the companies, participants and tele-tutors triggered the impulse to finally tackle the long-overdue necessity of updating the organisation of the production of goods and services in association with the introduction of IT applications.
- The available engineering, commercial and administrative skills and the new knowledge acquired by the participants in the course, enabled the expansion and intensification of marketing activities, the improvement of customer services and/or an extension of the goods and services produced by the company.
- The in-company learning phase enabled the firm to undertake an intensive examination of the suitability of the participant for work in this specific company and to test how far he was able to open up and manage new and useful fields of activity for the company.

Finally, the implementation of preceding measures such as those to establish suitability (cf. Dubiel and Schubert, 2002) was of considerable importance for the success of the skilling measure. This confirmed that the teaching of core competences including social competence is becoming increasingly important for subsequent higher-grade continuing training and skill training, especially against the background of a small-scale industrial structure.

4.1. Didactics and organisation of the courses

Vocational qualifications of the participants
As already mentioned, the previous qualifications possessed by the participants were a decisive factor for the success of the courses and were the basic pre-requisite for the participant's chance to re-enter the job market.

The fact that, even with relatively uniform pre-conditions in terms of formal qualifications, highly diverse combinations of different skills, interests and aptitudes still existed, confronted the teachers with a dual challenge. They had to take care that the existing differences did not develop into major obstacles for the progress of learning. This meant that the starting conditions for the participants had to be equalised through forerunning measures and at the start of the training course.

What was also important was that the potential participants had to have completed basic vocational training in a specific occupational field and also had to have practical work experience in a more or less complex sector.

Key qualifications and the motivation of the participants
As the *Telekompetenz* project was oriented to work-process-integrated learning, cardinal importance had to be attached to key qualifications such as self-organisation, communication skills and capacity for team work, thinking in terms of networks, etc. The participants selected for this project had already acquired these skills to a large extent.

What was also decisive for the success of the measure including the in-company learning phase with tele-tutoring was the motivation of the participants (cf. Weßling-Lünnemann, 1985). This factor was therefore one of the central criteria for selection of the participants. During the training course the experience made in previous ICT skilling measures was confirmed, namely, that participants with a high level of motivation are able to achieve above-average learning outcomes even if some gaps exist in their previous formal qualifications.

4.1.1. Canvassing partner firms for the in-company learning phase

Factors for the selection of partner firms:
Another essential factor for the success of efforts to place the participants in a working relationship in general and to create new jobs in particular, was the careful selection of partner firms. With due consideration of factors specific to the region, the firms and institutions selected for the learning projects with tele-tutoring support were assessed on the following grounds:

- whether they were, within the scope of their possibilities, willing in principle to offer permanent employment to the participants after completion of the skilling measure, provided the participant had the personal aptitude for the envisaged workplace; and
- whether the management of the company in question was basically interested in making use of IT applications to perform company tasks.

Apart from the basic willingness of the companies to meet these requirements, the following criteria were also to be considered when selecting the partner firms:
- a realistic assessment of the current or foreseeable need for IT-assisted production of goods and services;
- existing ICT potential and possible fields for the use of IT applications (e.g. PC work stations, ISDN, network facilities, access to Internet, remote data transmission);
- a minimum size of the enterprise which would ensure that it could provide the necessary personnel, technical and organisational resources for the implementation of the in-company learning phase including tele-tutoring and ensure that it ran smoothly.

As it was foreseeable that the learning projects would often have a strong impact on the internal operations of the company or would affect its external image, an essential pre-condition for successful project work was the involvement of a contact partner in the company with sufficient authority to take the necessary decisions.

The role of getting to know the company and the selection of learning projects in the classroom phase

The timely acquisition of partner firms facilitated cooperation with them. Difficulties often arose when it was necessary to define learning projects which met both the needs of the learner and the requirements of the company and which, at the same time, included the possibility of introducing new application forms of information and communication technologies to create new permanent jobs in the firm. Experience from the *Telekompetenz* project confirmed that the partner firms needed assistance from the educational establishments – all the more if they had had little contact with modern IC technologies up to then. This assistance consisted of:
- appraising what concrete advantages could emerge for the company from the use of information and communication technologies;
- defining promising learning projects in line with the specific features of the company;
- determining the demands the companies/institutions would place on the personality and performance potential of the participant;

- creating the technical and organisational pre-requisites for the use of IC applications in the firm.

4.1.2. *Differentiated teaching*

Differentiated teaching was a key function for the efficient design of the measure (see Figure 2), in particular for the contents of the learning projects used for work-process-integrated learning. The teachers and tele-tutors had the task of putting the participants in various interest groups corresponding to the specific requirements of the individual project tasks and giving them the specific group-oriented and task-oriented knowledge they would need to cope with the requirements of the in-company learning phase. This meant that all the teaching staff had to have the necessary didactic/methodological competence and a strong commitment to the project. Various features of the successful execution of these tasks were taken as examples of best practice and disseminated to all project partners. These examples contained features such as flexible reaction and adaptation to skill requirements which were not immediately apparent or whose dimensions were not foreseeable when the curricula were being drawn up.

If self-directed learning is to be effectively integrated in the overall project, some thought has to be given to it in advance. How should the teaching material be structured so that the learners can, if necessary, first learn how to set about exercising self-directed learning? The selection itself of the learning material for each module can be taken as the structure for the personalised learning approach. But this material is not pre-structured in the narrow sense of the term, it can only be re-arranged according to individual needs. But approaches which are oriented more to cooperative learning mainly depend on social contacts in the learning process, so that pre-structured tasks hardly play any role. Even the learning objectives sometimes remain open. In the case of tele-learning it will be increasingly important to combine these two approaches: i.e. combine the structured learning objectives, the tasks and the individual and time-flexible model of self-directed learning with the social exchange, the communication between the learners and the common application of what has been learned in practice. This calls for an explorative learning environment which permits the processes of self-initiated autonomous learning.

The feedback from the participating educational establishments and the Labour Offices at the end of the project showed that the differentiated teaching of participants and the approaches for personalised learning were the right methods for a differentiated vocational qualification geared to the needs of the economy and the labour market.

4.1.3. Project work in the in-company learning phase as a form of work-process-integrated learning

In the *Telekompetenz* model project an attempt was made to integrate the findings gained from the broad implementation the 'work-process-integrated learning' method in publicly funded skilling measures. Traditional training measures are increasingly confronted with the problem that, even if additional training is given after completion of the measure, the skills they taught no longer correspond to the rapidly changing needs of the labour market. The measures undertaken within the context of *Telekompetenz* were geared to the needs of companies primarily seeking people who were able to enlarge the basic theoretical knowledge they had acquired in their field in such a way that they could perform their tasks flexibly just-in-time and on-demand and could also assimilate new contents. This meant the enhancement and enlargement of skills which could be adapted rapidly to altered conditions and changing requirements, which permitted a shift of what had been learned between different fields of activity and its innovative application in new problem situations.

Exploitation of the potential of work-process-integrated learning, the sustainability of what has been learned, learning which is geared to current needs and is up-to-date, and the immediate transfer of newly acquired knowledge to ongoing work processes, have all been achieved within the framework of the *Telekompetenz* model project. The participants had the opportunity, not only of applying, consolidating and exercising what they had learned in the course of a precisely defined project, but they were also able to enlarge the relevant knowledge they required in a targeted manner. While executing the learning project the learner transferred theory into practice with the assistance of the tele-tutor and sustainably consolidated the newly acquired knowledge, skills and competences. To achieve this, it was important to structure the project tasks, to devise possible solutions, to plan individual resources, to detect gaps in knowledge and to find means of acquiring new knowledge, in other words, to achieve learning outputs in a self-directed manner in the direct work process. While executing the learning project, difficulties and tricky questions arose for which a just-in-time solution had to be found. These new solutions were immediately integrated in the work process and stored as newly generated knowledge. This enabled a blending of the learning and working worlds to form a constantly expanding universe.

One indispensable pre-condition for the practicability of work-process-integrated learning was the capacity of the learner to participate actively in the learning process and to search creatively for problem solutions. For some of the participants this adjustment to an active role in the learning process in the course of the *Telekompetenz* project was an tremendous challenge. But, autonomous activity and commitment earned their rewards for the learners. Firstly, they found recognition within the company as competent, flexible, creative and committed people and received the corresponding feedback. Secondly, through their self-responsible actions, e.g. in the planning and control of the work process or in the planning of their own resources, the participants developed a new feeling of self-esteem and gained more confidence in their own abilities. The execution of a learning project with an outcome which they themselves had planned and designed proved to be immensely important as a means of strengthening the self-confidence and self-assurance of the participants of the *Telekompetenz* project.

The success of the outcome was proved by the placement of the participants in the primary labour market and in the considerable number of new jobs created by the participants themselves in the course of the project.

5. The results of the *'Telekompetenz I'* project

In the course of the *'Telekompetenz* I' project it was possible, through the intensive networked cooperation of various institutions, to provide approximately 140 unemployed people with skills geared to the needs of small and medium-sized enterprises. The regular contact between the learners, the in-company instructor, the tele-tutor of the project and the tele-tutors in the different educational institutions established an effective network for the creative design and implementation of continuing training. Through this possibility of immediate feedback between the learner and his guiding instructor and also between the latter and experts competent for the problem in question, it was possible to solve problems and fill knowledge gaps within an extremely short time. In this model project it was possible, through training activities, to create new jobs which would not have been generated without the efforts of the participants undergoing training in the companies (see Figure 4). The data for this figure was collected at the end of the evaluation. The participants of one educational establishment were at that time still in the training process so the placement figures could not be included. That is why the total universe presented here is reduced to 117. Furthermore, it should be mentioned that, in the case of a another educational establishment, staff problems arose at the crucial point of transition from the classroom phase in the educational establishment to the learning phase in the company. This had an adverse effect on the success of the work in the partner firm and made the success ratio of this educational institution fall far below the average, and this had a negative influence on the total figures.

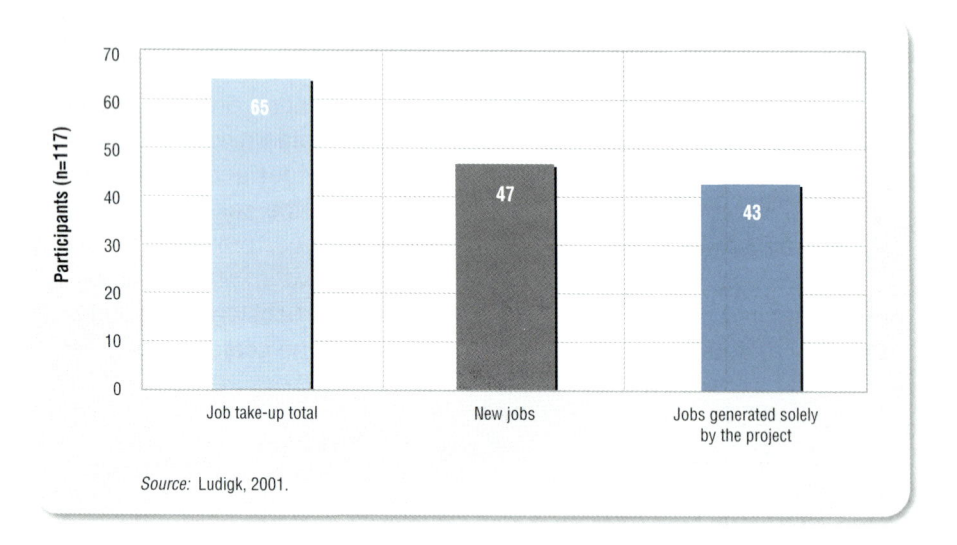

Figure 4. **Creation of jobs** (as of Nov. 2001)

[Bar chart showing Participants (n=117): Job take-up total = 65, New jobs = 47, Jobs generated solely by the project = 43]

Source: Ludigk, 2001.

6. Conclusions for the identification of skill requirements

As a whole, the evaluation of the 'learning by working' processes applied in the *Telekompetenz* project clearly showed that it is possible to generate new qualifications by initiating this approach of pro-active action in a formerly hazy area of activity (see Figure 5).

Important results are firstly, the training for dual qualifications and secondly, linkage of a basic qualification in the IT field with specific qualifications for application in an enterprise. Dual qualifications are generated through the combination with the commercial or technical knowledge which the participants had acquired in their earlier careers. The information provided by the company representative on the reasons for recruiting the person concerned shows what an important role this dual qualification plays.

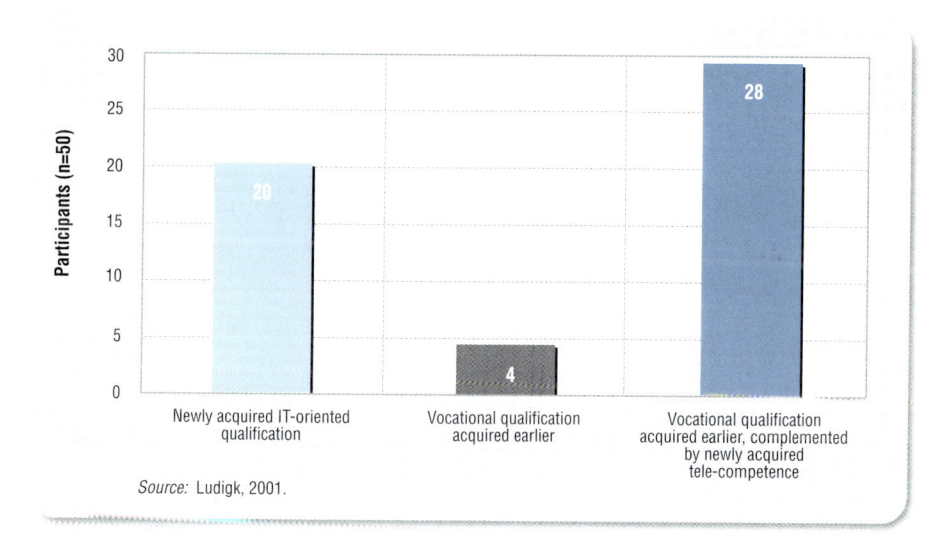

Figure 5. Decisive qualification for the hiring of the participants

Newly acquired IT-oriented qualification	Vocational qualification acquired earlier	Vocational qualification acquired earlier, complemented by newly acquired tele-competence
20	4	28

Participants (n=50)

Source: Ludigk, 2001.

Fields of activity for women

The results of the model project show that this form of skilling seems to be particularly suitable to offer women the opportunity of re-orienting their vocational careers to activities in the field of modern information and communication technologies. The practical skills taught in the skilling measure in modern methods of electronic data transmission and e-learning proved to be particularly helpful for women who, because of family commitments, were compelled to stay at home, for instance during parental leave, but who could quite easily find time for self-directed learning or tele-work, so as not to lose their contact with developments in their professional fields. What is more, these skills offer more opportunities for continuing vocational training or re-training, particularly in structurally weak regions where, without these options, an occupational activity would entail decisive changes in conditions affecting their personal lives. These include ownership of property (house or property) which, as participants said, offered material security for their future lives but tied them to their locality. In particular, participants from structurally weak regions – and a majority of the women – who spoke about their career developments said that they felt strongly bound by such factors.

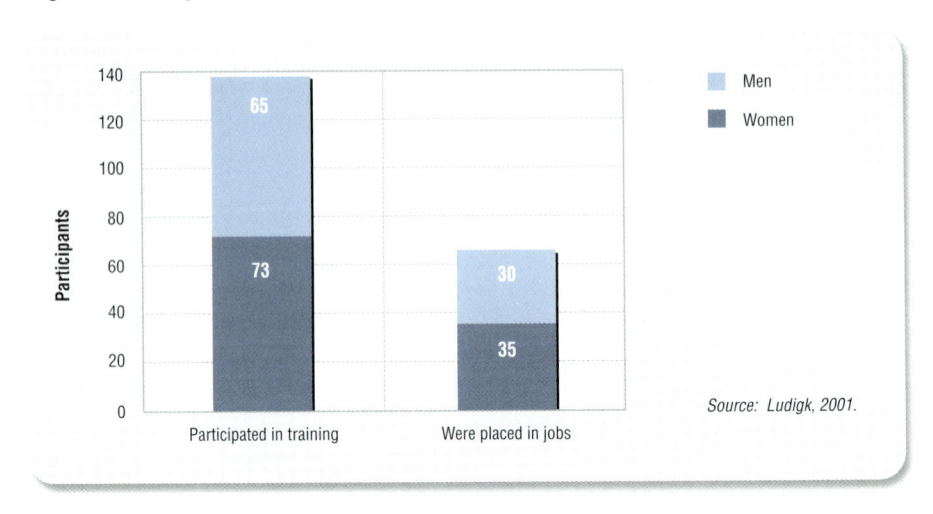

Figure 6. **Proportion of women in job placements** (as of Nov. 2001)

[Bar chart: Participated in training — Men 65, Women 73; Were placed in jobs — Men 30, Women 35. Source: Ludigk, 2001.]

Orientation of specialisation of IT knowledge
As indicated above, the contents of more extensive learning in the work process were at first derived from the coordination of the interests of the learners, the partner firms and the educational establishments. To achieve the practical relevance for the firm the intention was to coordinate the basic knowledge already possessed by the learner with the remaining training needs to be imparted by the educational establishment, and this was to be formulated in one or more learning projects. An overview of this process shows that the learning projects derived from this method were structured as follows:
1. introduction of modern information and communication technologies and their adaptation to company requirements;
2. presentation of the company and marketing with the use of IT applications;
3. direct utilisation of IT applications for sales through the installation of e-commerce applications and establishment of e-shops and suitable order-placing, sales and payment channels;
4. other application fields of modern information and communication media such as e-learning, information research, mobile computing.

To a certain extent these fields contain packages of combined skills, but it was not possible to determine at this point whether these would lead to further continuing training requirements in the future. The ongoing surveys now being conducted in the Telekompetenz II project will provide further information on this.

7. Final remarks

Through the innovative design of the training measures and their environment it has been possible, through pro-active action, to discover and not merely forecast a future (make SMEs aware of their latent needs).

In the course of this measure it was possible to verify the hypothetical theses through practical action.

Unemployed people were given targeted training for the application of modern information and communication technologies. The implementation of continuing training in the form of work-process-integrated learning led to a situation where the employees of the companies were directly integrated in the process of generating these modern IT applications. This in turn promoted the acceptance of IT applications. The production of these services in the direct working environment ensured that the company ordering these services had a direct influence on the end product. It also ensured that the product corresponded to the needs of the company and that the qualification of the learner was directly influenced by the company. In addition, the progress of work was directly visible and this facilitated the monitoring and evaluation of outcomes and enhanced the motivation of the learners. The company was in a position to get a clear idea of the competences of a potential employee.

In our opinion it is possible to transpose this method of pro-active creation of new skills can be considered if:
- there is a hazy situation with indistinct description of needs;
- the possibility exists of formulating a learning project;
- specialised skills are shaped through learning in the work process;
- participants' activities in the acquisition of these skills include the processing of further information and knowledge, i.e. they are trained as 'knowledge workers'.

Bibliography

Abicht, L.; Baldin, K.-M.; Bärwald, H.; Greim, R.; Schamel, E. *Ermittlung von Trendqualifikationen als Basis zur Früherkennung von Qualifikationsentwicklungen.* Vol. 1, 1999.

Abicht, L.; Bärwald, H. Trendqualifikationen in der IT- und Multimediabranche – Einstiegschancen auch für Erwerbslose. *BWP - Berufsbildung in Wissenschaft und Praxis*, 1/2002.

Abicht, L.; Schönfeld, P. Teletutoring in der betrieblichen Lernphase. Working material of the isw, 2000.

Bergleiter, S. *Didaktische Grundlagen des Lernens im Prozess der Arbeit.* Internal working paper of isw, 2002.

Dubiel, G.; Schubert, F. *Eignungsfeststellungen – handlungsorientiert.* Internal working paper of isw,, 2002.

Freikamp, H. Teletutoring - eine neue Generation medialen Lernens. *Europabrief* No 7, May 2001.

Freikamp, H. Neue Qualifikationen für das Teletutoring. *FreQuenz Newsletter*, 1/2002.

Hohenstein, A.; Wilbers, K.W. *Handbuch E-Learning – Expertenwissen aus Wissenschaft und Praxis.* Cologne, 2002.

Kerres, M.. *Multimediale und telemediale Lernumgebungen: Konzeption und Entwicklung.* Munich; Vienna; Oldenbourg, 1998.

Lüdigk, R. *Abschlussbericht zum Modellprojekt Telekompetenz.* Münster, New York, Munich, Berlin, 2001.

Rohs, M., ed. Arbeitsprozessintegrierte Weiterbildung in der IT-Branche. *In Arbeitsprozessintegriertes Lernen – Neue Ansätze für die berufliche Bildung.*, Münster; New York; Munich; Berlin, 2002.

S.n. Perspektiven für das Lernen in der Arbeit. *Kompetenzentwicklung*, Münster, New York, Munich, Berlin, 2001.

Weßling-Lünnemann, G. *Motivationsförderung im Unterricht.* Motivationsforschung Vol. 10, Göttingen, 1985.

Zimbardo, P. G. *Psychologie.* 5.ed., Berlin, Heidelberg, New York, 1992.

PART IV
Initiatives at regional level and in countries in transition

This Part presents several initiatives to early identify skill trends and requirements at regional level. Special attention is paid to activities in central and eastern European countries which have to cope with difficult problems in the process of transformation. The contributions illustrate that systems for the early identification of skill requirements display specific characteristics. Their design and method of implementation must therefore take into account the features of the region, sector and country in question.

Articles in Part IV

Ferran Mañé, Josep Oliver (E)
A note on the evolution of labour supply in Spain and its implications at regional level

Olga Strietska-Ilina (CZ)
Qualitative versus quantitative methods of anticipating skill needs: perspective of a country in transition

Pal Tamas (HU)
Skill markets in a learning society: transformation and vocational reforms in Hungary

Lewis Kerr (ETF/I)
A demand-side analysis of SME skills needs in regions of five candidate countries

A note on the evolution of labour supply in Spain and its implications at regional level [1]

Ferran Mañé, Rovira i Virgili University;
Josep Oliver, Autonomous University of Barcelona, Spain

A fast pace of technological change and unstoppable globalisation are creating a competitive environment where firms must come up with new products and produce them efficiently. These changes are decisively affecting the skills the workforce must bring to the labour market. Most research concludes workers have to upgrade their qualifications to command high wages or avoid unemployment. Alternatively, some research is pointing to potential problems of overeducation. The argument is the supply of workers with high skill levels is outpacing demand for such workers. The outcome is we find workers in jobs where a lower education or experience would be enough. Although debate on the potential mismatches between supply and demand for labour is not new, there is an important issue that may change its focus, namely the demographic transition experienced in most western economies. We see youth cohorts growing much smaller, females, especially older females, more attached to the labour market and an increasing role played by immigration. As a result, there will be high levels of uncertainty in the labour market, which means improving information on what the labour market will look like in the future becomes a key issue. Policy-makers, employers and families will need this information to prepare their strategies for dealing with all these changes successfully. This paper discusses the characteristics of this demographic transition in Spain, and presents the results of two forecasts, one for Spain as a whole and one for a part of it (the Catalan region). Comparing both analyses, it is clear there are severe imbalances on evolving regional labour markets, which call for policies at regional level.

---

[1] For a detailed analysis see Mañé and Oliver, 2001a, 2001b, 2002.

1. Labour force supply

Supply of labour has two dimensions: the first is the number of people available to develop working activities and depends on the relationship between inflows (how many people will enter the labour market in the near future) and outflows (how many people will retire). The second, more in qualitative terms, concerns the basic level of education potential new workers will bring onto the labour market. Both dimensions are obviously related as the educational level of those entering the labour market can be different from those who leave it.

1.1. Demographic evolution in Spain

During the past two decades, one of the most prominent social phenomena has been the increase in ageing of western societies. Coupled with a low level of mortality the main reason for this has been decline of the fertility rate. In Spain, this trend has been especially marked. Spain has gone from the highest fertility rate of OECD (except for Ireland) in 1977 (three births per woman) to the lowest in 1999 (1.1 births per woman) [2].

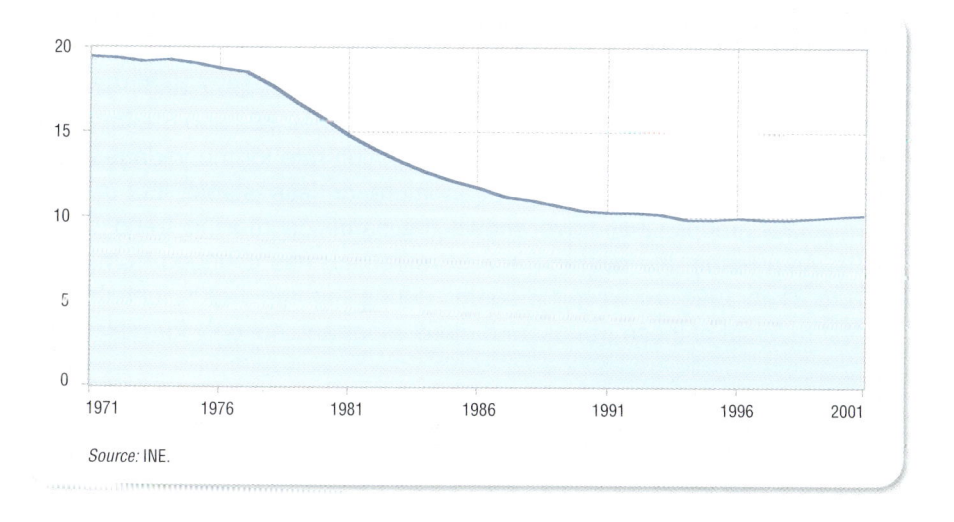

Figure 1. **Birth rates in Spain, 1971-2001** (Life births per 1 000 inhabitants)

Source: INE.

---

[2] There was a severe and continuous decline between 1976 and 1989, following some stabilisation from this moment. In fact, there is a current trend for the fertility rate to increase slowly. For basic data and comments on the economic implications for the demographic change in Spain, see Ahn (1998a).

In brief, in the late 1980s, the number of Spanish youth turning 16 years old was near 650 000 per year. This figure had gone down by the late 1990s to 450 000 per year. What could explain this dramatic decline in the fertility rate? Traditionally, it has been attributed to increasing rates of female labour force participation which postpones marriage and childbearing. Indeed, women have shown an increasing attachment to the labour market, moving from an activity rate below 30% in 1977 to slightly over 42% in 2001 among working-age females, and much more rapidly among younger women (for example, from 30% to 70% among those aged 25 to 34). However, as Ahn and Mira (1998a) defend, some other aspects may play a more important role. [3] These authors suggest that high youth unemployment and a rising proportion of temporary contract holders have brought enormous uncertainty on future careers and income as well as lower current income for many individuals and households. [4]

Without doubt, we have experienced a baby-burst. Besides, the situation will clearly not get better, but worse, even if members of these small cohorts change their family model towards one with more children. This dramatic decrease in the flow onto the labour market is combined with an opposite pattern from the outflow caused by retirement. Apart from a pure demographic reason (people reaching over 65 years old) [5], this increase in the number of people moving out of the labour market reflects a trend towards earlier retirement. Ahn and Mira (2000) report the decline in participation rates was substantial during the late 1970s and most of the 1980s for all male age groups over 50 years. Between 1977 and 1987 the participation rate declined about 20% for those in their 60s and 8% for those in their 50s. Since the late 1980s the participation rate for the youngest (50-54) and the oldest (65-69) has been more or less stable, but not for intermediate groups, that have shown the same decreasing trend of the 1980s. As a result, the average age of retirement has changed from 65 in 1970 to 61 in 1995. However, it seems during the late 1990s there was a modest reversal of these trends, and more important, not only for males, but

---

[3] They depart from some empirical evidence suggesting the negative relationship between fertility rates and female labour market participation does not hold any more. On the contrary, this relationship has become positive since the late 1980s in several OECD countries (Ahn and Mira, 1998b).

[4] In the mid-1990s, 45% of 29-year old males were still living in their parental home; in addition, the most dramatic decline in the fertility rate was among those aged 20-29 (in the last two decades has dropped by 70%). Note that unemployment has affected the youth population more than average.

[5] In fact, in Spain the 'baby-boom' generation is relatively younger than in other countries, which means the elderly population will grow more slowly. Note that we have moved from the largest generation ever in our country to a very small one in just a few years.

also for females (whose participation rate had hardly changed during the past two decades).

As stated before, the presence of retirement policies that encourage exit from the labour market have played an important role in explaining these trends (Alba, 1997; Blanco, 2000). Although use of these schemes during the 1980s was a way to help the restructuring of declining sectors or as a substitute for unemployment subsidies in depressed regions, this is no longer the case. In fact, early retirement has been used lately (especially in large firms) to substitute old workers with outdated skills by younger workers with more fitting qualifications. For several reasons, including the demographic trends just described (note in 1981 the net inflow to the labour market was nearly 370 000, decreasing to 276 000 in 1991 and only an expected 60 000 in 2001), we will have to substitute this policy for others focused on retraining these people.

Another topic to consider is the increasing number of foreign born residents because of immigration flows. In 1991, there were around 360 000 'official' immigrants. By 2000, this figure almost tripled. Official data also tell us they currently represent about 2% of the occupied population. But this number is clearly underestimated. First, we have a potential large number of illegal immigrants who, by definition, are not included in official statistics. In addition, there is a group running small stores and working as peddlers, which are difficult to include in some statistics. This inflow of mostly young males may change the demographic trend in future years, mainly because there is a political commitment to allow family reunification. As foreign-born females (especially Africans) show higher fertility rates than Spanish females, there could be a boost in the average number of children by family.

The stock of human capital in Spain

Without doubt, Spain has made a tremendous effort over the past years to improve the educational level of its youth. In fact, over the past 25 years, the Spanish educational system has experienced the fastest growth of all OECD countries. We can now say almost everybody stays in education up to 15 years old, while in 1975 fewer than half of 15-year olds were enrolled in high school.

There has also been an important evolution of the enrolment rate in non-compulsory secondary education. We have moved from a net enrolment rate of 40% for 17-year olds in 1975 to almost 79% in 1999. Although this change is impressive, we still have a low level of enrolment compared to other OECD countries. For instance, in 1999, countries like Belgium, Finland, France, Germany, Japan, the Netherlands and Sweden had net enrolment rates of over 90% for this group of 17-year olds.

Table 1. **Net enrolment rates in public and private institutions 1999; selected OECD countries**

	age 15	age 16	age 17	age 18	age 19	age 20
Austria	95	92	87	67	40	29
Belgium	100	98	96	85	74	63
Denmark	97	93	82	76	58	40
Finland	100	94	96	85	46	47
France	97	95	91	80	68	54
Germany	98	97	93	85	67	48
Greece	93	92	65	68	na	62
Ireland	96	92	81	74	49	42
Italy	88	79	73	69	47	35
Japan	99	95	94	na	na	na
Netherlands	102	107	95	80	55	57
Portugal	92	83	84	66	54	41
Spain	95	85	79	66	66	56
Sweden	97	97	97	95	46	46
United Kingdom	103	84	73	53	49	47
United States	107	88	82	63	50	38

Source: OECD. Education at a glance, 2001.

We also have a problem with vocational education. The number of students has consistently decreased since the early 1990s. This is worrying because we have a much lower number of youth enrolled in vocational education than most other countries. An important feature of our educational system is its bias towards the academic track. In 1999, 70% of all students enrolled in upper-secondary education were pursuing an academic curricula, in sharp contrast with Scandinavia and Germany, where it is normal to have around 60% of students enrolled in vocational secondary education. Nevertheless, more young adults already working or with some working experience are enrolling in vocational education to obtain further education. In fact, if this trend continues, it could make up for the reduction of youths directly entering the system from compulsory secondary level.

In sharp contrast, the number of people attending university has increased greatly, from 652 549 students (in 31 universities) in 1980 to 1 581 415 (in 62 universities) in 1999. If we look at gross enrolment rates, we can clearly see this increase: for 18 to 24 year olds, in 1990 this rate was 23%, while in 1999 it climbed to 32%. In clear contrast to the comments made about smaller enrolment in upper-secondary education, these rates are among the highest in the world.

Finally, the last issue worth noting is the distribution between short- and long-cycle studies. During the 1990s we observed an increase in the percentage of total students enrolled in short cycles, representing 40% in 1999. It is difficult to set a 'goal-to-achieve-figure', but we can interpret this increase in the number of people choosing short cycles in two ways. On the one hand, it may easily reflect, as the number of students increases, the 'quality' of the average student decreases, and they go for an easier pathway to get a university degree. On the other, these studies could have become a 'substitute' for a devalued vocational education. As already stated, vocational secondary education has a low level of consideration, and, until recently, we lacked a tertiary system of professional studies. [6]

2. Comparing the evolution of the Spanish and Catalan labour markets

The goal of this second part of the paper is to compare briefly the evolution of the Spanish and Catalan labour markets up to 2010. The main result is we can see severe labour shortages in Catalonia, but a more balanced situation for the whole of Spain. This means that in other regions, there must be high levels of labour surpluses. Before turning our attention to the results of both forecasts, we introduce a note on the methodology used in the two analyses.

2.1. The methodology used

The methodology used to calculate our projections is based on the *manpower requirement approach*. [7] In this approach, demand and supply forecasts are made independently and then compared. If supply does not match requirements (demand), labour market problems are predicted. Basic 'manpower' methodology is based on mechanistic methods of extrapolating past changes in economic structure and the composition of employment. Thus, the main flaw in this approach is its 'rigidity', as the trends of the past will continue in the future. Another key methodological flaw is this approach does

---

[6] Nevertheless, as noted before, this may be changing rapidly. In fact, over the past two years we have seen a decrease in the number of students pursuing a short university degree, which could reflect some students now prefer a more 'traditional' vocational education degree.

[7] See Van Eijs (1993) for a basic outline of this methodology.

not consider any feedback effects between demand and supply of labour.

On the *demand* side of our projections, we have followed what Fina et al. (2000) call a 'stage by stage procedure'. The first step is to forecast future economic growth (applying a macroeconomic model) and forecast employment growth from it, preferably at sector level. Unfortunately, such a model has not been developed to forecast employment growth breakdown at the level we need. Thus, we have calculated the average annual employment growth from 1985 to 2000. To divide this total employment growth among the different sectors of the economy, our hypothesis is it will follow a similar evolution (some industries losing and others gaining importance) to the one from 1994 to 2000. We compared the employment structure by industry in both years, and calculated the percentage change over the period considered. [8] This change was applied to the period 2000 to 2010.

Once the industry evolution is defined, the next step consists of calculating the occupational structure that comes out of it. To do so, we applied a method similar to the one just mentioned. We calculated the percentage change of the occupational structure by industry between 1994 and 2000 and applied this evolution to forecast future change.

The last step in forecasting labour demand between 2000 and 2010 consists of turning the changes in occupational structure into educational necessities. Again, we use the same technique and calculate the change in educational levels of employees by occupation and industry over the period 1994 to 2000 and we apply this evolution to forecast future change.

To make an accurate forecast of the future labour market situation, it is necessary to know the evolution of both demand and supply of the labour force.

The *supply* side has two dimensions: first, quantitative, which depends on demographic trends and individual decisions on labour force participation; second, qualitative, which reflects the human capital of the population.

On the first, the relevant population are already born because the projections are for 10 years. In a mechanistic way, we just moved up 10 years every population group divided by age and sex. [9]

It is more complex to calculate decisions on labour force participation, especially among females. To do so, we calculated the trends in labour force

---

[8] Some 'ad-hoc' restrictions are often imposed (for instance, some convergence to a specific structure observed in other countries) over the evolution of the sector structure of employment. The structure we end up having in 2010 seems in line with what we forecast, so we did not introduce any restrictions.

[9] Note that the main problem of our projection is we have not included adjustments for net migration or for mortality during working age.

participation by age and sex between 1992 and 2000 and we applied this evolution to forecast future change. It could be argued we should have used a longer period of time to capture trends in labour force participation correctly. Although, generally speaking, this is correct, in Spain we used to have a very low female activity rate. If we had used a longer period we would have overestimated the potential growth of female labour market participation. Using information from the early 1990s, once an important part of the work had been done, prevented us from making this mistake.

As stated before, we need to know not only how many people would be offering their services to the labour market, but also their level of education. Our hypothesis is that people over 25 years old in 2000 will not be acquiring more education, so they will keep the same level of education. Thus, only those below this age will change their human capital endowments. To project these changes we calculated the differences in educational attainment in the year 2000 for the groups of 26 and 36 years old. We applied the variation observed to incoming cohorts ([10]), checking that the projected increases in the quantity of people with every educational level considered were compatible with the number of people actually enrolled in every segment of the educational system.

2.2. Results

A summary of results appears in Table 2.

Results for the *Catalan* economy clearly show that with the current demographic structure, the Catalan population cannot supply, just by increasing their activity rate, the more than 420 000 new workers the economy will need. A major imbalance in the human capital demanded by firms and that supplied by individuals is also forecast. In conclusion, the Catalan economy will face severe problems in both labour shortages and skill gaps. To avoid these problems, we will have to increase labour force participation of our population, especially among women over 40. We will also need large flows of immigrants. In this way, we could solve the labour shortage problem, but we could create an even more important problem of skill gaps, unless we set up massive programmes of skill upgrading or, alternatively, we are able to attract highly-skilled immigrants.

The situation for *Spain* as a whole is different. The main conclusion from the projections until 2010 points to a balance between supply and demand of

---

([10]) It was not possible to use variations in educational attainment in two different points of time, because the classification methodology recently changed and the educational groups were not comparable.

Table 2. **Projection of labour force demand and supply by level of education 2010 in Catalonia and Spain**

	Demand	Supply total	NAIRU total	Supply net	Balance (5=1-4)	Deficit	Surplus
	1	2	3	4	5	6	7
CATALONIA 2010							
No education	103 183	178 237	12 319	165 918	62 735		62 735
Primary	1 176 652	1 381 113	63 188	1 317 925	141 273		141 273
Vocational training	567 078	482 571	14 476	468 095	-98 982	-98 982	
Upper-secondary	474 025	377 456	13 539	363 917	-110 108	-110 108	
Tertiary type-B	290 423	227 801	5 284	222 518	-67 905	-67 905	
Tertiary type-A and PhD	429 892	285 211	6 487	278 724	-151 168	-151 168	
Total	3 041 252	2 932 390	115 293	2 817 096	-224 156	-428 164	204 008
SPAIN 2010							
No education	790 555	329 086	11 717	317 369	-473 187	-473 187	
Primary	7 571 067	7 390 441	214 549	7 175 891	-395 176	-395 176	
Vocational training	2 850 529	3 725 055	222 932	3 502 123	651 593		651 593
Upper-secondary	2 180 103	2 428 243	130 079	2 298 163	118 060		118 060
Tertiary type-B	1 725 752	1 899 257	103 175	1 796 082	70 330		70 330
Tertiary type-A and PhD	2 375 383	2 424 288	172 741	2 251 547	-123 837	-123 837	
Total	17 493 389	18 196 370	855 193	17 341 175	-152 217	-992 200	839 983

Source: authors.

labour in the Spanish labour market over the next decade. High levels of unemployment may come to an end soon and no important skill mismatches are forecast.

It is clear Spain will have important regional tensions. The Spanish labour market is characterised by large regional imbalances. While female labour force participation is quite high and the number of immigrants is also high in some regions, in others the unemployment rate remains over 10% (coupled with low female labour market participation). As a result, the country will most likely need relevant improvements in the geographical location of either the labour force or productive capacity. Note that to move people from one part of Spain to another is difficult because of the important social and economic roles of family and social networks and different living costs (notably housing) in the Spanish regions. Policies are needed to deal with these problems.

One could argue that Spain has a long tradition (as other countries) in large national relocations of population (especially from the south to the north during the 1950s and 1960s), so it should not be problematic to go through a similar process. Regardless of personal costs most people bore, the main difference between former migration and what we may need in the future, is we will have to move females, not males. Males used to look for a job while their spouses stayed at home. This is no longer the case, because to make it economically viable to move a family to another region means finding two jobs, one for each adult member of the family (at least).

3. Policy implications for demographic transition in Spain

In these past 25 years, Spain has experienced several dramatic changes to the quantity and composition of labour supply which, most likely, will continue. Labour supply is shrinking because of the incoming cohorts. Two actions might counterbalance this trend. First, we could increase women's labour market participation. The problem is that females below 40 already have a high activity rate. It is over 40 where the rate is low. But this group is made up mainly of women with low levels of education, making it difficult for them to re-enter the labour market (although to some extent they are). The second action would be to defer males' retirement. Currently, more than 50% of 60 year-old males have already retired. They also have a low level of basic education, but in quantitative terms we should consider postponing their retirement, at least the more skilled. Obviously, another potential solution could be to increase the number of immigrants.

All these population groups (old men and women and immigrants) do not normally have high levels of education, which may create problems of skill gaps between the demand and supply of labour. Given this situation, the level of human capital incoming generations bring onto the labour market is important and as the number of youths decreases, it can become a dramatic problem. Spain must implement policies to ensure improving human capital does not get paralysed. ([11]) It is worrying that an important part of the youth population (under 35) only has primary or lower-secondary education. One could expect these people to receive much on-the-job training to make up for their low level of skills, but Spanish firms have not fully committed to this. Where they have, they have normally focused on their most skilled workers.

We would like to stress a final point on the unemployment rate. An

---

([11]) Even though Spain is doing a great job in improving the educational level of the population, it is none the less still true that the human capital level of the active population is one of the lowest among the most advanced OECD countries.

important cause of high unemployment rates (especially among young workers) in Spain during the past two decades was the massive entrance of baby-boom cohorts onto the labour market. This will completely reverse during the next two decades as the baby-bust cohorts enter the labour market. To some extent, the high number of unemployed has acted as a 'buffer' to avoid important skill mismatches, especially in the fast-growing service sectors. This may end soon, so firms will have to plan their human resource strategies much more carefully, and develop internal labour markets or engage much more intensively in training.

In brief, Spain can face either labour shortages or skill gaps. Where inflows to the labour market reduce, and the country is unable to increase the supply of workers it will most likely experience labour shortages. Skill gaps could also appear, but we believe they would be less important because in a labour market with excess demand, wages should increase more rapidly for high-skilled occupations, making people invest in human capital suitable for these occupations. Nevertheless, we do not rule out the possibility of simultaneous labour shortages and skill gaps. On the other hand, if Spain is able to attract more people to the labour market, their educational endowments and often their experience are low. This could easily produce skill gaps, unless, as stated before, wages increase for the most skilled occupations.

The last point to stress about policy implications is that the supply of labour will be very different across regions. Interregional mobility must be fostered by the correct set of policies, ranging from regional immigration to labour market and labour supply (both by helping women get onto the labour market and by ensuring a correct flow of educated youths) with special focus on regional characteristics.

Bibliography

Ahn, N.; Mira, P. *Job bust, baby bust: the Spanish case*. Working paper EEE12. FEDEA, Madrid, 1998a.

Ahn, N.; Mira, P. *A note on the changing relationship between fertility and female employment rates in developed countries*. Working paper EEE13. FEDEA, Madrid, 1998b.

Ahn, N.; Mira, P. *Labour force participation and retirement of Spanish older men: trends and prospects*. Working paper EEE 25. FEDEA, Madrid, 2000.

Alba-Ramírez, A. *Labour force participation and transitions of older workers in Spain*. Working paper 97-39. Carlos III University, Spain, 1997.

Blanco, A. *The decision of early retirement in Spain*. Working paper EEE76. FEDEA, Madrid, 2000.

Eijs, P. van. *The manpower requirements approach: background and methodology*. ROA-RM-1993/3E. Maastricht, 1993.

Fina, LL.; Toharia, L.; García, C.; Mañé, F. Cambio ocupacional y necesidades educativas de la economía española. *Formación y Empleo*, Sáez, F. (coord.). Fundación Argentaria, Madrid, 2000.

Mañé, F.; Alonso, J. Overview of the skill shortage problem in Spain. Report published in: European Commission. *The economic costs of the skill gap in the EU*. Tender Vc/2000/0196, coordinated by the Instituto per la Recerca Sociale, Milano, Italy, 2001a.

Mañé, F.; Oliver, J. *Mercat de Treball, Demografia i Sistema Educatiu a Catalunya a les Portes del S.XXI: Reptes i Oportunitats per a la Propera Dècada*. PIMEC-SEFES, Barcelona, 2001b.

Mañé, F.; Oliver, J. Forecasting educational necessities in Spain through 2010. In Schömann, K., ed. *Skill needs and the labour market*. Edward Elgar Publishing, UK, 2002 (forthcoming).

OECD. *Education at a glance*. OECD: Paris, 2001.

Qualitative versus quantitative methods of anticipating skill needs: perspective of a country in transition

Olga Strietska-Ilina, National Observatory of Employment and Training, Prague, Czech Republic

In a state of economic turmoil, transition countries face a challenge of how to identify future skill needs of the labour market. Insufficient data and short time series cause added difficulties. This paper considers the major advantages and disadvantages of different methodological approaches and their usefulness. Conventional macroeconomic forecasts produce valuable national results but are not yet reliable enough, or valid at regional level. Qualitative research at regional and sectoral levels provide necessary information on current skills required by companies but it lacks a longer-term perspective. Further, because of costs such research cannot be produced for each region and sector regularly and comprehensively. The Czech Republic in a transnational project 'Regular forecasting of skill needs' tried to integrate the two methodological mainstreams. The problems, challenges and future tasks that came into view as a result of this work are discussed in this paper. The follow-up work should end in establishing a system where different components can work complementarily and consistently together: regular macro level forecasts linked to qualitative information, periodical regional and sectoral surveys and analyses, and regular monitoring and analysis of emerging skills and occupational shortages.

1. Introduction

This paper presents some methodological issues and achievements in early identification of skill needs in the Czech Republic. These findings resulted mainly from a transnational project 'Regular forecasting of skill needs'. The paper therefore tackles the rationale, main idea, and some results for the Czech Republic. We shall first glimpse some advantages and disadvantages of different methodological approaches, and then we shall consider whether they can work complementarily, as illustrated in an example from pilot testing in the project. Finally, we shall tackle some problems arising and arrive at conclusions on research questions and future tasks.

2. Qualitative or quantitative methods?

Qualification needs analysis is an old topic in a new guise in many central and eastern European countries (CEECs) today. Under the old regime, central planning authorities were keen on drawing up rather detailed workforce plans for providing full employment. Planning in this area was a key issue in the overall exercise of meticulously planning demand in all aspects of the socialist economy. The methods employed were subordinated to this overall purpose. The results were used for changing manpower supply in line with demands of a centrally planned economy by regulating investment and available places in education and training in certain vocations and types of schools. Previous planning practices are widely associated with lack of democratic provision of training, and therefore remain unpopular till today.

After the fall of the communist regime these practices were totally abandoned and often institutions in charge of manpower planning were dissolved. For obvious reasons, the term 'planning' is not very popular in CEECs and the idea of forecasting labour market needs for qualifications and skills requires a heavy push (including lobbying and reasoning supported by scientific arguments) to prove that such measures are necessary. Sadly, not only decision-makers and civil servants often fail to see the point; academics are also often equally dismissive.

The transitional nature of the economy in the CEECs and global changes have ensured that forecasting is ever more challenging but at the same time ever more necessary. Slowly but surely countries in transition are developing various approaches to analysing future needs of the labour market.

Several years of ignorance in prognostic research have, however, created their own obstacles to development. Zecchini (1997) rightly noted that existing statistical services in CEECs are not prepared to measure facts not directly observable in all their detail. He further noted 'the tradition of precisely and meticulously quantifying facts related to the implementation of the central plan was suited to an era in which the economy was dominated by few large firms over which the government held strong control...' (p. 4). Under new circumstances, with a growing number of SMEs, self-employed and increasingly widespread flexible forms of employment, the statistical services are not prepared to measure economic trends in a longer-term development perspective. Comparable and reliable retrospective data with sufficiently lengthy time spans are simply not available. Companies in transitional turmoil are unable to foresee recruitment and redundancy in the nearest future.

Mere analysis of the current situation or a very short-term estimation of labour market needs is not enough for policy development in education which requires a perspective of at least four years of the educational cycle. Medium to long-term macro level forecasting has several weaknesses and gives only a partial answer. In the economic turmoil of a transitional economy many occupations become outdated, with some jobs disappearing or changing. Under these circumstances, information on the quality of the workforce needed is essential. To find an elegant methodological solution we decided to look at the experience of other countries in methods of analysis and anticipation of skill needs (see Strietska-Ilina and Munich, eds., 1999).

By quantitative methods we assume macroeconomic forecasts that identify medium to long-term labour market needs in numerical terms by occupation and qualification. By qualitative methods we understand various analytical approaches that try to anticipate both qualifications and skills needs, i.e. identifying not only numerical expression of demand but also providing qualitative information on the labour force required. Dividing methods into two methodological mainstreams - quantitative and qualitative – is only conventional. Such division has its own limits, as in fact both mainstreams employ elements of qualitative as well as quantitative methods.

Both quantitative analysis of manpower needs at macro level, and qualitative or semi-qualitative analysis of labour market needs (meso, micro, sectoral, etc.) have their own advantages and disadvantages. Medium- to long-term regular forecasting of manpower needs provides information on national employment trends which is useful for decision-makers, counselling services and individuals enabling them to choose their future career and type of study for the next four to five years. Producing the forecasts is not costly, once the method and all necessary data are available. Because of its 'futuristic' character, forecasting sounds attractive and exciting and plays a good informative role in raising public awareness of future trends. On the other hand, this is not the case in CEECs, where scepticism of forecasting and its added value prevails. Fear of forced planning of educational supply contradicts the nature of transformation to democratic principles in educational provision and in access to education and training. It is therefore important that all parties involved in forecasting have a common understanding of its objectives. It is not to ensure a perfect match between supply and demand (something hardly achievable anyway) but to provide information to those making their choice of education and career path.

As stated, macroeconomic forecasting cannot be performed in CEECs without a method adjusting to the economic turmoil and lack of data. Although quantified forecasts may be fairly detailed at national level, the reliability of results at regional level normally is questionable. Forecasting could be undertaken only for rather rough definitions of occupations and qualifications, which do not represent the actual picture of skills required. Also, forecasts can hardly consider newly emerging hybrid occupational profiles, whose share of the labour market increases with the greater involvement of modern information technologies in production and services. Conventional forecasts therefore lag behind the process of innovation, becoming hostages of revisions of classifications and systems of occupations and qualifications.

Analysis of labour market needs could be carried out by qualitative and semi-qualitative methods, performed at a sectoral or regional level. Although methods may and usually do require a questionnaire survey, contextual analysis, in-depth interviewing, focus groups, etc., the core principle is putting people from the demand and supply sides together with experts and other partners to discuss the results of surveys, verify available statistics, and validate occupational profiles. The highest added value of such an approach is not only in the result itself but also, and perhaps even more so, in discussions and attempts to develop common understanding and to achieve, if not a consensus at least a compromise. This approach is therefore more proactive than traditional manpower forecasting. In addition, anticipating labour market needs may bear 'soft' prognosis, developing scenarios rather than 'hard' linear quantified forecasts. We must, however, consider that such methods of anticipation also have several drawbacks. They are not pure scientific research, they stem from cooperation with social partners and industry experts, and therefore they deliver their opinion on where industry stands. Results may not be fully objective and final, and may be vulnerable to objective developments in the socio-economic or even cultural contexts.

Such analyses are always subject to the commitment of partners and experts involved. Methods used as a part of the overall anticipation exercise are often costly, are of one-off rather than regular character, and produce a forecast limited in its time perspective.

Finally, both qualitative forecasting and quantitative anticipation methods are based on current data or judgements and therefore build a view of future developments from the static perspective of today. They lack the dynamism of actual development, and perhaps only the scenarios approach may partially solve the problem. The qualitative approach of scenarios development is, however, subject to the limits of the human mind's ability to imagine the future while at the same time bound by determined criteria.

Table 1. **Quantitative vs. qualitative analyses: pros and cons**

Quantitative analyses (macro level)		Qualitative analyses (regional/local/sectoral)	
PROS	CONS	PROS	CONS
■ Results available at the level of economy ■ Medium to long-term forecast ■ Cost-efficient ■ Attractive because of its future-oriented nature ■ Raises public awareness ■ Objectiveness of data (neutral to subjective judgements) ■ Serves various target groups ■ Data may suit counselling and guidance nationwide ■ Regular character	■ Lack of reliable retrospective data in CEECs ■ Lack of macroeconomic forecast data in the Czech Republic ■ Sensitive to unstable contexts ■ Scepticism in transitional societies ■ Problematic reliability at more detailed level ■ Occupational forecast may be only roughly translated to qualifications, no qualitative information on skills ■ Brings to the forecast a view of the state of the art and past trends	■ Reliability at sectoral or regional level ■ Detailed information ■ Information on the quality of required labour force ■ Possibility to update occupational profiles ■ Scenarios and shared diagnoses facilitate shared commitments ■ Shared commitments facilitate implementation	■ Results are available for limited territories or industries ■ Limited target level and number of users ■ Indispensability of involvement of experts and practitioners from the relevant field; difficult to commit partners ■ Short- to medium-term perspective ■ Second-hand judgement; subjective ■ Costly ■ One-off actions, difficult to introduce regularity

Considering the pros and cons of quantitative forecasts and qualitative analyses (summed up in Table 1), we have asked ourselves whether we need to make a choice between the two mainstream methodologies. Each method appears imperfect and inadequate on its own but may serve well by providing valuable information to a more complex and integrated methodological system. This is how the project 'Regular forecasting of skill needs: comparative analysis, elaboration and application of methodology' (*LABOURatory*) was initiated. [1]

3. The project

The objective of the project was to suggest a mid-term (five-year) forecasting model for producing information on future national trends useful for decision-makers, guidance services and individuals. We were, however, aware that considering the lack and deficiency of data structures on education and employment, the results would not be valid at regional and industry levels. Therefore, the project team also tried to work out an anticipation mechanism for analyses at regional or sectoral levels.

The project brought together various expertise from the experience of partners in applying different types of methods. The outcomes are therefore the result of collaborative work between the two project mainstreams - one part of the partnership worked mainly on elaborating and improving quantitative forecasting models and another on qualitative analyses. The difficulty in introducing a joint approach and a common understanding among partners specialised in each of the methodological mainstreams speaks for itself. For decades analyses, although undergoing significant methodological developments, were worked out in parallel. Research institutions supplying the results of macroeconomic skill forecasts at national level worked separately, and with limited exchanges of methodological ideas, from institutions performing analyses of skill needs in specific sectors and regions. The former were linked to national policy-making, while the latter, by looking at micro level demand, were driven mostly by the need to provide specific

---

[1] The project was implemented with the support of the Leonardo da Vinci programme. It involved a trans-European partnership [Czech National Observatory of Employment and Training (project leader), the Czech Centre for Economic Research and Graduate Education at Charles University, the Dutch Research Centre for Education and the Labour Market, the Irish Economic and Social Research Institute, the Regional Employment and Training Observatory of Burgundy, the French private consultancy company Quaternaire, an interinstitutional research team in Poland, and the National Observatory and regional HRD Fund of Slovenia]. The project lasted for over two years (1998-2001).

information to schools and training organisations on the quality of the labour force required. The idea was as unique as was it simple: to link the two different approaches and research experiences and make them work together.

The results of the project could be seen as a testing stage which helped to identify methodological problems rather than introduced ready-made answers and solutions. We believe, however, this is already a big step forward. We shall now look at some successes and failures from the findings of the Czech project team.

3.1. Phase 1: The quantitative model

One of the suggested quantitative models in the Czech Republic is macroeconomic forecasting elaborated by the Centre for Economic Research and Graduate Education (CERGE) based on the Dutch model of the Research Centre for Education and the Labour Market (ROA). The Czech team faced many data limitations. Therefore the model is not yet fully functional or reliable. It requires further efforts in research and enrichment with data. The model compares the forecast of demand for labour by education or occupation with the projected supply of labour. The model is presented in Figure 1.

The model considers expansion demand, based on the macroeconomic projection of employment by industry, and replacement demand which captures the need to replace workers (e.g. due to retirement). Because of data limitations the forecast is only available for a maximum of 50 occupational clusters and 59 educational types (see Annex 1). The major drawback is the absence of a reliable macroeconomic forecast of employment by industry in the Czech Republic. These important data were therefore substituted by the available demand-side macromodel 'Hermin', which was not initially designed as a standard forecasting model. It is also not sufficiently detailed at industry level to supply reliable information on employment demand. Elaboration of a standard macroeconomic sectoral model is therefore an important task for the future.

The CERGE-model is mainly based on the labour force survey (LFS) and on the labour supply projection from statistical records on enrolments by education. Developing the model involved many efforts in matching different classification systems and clustering occupations to ensure data validity. [2] The model eventually predicts shortage by type of education (Annex 2, Figure 1A) and introduces two indicators: first, future labour market prospects

---

[2] Full information on the model and its methodology is available in Munich, D. et al. (2001).

Figure 1. **Czech Forecasting Model (ROA-CERGE)**

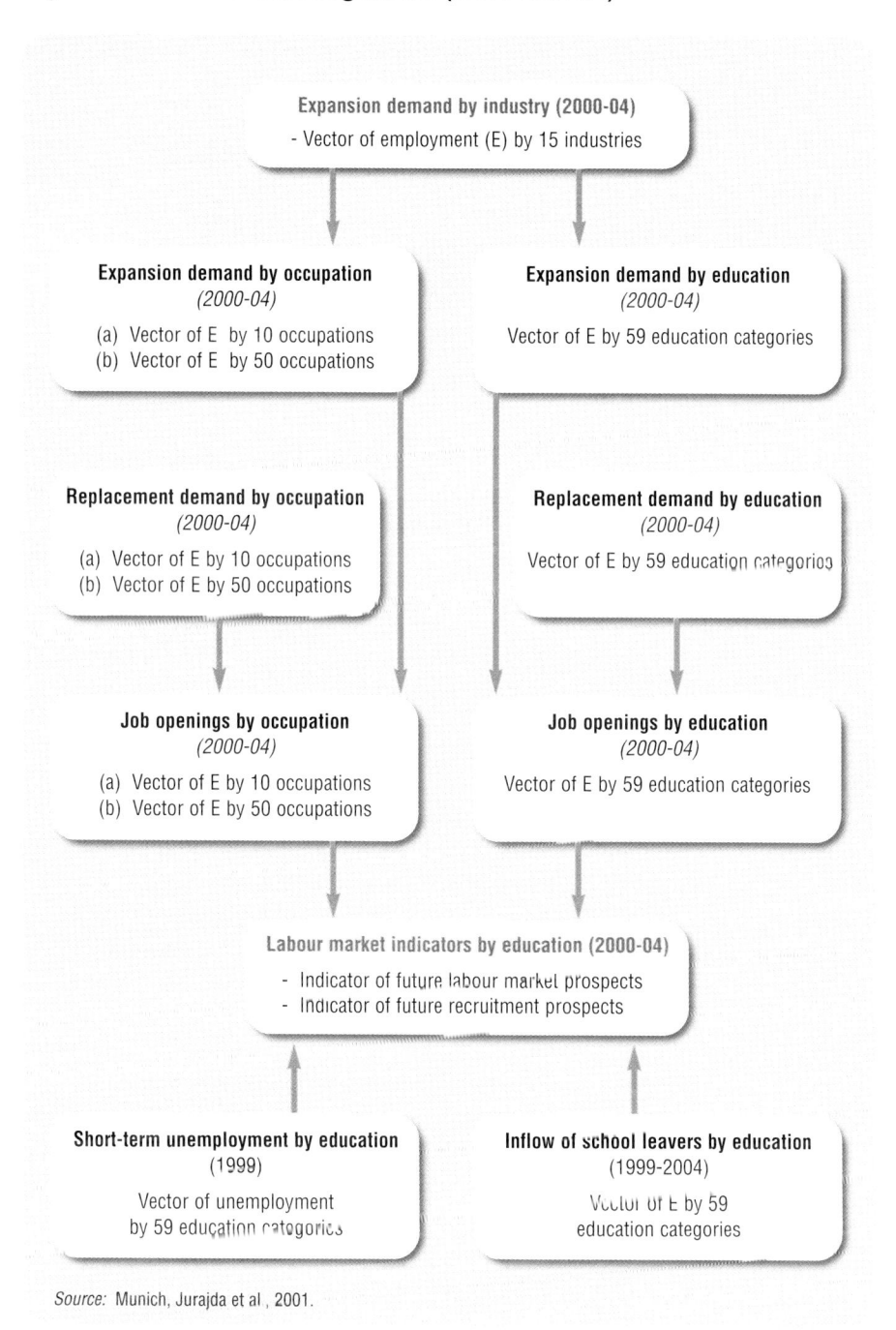

Expansion demand by industry (2000-04)
- Vector of employment (E) by 15 industries

Expansion demand by occupation
(2000-04)
(a) Vector of E by 10 occupations
(b) Vector of E by 50 occupations

Expansion demand by education
(2000-04)
Vector of E by 59 education categories

Replacement demand by occupation
(2000-04)
(a) Vector of E by 10 occupations
(b) Vector of E by 50 occupations

Replacement demand by education
(2000-04)
Vector of E by 59 education categories

Job openings by occupation
(2000-04)
(a) Vector of E by 10 occupations
(b) Vector of E by 50 occupations

Job openings by education
(2000-04)
Vector of E by 59 education categories

Labour market indicators by education (2000-04)
- Indicator of future labour market prospects
- Indicator of future recruitment prospects

Short-term unemployment by education
(1999)
Vector of unemployment by 59 education categories

Inflow of school leavers by education
(1999-2004)
Vector of E by 59 education categories

Source: Munich, Jurajda et al., 2001.

for those looking for jobs (Annex 2, Figure 2A), and second, future recruitment prospects for employers (Annex 2, Figure 3A).

Developing the model in a transition economy with huge restructuring and introducing technological innovation was a breakthrough in prognostic research. We have to consider, however, the fact the forecasting model relies on past data series whose pattern might be altered significantly under economic transition and qualitative changes on the labour market. Also the results of the forecast are too general. Because of the limited size of LFS, the model cannot be interpreted at regional level. This represents an important constraint: regional mobility of labour is low in the Czech Republic, and the national labour market therefore is to a certain extent composed of regional submarkets (Munich et al., 2001). That is why more regional qualitative analyses appear an important additional source of information.

3.2. Phase 2: The qualitative survey on tourism in a selected region

The pilot analysis of qualification and skill needs in tourism was held in one selected region in three countries (Czech Republic, France and Slovenia). The strikingly similar results for the three countries are briefly summarised in the Table 2 ([3]).

The Czech team employed rather a straightforward method:
- analysis of sectoral development at European, national and regional levels;
- analysis of policy plans and developments;
- socio-economic analysis of the region;
- company survey (24 face-to-face interviews with a qualitative questionnaire);
- several focus groups with experts from the region and firms;
- SWOT analysis;
- development of scenarios.

Pilot results of a macroeconomic forecast were used as one source of information. Thus, both quantitative and qualitative methods were applied as additional to each other (see below).

([3]) The synthesis and detailed results of the three surveys can be consulted in Strietska-Ilina, O. et al. (2001); Zelenka, J. et al. (2001); Giffard, A. and Guegnard, K. (2001); and Karnicnik, M. et al., (2001).

Table 2. **Required skills in the sector of tourism in selected regions**

Slovenia - Podravje region	Czech Republic - North West	France - Burgundy
German language **English language**	**Language knowledge**	**Language knowledge**
Social communication	Social communication Managing and working with people	
Food preparation *Food/desserts decoration*	Manual skills specific to the sector Broad professional base Technical skills Specific professional knowledge	**Hygiene, food security** *Conservation techniques, lighter cuisine, more diversified food*
IT skills	IT skills	**IT skills**
Designing travel arrangements	Strategic planning Creativity	
Commercial skills Selling travel arrangements Marketing	**Financial skills** Sales skills **Marketing**	Sales skills
Expertise in wine		
Management skills	*Management skills*	

Note: This table sums up the required skills as mentioned by companies during the survey. **The shaded** sections indicate those most needed, the skills *in italics* are those mentioned by some, and the skills in normal characters are rarely mentioned.

3.3. Phase 3: Integration and some results

The qualitative sectoral analysis included confrontation with major trends displayed in the quantitative forecasting model. During this phase, we discovered several drawbacks in the quantitative macro level forecasts, which we will consider in our follow-up work. Thus, the two methods present a complex methodological cycle (Figure 2).

Figure 2. **Methodological cycle**

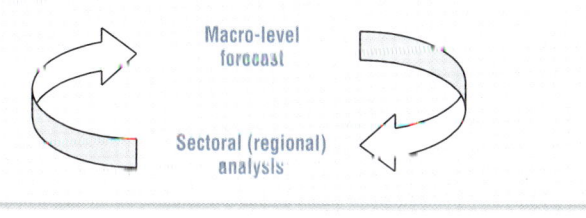

This was only a first step towards integration of the two approaches. Much still needs to be done. To make this phase more understandable, we shall briefly illustrate this research step with one specific line of reasoning.

The first problem we faced was the definition of tourism. In our qualitative survey we assumed tourism includes hotel and catering as well as travel agencies and tourist information centres. This did not correspond to the conventional division by industry in the NACE classification, used in the macroeconomic projection. Results of the mid-term macroeconomic employment forecast in the hotel and catering industry (Annex 2, Figure 4A) in fact corresponded to predicted employment trends in qualitative scenarios: fairly modest but steady employment growth is forecast whereby the pessimistic qualitative scenario assumed slight growth or stagnation of employment opportunities. Apart from the numerical forecast, the qualitative scenarios considered such factors as entrance to the EU, access to structural Funds, introducing the new concept of government policy in tourism in the Czech Republic, and many others.

The qualitative analysis showed a twofold nature of trends in tourism. The attractiveness of the hospitality sector is largely linked to its traditional nature, with old roots and long-standing customs. Its traditional character represents the mainstream, conservative, part. It is often characterised by high labour turnover, high proportion of low-skilled workers, and low investment in training employees. This traditionalism is in contrast with dynamism. New and modern forms of organisations with complex and comprehensive information systems [4], such as tourist information centres, represent dynamic features and, most importantly, a driving force for development. This dynamic part is characterised by vast application of information and communication technologies (Zelenka et al., 2001). The key to success in the tourism business is therefore a highly qualified, multiskilled labour force capable of providing traditional services with new technologies, and offering complex travel packages maximally adjusted to the diverse expectations of clients.

Let us now look at the macroeconomic forecast for the three most common educational categories for tourism. We are already aware of the inadequate detail in educational categories. We need therefore a compromise for selecting categories that suit the educational fields we are interested in (e.g. gastronomy, hotel and tourism, cook, waiter, etc.). We need to select a higher level of groupings, where the educational fields in question are combined with 'kin' fields. These are for instance: No 12 of the project code (see Annex 1) -

---

[4] Such information systems integrate information from travel agencies, hotels, transportation, guides, interpreters, regional development agencies, local administration, etc.

trade and services at apprenticeship level, No 43 - economics, trade and services at secondary vocational education level with final exam, and No 55 - economics, trade and services at higher education level.

Let us first see the mid-term supply and demand on the labour market for these three educational categories. Trade and services at apprenticeship level (No 12), and especially economics, trade and services at higher education level (No 55) are forecast to be in excess supply (negative values, Annex 2, Figure 1A); unlike economics, trade and services at secondary vocational education level with final exam (GCSE, No 43) where there will be a significant shortage (positive value, Annex 2, Figure 1A). Roughly the same trend is forecast by the indicator of future labour market prospects (Annex 2, Figure 2A), and the indicator of future recruitment prospects (Annex 2, Figure 3A).

The trend of shortage and surplus qualifications was determined by the traditional nature of the sector where skill needs are mostly targeted at the intermediate level of qualifications (four-year vocational education with final exam providing GCSE). With greater involvement of modern technologies, low-qualified workers can no longer keep up with the needs of businesses. In fact, apprenticeship-type school leavers (mostly three-year vocational programmes) were the only category whose quality was criticised by employers in our qualitative survey. The surplus of higher education graduates in relevant fields of education cannot, however, be interpreted in the same straightforward way. In cases of shortage of intermediary qualifications, excess supply of higher education graduates in similar study fields may force them to occupy jobs initially designed for lower levels of qualification. This is an important observation for methodological findings, as the current macroeconomic forecasting model does not include these substitution effects. The latter are likely to be especially important during economic transition and significant skill mismatch (Munich et al., 2001). Incorporating substitution effects into the forecasting model is therefore a future task.

Apart from possible compensatory effects of demand in workers with intermediary skills being replaced by higher qualified labour, it is also important to consider the effects from changes in the sector. Current stress on providing traditional services with predominantly lower-skilled labour could change markedly demand during qualitative development in the sector. Should new technologies continue to be the driving force and its share in the sector grow further, the forecast based on past trends will be overturned. Growing demands from employers for use of information technologies, integration trends in regional socio-economic and territorial planning, including infrastructure and the environment, and the growing importance of information networks at various levels are increasing demands for comprehensive services in tourism. This, in turn, increases the need for higher qualifications and skills. Expert surveys have shown that demands on the skills and professionalism of middle management will grow. In such a scenario, more people with top-level qualifications in relevant study fields will be needed and university graduates in economics and business subjects will enjoy increasingly good job prospects. The question, however, arises of how far the trend will be affected by the rather modest wages on offer in the tourism sector (Zelenka et al., 2001).

This is one of many examples we found during the integrative phase of the project. Trying to combine results of the quantitative forecasts and the qualitative sectoral analysis was pilot testing only and many problems remain unsolved. However, it helped to provide some conclusions on improving the forecasting technique, the data and their structures. For instance, it became clear that clustering occupations and grouping educational types provide inadequate information for drawing any significant conclusions from quantified forecasting. Therefore, in future much work will be needed to provide information at disaggregated levels.

4. Some conclusions, further challenges and tasks

The project was only a first attempt at integrating different methodological approaches. The Czech team has now started follow-up work planned during 2002 and 2003. [5]

Much work on harmonising data structures for qualitative and quantitative components, and on improving data input, structures and methods is needed in future. The first attempts at integrating the quantified forecast by occupation and education with qualitative information on skills needs proved useful. It would be naïve, however, to imagine that to produce a reliable and sufficiently detailed interpretation of the macroeconomic forecast, it is necessary to run another qualitative survey and research in every region and sector. Although such surveys are important and useful, they are also costly and time-consuming. Such studies should be undertaken in special circumstances, for instance, in a sector where a significant skill shortage is forecast, or where supply provides enough qualified workers for certain occupations but they choose different occupations leaving demand unfulfilled.

---

[5] All follow-up activities are supported by the Czech Ministry of Labour and Social Affairs.

We are now looking for a nationwide perspective of skill needs at an early stage with enough detail, more reliability and some information on the quality of the required labour force. To succeed without needing to run extra surveys for each sector and region, we now face the major challenge of linking the macroeconomic forecasting model to the 'Integrated system of typal positions' ([6]) (ISTP). ISTP is genuinely an information system which currently includes a catalogue of more than 1 000 standardised working positions with a description of each working activity, and its requirements for skills, personal aptitudes and educational background. Further, each working position is linked to the classification of educational fields used in supply-side statistics and to over 500 occupations. It is an open system complemented and updated continuously with the direct involvement of social partners.

It is obviously of high relevance for forecasting labour market training and education needs. Describing each working activity for the whole set of standardised working positions provides a unique opportunity to study substitution between occupations. ISTP links the highly stratified fields of the Czech education system to a catalogue of occupations, providing a labour market forecaster with a solid base for aggregating occupations and translating macroeconomic forecasts into information on the quality of qualifications and skills required. Such integration, however, demands further clustering of occupational groups in ISTP and richer data input (e.g. extension of the LFS sample) for the forecasting model. We are also looking at using alternative data sources to LFS to ensure more detail in forecasting results.

The greatest challenge is to ensure the various methodological approaches complement one another in identifying skills needs and the system works regularly. This will require developing interinstitutional cooperation for data supply, interpretation and dissemination as well as producing a system for ordering, tendering, financing and recognising results of analyses of skill needs. A major development will be to ensure legitimacy of the system, whereby tripartite arrangements (between both sides of the industry and the government) are indispensable.

Another challenge is to guarantee accuracy of results and reliability of analysis over time. Considering the unstable profiles of occupations and general changes in the world of work influenced by global developments, it is ever more important to find a way to make cooperation between experts and social partners ongoing. Particular stress therefore was put on verifying

---

[6] ISTP was developed by the Czech company Trexima with the support and initiative of the Ministry of Labour and Social Affairs.

results in focus groups with direct involvement of experts, social partners and educators, where the process of verification progressed to 'shared diagnosis' and collective commitments. Such activities should be more actively used in future where scenario building may become a justifiable qualitative part of a macroeconomic forecast. This could make it possible, for instance, to verify macroeconomic sectoral employment forecasts with the help of Delphi methodology and later design scenarios with direct involvement of experts, practitioners and politicians. It is important identified needs receive the necessary recognition for possible follow-up measures at policy and implementation levels. Scenario building and shared diagnosis increases commitment of participants to further implementation steps.

Another important challenge emerges from the qualitative change on labour markets in CEECs. Evidence in the Czech Republic shows that almost 90% of companies increased demands for quality of the workforce over past two years (Kaderabkova, Strietska-Ilina et al., 2001). Restructuring and the high rate of technological change in CEECs brought about the problem of skill gaps and qualification shortages. One third of Czech companies consider skill shortages a problem. In more dynamic and new technology-oriented sectors about half of companies are aware of skill shortages on the labour market. The higher the level of occupation, the more skill shortages are reported by firms. The shortage skills reported across sectors and levels of occupations are mostly social skills, foreign languages and IT skills.

About one quarter of all companies experience recruitment difficulties at all occupational levels. However, the reasons are different: lower skill occupations are often difficult to fill because of poor working conditions, lack of job stability, low wages, etc., while more skill demanding vacancies are often difficult to fill because of shortage of appropriate qualifications on the labour market. Shortage occupations are reported sporadically. Most are either specific with hybrid specialisation requirements (such as doctors with clinical accreditation for work in spas, publicity workers with thorough ICT skills for work in tourism), or linked to fast developing businesses in dynamic industries (IT educators, programmers, system analysts, etc.). The qualitative change on the labour market is also shown in changing occupational profiles. Although the latter are reported by only 8% of firms, multiskilling and job interchange are often introduced by employers (40% and 44% respectively; see Kaderabkova et al., 2001) leading to a larger share of hybrid occupational profiles and demand for combined skills.

Shortages of skills and qualifications on the labour market is made worse by low awareness in CEECs against often better awareness and therefore more thorough policy measures in neighbouring EU Member States. The latter often introduce attractive packages for foreign qualified workers which can cause an increase in the brain drain in CEECs. It is therefore important to have a transparent system for monitoring and early recognition of skill shortages on the labour market. This task shall be tackled in the Czech Republic in 2002-03 by developing a methodology and conducting a pilot analysis of skill shortages and shortage occupations in the Czech Republic. The analysis shall include an investigation of existing methods, a questionnaire survey among regional employment services on repeatedly announced job vacancies, a survey among personnel agencies, analysis of vacancy advertisements in the media, focus groups and interviews on new occupations and job profiles, a company survey, an analysis of needs and shortages recorded by investors, and others. Identifying and monitoring skill shortages on the Czech labour market should then become an integral part of the overall system of early identification of skill needs in the Czech Republic.

The project should end in establishing a system where different components can work complementarily and consistently together: regular macro level forecasts possibly linked to the ISTP information system, periodical regional and sectoral surveys and analyses, and regular monitoring and analysis of emerging skill shortages and shortage occupations. The Czech team has also come with a proposal to set up a national information platform to incorporate information on various activities in early recognition of skill needs at national, regional and local levels. Such platform can be a useful reference point for researchers and practitioners. Exchanging knowledge on modern methods of research on early recognition of skill needs appears useful at European level. Further, the Czech team would welcome the creation of an international network of researchers preferably including countries outside Europe where much forecasting research has brought interesting high-quality results. Such a network must bring together researchers applying conventional macroeconomic quantitative forecasting and those performing qualitative research to enable both sides to share their experiences and find common solutions.

References

Giffard, A.; Guegnard, K. Forecasting methodology for qualification and training needs: the case of the hotel and catering sector in Burgundy - France. In Strietska-Ilina, O. et al.; Havlickova, V., tech. ed. *Forecasting skill needs: methodology elaboration and testing.* Prague: National Observatory - NVF, 2001, pp. 315-340.

Kaderabkova, A.; Strietska-Ilina, O. *Human resources in the context of regional development. Company skills survey in selected industries of North West Bohemia.* Prague, Turin: European Training Foundation, 2001.

Karnicnik, M.; Luzar, D.; Gerzina, S. Analysis and forecasting of the training needs in the sector of tourism - Podravje region - Slovenia. In Strietska-Ilina, O. et al.; Havlickova, V., tech. ed. *Forecasting skill needs: methodology elaboration and testing.* Prague: National Observatory - NVF, 2001, pp. 341-364.

Munich, D.; Jurajda, S.; Babeckij, J.; Stupnickyy, O. Regular forecasting of training needs: quantitative models for the Czech Republic. In Strietska-Ilina, O. et al.; Havlickova, V., tech. ed. *Forecasting skill needs: methodology elaboration and testing.* Prague: National Observatory - NVF, 2001, pp. 17-129.

Strietska-Ilina, O.; Munich, D., eds.; Havlickova, V., tech. ed. *Forecasting education and training needs in transition economies: lessons from the western European experience.* Prague: National Observatory - NVF, UIV, TAURIS, 1999.

Strietska-Ilina, O.; Giffard, A.; Guegnard, K. Regional and sectoral analyses as a methodology of forecasting labour market needs. Case study: the hotel, catering and tourism sector in the Czech Republic, France and Slovenia. In Strietska-Ilina, O. et al.; Havlickova, V., tech. ed. *Forecasting skill needs: methodology elaboration and testing.* Prague: National Observatory - NVF, 2001, pp. 221-230.

Zecchini, S. Transition approaches in retrospect. In Zecchini, S., ed. *Lessons from the economic transition: Central and Eastern Europe in the 1990s.* Dordrecht, Boston, London, 1997, pp. 1-34.

Zelenka, J.; Strietska-Ilina, O.; Havlickova, V.; Beranek, J.; Riha, J. Qualification and skill needs in the sector of tourism: the case of North West Bohemia - Czech Republic. In Strietska-Ilina, O. et al., eds. *Forecasting skill needs: methodology elaboration and testing.* Prague: National Observatory - NVF, 2001, pp. 231-314.

ANNEX 1
Educational classification
(LFS-based, linked to national classification)

PC	Education	Specialisation	PC	Education	Specialisation
1	Without school education	No	29	Apprenticeship with GCSE	Chemistry, food industry
			30		Textile, clothing industry
2	Primary (9 years)	No	31		Wood processing, shoe industry
3	Grammar school with GCSE	No	32		Construction
4	Apprenticeship	Machine control and operation	33		Agriculture and forestry
5		Mechanical engineering, metallurgy	34		Trade, services
			35		Other
6		Electrical engineering, transport, communication	36	Secondary vocational with GCSE	Natural sciences
			37		Mechanical engineering
7		Chemistry, food industry	38		Electrical engineering
8		Textile, clothing industry	39		Construction
9		Wood processing, shoe industry	40		Other technical subjects
10		Construction	41		Agriculture, forestry
11		Agriculture and forestry	42		Health
12		Trade, services	43		Economics, trade, services
13		Other	44		Law
14	Secondary vocational	Natural sciences	45		Teacher-training
15		Mechanical engineering	46		Other social subjects
16		Electrical engineering	47		Other sciences and disciplines
17		Construction	48	Higher education	Natural sciences
18		Other technical subjects	49		Mechanical engineering
19		Agriculture, forestry	50		Electrical engineering
20		Health	51		Construction
21		Economics, trade, services	52		Other technical subjects
22		Law	53		Agriculture, forestry
23		Teacher-training	54		Health
24		Other social subjects	55		Economics, trade, services
25		Other sciences and disciplines	56		Law
26	Apprenticeship with GCSE	Machine control and operation	57		Teacher-training
27		Mechanical engineering, metallurgy	58		Other social subjects
28		Electrical engineering, transport, communication	59		Other sciences and disciplines

PC = Project Code
Source: Munich, Jurajda et al., 2001.

ANNEX 2

Figure 1a: **Shortage by type of education, 2000-2004**

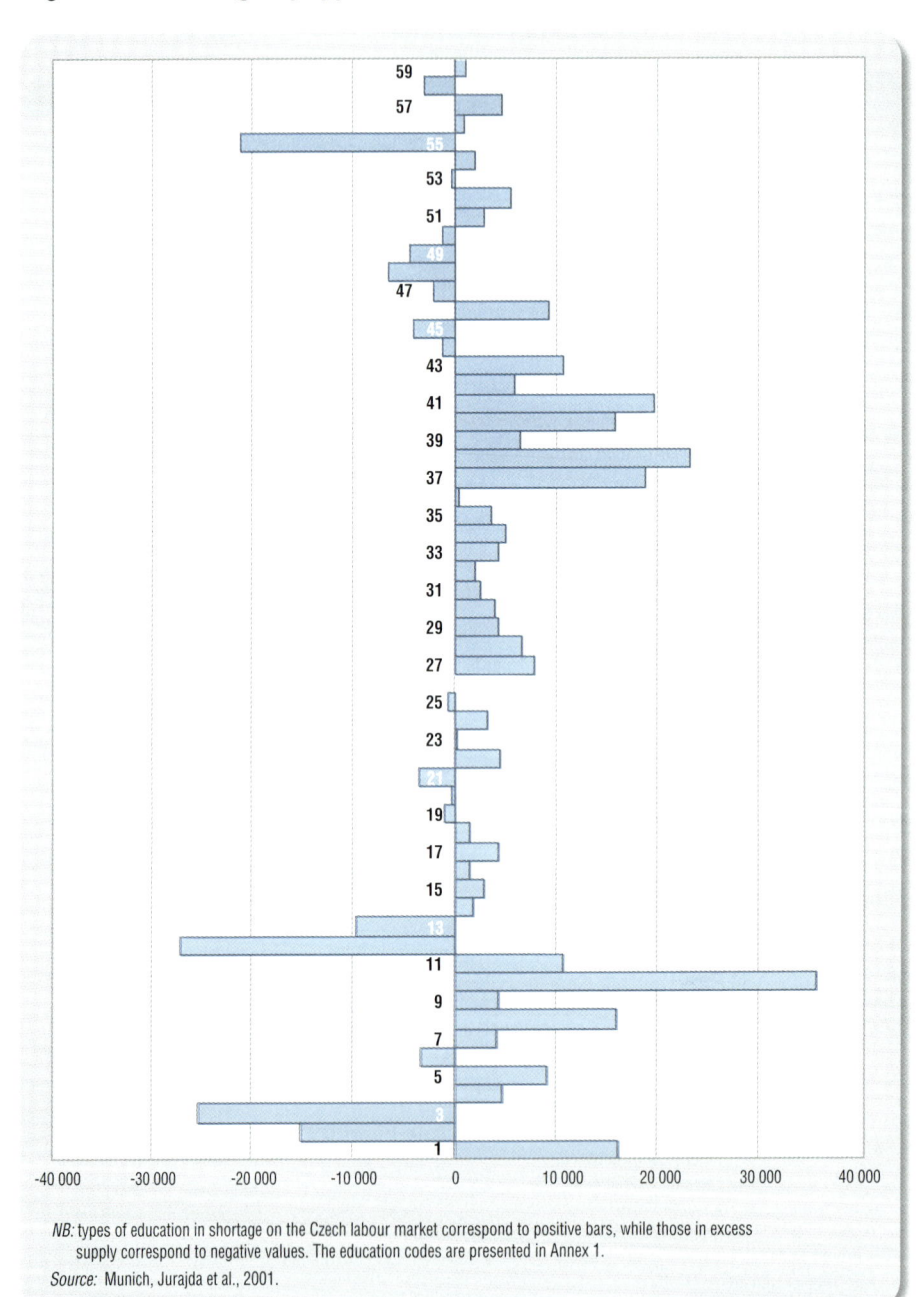

NB: types of education in shortage on the Czech labour market correspond to positive bars, while those in excess supply correspond to negative values. The education codes are presented in Annex 1.

Source: Munich, Jurajda et al., 2001.

Qualitative versus quantitative methods of anticipating skill needs: perspective of a country in transition | 261

Figure 2a: **Indicator of future labour market prospects, 2000-2004**

NB: When the indicator of future labour market prospects takes on values larger than 1, workers with the given education will find it harder to find employment. The education codes are presented in Annex 1.
Source: Munich, Jurajda et al., 2001.

Figure 3a: **Indicator of future recruitment prospects, 2000-2004**

NB: Higher values (more than 1) of the indicator of future recruitment prospects signal good recruitment prospects for firms. Low values correspond to problems in recruiting workers with the given type of education. The education codes are presented in Annex 1.

Source: Munich, Jurajda et al., 2001.

Figure 4a: **Employment in hotels and catering – forecast up to 2000-2005**

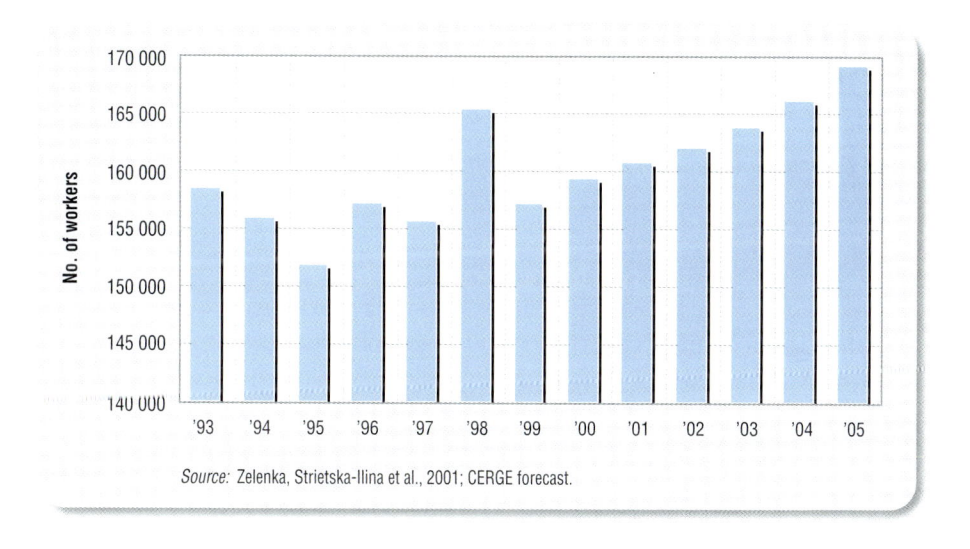

Source: Zelenka, Strietska-Ilina et al., 2001; CERGE forecast.

Skill markets in a learning society: transformation and vocational reforms in Hungary

Pal Tamas, Hungarian Academy of Science, Budapest, Hungary

Discussions on 'the knowledge economy' have proliferated in recent years and are tightly linked to policy prescriptions, management strategies and fundamental changes in work, education and leisure. By putting new slants on academic debates about the character of knowledge, labour and learning, many actors in this discourse believed that they could suggest progressive practical reforms based on sound theoretical foundations.

This paper attempts to raise a number of questions on some of the theoretical underpinnings. The main thesis is that the increased intensity of knowledge pervading labour and production in modern sectors of transformation economies could possibly change the nature of employment relationships, leading to increased national variability in control of the labour process and the firm. This could be encouraged through policy intervention and would lead to an evolving skill system characterising national forms of capitalism emerging in the region.

1. The framework: knowledge markets and territories

A focus on the learning economy of the new central and eastern European countries (CEECs), in contrast to those investigations that addressed the structural limits to learning, raised the possibility of a learning economy creating contextual conditions of endogenous development.

Different national institutional frameworks support different forms of economic activity. Coordinated market economies have a competitive advantage in diversified quality production. Uncoordinated market economies, in comparison, are most competitive in sectors based on radical innovative activities (Soskice, 1999). Coordinated systems are connected with the post-Fordist development path based on competitive advantage (Porter, 1990). Uncoordinated economies combine this with comparative advantage based upon neo-Fordist developments. The tendencies in the latter depend upon the technological parameters of the particular market sector.

The best performances from coordinated economies are found in diversified quality production of relatively complex goods. In contrast, the most successful uncoordinated economies perform best utilising the knowledge generated from national innovation systems.

Judged from this perspective, the Hungarian economy, actively reformed in the 1990s, represents a polarised mixed case. There is still a significant concentration on labour intensive low tech industries, yet there are also numerous 'A-'level high tech industries.

The, on average, low level of skills of workers in the labour intensive low tech industries creates aggregated structural problems for this part of the Hungarian economy, particularly when exposed to global competition from countries in regions with even lower costs (e.g. south east Europe). The changing commitment of the firms to their expressed and latent needs - not only but primarily in the low technologies - also influences the professional involvement of employees. Without commitment from the enterprise (or the organisation in general) to the individual, a reciprocal commitment of the individual to its organisational environment cannot be expected (Lazonick, 1994).

The institutional competitive advantage of semi-coordinated market economies, like the central and eastern European ones, seems to be founded on the upgrading of existing technological trajectories in manufacturing industries (Asheim, 2000) characterised by interactive innovation models.

In this respect it is important to remember (Freeman and Perez, 1988) that knowledge diffusion very strongly depends on the socio-institutional framework. The learning and absorbing capacity of the respective society, the configuration of social capital in the national innovation system and the proximate access to high quality educational facilities are becoming crucial for economic performance.

With regard to 'configurations of development', it is necessary to determine whether basic factors (population mobility, information infrastructure, technology transfer patterns, etc.) help produce an autocentric development trajectory, or build negative combinations which generate different forms of 'blocked development'.

In the Hungarian and CEEC case two groups of factors contributed decisively to the re-industrialisation and rapid economic development during the 1990s: socio-structural factors ('socialist market' reforms of the late

1960s and a relatively even stratified distribution of knowledge) and politico-institutional factors (mobilising effects of political transformation, identification of professionals as *intelligentsia*, well-constructed 'exit' strategies for labour conflicts, etc.). Despite early attempts in the transformation to discredit egalitarianism - identifying it with socialism - some social and psychological structures remained relatively egalitarian. That is a new aspect for this particular European area, though some comparative studies have already underlined the importance of a sort of egalitarianism for the Scandinavian economic development success story (Berend and Ranki, 1982). This primacy meant that cooperation became a more central dynamic force of transformation in the 1990s rather than competition driven by external factors.

The new knowledge-based central and eastern European economies are Soskice (1999)-type coordinated market economies. But these structures could also be easily interpreted as 'learning economies' (Lundvall, 1996). However, the transition from Fordism to post-Fordism in this part of Europe is not complete and perhaps, because of some parallel neo-Fordist tendencies, will not be completed in the immediate future. Despite this, according to a new theoretical understanding, innovation in this system is an interactive learning process, embedded both socially and geographically (Lundvall, 1992). This means that institutional and socio-cultural structures, and the skill structures they encompass, should be viewed as necessary prerequisites for countries and regions to be competitive in a post-Fordist economy (Asheim, 2000).

In this sense, strategic parts of the learning process are localised and related to the historical trajectories of a country, or of regions. Such territorial 'context-conditions' (Dosi, 1988), or 'territorialisation' (Storper, 1997) are related to moments of competitive advantage. The country-specific skill and motivation structures could, together with the related institutional configurations and organisational innovations, contribute to the formation of learning regions (Asheim, 1996). Developments in a number of central and eastern European regions (like Western Hungary, Malopolska in Poland, the Bratislava Region in Slovakia) support this institutionalist thesis very strongly. The learning region - including the actors in vocational and professional training – is, in this perspective, a developmental coalition.

The formal infrastructure of training institutions, or more exactly the personal networks created among their trainees, can significantly contribute to the creation of trust in the region, though there is a need for other forms of trust and trust creation if this is to function properly. Following Sabel (1992) we could speak here about a sort of 'studied trust' promoted by the training networks. Naturally, we will be unable to preserve a reasonable degree of trust without a minimum of social cohesion, and skills represent an important means from this point of view.

We could operate here with a concept of social capital as a structural property of larger groups (Woolcock, 1998) underlining that not all cultural settings automatically represent it. But there is still an open question: how fragmented are the obligations, expectations and norms governing the behaviour of individuals in a post-socialist society in this respect?

With regard to the Hungarian or other central and eastern European economies, the concept of 'learning regions' could be used in two different ways. The first approach emphasises the role played by collective learning and cooperation in territorial clusters and networks in order to promote the local (national) firms in the global learning economy. The second approach conceptualises learning regions as territorially based development coalitions with intra- and interfirm learning organisations (Asheim, 2000).

2. Skills supply and vocational training in transition

Since the early 1990s, the CEECs moving to democratic market economies have faced radical socio-economic change. In all countries the number of workers employed in industry was reduced. The reduction in the labour market in Hungary was more substantial than in the other countries of the region.

Dividing the industries of the transition economies according to the Neven-scheme into five clusters ([1]) by the capital and skill intensity of labour (Kaitila, 2001, p. 21-22) results in a detailed map of skill intensity in the region. The comparative advantage of countries revealed in this way reflects the quality of labour employed by the specific industries. The peculiarities of skill needs in Hungarian enterprises can then be interpreted using Kaitila's (2001) data referring to the broader central and eastern European context.

We see that in 1998 Category 4 (relatively capital-intensive industries but with low skill-intensity of labour) emerges as the most important cluster in the region. The share of that category varies between 24 % in Romania and 73 %

([1]) Category 1 are high-tech industries intensive in human capital. Category 2 uses intensive human capital with little physical capital. Category 3 is intensive in labour with relatively little physical capital. Category 4 includes industries intensive both in labour and capital. Category 5 includes food-processing industries (see Kaitila, 2001, p. 21).

in Latvia (not in Table 1) with the 40% of Hungary in between. Combining categories 3 and 4, the low-skills intensive industries emerge as dominant parts of the national economy representing 58% in Hungary. Category 1 is quite pronounced for this country as well. Regarding the comparative advantage of this economy, Category 2 is also important. Category 3, with low intensity in skills and capital, has experienced a significant decline since 1993 (Table 1). The country has moved significantly towards a model with increased skill-intensity in its comparative advantage (at the same time adding to its capital intensity, but this is not a major point for our arguments in this paper).

Table 1. **Industrial dynamics in central European transition economies, 1998, 1993-98 (%)**

	Category 1	Category 2	Category 3	Category 4	Category 5	Category 3-4
1998						
Hungary	25.3	15.5	18.1	39.9	1.2	58.0
Czech Republic	5.2	19.2	14.7	58.7	2.2	73.4
Poland	6.9	8.1	33.0	45.4	6.6	78.4
Romania	1.6	6.2	66.9	24.4	0.9	91.3
Slovakia	6.5	10.9	19.5	60.4	2.7	79.9
1993-1998						
Hungary	15.9	3.0	−20.8	6.1	−4.1	−14.7
Czech Republic	−2.1	7.3	−12.3	10.8	−3.7	−1.5
Poland	1.3	2.0	−8.8	7.6	−2.1	−1.2
Romania	−1.3	2.9	−2.6	2.7	−1.7	0.0
Slovakia	−1.0	3.8	−14.1	17.2	−5.9	3.1

NB: Category 1: high-tech and human capital intensive industries; category 2: human capital intensive with little physical capital; category 3: labour intensive with relatively little physical capital; category 4: both labour and capital intensive industries; category 5: food-processing industries.

Source: Kaitila, 2001, p. 23.

Starting from the last wave of modernisation, lasting from the 1960s until the1970s, countries of the region have witnessed an increase of labour market participants obtaining secondary and higher educational qualifications. The changes in Hungary in comparison with countries in other regions, especially in south-eastern Europe, are not very positive in this respect (Table 2). However, 76% of the age group 30-39 years obtained at least upper secondary level in 1998 compared with the EU average of 65.8% in 1999 (ETF, Key indicators, 2001, p. 4). During the 1996-1998 period the educational attainment level in the 25-29 category did not change significantly in CEECs.

Table 2. Educational attainment of the population by age groups, central European countries 1998 (%)

Level of education	Hungary		Czech Republic		Poland		Slovakia		Romania	
Age	50-59	30-39	50-59	30-39	50-59	30-39	50-59	30-39	50-59	30-39
ISCED 3	33	62	71	78	25	37	59	79	28	73
ISCED 5-7	13	14	9	12	10	10	8	10	16	12
At least ISCED 3	46	76	80	90	35	47	67	89	44	85

ISCED 3 - upper secondary education; ISCED 5-7 – higher education.
Source: ETF. Key indicators, 2001, p. 4.

The CEEC average participation rate for vocational training by 14-16 year-olds in the 1990s (varying between 40-70%) was significantly higher than the EU average (22% in 1996) due to the fact that in central and eastern Europe 15-16 years is the most common age for entering the vocational education system. The Hungarian data in that respect are in line with the median of this region.

3. State-socialist prehistories: a debate about skills

A certain kind of skills discussion was already taking place in Hungary in the 1980s. The problem of skills mismatches was at the core of emerging debates on the (in)efficiency of the existing (at that time) state socialist order. The skills problem is - in different (in)direct forms - also present today, a major focus being the overeducation of the population in comparison to the actual needs of industry. In the former regime local skill supply was mainly judged as of high quality. Critics analysing the demand-supply imbalance of that time were usually critical not just of the supply structure but also of the rigid demand side which underestimated the human talent and skills of the available labour force. This led to general criticism of the governance of the late command economy.

The debate was concentrated on the underutilisation of higher professional and technical skills, the absence, or unequal presence, of managerial skills and the unsatisfactory development of foreign language and other cross-cultural communication skills. The oversupply - or more exactly the perception of it - can be understood in hindsight as positive, as a resource for future growth and development of society after radical reform. The reform proposals of the late 1980s, examining the importance of skills held by individuals, usually considered the relationships between skills and outcomes at the national level. Systematic studies of the problem were very rare, almost nonexistent, and if they were done, typically did not indicate which particular skills could be most productive, or would be after the reforms. Very few studies attempted to evaluate the effect of specific skills, such as those of technologists in engineering industries, economists and lawyers in company management in the planned economy, or changes in skills of female workers and their career strategies.

The traditional skills demand approaches of the former state socialist years are still present. However, rigid manpower planning had disappeared, and there is no longer faith in the accuracy of forecasts about the volume of new entries to a given occupation. However, the ministries (of education and labour) - determining the needs of the national economy - continued to control enrolment into and graduation from educational institutions. Until the 1980s, internal power plays in schools and colleges focused on officially forecast student numbers in the departmental profile. Existing departments in higher education - partly as a result of this situation - were subdivided into departments with their own 'speciality' (a degree profile of its own on graduation from the school), and those which were forced to survive without it.

Low skills vocational training policies, due to the more moderate or less expressed symbolic value of training, were less directly performed, but were guided by school interests almost as strongly as in higher education. The 'school – industrial ministry – national educational administration' triangle of interests in establishing new programmes was usually guided behind the scenes, or at least influenced by the interest of the educational institution.

The major theme for educational policy debates of that time was not the skill supply problem (no-one really believed in the existence of a significant skill demand on the part of the national economy) but the simultaneous unilinearity and multi-linearity of the educational system, both on entry to traditional vocational training for school leavers and inside higher educational institutions.

The system, developed from the 1950s until the 1960s, was multi-linear at the starting points of vocational training and unilinear in its philosophy in higher education. The reforms tried to integrate, but also differentiate, the system - referring to existing skill profiles, but not seriously measuring them. They tried to incorporate vocational training institutions into the 'normal' secondary educational level. Vocational-secondary schools, already established in the 1970s, in principle offered graduation examinations preparing for college entrance examinations in combination with the traditional vocational training. The over-ambitious goals regarding quality were never reached by those schools. So, debates about the possible compromises leading to better-suited skills packages continued into the 1990s. However, those ideological motives underlying temporary attempts in some socialist countries, like the former GDR or Romania, to accommodate the vocational moment in different forms in an integrated secondary system were not present in Hungary. The traditional skills transmitted by vocational schools were not at all identified by serious experts influencing the policies on 'working class' life experiences, incorporating some higher ideological meaning for the prospective pupils. The debates about the vocational dimension of the system, in this case, were just pragmatic.

From the late 1980s we observed a new trend, with changes of the wage inequality driven by changes in the supply and demand for skills. But it is still hard to argue that the reduction of wage inequality was a result of the rapid rise in the supply of skills in the 1980s (as measured by educational attainment) while the subsequent rise of wage inequality in the 1990s was due to a new demand structure for skills (as measured by the industrial structure and occupational shifts). Some theories try to explain the change using political-environmental arguments (transformation returns the country to the traditional, 'pre-communist' international division of labour, etc). Of those theories using non-political elements two are advanced more frequently (e.g. Berman et al., 1994; Wood, 1994). One holds that skill-biased technological change and especially the arrival of multinational corporations in the 1990s increased the demand for skilled personnel. According to the alternative explanation, increased international trade, with the opening the of central and eastern European economies, destroyed manufacturing potential for low-skilled industrial goods in different sectors (like food processing or clothing industry) which increased the demand for unskilled workers, generating the main force behind the rise of wage inequality. The skills supply-demand ratio could be characterised by the qualifications-wage relationship of the 1990s. While normally the level of education can increase wage level substantially, the data show that in this general stratification perspective the labour market was not too sensitive to qualifications (see Table 3).

Table 3. **Differences in relative wages by educational level of employees in the Hungarian competitive and budget sectors 1998**
(average of the national economy = 100%)

Educational level	Competitive sectors	Public sectors
8-years primary school	68.7	53.1
Vocational school	80.9	63.9
Secondary vocational	107.6	79.8
Secondary grammar	107.6	81.2
Technician	134.3	102.0
College	209.5	103.7
University	304.9	156.5
Total	**104.9**	**90.0**

Source: KSH: A KSH Jelenti, 1999, p. 7.

4. Hungarian vocational training strategies

Vocational training in Hungary was adapted to the structural transformation of the 1990s by relatively small and diverse steps, rather than on the basis of systematic reform. Training institutions reacted to changes in the national economy restructuring the labour market, employment strategies, the emerging new ownership structure and the transferred management styles and philosophies. After a few years of uncertainty the sector had stabilised by the second half of the 1990s.

In institutions of vocational education (secondary vocational schools, apprenticeship schools, other general and special vocational schools, labour development centres and commercial training units) there was a general shift in emphasis from forms which lead to lower qualifications towards those which provide higher ones (Köpeczi-Bocz, 2000, p. 22). Since 1998, vocational training can start at the ninth or tenth year of schooling and the previous form of apprenticeship is set to disappear in the near future. For a number of occupations with more complex skill structures, e.g., for electronics technicians, an additional 13th school year is an integral part of secondary vocational training.

In 1997, the government launched a new form of practical post-secondary training course, mainly of two years duration, integrated as AIFSZ programs

(Accredited Higher Education in Schools). In 1993 the Ministry of Education reached an agreement with those sectoral ministries in charge of various vocational qualifications about a national register of vocational qualifications and the procedures governing related examinations. Both the register and the rules have been amended and modified several times since (Köpeczi-Bocz, 2000, p. 24). The original register in 1993 was compiled in tripartite committees of employers, employees (unions) and government representatives. Its modification is now in the hands of a special subcommittee of the OSZT, the National Council of Vocational Qualifications. The social partners, chambers of industry and the state administration also take part in the preparation of its decisions. The National Vocational Qualification Register organises state-recognised qualifications in this area (including such parameters as organisation and duration of training, requirements for entry and suggestions on the theoretical and practical parts of it). The structure of the skills supply in a quantitative sense, therefore, is fixed by the register.

The number of qualifications included is changing continuously but the modifications are not too significant.[2] During the mid-1990s a new unification of the system took place based on the requirements of the Register with the mandatory introduction of a new central curriculum from 1 September, 1998. In most cases, the duration of training is two years. The pre-qualification level of the programmes has not changed to any significant degree during this period. In 1996 a total of 47 of the qualifications did not require pre-qualifications; in 1999 this figure was 43. Elementary school pre-qualifications were required in 1996 for 412, and 407 qualifications in 1999. Secondary and higher degrees were pre-requisite for 463 and 11 qualifications respectively in 1996, and 492 and 9 in 1999 (Köpeczi-Bocz, 2000, p. 53).

At the same time, as a result of the economic transformation and privatisation, the total number of practical training places/enrolments (in apprenticeship schools, in companies, outside the school system) fell dramatically, by about 50% between 1990 and 1998 (Table 4). Vocational training was, to a certain degree, integrated into general public education (e.g. its supervision was transferred from branch ministries to the educational administration, a special fund was created). Nevertheless, with the exception of short-time retraining programmes, responsible actors in the business sector and economic policy makers generally lost interest in the vocational

---

[2] In 1993, 955; in 1996, 933; in 1999, 951; and in 2000, 932 vocational qualifications were listed.

training problem. The general feeling among the business elite seemed to be that if a government body was interested in the coordination and maintenance of the system, it should be left solely in charge. As long as the system functioned more or less according to its basic mandate, the new business elite was ready to use it as a service (believing that the transfer of obligatory fees as a percentage of their gross wage costs to the Vocational Training Fund (VTF) was already paying for it). The VTF transfer now amounts to approximately one third of enterprise contributions to vocational training. During the 1990s, the total value of local training by companies slightly decreased, allowing for inflation, but direct subsidies to schools increased substantially, mainly as a result of donation of equipment.

Table 4. **Hungarian vocational training: structural changes 1990/91 - 1997/98**

Training	Enrolment numbers 1990/91	Enrolment numbers 1997/98	Enrolment (%) 1990/91	Enrolment (%) 1997/98
Heavy industry	79 975	44 015	38.2	33.2
Light industry	40 787	23 075	19.5	17.4
Trade	25 679	17 324	12.3	13.1
Construction	23 753	13 945	11.3	10.5
Agriculture, food processing	18 586	12 028	8.9	9.1
Catering	10 287	12 022	4.9	9.0
Transport, other services	10 304	10 228	4.9	7.7
Total	209 371	132 637	100.0	100.0

Source: Benedek, 1999.

In the last four to five years significant improvements have taken place, adding different open vocational and professional training forms to the existing system. Up to March 1998, 1024 organisations received a state certificate, allowing them to engage in vocational training. Of these, 37% are supported by publicly funded schools, colleges, state-owned training centres, 12.4% by non-profit institutions, and 50.5% are represented by commercial firms. Some 75% of the institutions listed in the official records of the authorities are engaged in training as their core activity.

The National Statistical Data Collection Programme recorded that, in 1998, 16% of the people involved in this form of training were funded by their own resources (i.e. paid tuition fees). Fees were paid by employers for 11%, the Labour Centre for 18% and by the VET contracts in 4% of the cases. A total of 51% of the answers indicated other sources (which means that, in most cases, they did not want to answer at all).

At present, it is difficult to name the main motives for the reforms: the need to put in place internationally widespread forms of training, or the disinterestedness of the new business elites in non-core activities in their enterprises. In more general terms, the socialist enterprises before 1989, in addition to their primary production functions, played important roles in training, welfare and recreation. As much as they could without disturbing the social peace inside the factories, the new owners tried to abolish a good part of those non-primary production related services. Vocational training was affected by that tendency as well. However the number of training units, especially in the economically more advanced regions, started to grow again in the late 1990s. The maintenance of their quality standards is carried out by the chambers of trade or industry.

During the reforms of the vocational training systems in 1999, compulsory schooling was increased to 18 years for new entrants. In the new scheme, vocational specialisation takes place after 16 years, so the old apprenticeship system will gradually disappear.

A National Evaluation and Examinations Centre, together with a network of regional offices, was set up in 1999 to provide quality control of vocational training.

The initial system continues to move away from one offering mainly basic vocational training to a structure providing intermediate and higher vocational education. The characteristics of this are later specialisation, combination of a curriculum leading to upper secondary school examination with traditional vocational training, and development of post secondary technical education programmes.

The regulations from 2000 increased the employer's contribution to the Vocational Training Fund to 0.5% of the 1.5% levy (up from 0.2%) which the companies can retain to train their own employees.

Since 1999 a Register of National Vocational Qualifications has provided a standard for all vocational training inside and outside of the public education system. An Adult Education Act is under preparation.

The whole education sector is influenced by the basic fact that, with the general decline of the population, the number of children entering secondary education has been declining every year. In 1997-1998 one third of young people in secondary schools attended 'uni-prep' grammar schools and two-thirds secondary vocational schools. However, the older-type apprenticeship schools during the 1990s remained important parts of the training system. While the number of school-leaving students in vocational secondary schools was growing (despite the decreasing number of students in the whole educational system) from 28 701 in 1991/92 to 43 930 in 1998/99, the relevant numbers for apprenticeship institutions were 51 558 and 38 871 in the same years. A significant proportion of those attending the vocational higher education continued their studies in the college system, with the number of students starting to increase rapidly in the late 1990s (e.g. from 199 000 in 1996 to 258 000 in 1998). While the number of students in industrial, technical, economic and commerce schools increased significantly, it declined substantially in the agriculture and health-related fields (Köpeczi-Bocz, 2000, p. 30).

The skill sets of the Romany groups - the largest ethnic minority in Hungary, representing 5-7% of the entire population - is different from that presented by the average population. The dropout rates for Romany students show a certain improvement in recent years. However, even in the early 1990s, of a given generation of first year pupils more children dropped out of primary school than successfully completed it. The proportion of Romany children enrolled in secondary schools during the 1990s was declining, in a period in which among the general population the number of students in the secondary school is increasing significantly.

Table 5 shows the changing qualification structures of employed and unemployed people. Compared to those with higher education, the risk of unemployment is approximately 2.5 times as high for those who have completed education at secondary grammar or other school, four times for those with vocational secondary school degrees and six times as high for those who only completed primary school (Köpeczi-Bocz, 2000, p. 35).

Among the registered unemployed, more than 40% had attended to only eight classes of primary school or less, while among those unemployed at the beginning of their career, lower qualifications represented a total of 25%. This indicated that the strategies among the registered unemployed were, to a certain degree, different between generations. In 1998, those registered as unemployed at the beginning of their career included 3.2% whose school qualifications were less than eight school years; 4.4% who finished primary school; 6% who finished vocational school; and 6.7% from the group with higher educational degrees (Köpeczi-Bocz, 2000, p. 51).

In 1997, 16.3% of young people leaving school had completed college, or university degrees, though, in the same year, so had 5.3% of registered unemployed school leavers. An opposite trend could be observed with other qualification levels, with 11.7% of school leavers completing grammar, and

20.5% vocational secondary schools. However, at this time 16% of the first, and 23.6% of the second qualification groups were registered among the school-leaving unemployed.

Table 5. **Employed and unemployed persons by educational attainment, Hungary 1992-98 (%)**

Year	Uncompleted primary school	Completed primary school	Apprentice or vocational school	Grammar or other second. school	College or university degree	Total	Total (1 000)
Employed persons							
1992	3.5	25.6	26.8	29.6	14.5	100.0	4 025.7
1995	1.3	22.3	30.2	30.7	15.4	100.0	3 622.8
1998	0.8	21.2	30.7	31.3	16.0	100.0	3 693.3
Unemployed persons							
1992	6.8	37.4	31.8	20.4	3.6	100.0	444.2
1995	4.1	34.9	36.7	20.3	4.1	100.0	416.5
1998	4.2	34.2	33.7	23.9	3.9	100.0	302.8
Unemployment rates							
1992	17.5	13.9	11.6	7.1	2.7	9.9	–
1995	26.2	15.2	12.3	7.1	3.0	10.3	–
1998	29.2	11.7	8.3	5.9	1.9	7.6	–

Source: CSO LFS.

5. Special skill markets

The special skills most appreciated in the labour market are managerial, computer related, and foreign languages. During the 1990s a market was emerging for special training courses on these subjects, both inside and outside of the general educational programmes.

Most larger companies, and practically all multinational high tech manufacturers, retrain their managers within the enterprise; major firms have their own educational departments. According to a survey, the percentage of wages spent on training varies from 0.4% to 6.5%: the agricultural processing industry spends 0.4%; the public service sector spends 1.5-2%; the chemical industry 1.6%; and heavy industry 2-3%. As the most serious spenders, the electronics industry and the financial sector are worthy of mention.

The relationship between in-house training and those courses offered by external providers varies in different branches. In addition to the technological and management traditions of the sectors, the position of local providers and their special arrangements with leaders of human management services inside enterprises are the most important factors explaining the local organisational differences in training. The differences are not segregated along high-tech/low-tech lines. In the most important Hungarian technology-intensive sectors, e.g. electronics, the majority of programmes are provided in-house. In contrast, the pharmaceutical industry's programmes are carried out by external providers. In the car import industry they are usually in-house but in the agricultural sector they are largely supplied by external providers.

International surveys of student achievements could be also used as important maps of skills in the student population. Data generated in the 1995 IEA TIMSS survey show ambivalent results for Hungary (Table 6). Mathematical and science skills were measured among fourth grade pupils and school leavers. While in this international comparison Hungarian results are good among the youngest groups, they are well below the international average for the school leavers. In this study the mathematical achievements of the school leavers were rated 14th and science achievement 18th place among 21 nations. Results from the younger classes were much better: the fourth grade pupils were 14th from 25 and in the Eighth grade 9th out of 41 nations.

Table 6. **Mathematical skills measured in the TIMSS survey comparative data, scores measured in the distance from the international average, 1995**

Country	3. grade	4. grade	7. grade	8. grade	school leavers
Hungary	6	19	18	24	−17
Czech Republic	27	38	29	51	−34
USA	10	16	−8	−13	−39
Iceland	−60	−55	−25	−26	34
Norway	−49	−27	−23	−10	28
New Zealand	−30	−30	−12	−5	22
Slovenia	18	23	14	28	12
Austria	17	30	25	26	18
Canada	−1	3	10	14	19
Netherlands	23	48	32	28	60

Source: Vári, 1998.

6. Future prospects for the system

There are no available comprehensive studies about the future skill needs of industry or sub-sectors in the country. However, interested policy makers can consult qualitative statements projecting selected international trends expected in given industrial or economic sectors into the local conditions. The only comprehensive vision of the market is the *Educational and human capital* chapter of the National Technology Foresight exercise in 2000. ([4]) The results of a Delphi expert survey ([3]) on national human capital prospects provided in the framework of this programme would be particularly relevant in the context of our investigations. Major factors influencing the condition of the Hungarian education system are presented in Table 7.

Table 7. **Factors influencing the actual situation in Hungarian education. Delphi expert evaluation, 2000 (% of all nominations)**

	Scientific-technological knowledge and creativity	Practical utilisation of innovations	Production, service quality level	Regulation, administration quality level	Quality level in Hungary, total
General lifestyle	–	33.0	27.5	26.9	27.7
Vocational training	37.7	34.6	36.5	35.9	36.6
Public education	38.9	36.8	33.8	34.1	34.4
Higher Education	36.0	35.6	34.8	35.2	34.6
Total	**37.8**	**35.4**	**34.1**	**33.8**	**34.4**

The following ten items are seen as the most probable positive events expected to influence the quality of human capital (also represented by the skill structure); the supposed year of realisation is given in brackets:

([3]) The programme was provided by the State Committee for Technological Change (later Ministry of Education) in 1997-2000. The Working Group for Education Policy was coordinated by Andras Semjen. The author was a member of the Steering Committee of the entire National Foresight programme, publishing the synthesis country report.

([4]) Some 206 experts took part in the first round of this survey; there were 151 in the second. The participants were asked to select events or turning points in trends with the highest probability from a larger list, evaluate them as positive or negative and judge the intensity of their social, economic, regulatory-administrative (political) and environmental impacts. The experts represented the private sector, the research establishment and the governmental machinery.

(a) More than 90% of school leavers (including those from the higher education sector) should complete some kind of vocational and professional training (2015);
(b) communication skills in two foreign languages would be part of high school final examinations (2013);
(c) the fundamental equivalence of European vocational and professional degrees is basically accepted (2012);
(d) due to EU accession, resources available for human capital development are doubled in the country (2015);
(e) the proportion of registered unemployed in Hungary will be permanently under 5% (2013);
(f) at least 80% of the 18-19 years old pass high school final examinations (spending 12 years in the education system) (2014);
(g) rich multimedia online environments are available in each school (2021);
(h) participation in different continuos educational and training forms is broadly accepted in the society (2014);
(i) the proportion of GDP spent for higher education is at least 1.5% (2013);
(j) at least 83% of the potentially employable labour force is actually employed (2014).

Between 3-9% of the experts believe that these conditions are not achievable at all in Hungary. The limiting factors mentioned most frequently as seriously affecting the realisation of these prospects are: population structure; lifestyle; public education impedes social and moral development; plus, in vocational and professional training, economic aspects (resource scarcity). Market limitations are at their highest in vocational training. Political regulation, popular viewpoints and a 'low distribution-redistribution profile' make solutions based on lifestyle modification especially problematic. A shortage of existing skills is the most serious limitation on developments in the public school system. Technological (and R&D) factors (their absence or non-satisfactory level) more often govern vocational training and labour market adaptation (Table 8 and 9).

Table 8. **Most probable changes in the Hungarian system of vocational education. Delphi factor evaluation, 2000 (nominations, %)**

Events-Factors	Creativity	Utilisation of innovations	Production, services	Regulation, administration	Standards in the country, total
90% of school leavers with vocational training	–	–	40.5	41.7	38.6
2 foreign languages in high school final examinations	–	–	36.5	38.6	37.7
European equivalence of vocational degrees	–	–	44.0	43.8	40.0
2x larger resources in human capital development due to EU membership	–	–	36.8	37.0	36.5
Registered unemployed below 5%	–	37.3	40.0	37.7	38.2
80% of the 18-19 year olds with High School diplomas	–	–	41.2	43.8	40.2
Multimedia demonstration, on-line in each school	36.6	34.7	34.2	38.4	36.0
Continuous education broadly accepted	–	–	40.0	38.6	37.7
1,5% of the GDP used for higher education	–	–	29.1	29.5	32.6
Min 83% of adult labour potential is used	–	35.5	38.4	36.8	37.1

Table 9. **Assessment of expected impacts for the vocational education system in Hungary. Delphi survey, 2000 (nominations, %)**

	Economic impact	Social impact	Environmental impact	Total impact
90% of school leavers with vocational training	91.1	93.5	73.4	93.1
2 foreign languages in high school final examinations	91.8	92.5	67.5	93.0
European equivalence of vocational degrees	90.2	91.2	-	91.8
2x larger resources in human capital development due to EU membership	91.4	88.9	71.3	91.3
Registered unemployed below 5%	88.3	91.3	61.4	91.0
80% of the 18-19 year olds with High School diplomas	87.8	91.5	78.3	90.8
Multimedia demonstration, on-line in each school	89.0	90.3	75.0	90.8
Continuous education broadly accepted	88.5	90.7	70.6	90.8
1.5% of the GDP used for higher education	86.7	90.5	70.7	89.9
Min 83% of adult labour potential is used	87.0	89.5	56.8	89.6

The overwhelming majority of the experts in the survey believe that changes in this area should be based first of all on local (national) research or development. The proportion of those who believe that 'ready-made' packages could be obtained from the international market or transferred easily *en bloc* to Hungary is negligible, although in the higher education group the acceptance of the possibility of licence or know-how utilisation is higher.

The Foresight exercise compares five possible future scenarios for the system: knowledge intensive combining of private and public sources; state-dominated human capital development; human capital development based on private resources; a 'dinosaur model' of human resources (continued structural underdevelopment); and a 'future-oriented satellite' situation (significant overeducation of workers waiting for a better future without paying to much attention to the actual situation). The research group compares all five with regard to knowledge intensity, freedom of action, equality of options, social integration, the division between state and the private actors and accessibility of resources. It ultimately states a preference for the first scenario.

7. Conclusions

Visions of an overeducated, or overtrained, labour force easily available in the labour market are prevalent in the country as myths and still alive in public opinion but industrial policy concepts are no longer dominated by them. Decision-makers, both in the education and economic policy generally consider that the skill demand landscape is becoming more fragmented and rapidly changing. Therefore, the space for local actions and solutions to upgrade skill structures in the last five to six years has expanded significantly. This does not mean that the educational bureaucracy has disappeared, but its former competences in important areas have been transformed.

The appearance or modernisation of high-tech sectors (especially when represented by local divisions of multinationals) in countries like Hungary does not automatically lead to mass upgrading of the labour force. Most skill-intensive jobs in high tech manufacturing facilities are highly specialised and not easily transferable to other industries. At the same time, we can observe emerging islands of excellence, especially in information and communication technologies, in joint projects of multinational businesses and local educational institutions (a well-known reference point in Hungary are the cooperative efforts of the Ericsson company with the Budapest Technical University in upgrading advanced training facilities).

In the education market there is a significant demand from the population for more training or, more exactly, for more qualification certificates. That growing pressure for more diplomas and degrees (from foreign language certificates to PhDs) is well understood as a political message by the educational bureaucracy and is becoming - together with the particular interests of the administrative elites - the major motivational force behind reform. At present, industrial interests for the most part are of secondary importance.

Reforms of vocational education in the country are still dominated by ambitions relating to skills supply side regulation. This does not mean that in some sectors, e.g. information technologies, revealed demand for industrial skills would be absent.

This case study indicates the importance of skills, as bottom-up building elements of the learning economy, or 'learning region'. The ambitious, upwardly mobile, modernising population, upgrading its own skills, is an increasingly important element in industrial siting decisions of new central and eastern European capitalism.

References

Arbeitsstelle für Vergleichende Bildungsforschung-Bochum. *The European house of education - education and economy - a new partnership.* Background paper. Conference of the European Ministers for Education, Budapest, 24-26 June 1999.

Asheim B. T. *Industrial districts as 'learning regions' - A condition for prosperity?* European Planning Studies. Vol. 4 (4) 1996, pp. 379-400.

Asheim B. T. *The learning firm in the learning region - workers participation as social capital.* Rebild, DK, DRUID Summer Conference, June 15-17, 2000.

Benedek A. *Szakoktatas es gazdasag* [Vocational training and the economy]. Research Report. Budapest, OM, 1999.

Berend, I.; Ranki, G. *The European periphery and industrialization, 1780-1914.* Cambridge, 1982.

Berman, D. R. *State and local politics.* Madison, 1994.

Dosi, G. The nature of the innovation process. In Dosi G., ed. *Technical change and economic theory.* London, 1988, pp. 221-238.

ETF. *Review of progress in vocational education and training reforms of the Candidate Countries for accession to the European Union in the light of developments in European policy on vocational training.* Turin: European Training Foundation, 2000.

ETF. *Key Indicators 2000. Vocational education and training in Eastern and Central Europe.* Turin: European Training Foundation, 2001.

ETF. *Review and lessons learned of Phare Vocational education and training reform programmes 1993-1998.* Turin: European Training Foundation, January 2001.

Freeman C; Perez C. Structural crises of adjustment. Business cycles and investment behaviour. In Dosi, G. et al., eds. *Technical change and economic theory.* London, 1988.

Halasz, G.; Lannert, J., eds. *Jelentés a magyar közoktatásról 2000* [Report on the Hungarian public education system 2000]. Budapest, 2000.

Horvath, R.; Ábrahám, Á.; Hprvath, T.; Köpeczi-Bócz, T. *Background study on employment and labour market in Hungary.* Turin: European Training Foundation, 1999.

Kaitila, V. *Accession countries' comparative advantage in the internal market - a trade and factor analysis.* Helsinki, BOFIT Discussion Papers, 2001/3, 2001.

Köpeczi-Bócz, T. *Report on the vocational education and training system in Hungary 1999.* Turin: European Training Foundation, 2000.

Lannert, J. *A közoktatas szerkezetének alakulása Magyarorszagon* [Structure of public education in Hungary]. Budapest, OM TEP Working paper, 2000.

Lazonick, W. *Creating and extracting value - corporate investment behavior and American Economic Performance.* STEP-Report, no.20. Oslo, STEP Group, 1994.

Lundvall, B.-A., ed. *National systems of innovation.* London, 1992.

Lundvall, B.-A. *The social dimension of the learning economy.* DRUID Working Papers No. 96-1. Aalborg: Aalborg University, 1996.

Márian, B. *A közvélemény a közoktatásról* [Public opinion about the public education]. Research Report. Budapest, 1999

McIntosh, S.; Steedman, H. *Low skills - a problem for Europe.* Final Report to DG XII of the EC on the New Skills Programme of Research. ERB-SOE2-CT-95-2006(TSER), TSER. Brussels, 1998.

Mursak, J. The relevance of key qualifications in the transition process. *In* ETF, ed. *Qualification challenges in the partner countries and Member States.* Turin: European Training Foundation, 1997.

Porter, M. *The competitive advantage of nations.* London, 1990.

Sabel, C. Studied trust - building new forms of co-operation in a volatile economy. *In* Pyke, F.; Sengenberger, W., eds. *Industrial districts and local economic regeneration.* Geneva: ILO, 1992, pp. 215-250.

Shaw, S. *Development of Core Skills Training in the Partner Countries.* Torino: ETF, June 1998

Soskice, D. Divergent production regimes - uncoordinated and coordinated market economies in the 1980s and 1990s. *In* Kitschelt, W. et al., eds. *Continuity and change in contemporary capitalism.* Cambridge, 1999, pp. 101-134

Storper, M. *The regional world. Territorial development in a global economy.* New York, London, 1997.

Vámos, D. *A fels_oktatas financialis kérdései es gazdasagi helyzetenek alakulása* [Financial questions and the higher education economy]. Budapest, OM TEP Working Paper, 2000.

Vári, P. *A TIMSS vizsgálat magyarországi eredményei* [Results of the TIMSS survey in Hungary]. Research Report. Budapest, OKI, 1998.

Wood, A. *North-South trade, employment and inequality. Changing fortunes in a skill-driven world.* Oxford, 1994.

Woolcock, P. G. *Power, impartiality, and justice.* Aldershot, 1998.

A demand-side analysis of SME skills needs in regions of five candidate countries

Lewis Kerr, European Training Foundation (ETF) [1], Turin, Italy

The paper reports on the objectives, methodology and findings of a demand side skills survey in regions in five candidate countries. The objectives of the survey were: to undertake an in-depth qualitative assessment of emerging regional SME skills needs; to examine demand-side perspectives in the context of local supply-side infrastructure; and to prepare the context for the development of intervention strategies. The exercise covered 952 small and medium sized companies in 15 sectors and five regions within economies that are at different stages of the transition process. The origins of the survey instrument employed lie in a nationwide exercise carried out in the UK during the course of the 1990s, called the Employers Manpower and Skills Practices Survey (EMSPS).

1. Introduction

This paper [2] reports on a company skills survey carried out in regions of five candidate countries during 2001. [3] The survey, which was commissioned and managed by the European Training Foundation, had three primary objectives:
(a) to undertake an in-depth, demand-side qualitative assessment of emerging regional small and medium sized enterprise (SME) skills needs;
(b) to examine demand-side perspectives in the context of local supply-side infrastructure, i.e. the provision of training in the public and private sectors;
(c) to prepare the context for the development of intervention strategies.

---

[1] until July 2002.
[2] The paper draws heavily on the Cross-Country Survey prepared by Jim Twomey of Pion Economics for the European Training Foundation.
[3] North-West Bohemia (Czech Republic), South Estonia, South Great Plain (Hungary), Lithuania and Lubelskie Voivodship (Poland).

2. The survey

The survey covered companies in a variety of sectors across very different regions within economies that are at different stages of the transition process. The regions have per-capita GDP levels that range from 26% (Lubelskie Voivodship) to 53% (North-West Bohemia) of EU 15 levels with a corresponding variation in employment profiles.

A total of 952 companies were surveyed in 15 sectors which were representative of the companies operating in the respective regions. With the exception of North-West Bohemia, the companies surveyed were overwhelmingly small (less than 50 employees), which again reflected the norm in the various regions.

The survey tool, which was adapted from a questionnaire developed for a similar survey carried out in North-West England, comprised six sub sections covering:
(a) The workforce and processes of change;
(b) turnover of employees;
(c) skills and recruitment;
(d) training and development activities;
(e) in depth questions on the skills shortages in particular occupational groups;
(f) beyond the establishment – the business environment.

The survey was based on the premise that the demand for skills, their deployment and use by employers within the productive processes are all critical aspects of the wider regional development process. More fundamentally, the basic premise of the survey was that competitive pressure is likely to result in a gap between the actual and required performance of an enterprise. This gap can be bridged in a number of ways, among them: the development of new products; increasing market share; or increasing efficiency through the introduction of new technologies. Whichever solution is adopted will result in a gap between the actual and required skills of the workforce.

In this context, the survey sought to establish whether firms:
- ever take stock of the skills inherent within their workforce and, if so, the basis on which that judgement is made;
- ever consciously examine the skills of their workforce in relation to the development of the products they supply or the markets they serve;
- whether SMEs actively consider skills as an element contributing to their competitiveness;

- consider the acquisition of skills by their workforce as a benefit or cost;
- fail to recruit graduates/school leavers due to lack of awareness, accessibility, cost, lack of work experience or other reasons; and
- respond to such issues differently depending on their particular size, sector/market or level of turnover.

It should be emphasised that the survey provided qualitative rather than quantitative data. The sample was too small to allow for a statistically reliable analysis, but the methodology adopted allowed for this. After the initial analysis of the findings of the survey, they were presented to focus groups comprising the original interviewees and other stakeholders for verification. Thus some confidence can be placed in the conclusions drawn from the survey.

3. The operating environment

In the course of interviews, firms were asked a number of questions designed to provide details about the trading and operating environment in which they function.

3.1. Market conditions and financial turnover

In the two years prior to the exercise, the majority of organisations in the survey regions indicated a situation of expanding markets and turnover. The only exception, for the former, was in Lubelskie where the proportion of firms reporting market growth was some 30% in comparison to figures between 55% and 73% elsewhere. Figures for financial turnover also reflected a generally favourable trading situation with a majority of firms in each area reporting growth.

3.2. Employment and productivity

While the trading environment for participating companies was relatively buoyant, follow-through to employment was much more muted. Employment growth was reported by between 30% and 40% of firms across the regions but this was balanced by similar proportions reporting employment loss. In the case of South Estonia and Lubelskie, the share of firms indicating decline was marginally higher than that reporting expansion.

Much of the employment loss took the form of redundancy with large numbers of firms reporting this form of separation over the course of the two years preceding the survey. Prospects for the following two years were, however, somewhat brighter with significant reductions in expected redundancies (Figure 1).

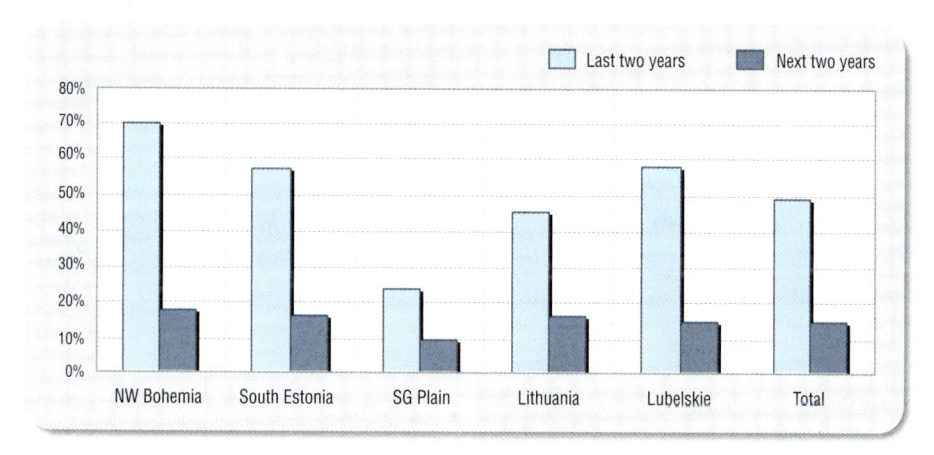

Figure 1. **Redundancy patterns**

Another contributory factor for the employment profile was related to productivity growth which was cited as highly significant in all regions ranging from around 50% in Lubelskie and South Great Plain to over 70% in the case of South Estonia and the North-West Bohemia. Figures of this scale will invariably have impacted to restrain employment growth in the face of market expansion. Some productivity decline was evident but was relatively limited.

3.3. Competitive response

There was evidence that firms in the survey regions had responded to the dynamics of the trading environment by attempting to improve their competitive position in the market place. There had been some attention to product design but more emphasis had generally been placed on product/service range and quality - between 50% and 71% of companies reported attempts to increase their product/service range and 75% to 93% reported increased attention to quality. Some 70% to 80% of firms had introduced new products/services (the figure for Lubelskie was somewhat lower than elsewhere at 40%) though much of this activity had focussed on existing ranges or related fields. Significantly fewer numbers of firms had introduced completely new products/services despite four out of the five regions reporting more than 20% of organisations with some form of R&D activity on-site.

Companies had also introduced changes in order to reduce costs, further promote productivity and improve quality. Between 70% and 80% had sought to lower costs and to increase productivity but between 80% and 90% had sought to improve quality. There was some variation across regions but the profiles are all consistent.

3.4. Competitive Priorities

The importance attached to quality and quality improvements within survey organisations was reflected in the findings of questions that sought to elicit the relative weight attached to key competitiveness factors such as price, quality, responding to customers, marketing and advertising, product differentiation and availability/delivery.

Weighting the reported results by the numbers of firms in each region, the dominant factor was defined as quality with an average rating of 93%. This was followed by responding to customers (84%), price (75%), availability/delivery (71%), marketing/advertising (49%) and product differentiation (42%).

It is difficult to make observations with just five cases, but there was some evidence to suggest that while organisations in all regions attach great importance to quality, more importance was attached by those who export a higher proportion of their goods and services. There was no such evidence with regard to price or marketing/advertising, but some moderate evidence of links between exporting, product differentiation and availability/delivery.

3.5. Organisational change

Alongside more detailed questions about skills and training issues that are discussed in later sections, the initial review of trading context attempts to examine whether the variety of market pressures that organisations have been subject to have promoted any particular set of organisational changes. Overall, the most common form of change appears to have been job interchange though significant variation was present between regions. This was followed by introduction of Total Quality Management (TQM), multi-skilling and job redesign. Adoption of just-in-time scheduling ranks low on the list of responses.

3.6. Human resource development response

Precisely how this profile of change feeds back into generic human resource development (HRD) was investigated by another series of survey questions which invited organisations to indicate the nature of management focus on employee development. The dominant HRD activity across the set of regions as a whole had been to develop employees for improved customer service. This was followed closely, however, by the desire to raise general competence and promotion of teamwork.

Asked to evaluate whether their general workforce met their organisational needs, the proportion indicating that the workforce was a major strength lies at around 40% for South Great Plain and Lubelskie, 30% for North-West

Bohemia, 17% for Lithuania and 12% for South Estonia (Figure 2). Such figures would tend to indicate that substantial numbers of employers across the regions believe that scope exists to improve the capabilities and contribution of their current workforce.

Figure 2 also reports the proportions of employers who perceive the quality of their workforce to be better than that of competitors. On the whole, this tends to be smaller than the proportion viewing their workforce as a major strength indicating some concern over workforce quality.

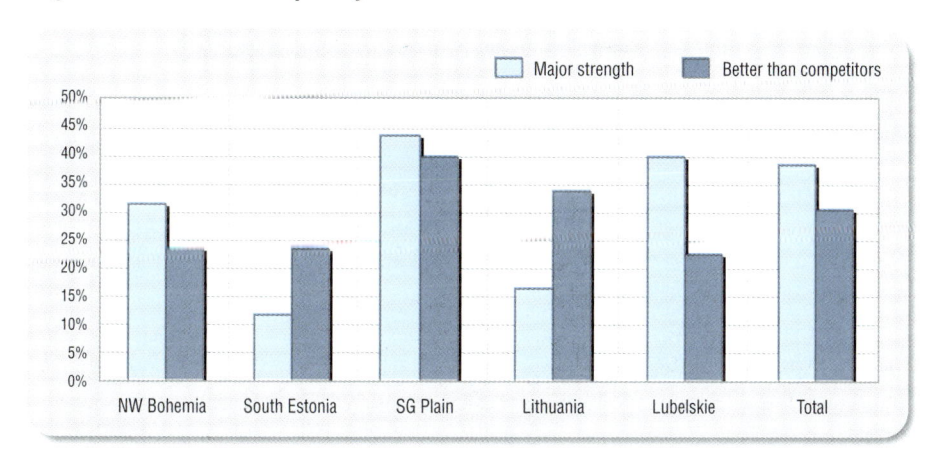

Figure 2. **Workforce quality**

4. Skills and recruitment

Having established a series of contextual parameters, the survey instrument focused on specific issues relating to skills and skills shortages.

Occupational change and labour turnover

The nature of the profiles suggests that many organisations had been undergoing a sustained process of development in recent years. This is generally reinforced by the number of companies who reported experiencing a change in the distribution of occupations internally within their organisations. Over 50% of companies in South Estonia, Lithuania and Lubelskie reported such change though the figures for the South Great Plain and North-West Bohemia are lower at 33% and 25%.

Employee turnover levels were relatively moderate in most instances but there is evidence that some employers were facing difficulties. Over 20% of companies in South Estonia and South Great Plain areas reported labour turnover greater than expected. This is broadly double that in Lithuania and Lubelskie and North-West Bohemia.

Problem occupations, in terms of turnover, appear remarkably consistent across all five regions. Elementary occupations, craft and plant and machine operators are the most common.

4.2. Skills requirements and shortages

There is widespread recognition among survey companies that the skills required of their workforces have increased over the last two years. A minimum of 80% and a maximum of 95% of firms acknowledge that demands placed on the skill-sets of employees have increased (Figure 3).

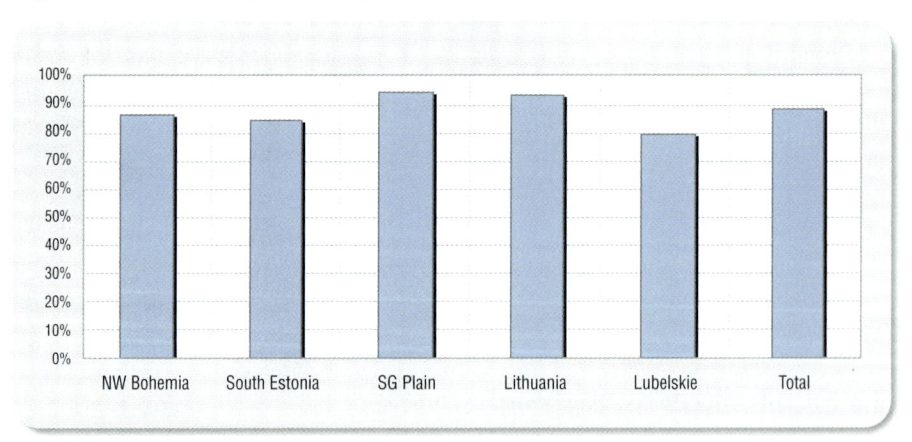

Figure 3. **Increasing skill requirements**

This is generally reinforced by the proportion of organisations ranking skills as 'very important'. What is interesting, however, is to compare the difference between the proportion of firms ranking their workforce as a major strength and the proportion ranking skills as very important. Figure 4 shows that the latter generally exceeds the former by a significant margin suggesting that employers have some concerns about the skills capability of their workforce.

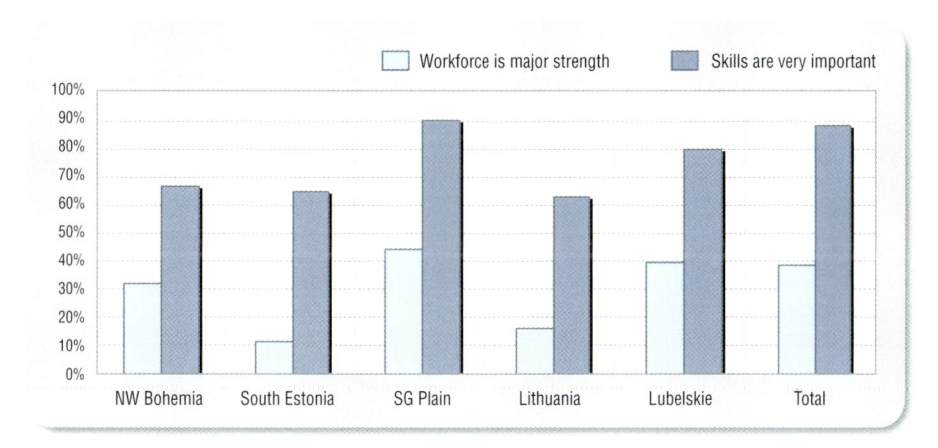

Figure 4. **Workforce skills capability**

Confirmation of these concerns is given through estimates of skills shortages which are defined as situations where employers have not been able to identify anyone in the labour market with appropriate skills to undertake a specific task or have been 'making do' with existing but inappropriately skilled staff. Between 28% and 65% of employers report such shortages suggesting that between 1 in 4 and 1 in 2 employers are facing difficulties. Even at the lower end of the spectrum, these are not insignificant magnitudes and suggest that the competitiveness of firms in all regions is being constrained.

The occupations creating difficulties are again relatively consistent across the set of regions participating in the exercise. Craft occupations are identified by four of the five regions, technical occupations are identified by three regions and service/sales and professional occupations are identified by two regions. The skills identified as being in particular short supply include technical skills, communication skills, language and creativity.

Figures 5 and 6 provide a simple cross-tabulation between the proportions of employers reporting skills shortages and the proportions reporting market and productivity growth. It is difficult with only five observations, and some care should be taken in assigning causality, but there exists *prima-facie* evidence that skills shortages are more pronounced in organisations experiencing strong market and productivity growth. Such a conclusion tends to be given a degree of support in those regional reports that undertake a similar exercise.

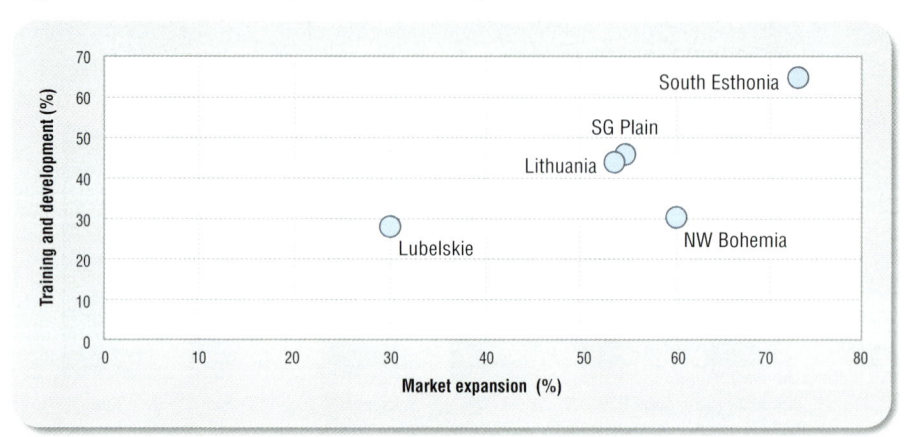

Figure 5. **Skills shortage and market growth**

[Scatter plot: Training and development (%) vs Market expansion (%). Points: South Esthonia, SG Plain, Lithuania, Lubelskie, NW Bohemia]

Figure 6. **Skills shortage and productivity growth**

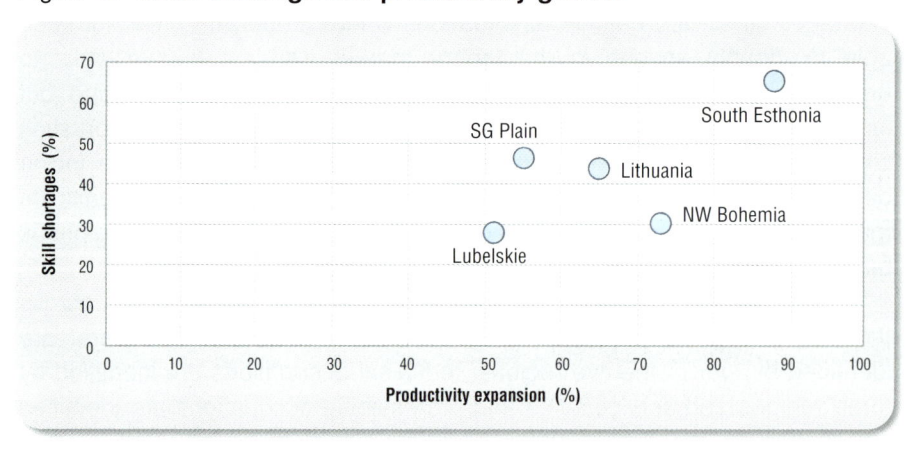

[Scatter plot: Skill shortages (%) vs Productivity expansion (%). Points: South Esthonia, SG Plain, Lithuania, Lubelskie, NW Bohemia]

4.3. Skills assessment

Organisations were asked to indicate whether, and the frequency with which they undertake assessment of workforce skills. The results show some variation between regions. In the North-West Bohemia, South Estonia and South Great Plain samples, some 80% to 90% of employers claim that they have previously assessed the skills of their workforce. In Lithuania the figure is 59% and in Lubelskie 17%.

Some of the focus group activity suggests that the high nature of some of these figures may reflect employer variation/misunderstanding of the concept of 'skills assessment' and indicates that some care should be taken in interpreting this attribute. Figure 7 suggests the not too surprising finding that more extensive skills shortages tend to be discovered as higher levels of skills assessments are performed.

Figure 7. **Skills shortage and skills assessment**

It is instructive to note that the survey also enquires about the regularity with which employers undertake assessments. It is, of course, one thing to have undertaken an assessment but it is another to set in motion procedures to review skills development. Figure 8 shows that the proportion of companies undertaking regular assessments is generally lower than the proportion that have undertaken at least one assessment.

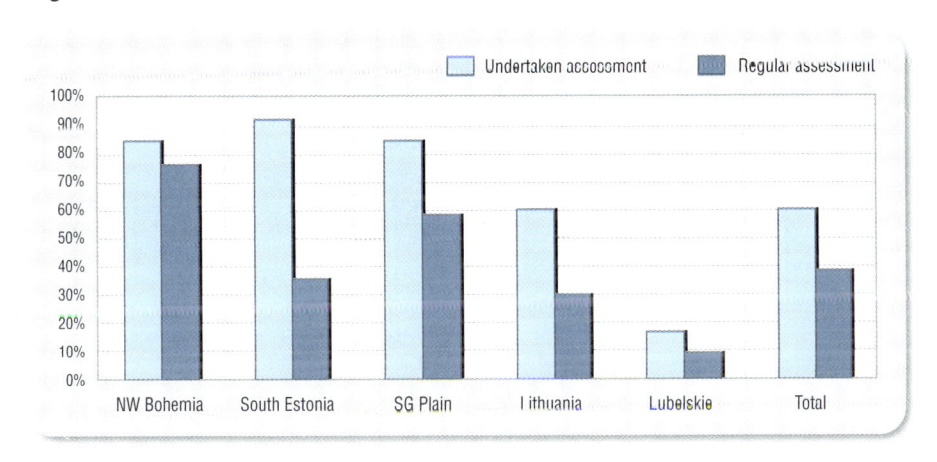

Figure 8. **Skills assessment**

This is not a surprising finding but there do appear to exist substantial differences across regions. The differential is smallest for North-West Bohemia where regular assessments are claimed by 90% of all those who have ever undertaken an assessment though again some care is required in the light of differing interpretations of 'regularity'.

In terms of capacity to evaluate current and future skills needs, what evidence is available suggests that organisations that already had some experience in this area tend to feel that they have the internal capacity to address the issue and vice versa. Hence 83% of North-West Bohemia firms have undertaken an assessment and 88% feel comfortable about capacity in this area whereas 17% of Lubelskie firms have undertaken an assessment and only 14% feel capable of so doing. It is also interesting to note that access to external intelligence on skills is very limited in the case of Lubelskie relative to other regions. Overall, there is some suggestion that firms feel a little less secure about evaluating future skills needs with positive response rates falling by between 10% and 20%.

4.4. Responsibility for skills development

With relatively large numbers of firms reporting some degree of prolonged skills shortage, the survey exercise invites employers to express their opinion as to the nature of responsibility for the development of workforce skills. Figure 9 provides the findings of this process.

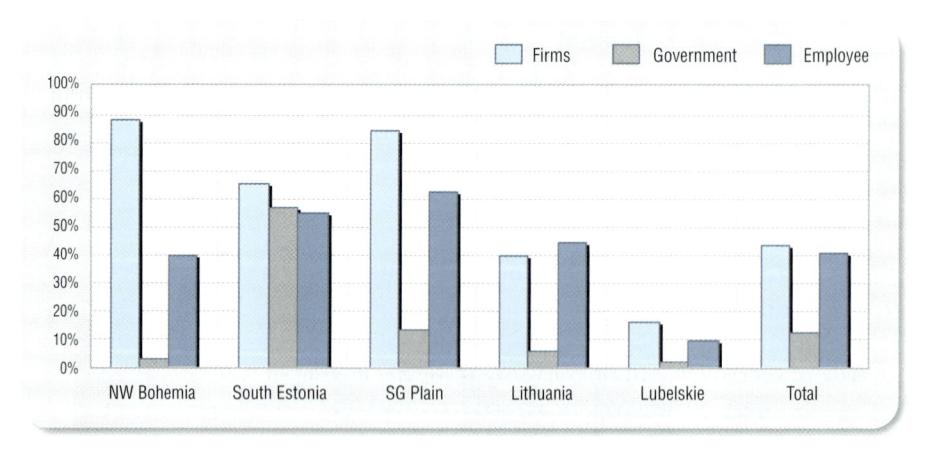

Figure 9. **Skills responsibility**

Variation across the study regions is evident but in most cases employers appear to take the view that they are key agents for skills development. Over

80% of employers in North-West Bohemia and South Great Plain areas cite themselves as bearing responsibility with figures of over 60% for South Estonia and around 40% for Lithuania. There is a marked drop in the response from Lubelskie where only 17% report in a similar manner. Such variation is not necessarily inconsistent with the differential nature of the latter area evident in other responses.

Alongside recognition of their role, employers also believe that employees have an important contribution to make to their own skills development. Over 50% of employers place some emphasis on employee own development in South Estonia, South Great Plain and Lithuania with figures of 40% for North-West Bohemia and 10% in Lubelskie.

With the exception of South Estonia, the role and responsibility of government in skills development is seen as very limited.

4.5. Recruitment of school-leavers and graduates

Recruitment of school leavers is relatively widespread across all survey regions. When asked if they have recruited any school leavers over the previous years, most regions report a figure between 40% and 55%. South Great Plain is the exception in reporting a figure of some 78%. The same broad profile exists in terms of university graduate recruitment – most regions indicate a figure of some 20% to 25% while South Great Plain reports a figure of 51%.

It is difficult to make generalisations but there are some signs that regions with greater skills shortages are relatively more likely to recruit school-leavers and university graduates. To balance this, there is no significant evidence of a relationship between productivity growth and school-leaver/graduate recruitment which may confirm the role of downsizing and capital development in the former rather than any supply-side skills improvement in the workforce.

4.6. Recruitment and vacancies

Information on whether vacancies have been difficult-to-fill (DTF) presents an interesting contrast to data on skills shortages. It has been common, in many skills studies, for employers to interpret vacancies that are difficult-to-fill as evidence of skills shortage though they may equally reflect the nature and quality of employer attempts to secure appropriately qualified staff.

Figure 10 details the skills-shortage/DTF vacancy profile. DTF proportions for the North-West Bohemia and South Estonia regions are relatively close to the skills-shortage proportions (25% compared to 30% for the former and 57% compared to 65% for the latter) with the result that one cannot rule out the role of DTF vacancies in determining claims of skills shortages. In contrast, there exists a substantial difference for Lithuania (23% compared to 44%) suggesting a clear indication of a structural skills deficit among sampled organisations.

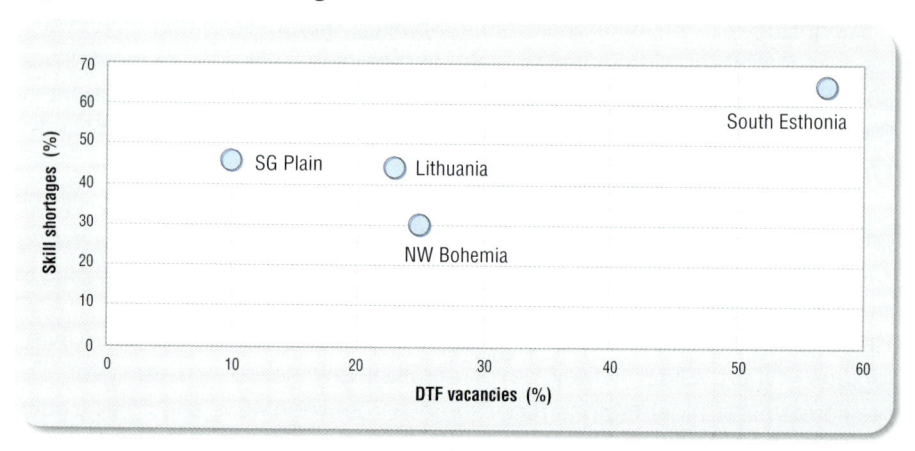

Figure 10. **Skills shortage and DTF vacancies**

Firms reporting DTF vacancies were also asked to indicate their impact on organisational performance. Among the subset of such firms, the highest response relates to lower profitability and is followed by bottlenecks/reductions in efficiency and reduced forward planning. Relatively few companies report any significant impact in terms of staff morale. Responses to the existence of DTF vacancies is dominated by an attempt to increase productivity and the job range of staff – making existing staff achieve/produce more – followed at some distance by increased overtime. The decision to undertake more training is relatively limited.

5. Training and human resource development

Once the issue of skills shortages has been investigated, the survey instrument turns to the way in which organisations address training and general HRD development.

5.1. Provision of training

Organisations were asked to report whether any training and development activities are provided for employees above and beyond routine induction and any activities that are required by specific legislative requirements.

Responses are generally high, ranging from some 40% in the case of Lubelskie to some 90% in the case of South Estonia. ([4])

Figures 11 and 12, on the other hand demonstrate that the training profiles reported are broadly consistent with a-priori expectations. Figure 11 shows that the proportion of organisations providing training within sample regions increases in line with the level of market expansion. Figure 12 indicates that the same is broadly true in terms of productivity growth.

Figure 11. **Training and market expansion**

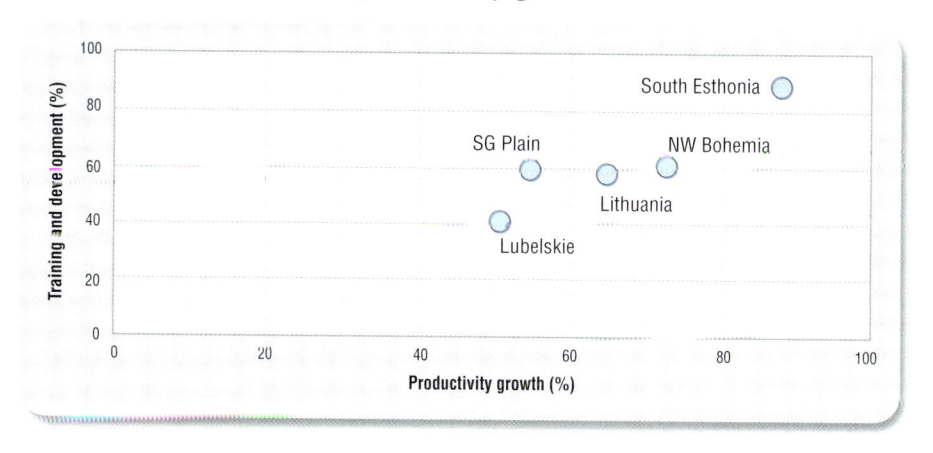

Figure 12. **Training and productivity growth**

([4]) This figure may be connected to high import level of capital equipment with associated supplier provided training.

Figure 13 provides an additional perspective and shows, as one might expect, an inverse relationship between training provision and assessment of workforce quality. Where firms in sample regions feel that their workforce is weak they appear to invest in higher levels of training. Figure 14, finally, suggests that firms also tend to relate investment in training to the level of perceived skills shortage. Training proportions generally exceed skills shortage levels by a factor of some 30% to 40%, the only exception being North-West Bohemia where the excess is some 100%.

Figure 13. **Training and productivity growth**

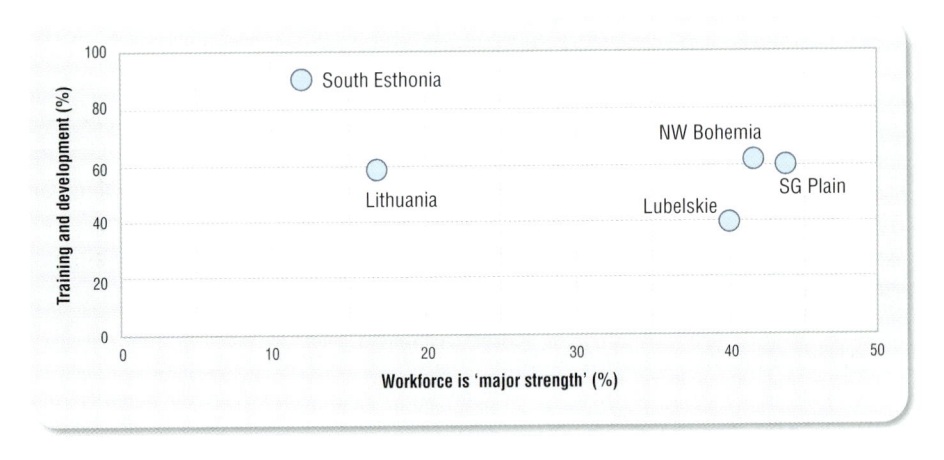

Figure 14. **Training and skills shortage**

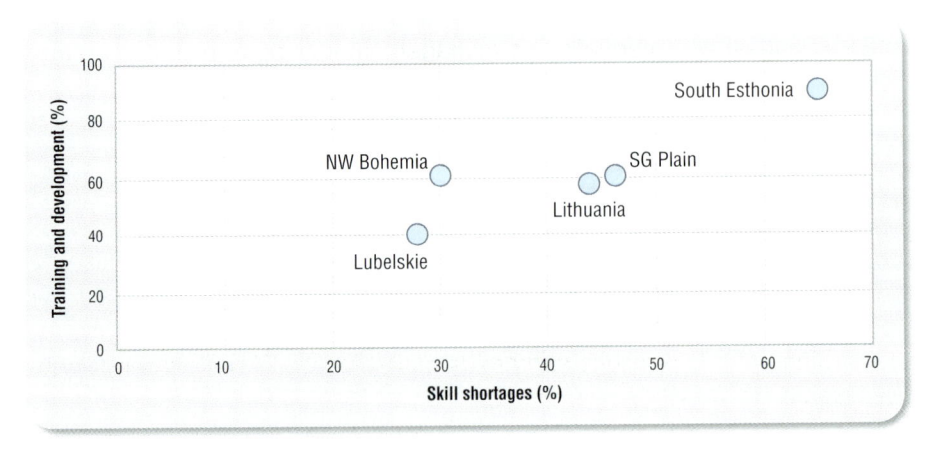

5.2. Training intensity

As a balance against high reported training levels, the survey tool asks employers to detail the proportion of employees who have participated in such activities over the previous 12 months. Comparisons are difficult due to differences in regional reports but the evidence that is available suggests that:
- North-West Bohemia - higher proportions of companies provide training for administration, technical and senior officials with highest number of training days provided for technicians and senior managers;
- South Estonia – senior/professional and craft occupations receive highest number of training days with lowest number for plant/machine operators and elementary workers;
- South Great Plain – highest number of training days allocated to administration with little variation elsewhere.

What evidence exists raises the suggestion that there may exist an element of skill–bias in some of the study areas – greater training being provided to those occupational groups with a relatively greater stock of initial skills. Additional questions also indicate that the nature of training provision conforms to this general pattern with higher skilled workers tending to receive more formal and systematic training investment.

5.3. Graduate and management training

The proportion of companies providing training for graduate entrants varies between regions. Figures for Lubelskie and South Estonia are equal to or less than 5% whereas that reported for South Great Plain is 20%. Management development structures are more prevalent than those for graduates but are still reported by only 30% of organisations at most. Such figures suggest that graduate and management training remains an area of relative under-investment across most of the regions.

5.4. Performance and training assessments

The proportion of firms undertaking assessment of employees shows a clear divide across the sample areas. At one end of the spectrum lie Lubelskie and South Estonia with responses around 90% and at the other lies Lithuania with 27%. The figure for Lubelskie is noticeably high in relation to some of the other responses cited elsewhere in the report. Figure 15 provides further information on training provision, results and needs assessments. Three regions (North-West Bohemia, South Estonia and South Great Plain) have a higher proportion of companies providing training than assessing training needs. In Lithuania there is a rough balance whereas in Lubelskie the proportion assessing needs vastly exceeds the proportion providing training support.

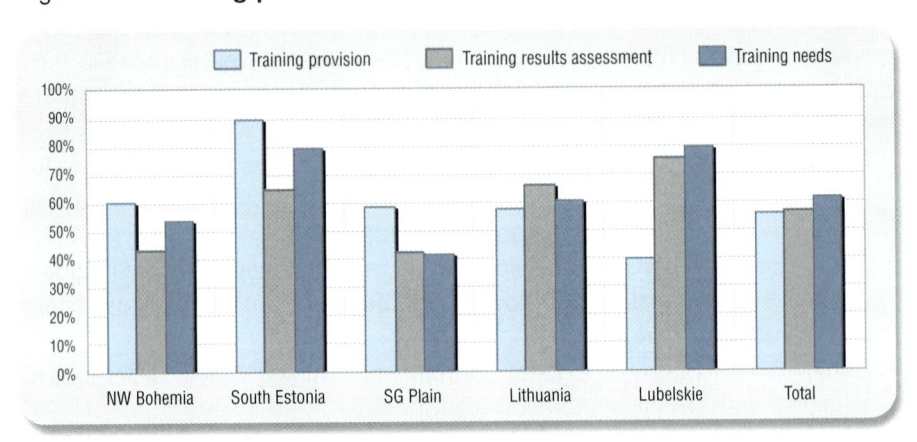

Figure 15. **Training profiles**

5.5. Integrated human resource development

The general responses of companies to questions regarding skills and training issues indicate that many employers are aware of the importance of these considerations in the context of growth and development.

However, evidence from the survey exercise indicates the general absence of a coherent and integrated HRD framework in many of the regions. Figure 16 reports the proportion of companies who claim that they have business/training plans and the proportion that cite that the latter is linked to the former. The proportion with training plans varies from just over 15% to just 35% and is lower than the proportion with business plans in all instances.

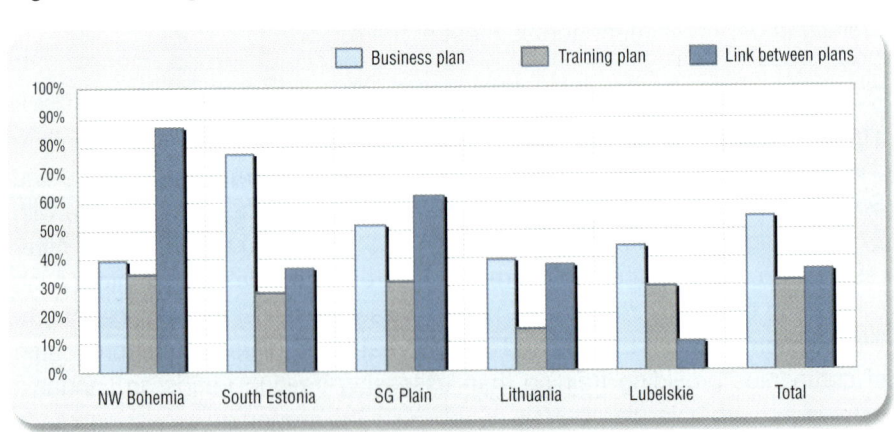

Figure 16. **Integrated HRD infrastructure**

In terms of bringing together business and HRD planning, and despite the fact that the survey results clearly profile the connection between HRD and growth, there is a variable performance in terms of organisations formally linking together business and HRD policies. This generally represents a significant lost opportunity and a major area of potential future activity.

6. Conclusions

The exercise reported in this document has represented a commitment of a large number of persons and organisations in the study regions. It has also been an important exercise for three primary reasons, namely it has:
- provided a coherent way of assessing demand-side skills and training issues 'in context';
- addressed the type of issues that will need to be considered in the progression towards Structural Funds Programming; and
- assisted the development of 'evidence-based' labour market intelligence needed to secure and access an adequate resource base for human resource development policy interventions.

Despite the variation in regions and sample sets, the exercise has provided a profile of demand-side considerations and attitudes that are broadly consistent across regions. The study has pointed to a number of potential deficiencies and inconsistencies in employer perspectives towards human resource development within their organisations and assisted regional organisations to form an initial set of recommendations designed to enhance opportunities for growth.

Analysis of the results also indicates that there exists an underlying rationality across the sample set in terms of patterns of responses to underlying difficulties. Skills shortages and training levels appear to be more pronounced in regional companies experiencing strong market and productivity growth as well as being positively related. This is a promising outcome but the evidence remains that large numbers of employers undervalue the potential contribution of employees and adopt a structured approach to human resource development.

The challenge for regional bodies is to take the results of the exercise forward, to establish mechanisms to implement proposed recommendations through existing/new partnerships and to monitor progress and improvement. Other considerations include that of replicating the exercise within other regions (already the case in Hungary) and over time. All labour market intelligence is time limited in relevance as economic conditions, policy interventions and organisational development combine to alter the fundamentals of the labour market.

Résumé and perspectives

Identification of future skill requirements. Activities and approaches for European cooperation

Manfred Tessaring, *European Centre for the Development of Vocational Training (Cedefop), Thessaloniki, Greece*

Starting out from the processes of social and economic change impacting on education and training, the following article addresses the resulting need for the early identification and timely forecasting of qualifications and skills and their implementation in educational and training policy and practice. It documents the wide range of activities and approaches to the forecasting of skills and occupations in the various European countries. Finally, conclusions are drawn for the creation of greater transparency and with a view to more intensive European cooperation – by means of information exchange, networking, information databases and the establishment of a website.

1. Introduction

In contrast to the great social utopias of the past, and equally unlike the attempts of the 1960s and 1970s to find and project laws and rules of socio-economic change, there has been a change in the objectives and approaches of forecasting in various fields – education, training, the labour market, technology, etc. This is partly due to the fact that the developed industrialised and post-industrial societies are now characterised by a dynamic of increasing openness, flexibility, complexity and therefore also uncertainty. The 'mega trends' impacting on education and training, e.g. globalisation and internationalisation of economies, job markets and even of education and training systems, demographic transition and the transformation towards an information and knowledge based society in the context of lifelong learning can be taken as familiar ground which need hardly be discussed in detail in the context of this article. (¹) However, these trends affect the education and training systems of European countries to a different extent: these systems vary considerably across countries and so does the educational attainment of populations (Figure 1).

Figure 1. **Educational attainment of the population aged 25-64 years in Europe, 2001 (%)**

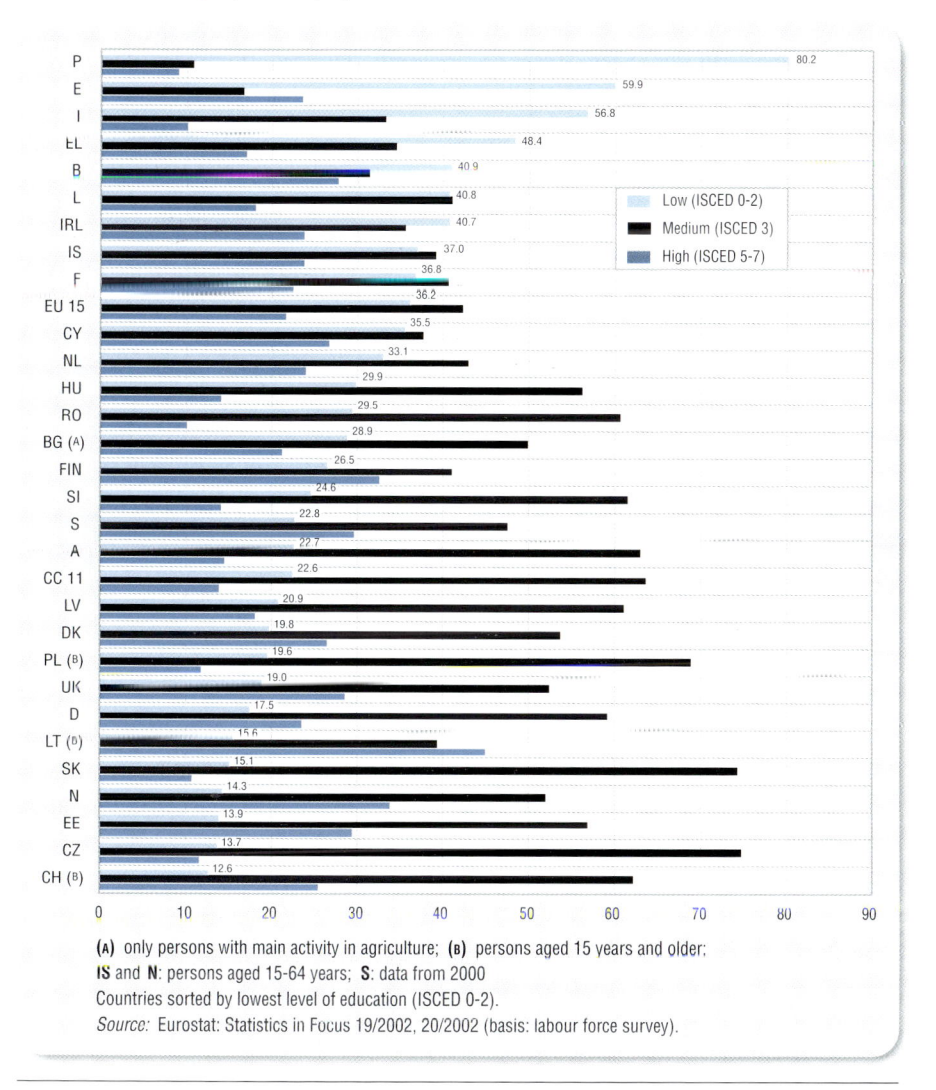

(A) only persons with main activity in agriculture; (B) persons aged 15 years and older;
IS and N: persons aged 15-64 years; S: data from 2000
Countries sorted by lowest level of education (ISCED 0-2).
Source: Eurostat: Statistics in Focus 19/2002, 20/2002 (basis: labour force survey).

(¹) Cf. inter alia the summaries in Cedefop's first two Reports on Vocational Training Research in Europe (Tessaring, 1999; Descy and Tessaring, 2002) and the extensive bibliographies indicted in both reports.

Against this background, the question of the nature of skills and qualifications which are 'fit for the future' and how they can be designed and implemented in curricula and educational/training routes are increasingly gaining in importance. Appropriate measures call for substantiated findings on skill requirements in a longer-term perspective as well as information on new qualifications, competences and requirements which have not yet been defined by statistics and classifications. Early identification of future skill requirements is of the utmost importance for political decisions on the design of education and vocational training systems. This is already evident when one considers the time lag between the occurrence of an event triggering new or substantially different skill requirements and the point in time when the first cohorts leave the system with these new skill profiles: depending on the training system of the country in question and the relevant institutional, legal and formal regulations [2], there may be a time lag of as much as 10 years between the two events (see Figure 2). This is also the approximate time frame which projections should at least cover if their results are to be policy-relevant and not arrive too late. More long-term projections are necessary for fundamental reorientations or redesign of the education and training systems.

Figure 2. **Estimated time lags** [3] **between new skill requirements and job market entry of the first cohorts with the new skill profiles**

Triggering event: New skill requirements (e.g. due to technological innovation)	Time lag	Cumulated time lag
Recognition and identification of new skill requirements	0.5-1 year	–
Design/revision of skeleton curricula in initial training	0.5-1 year	1-2 years
Implementation in the training system	1-3 years	2-5 years
Young people commence training in the revised training programmes	0.5-2 years	2.5-7 years
Completion of training, job market entry of the first cohorts with the new skill profiles	2-3 years	4.5-10 years
Passage through working life	–	35-45 years

Source: based on Descy and Tessaring, 2002, p. 300.

---

[2] E.g. duration and permeability of training courses, involvement of the social partners, government, chambers, etc., competence and implementing regulations.
[3] Dependent on national institutional, legal, formal, etc. factors.

The fundamental objectives of such efforts are on the one hand, at individual level, career and personal advancement, identification with work and optimal design of individual life and career biographies, and prevention of unemployment, inappropriate employment and the exclusion of disadvantaged groups, which can be decisively achieved by means of appropriate and targeted education and training provision, at the level of society as a whole, on the other hand. And finally, since the achievement of all these aims is virtually inconceivable without a sufficient number of adequate jobs – or a flourishing development of the economy to decisively facilitate the process – information on the future requirements of work in enterprises is of central importance to meet the challenges of the future.

A majority of scientists and political and economic stakeholders agree that flexibilisation of work and working careers, the dissemination of information and communication technologies in virtually all areas and the growing role of 'knowledge' are increasingly calling for flexible, broadly based and transferable skills – in parallel with and complementary to 'traditional' specialised skills and working qualities.

At the same time, however, openness, flexibility and the change of meaning emerging in many countries with the movement away from (formal) 'qualifications' towards a more comprehensive understanding of 'competence', which includes non-formal and informal forms of learning and knowledge acquisition, is making it increasingly difficult to anticipate and define the knowledge, skills and competences which will be required in the future. Whereas it was previously a question of applying an 'equilibrium approach', and detecting and forecasting functional and formal qualifications at a high level of aggregation, e.g. with the aid of production functions or econometric processes, today the focus is increasingly on more comprehensive and qualitative approaches which are not intended to replace, but to supplement the 'traditional' methods and provide differentiated and exploitable information on changing trends in work requirements.

It should hereby be pointed out that efforts to identify and forecast skill requirements decisively depend on the type of education and training system and the job markets in the country in question: the question as to what is to be forecast and how this forecasting is to be conducted will be seen in a completely different light in vocationally-oriented labour markets with nationally defined training and qualification standards than in countries with predominantly competition-based or internal labour markets. Other factors which will play role, to mention but a few examples, are differences in planning and control and the participation of the various societal groups (governance) at centralised, decentralised/regional or sectoral level, as well as the increasingly indistinct boundaries between general and vocational education and training and continuing training in many countries. So it is hardly surprising that there is such a broad spectrum of objectives, approaches and forms of implementation in the various European countries, as demonstrated by this volume.

2. Approaches to identify future qualification and skill requirements

A whole series of quantitative approaches to the forecasting of the supply and demand of skills and jobs have been developed in recent decades, ranging from macroeconomic projections to surveys among enterprises and the workforce at micro and meso level, including the regional and sectoral level (for an overview see: Tessaring, 1998, 1999; Wilson 2001, Descy and Tessaring, 2002). However, although they may be consistent within a given socio-economic framework and important for fundamental long-range policy strategies in view of their long-term character, macro approaches cannot provide detailed insights into specific and new qualification and skill requirements. Furthermore, long-term projections are of only limited relevance for individuals standing before educational/training or career decisions and expecting information on employment prospects in the coming years. Similarly, most enterprises are more interested in short- and medium-term skill trends. On the other hand, specific findings on skill developments at micro and meso level cannot always be generalised. Moreover, they generally tend to refer to present skill requirements or needs foreseeable in the short or medium term.

These are some of the reasons why the European countries are in search of methods, approaches and data from which they can derive information on future skills and new qualifications not yet delivered by the education and training system. In complement to quantitative approaches, qualitative methods, e.g. Delphi or scenario methods, are increasingly applied, often 'enriched' by quantitative information relating to the various areas of relevance to the development of education and training (e.g. demographic or macroeconomic trends, job market structures, social developments, etc.). By drawing on expert knowledge from various areas, the aim of these approaches is to place possible and/or expected alternative education and training trends in a wider context as a means of deducing appropriate strategies and responsibilities.

The decisive difference between these and quantitative methods is not only that trends on both the supply and demand side can be dealt with simultaneously (e.g. skilling and integration problems of disadvantaged persons; the impact of changes in the distribution and organisation of labour in enterprises on the members of the workforce and their qualifications; identification of possible strategies and their effects), but also that 'anticipation' is no longer based on understandable calculations backed up by figures, but takes place 'in the minds' of experts consulted, on the strength of their knowledge and their sources of information. It is therefore of decisive importance for the quality and relevance of these approaches that they be theoretically substantiated, that the 'right' and relevant questions are asked and, above all, that suitable experts are found from all fields of activity (research, politics, business, social partners, etc.) and prompted into constructive cooperation.

The variety of approaches documented in the present volume, not only between European countries, but also within national borders, raises a further, by no means insignificant problem: How can the findings obtained via the different channels be collated, compared and rendered exploitable for policy action at national or EU level? For example, what findings are produced by a highly aggregated macro economic projection of skill requirements in interaction with a set of scenarios or sectoral, regional or company projections which have been established in isolation? Thus there may and will always be contradictions between macroeconomic and separately established sectoral or job-specific projections or enterprise surveys – just as there are contradictions between quantitative and qualitative projections. The reasons for these contradictions lie in differences in the time horizon, the depth of aggregation, the information and data basis and the methods. The decisive question is: how do those responsible for the planning and management of the education and training system handle these contradictions? What can be done to place their decisions in a reliable and reasonable framework which is not dominated by the interests of individual groups? And, last but not least, what conclusions can be drawn for the delivery of information to guide the educational/training and career decisions of the individual?

These are questions which can evidently only be briefly touched upon in the present context and how the findings can be rendered exploitable for political action will depend on the further continuation of the project. The following sections seek to provide the reader with an overview of relevant activities at both European and national level. With no pretensions of exhaustiveness (⁴), this overview is to be extended in the course of future project phases. The editors would be grateful for corresponding information and the indication of contacts.

3. Forecasting and early identification activities

3.1. Activities at European and international level

At the European level, the European Commission has and continues to support a number of related projects, particularly in its programmes Leonardo da Vinci and Targeted Socio-economic Research (TSER) and their follow-up programmes, and also within the framework of the European Structural Fund.

As early as in 1994, the European Commission expressly called for projections at national, regional, local and enterprise level: 'Vocational training should be coordinated with the needs of enterprises and individuals. The question is raised, how these needs could be considered, how changes of demand could be identified and how foreseeable changes could be anticipated and on which level' (p. 36). The Commission's comments on demand forecasts were as follows:
- 'as a tendency there are indications that improved demand forecasts are required;
- changes have to be anticipated better, concerning the national, regional, local and enterprise level;
- the European Community is asked to take initiatives in order to make the data collected available and comprehensible.' (ibid.)

In 2002, the European social partners – the European Trade Union Confederation (ETUC), the Union of Industrial and Employers' Confederations of Europe (UNICE) and the European Centre of Enterprises with Public Participation and of Enterprises of General Public Interest (CEEP) – adopted a 'framework of actions for the lifelong development of competencies and qualifications' (European Trade Union Confederation, 2002). The first of the four priorities is to 'identify and anticipate the competencies and the qualifications needed'. The text continues: 'Identifying competencies and qualifications needs and anticipating their development represents a complex task given the numerous socio-economic factors which must be taken into consideration, but it is imperative nevertheless' (p. 3). The implementation of this objective is envisaged by the social partners at two levels: at enterprise

---

(⁴) The contributions to this volume also make reference to further skill requirement forecasting and early recognition initiatives.

and at national/sectoral level. As far as the practicalities are concerned, the following measures, among others, are considered necessary: (1) work in partnerships with education and training providers at all levels; (2) develop networks to collect information and exchanges experiences, including by making effective use of the existing European instruments such as the European monitoring centre for change or Cedefop. (p. 3 f.)

A number of forecasting activities conducted in recent years at both European and international level are presented in the following.

1. In the 'Employment in Europe' reports, the *European Commission/Eurostat* publishes information on sectoral employment growth at irregular intervals. Those sectors identified as sectors with high (previous and expected) growth are generally those in which the proportion of the lesser skilled is lower than elsewhere. However there is no explicit break-down of sectoral growth according to skills or occupations.

2. The Institute for Prospective Technological Studies (IPTS), one of the institutes of the Joint Research Centre of the European Commission, has presented a series of – qualitative and quantitative – forecasting studies in recent years which also touch upon aspects of education, training and skilling.

   - In the framework of the 'Futures' project, launched in 1998, the IPTS brought together a considerable number of experts and decision-makers from the business and scientific communities and politics. The project is designed to provide insights into trends in the demographic, social, economic, skilling and technology fields as well as their impact on competitiveness and employment up to 2010. The reports drawn up in the framework of this project comprise analyses and trends of various socio-economic aspects of European society, whereby the focus is on their relationship with technological development. The conclusion of future trends is not or only partially based on projections in the technical sense, but is largely the reflection of estimates and assessments of the participating experts or takes the form of scenarios. The reports were discussed and summarised in five panels: demographic and social trends; ICT and the information society; natural resources and the environment; the political and economic context; life sciences and the frontier of life. The panel study and the research reports are published in the 'Futures Report series' (further details at: http://futures.jrc.es).

   - In 2000, in cooperation with the European Science and Technology Observatory (ESTO) network, the IPTS launched a projection of the impact of technologies on the economy and employment in the EU. The starting point of this initiative is the 'Technology and Employment Map'

of the afore-mentioned Futures project. In the framework of two simulation models and using an approach which is a combination of qualitative and quantitative analyses, the network projects the impact of various technologies on productivity, consumption and consequently on growth and employment on the basis of a number of alternative technology policy scenarios up to the year 2020. The projections include sectoral skill requirements, but only for highly aggregated skill levels. The results are supplemented by statements on skill supply and – in comparison with demand – estimates of future skill bottlenecks in the field of technologies and research and development. A preliminary project report was prepared in December 2001 (IPTS, 2001).
- In 2001, in conjunction with the Information Society Technologies (IST) Advisory Group, DG Information Society and 35 European experts, the IPTS published a series of scenarios on the future development of information and communication technologies taking account of the following critical factors: (a) socio-political factors; (b) enterprise and industrial models; (c) the demand for key technologies for 'ambient intelligence' 2010. The scenarios also included aspects of learning, human resources management and competences (European Commission, 2001).

3. In 1999, *Cedefop,* along with the *European Training Foundation* (ETF) and the *Max-Goote Expert Centre* (University of Amsterdam) initiated a scenario on vocational training in Europe with the participation of five EU Member States and five central and eastern European countries: Germany, Greece, Luxembourg/Belgium, Austria, the United Kingdom, the Czech Republic, Estonia, Hungary, Poland and Slovenia.

The scenario is based on a Delphi survey among several hundred vocational training experts per country, asked to name expected trends, strategies and players in the field of vocational training. The findings provide an insight into possible and probable developments of vocational training systems (up to approx. 2010), by examining trends in the following three important contexts:
(a) the economy and technology,
(b) employment and the job market,
(c) training, skills and knowledge.

The project also provides information on possible strategies and players in the field of vocational training. The first phase of this project was concluded in the spring of 2000, the second at the end of 2001. A report on the findings of Phase I is already available (Sellin et al., 2000) and a document on the findings of Phase II is currently being drawn up by

Cedefop (Van Wieringen et al., forthcoming; further information at the Cedefop Electronic Training Village: http://www.trainingvillage.gr).
4. The *European Commission's Forward Studies Unit* conducted a project entitled 'Scenarios Europe 2010. Five possible futures for Europe' (European Commission, Forward Studies Unit, 1999). The project draws on the expertise of European Commission officials in a process of brainstorming and reflection. The scenarios encompass all the important aspects of European development: markets, the economy, employment and technologies; social, political, demographic, cultural and changing values; globalisation and EU enlargement; the role of national and European organisations, social partners and NGOs, etc.
The scenario may be accessed on the Internet (EN, FR, DE, IT) at http://europa.eu.int/comm/cdp/scenario/index_en.htm.
5. In 1990, the *OECD* launched the 'International Futures Programmes', consisting of four interrelated and mutually supportive elements:
    (a) OECD Forums for the Future: a platform for informal, high-level meetings with the aim of testing new ideas, developing fresh perspectives on problems and advancing the understanding of strategic economic and social issues;
    (b) OECD Futures Projects: targeted and multidisciplinary research and policy analysis on certain subject areas which are in particular from the Forum conferences;
    (c) OECD Future Studies Information Base: a documentation system (CD ROM) providing the key findings and conclusions of published and unpublished literature worldwide;
    (d) OECD International Futures Network: a global network of some 600 persons from government, the economy, research, who share a mutual interest in long-term developments and related policy aspects.

Information at: http://www.oecd.org/sge/au/

3.2. Initiatives on the early recognition of skill requirements at country level

The following provides a summary of selected activities relating to the forecasting and early recognition of skill requirements in a number of European and OECD countries. These initiatives encompass a wide range of quantitative and qualitative approaches at the level of sectors, occupations or qualifications, derived from both statistics or information drawn from enterprises and experts. In the first instance, a number of projects providing an overview of activities in several European and non-European countries are presented. This is followed by an attempt to summarise these and other activities, drawing on both information from the various contributions to this volume as well as additional sources.

3.2.1. *Overviews of forecasting activities in various countries*

1. *Frequenznet/Social Science Research Centre Berlin (WZB): OECD countries*
In the project 'Qualification needs in the OECD countries', sponsored by the German Ministry of Education and Research (BMBF), WZB conducts research into how skill requirements are detected and – on the basis of the example of the health, information technology, metal-working and electrical engineering sectors – how new skills are implemented in Germany. This activity on the identification of skill requirements in OECD-countries is part of the 'FreQueNz' research network.

The project analyses micro-economic models in a string of OECD countries and on the basis of this information and other elements, carries out cross-country comparisons, in particular in a number of specific sectors (services, computers, health and care). Following the pilot phase, concluded in 1999, a network of experts from eight OECD-countries was set up. The network's findings are available on the Internet platform at http://www.frequenz.net.

A further activity in the framework of this project was the organisation of a joint workshop of Franco-German occupational and training research experts (26-27 October 2000) which addressed the following issues: (a) quantitative aspects and skill structure; (b) new approaches in the field of the early recognition of skill requirements; (c) sectoral analyses with a view to identifying skill requirements; (d) regional analyses with a view to identifying skill requirements.

Publications: Gülker, Hilbert and Schömann, 2000; n.n., 2000; Schömann, 2001.

2. *Cedefop: European trends in the development of occupations and qualifications*
This publication features a summary of contributions to Cedefop's 'Ciretoq' network. Vol. I summarises the main macro-trends in the development of occupations and qualifications against the background of social, economic, technical and cultural challenges. Vol. II features contributions by scientists from various disciplines, touching upon the following subject areas: (a) the socio-economic context and systems development; (b) development of supply and demand in initial vocational training; (c) competences and qualifications' development in the light of continuing education/training and lifelong learning; (d) inter-enterprise and in-company developments and local/regional competition; (e) teaching and learning languages; (f) EU

programmes and outcomes of vocational education and training research; (g) activities of Cedefop's network for 'European trends in occupations and qualifications.'

Publications: Sellin, 1999; Sellin, ed., 2000.

3. *Cedefop: Reports on vocational training research in Europe*
Since 1998, Cedefop has been publishing regular Reports on vocational training research in Europe covering a wide range of issues. The reports include a presentation and analysis of the latest forecasts on skill supply and demand. The research reports consist of a comprehensive background report with contributions from reputed scientists, as well as an extended synthesis report, featuring a summary and a critical appraisal of this and other research studies.

An article in the first research report (1998/99) addresses 'the future of work and skills – visioning, trends and forecasts' (Tessaring, 1998). Starting out from fundamental processes of change in society and work in enterprises, the contribution presents approaches and findings of both quantitative and qualitative skill and job supply in various EU countries (Germany, Ireland, Netherlands, Finland, United Kingdom).

The second research report (2001/02) includes an article by Wilson (2001), entitled 'Forecasting skill requirements at national and company levels' in which the author gives a critical appraisal of forecasting approaches used so far and weighs up their pros and cons. The article provides a detailed overview of quantitative and qualitative forecasting activities at national level in various EU and non-EU countries and of relevant activities at regional and local level. The contribution also features a discussion of skill projections at enterprise level. The synthesis report provides information on the latest forecasts and scenarios in Germany, France, Ireland, the Netherlands, Finland, Sweden, the United Kingdom and a number of central and eastern European countries.

Publications: Tessaring, 1998, 1999; Descy and Tessaring, 2002; Wilson, 2001.

4. *National Observatory of Employment and Training, Czech Republic:*
   LABOURatory for the regular forecasting of training requirements
The Leonardo da Vinci project 'Regular forecasting of training needs: comparative analysis, elaboration and application of methodology, "LABOURatory"', sponsored by the European Commission, was set up in 1998. The aim of the project is to draw up forecasting methods applicable not only to western but also to eastern European countries. The project is

coordinated by the Czech National Observatory of Employment and Training, (NTF; project leader: O. Strietska-Ilina). The LABOURatory members come from the Czech Republic (CERGE), France (OREF and the private-sector corporate consultancy, Quaternaire), Ireland (ESRI) and the Netherlands (ROA), as well as two national observatories and independent experts from Germany (IAB) and other countries.

The project's first step was to take stock of forecasting activities in the Czech Republic, France, Germany, Ireland, the Netherlands, Poland and Slovenia. The second phase of the project involved the presentation of methods and models used in forecasting training needs and their application in various countries: quantitative models and their application in the Czech Republic; comparative analyses and forecasting activities in Poland; regional and sectoral methods (case studies for the hotel, catering and tourist trade in the Czech Republic, France and Slovenia). The publication includes an overview of the methods, applications and findings as well as the conclusions on possible improvements to the methods.

Publications: NTF, 1999, 2001.

5. ETF: Skill needs of SMEs in regions of five candidate countries
In 2001, in cooperation with national partner organisations, the ETF carried out a survey on skill needs in specific regions of five candidate countries (north west Bohemia/Czech Republic, southern Estonia, the southern Hungarian plain, Lithuania and the Lubelskie district of Poland). The purpose of the survey was to conduct an intensive qualitative assessment of emerging regional skill requirements in small and medium-sized enterprises (SMEs), to examine demand-related perspectives in the context of the local infrastructure supply and to prepare the development of intervention strategies. The survey included 952 SMEs from 15 sectors in five regions located in economies in various phases of the transition process.

See the contribution by L. Kerr (in this volume) for further details.

6. Career Space Consortium: the demand for ICT skills in Europe
The Career Space Consortium, comprising a number of major electronic companies alongside the European Commission, has set itself the aim of analysing information on the situation and perspectives of skills and skill requirements in the field of information and communication technologies in Europe and to draw up appropriate recommendations for education and training policy – in particular with a view to narrowing the current ICT skills gap.

For further details, see the contribution by M. Curley (in this volume).
A further report on this subject has been published by Cedefop (2001).

3.2.2. *Overview on national forecasting activities*

With no pretension that the information is exhaustive, up-to-date or correct in every detail, the following table gives an overview of the institutions in Europe involved in skills and occupational forecasting activities as well as the approaches applied. Further information and source references can be obtained from the individual contributions in this volume as well as the bibliography. The editors would be grateful for any corrections or additional details.

4. Summary and future cooperation

Identifying and forecasting future skill requirements – at the level of individuals, enterprises and society as a whole – and implementing these requirements in the framework of the education and training system has long been the subject of intensive research efforts and political discussion. Societies characterised by rapidly changing social and economic conditions, increasing openness, permeability, complexity, and therefore uncertainty, are seeking new, alternative or complementary instruments for the early identification of skill requirements and their implications for the design of education, initial vocational training and continuing training. Such approaches consider the future skill requirements of target groups, enterprises, sectors and regions and increasingly incorporate options and alternatives for policy and strategic actions.

In this context, the objectives of the early identification of skill requirements may in fact differ substantially:
- Projecting future developments/trends of supply and demand of existing (formal) qualifications;
- Forecasting changing skill profiles in a given occupation or sector;
- Identifying newly emerging skills and requirements;
- Analysing the increasing or declining significance of contents or elements within specific qualifications;
- Detecting new configurations or bundles of skill elements in a given activity;
- Taking into consideration (formally, non-formally or informally acquired) competences instead of purely formal qualifications, etc.

Table 1. National skill requirement forecasting and early identification activities
(The abbreviations are explained in the annex)

Country	Institution	Approach/Method/Data sources	Comments
Czech Republic	CERGE-EI, RILSA, NOET-NTF	Macro-economic projection model: extension, replacement and recruitment demand; those leaving the education/training systems; balancing supply and demand.	Based on the ROA and ESRI forecasting models; implemented within the Leonardo project, 'LABOURatory'.
	NOET-NTF, Trexima, Ministry of Labour and Social Affairs	Skill needs analyses, short to medium-term qualitative-type projection – sectoral and regional (e.g. tourism sector in the region of north west Bohemia).	
	NOET-NTF/ Trexima/RILSA supported by Ministry of Labour and Social Affairs	Integration of macro-economic forecasts in an 'integrated system of typical positions' (ISTP) to determine qualification requirements and training needs.	In the set-up phase
	NOET-NTF supported by Ministry of abour and Social Affairs	Research into skill shortages, elaboration of methodology of regular monitoring of skill shortages.	in the development phase
Denmark	AKF	Macro-economic projections of labour demand according to level of education/training and sector at national and regional level; projection of labour supply according to education/training categories based on demographic trends.	in the development phase
	Regions	Short-term forecasting of skill requirements in the regions, combination of job market data with panel data from surveys among enterprises and experts.	
Germany	IAB/Prognos	Long-term macro-economic demand projections per sector, qualification level and field of activity; carried out on an irregular basis since 1986.	
	IAB	Projection of labour force supply and the those leaving education/training on the basis of the educational accounting system (BGR) (on an irregular basis).	
	KMK	Projection of scholars, students and those leaving the education/training system; on a regular basis.	
	BLK	Macro-economic projection of skill supply and demand (on an irregular basis).	On the basis of various projections (of e.g. IAB/Prognos, etc.)
	FreQueNz	'Early recognition of skill requirements'; sponsored by BMBF; 8 participating research institutes. Approaches: job vacancy analysis; reference enterprise surveys; examination of regional continuing training provision; examination of the skill supply of vocational schools and colleges; utilisation of the network of specialised associations and chambers; development of methods for the ongoing observation of skill trends; skill trends in the service sector; identification of trendsetters; comparative international studies; skill structure report; skills report and skill trends – online.	Further details in the relevant articles in this publication or at the FreQueNz website: ww.frequenz.net
	Research institutes, *Länder*	Projections produced on an irregular basis by various universities, research bodies and the *Länder*.	
	BIBB	Econometric simulation and forecasting model of industrial vocational training (training place supply and demand).	In the development phase
Spain	FORCEM	Observation of skill and training requirements, including the sectoral and occupational level.	
	Autonomous regions	Observatories to identify skill requirements at regional level.	
	OBINCUAL/ Ministry of Employment	Network to identify key qualifications/skills and sectors and future trends in occupations, jobs and occupational profiles; scenarios, Delphi surveys, etc.	In the set-up phase
France	BIPE	Macro-economic projections of skill and recruitment requirements per occupational category, sectors and (to a certain extent) region; supplemented by scenarios.	
	OREF	Qualification needs at national, sectoral, regional and local levels; skill supply and projection of school-leavers and those coming out of training; employment perspectives.	

Country	Institution	Approach/Method/Data sources	Comments
France	Céreq	Changing skill requirements on the basis of expert/enterprise surveys and job market analysis.	
Finland	Central Office for Education	Projections of occupational and skill trends (supply and demand), since 1976.	
	Ministry of Employment	Manpower supply and demand: short- and long-term trends	
	National Board of Education	Medium- to long-term macro-economic projections of manpower supply and demand per educational/training and occupational category, combined with scenarios and experts' forecasts.	
Ireland	ESRI	Regular macro-economic projections of skill requirements per sector.	
	FORFÁS/ Expert Group on Future Skill Needs	Short- and medium-term forecasting of the supply and demand of skilled manpower in certain sectors and areas, in particular ICT and research.	
Italy	Government, network	National surveys on short- and medium-term job and skill requirements per sector; surveys on regional and occupational skill needs; scenarios; annual recruitment needs; medium-term macro-economic forecasts.	Coordinated by the Ministry For Employment and Social Affairs
	Regions	Various skill requirement projections	
Netherlands	ROA	Short- and medium-term macro-economic projections of skill supply and demand according to sector; incorporation of mobility and substitution processes; projection of school-leavers.	
	Max-Goote Expert Centre	Scenarios of educational and training trends.	
Poland	Various organisations, government	Projection of skill requirements.	Preparatory work; projection of global labour supply available
	National Observatory	Short- and medium-term projection of manpower requirements according to sector, occupation and educational/training level, including a regional structure; projection of those leaving the education/training system and manpower supply.	Implemented within the context of the Leonardo project 'LABOURatory'
Portugal	Ministry of Employment	Surveys on the short-term training requirements of enterprises according to sector and region.	
Slovenia	HRDF	Surveys on the training requirements of enterprises (in certain regions).	
		Development of the tourist sector and training requirements (in certain regions).	Implemented within the context of the Leonardo project 'LABOURatory'
Sweden	Central Statistical Office	Projection of recruitment requirements and transitions from education/training to employment; Balance of supply and demand.	
	Swedish Foresight	Projection of long-term technical, social and economic trends (including education and training) and their interaction on the basis of an expert panel and additional information.	
United Kingdom	IER	Macro-economic long-term projection of manpower requirements according to qualification levels, including regional and local structures; forecasts of those coming out of training; on a regular basis.	
	DfEE	Compilation and analysis of job market trends, on a regular basis.	
	DfEE/Skills Task Force	Skill requirement projections.	
	NIESR	Qualitative projection of training requirements.	
	QCA, London University etc.	Scenarios on skill requirements in various sectors and regions.	Partially in the set-up phase

As the contributions to this volume and the contents of the present article show, the channels and the approaches used in the various countries and by the different scientists are extremely diverse. Some countries have already made considerable progress, whereas others are still at the beginning of the process – either due to a lack of relevant experience and skills, or because the relevant organisational infrastructure or support on the political level is not yet sufficient. Access to this information is frequently difficult and cooperation across national borders – despite a certain degree of progress in the recent past – is not yet well-developed.

So, from this perspective, this publication of the proceedings of the conference on 30-31 May 2002 is not only to be seen as an inventory of the activities in the various European countries, but could also provide the starting point for future intensive cooperation – both between scientists and research institutions from different countries, as well as between researchers, policymakers and practitioners. Both aspects are of the utmost importance: exchange of experience and transnational research cooperation should serve as a driving force for the further development of methods and approaches. The involvement from the very outset of policymakers and practitioners – including the social partners – is designed to raise awareness among the stakeholders of the relevance of and the need for a future-oriented design of education and training – based on concrete information and recommendations – and thereby encourage them to support corresponding efforts in terms of personnel, finance and organisational resources.

In concrete terms, cooperation and transparency could be promoted in the following ways:
- Mutual *exchange* of experience on methods, approaches, new and planned projects and the outcomes of early recognition initiatives in the framework of regular specialised conferences and/or bi- and multilateral meetings of researchers and stakeholders. The Berlin conference on 30-31 May 2002 in Berlin is to be followed up by a second conference in the spring of 2003. The results of the conference should be published and made available via the Internet. The drawing up and ongoing update of an 'early recognition handbook' and a 'European skills development report', also posted on the web, should also be envisaged (by analogy to the 'qualifications report' of the early recognition initiative in Germany).
- Establishment of a cross-country *network* – incorporating the EU candidate and other countries – along the lines of what has been done in the context of e.g. the LABOURatory project (NTF, 1999 and 2001) and in the WZB project's early recognition initiative. This network would require an

organisational framework with corresponding personnel and financial resources. A further aim is to build up an *information and documentation database* with the participation of all network members and including other external sources.
- Establishment of a *website* or an extranet to create greater transparency and as a discussion platform for the members of the network. Corresponding infrastructures are already available, e.g. website of the early recognition initiative (www.frequenz.net), Cedefop's Electronic Training Village (ETV) (www.trainingvillage.gr), the research platforms 'Cedefop Research Arena' (CEDRA; http://www2.trainingvillage.gr/etv/cedra/default.asp) and the 'European Research Overview' (ERO) of Cedefop and WIFO (Wissenschaftsforum Bildung und Gesellschaft e.V.; http.//www.b.shuttle.de/wifo/vet/ero.htm). A further possibility to be envisaged is the creation of an extranet in the context of the EU CIRCA network (Communication & Information Resource Centre Administration; http://forum.europa.eu.int/), which is however only accessible to registered members. Cedefop has already set up a number of interest groups for specific projects and activities in the framework of this extranet.

Bibliography

Cedefop. *Generic ICT skills profiles. Future skills for tomorrow's world – Career Space.* Cedefop Panorama. Thessaloniki 2001.

Descy, P.; Tessaring, M. *Training and learning for competence. Second report on vocational training research in Europe: Synthesis report.* Cedefop Reference series, Luxembourg: EUR-OP, 2002 (also available in DE, FR and ES).

European Trade Union Confederation. *Framework of actions for the lifelong development of competencies and qualifications.* European Trade Union Confederation (ETUC), Union of Industrial and Employers' Confederations of Europe (UNICE), European Centre of Enterprises with Public Participation and of Enterprises of General Economic Interest (CEEP), Brussels, 28 February 2002.

European Commission, Forward Studies Unit. *Scenarios Europe 2010. Five possible futures for Europe. Working paper July 1999.* Gilles B., coord.; Michalski, A.; Pench L.R. Brussels 1999 (also available in FR and IT); http://europa.eu.int/comm/cdp/scenario/index_en.htm).

European Commission. *Vocational training in the European Community: challenges and future outlook: Follow-up to the Commission memorandum* on vocational training in the European Community in the 1990s. Luxembourg: EUR-OP, 1994.

European Commission. ISTAG. *Scenarios for ambient intelligence in 2010.* Final report compiled by K. Ducatel et al. IPTS Seville, IST. Luxembourg 2001.

Eurostat. *Statistics in focus*, 19/2002 and 20/2002, Luxembourg, 2002.

Gülker, S.; Hilbert, C.; Schömann, K. *Lernen von den Nachbarn. Qualifikationsbedarf in Ländern der OECD.* Bullinger, H.-J., ed. Qualifikationen erkennen – Berufe gestalten, vol. 3. Bielefeld 2000.

IPTS (Institute for Prospective Technological Studies). *Impact of technological and structural change on employment. Prospective Analysis 2020. Synthesis report.* Report to the Committee on Employment and Social Affairs of the European Parliament. Seville (draft), December 2001.

NTF. *Forecasting education and training needs in transition countries: Lessons from the western European experience.* Prague 1999.

NTF. *Forecasting skill needs: Methodology elaboration and testing.* Prague 2001.

N.N. Qualifikationsbedarf in OECD-Ländern. *WZB-Mitteilungen* 87, March 2000, p. 17-18.

Schoemaker, P.J.H. Scenario planning: A tool for strategic thinking. *Sloane Management Review*, Winter 1995, pp. 25 ff.

Schömann, K. *Qualifikationen von morgen. Ein deutsch-französischer Dialog.* Bullinger, H.-J., ed. Qualifikationen erkennen – Berufe gestalten, vol. 5. Bielefeld 2001.

Sellin, B. et al. *Scenarios and strategies for vocational education and training in Europe. European synthesis report on phase I.* Max Goote report. Amsterdam 2000.

Sellin, B. *European trends in the development of occupations and qualifications – Vol. I.* Cedefop Reference Document. Luxembourg: EUR-OP, 1999 (also available in FR and DE).

Sellin, B., ed. *European trends in the development of occupations and qualifications – vol. II: Findings of research, studies and analyses for policy and practice.* Cedefop Reference Document. Luxembourg: EUR-OP, 2000.

Tessaring, M. *Training for a changing society: a report on current vocational education and training research in Europe 1998.* Cedefop Reference Document. Luxembourg: EUR-OP, 1999 (Synthesis report; also available in FR, DE and ES).

Tessaring, M. The future of work and skills – visions, trends and forecasts. *In* Tessaring, M., ed. *Vocational education and training – the European research field.* Background report 1998, Vol. I. Luxembourg: EUR-OP, 1998, p. 271-317.

Van Wieringen et al. *Future education: learning the future. Scenarios and strategies in Europe* (in the course of preparation).

Wilson, R.A. Forecasting skill requirements at national and company levels. *In* Descy, P.; Tessaring, M., eds. *Training in Europe. Second report on vocational training research in Europe 2000: background report.* Cedefop Reference series. Vol. II. Luxembourg: EUR-OP, 2001, p. 561-609.

Annex

List of authors

Lothar Abicht
Institut für Strukturpolitik und
Wirtschaftsförderung Halle-Leipzig e.V. (isw) /
Institute of Structural Policies and Economic
Development
Halle (Saale), Germany
E-mail: isw.halle.abicht@t-online.de
www.isw-online.org
www.frequenz.net

Gert Alaby
Socialstyrelsen / The National Board of Health and
Welfare
Stockholm, Sweden
E-mail: Gert.Alaby@sos.se
www.sos.se/sosmeny.htm

Norbert Bromberger
Forschungsinstitut für Berufsbildung im
Handwerk an der Universität zu Köln (FBH) /
Research Institute for Vocational Education and
Training in the Crafts Sector at the
University of Cologne
Cologne, Germany
E-mail: Norbert.Bromberger@uni-koeln.de
www.uni-koeln.de/wiso-fak/fbh/
www.frequenz.net

Frank Cörvers
Dutch Research Centre for Education and
the Labour Market (ROA)
Maastricht University, Faculty of Economics and
Business Administration
Maastricht, The Netherlands
E-mail: F.Coervers@ROA.unimaas.nl
E-mail: secretary@roa.unimaas.nl
www.fdewb.unimaas.nl/roa/home.htm

Mike Coles
The Qualification and Curriculum Authority (QCA)
London, United Kingdom
E-mail: ColesM@qca.org.uk
www.qca.org.uk

Martin Curley
Intel Corporation
Leixlip, Ireland
E-mail: Martin.G.Curley@intel.com
www.intel.com

Helen Diedrich-Fuhs
Kuratorium der Deutschen Wirtschaft für
Berufsbildung (KWB) / German Employers'
Organisation for Vocational Training
Bonn, Germany
E-Mail: Diedrich-Fuhs@kwb-berufsbildung.de
www.kwb-berufsbildung.de

Mario Gatti
Instituto per lo Sviluppo della Formazione dei
Lavoratori / Institute for the Development of
Workers' Vocational Training (ISFOL)
Rome, Italy
E-mail: m.gatti@isfol.it
www.isfol.it

Gerd Gidion
Fraunhofer-Institut für Arbeitswirtschaft und
Organisation (FhIAO) / Fraunhofer Institute for
Industrial Engineering
Stuttgart, Germany
E-mail: gerd.gidion@iao.fhg.de
www.pm.iao.fhg.de
www.frequenz.net

Gerard Hughes
The Economic and Social Research Institute
(ESRI)
Dublin, Ireland
E-mail: gerry.hughes@esri.ie
www.esri.ie

Lewis Kerr
until July 2002: European Training
Foundation (ETF)
E-mail: lewis.kerr@ntlworld.com

Joan-Louis Kirsch
Centre d'Études et de Recherches sur les Qualifications (Céreq) / Centre for Research on Education, Training and Employment
Marseille, France
E-mail: jlkirsch@cereq.fr
www.cereq.fr

Manfred Kremer
Bundesministerium für Bildung und Forschung / Federal Ministry of Education and Research
Bonn, Germany
E-mail: Manfred.Kremer@BMBF.Bund.de
www.bmbf.de

Helmut Kuwan
Helmut Kuwan - Sozialwissenschaftliche Forschung und Beratung München / Social Research and Consultancy Munich
Munich, Germany
E-Mail: Helmut.Kuwan@supplier.nfoeurope.com
www.HK-Forschung.de

Tom Leney
Institute of Education, University of London
London, United Kingdom
E-mail: leney@easynet.co.uk
http://ioewebserver.ioe.ac.uk/ioe/cms/get.asp?cid=1397&1397_1=2048

Ferran Mañé
Rovira I Virgili Universitat, Department d'Economia / Rovira i Virgili University, Department of Economics, Reus, Spain
E-mail: fmv@correu.urv.es
www.urv.es

Josep Oliver
Universitat Autònoma de Barcelona / Autonomous University of Barcelona, Applied Economics Department
Barcelona, Spain
E-mail: josep.oliver@uab.es
www.uab.es

Jordi Planas
Institut de Ciències de l'Educació (ICE) - Universitat Autonoma de Barcelona (UAB) / Education Sciences Institute – Autonomous University of Barcelona
Bellaterra (Barcelona), Spain
E-mail: jordi.planas@uab.es
www.ub.es/ice

Susanne Liane Schmidt
Fraunhofer-Institut für Arbeitswirtschaft und Organisation (FhIAO) / Fraunhofer Institute for Industrial Engineering
Stuttgart, Germany
E-mail: Susanne.Schmidt@iao.fhg.de
www.pm.iao.fhg.de
www.frequenz.net

Kathrin Schnalzer
Fraunhofer-Institut für Arbeitswirtschaft und Organisation (FhIAO)/Fraunhofer Institute for Industrial Engineering
Stuttgart, Germany
E-mail: kathrin.schnalzer@iao.fhg.de
www.pm.iao.fhg.de
www.frequenz.net

Klaus Schömann
Wissenschaftszentrum Berlin für Sozialforschung (WZB) / Social Science Research Center Berlin
Berlin, Germany
E-mail: klaus@wz-berlin.de
www.wz-berlin.de
www.frequenz.net

Jerry J. Sexton
The Economic and Social Research Institute (ESRI)
Dublin, Ireland
E-mail: Jerry.Sexton@esri.ie
www.esri.ie

Stavros Stavrou
European Centre for the Development of
Vocational Training (Cedefop)
Thessaloniki, Greece
E-mail: sts@cedefop.eu.int
www.cedefop.eu.int
www2.trainingvillage.gr

Olga Strietska-Ilina
National Observatory of Employment and Training
National Training Fund
Prague, Czech Republic
E-mail: strietska-ilina@nvf.cz
www.nvf.cz/observatory

Pal Tamas
Hungarian Academy of Science, Institute of Sociology
Budapest, Hungary
E-mail: H8756tam@ella.hu

Manfred Tessaring
European Centre for the Development of
Vocational Training (Cedefop)
Thessaloniki, Greece
E-mail: mt@cedefop.eu.int
www.cedefop.eu.int
www.trainingvillage.gr

Miriam Thum
Infratest Sozialforschung / Infratest Social Research
Munich, Germany
E-mail: miriam.thum@nfoeurope.com
www.infratest-sofo.de
www.frequenz.net

Rainer Werner
Institut für Strukturpolitik und
Wirtschaftsförderung Halle-Leipzig e.V. (isw) /
Institute of Structural Policies and Economic Development
Halle (Saale), Germany
E-mail: werner@isw-ev.de
www.isw-online.org

Peter Wordelmann
Bundesinstitut für Berufsbildung (BIBB) /
Federal Institute for Vocational Training
Bonn, Germany
E-mail: wordelmann@bibb.de
www.bibb.de

Beate Zeller
bfz Bildungsforschung / bfz Vocational
Training Research Department of the Bavarian Employers' Associations
Nuremberg, Germany
E-mail: zeller.beate@bf.bfz.de
http://bildungsforschung.bfz.de
www.frequenz.net

Abbreviations

Country abbreviations

A	Austria
AL	Albania
B	Belgium
BG	Bulgaria
CC	Candidate Countries
CEECs	Central and Eastern European Countries
CH	Switzerland
CY	Cyprus
CZ	Czech Republic
D	Germany
DK	Denmark
E	Spain
EE	Estonia
EL	Greece
EU	European Union
F	France
FIN	Finland
GDR	former German Democratic Republic
HU	Hungary
I	Italy
IRL	Ireland
IS	Iceland
L	Luxembourg
LT	Lithuania
LV	Latvia
N	Norway
NL	Netherlands
P	Portugal
PL	Poland
RO	Romania
S	Sweden
SK	Slovakia
SL	Slovenia
UK	United Kingdom

Institutions and organisations
(in brackets: country)

* unofficial translation

AFNOR	Association Française de Normalisation / French Association for Standardication
AKF	Institute of Local Government Studies (DK)
bfz	Berufliche Fortbildungszentren der Bayerischen Wirtschaft / Vocational Training Research Department of the Bavarian Employers' Associations (D)
BIBB	Bundesinstitut für Berufsbildung / Federal Institute for Vocational Training (D)
BIPE	Bureau d'Informations et de Prévisions Économiques / Bureau of Information and Economic Forecasting* (F)
BLK	Bund-Länder-Kommission für Bildungsplanung und Forschungsförderung / State-Federal Committee for Educational Planning and Research Promotion (D)
BMDF	Bundesministerium für Bildung und Forschung / Federal Ministry of Education and Research (D)
CBS	Centraal Bureau voor de Statistiek / Statistics Netherlands
Cedefop	European Centre for the Development of Vocational Training (EU)
CEEP	European Centre of Enterprises with Public Participation and of Enterprises of General Economic Interest
CÉREQ	Centre d'Etudes et de Rechorches sur les Qualifications / Centre for Research on Education, Training and Employment (F)
CERGE-EI	Center for Economic Research and Graduate Education at the Economic Institute (CZ)
CGFP	Consejo General de la Formación Profesional / General Council for Vocational Training (E)

CPB	Centraal Plaanbureau / Bureau for Economic Policy Analysis (NL)		Education Sciences Institute – Autonomous University of Barcelona (E)
DfEE	Department for Education and Employment (UK)	IDC	International Data Corporation
DG	Directorate General (of the European Commission) (EU)	IEA	International Association for the Evaluation of Educational Achievement
DTI	Department of Trade and Industry (UK)	IER	Institute for Employment Research (UK)
EICTA	European Information and Communications Technology Industry Association	IHK	Industrie- und Handelskammer / Chamber of Industry and Commerce (D)
EITO	European Information Technology Observatory	ILDC	National Careers Guidance Information Centre* (NL)
ESRI	Economic and Social Research Institute (IRL)	ILO	International Labour Office
ESTO	European Science and Technology Observatory	INCUAL	Instituto Nacional de las Cualificaciones / National Institute for Qualifications (E)
ETF	European Training Foundation (EU)		
ETUC	European Trade Union Confederation	INE	Instituto Nacional de Estatística / National Institute of Statistics (E)
FÁS	Training and Employment Authority (IRL)	INEM	Instituto Nacional de Empleo / National Employment Institute (E)
FBH	Forschungsinstitut für Berufsbildung im Handwerk an der Universität zu Köln / Research Institute for Vocational Education and Training in the Crafts Sector at the University of Cologne (D)	IPTS	Institute for Prospective Technological Studies (EU)
		ISFOL	Istituto per lo Sviluppo della Formazione dei Lavoratori / Institute for the Development of Workers' Vocational Training* (I)
FhIAO	Fraunhofer-Institut für Arbeitswirtschaft und Organisation / Fraunhofer Institute for Industrial Engineering (D)	IST	Information Society Technology
		ISTAT	Istituto Nazionale di Statistica / National Institute of Statistics (I)
FORCEM	Fundación para la Formación Continua / Foundation for Continuing Training* (E)	ISTP	Integrated System of Typal Positions
		isw	Institut für Strukturpolitik und Wirtschaftsförderung Halle-Leipzig e.V. / Institute of Structural Policies and Economic Development (D)
FORFÁS	The National Policy and Advisory Board for Enterprise, Trade, Science, Technology & Innovation (IRL)		
		IW	Institut der deutschen Wirtschaft Köln / Institute of the German Industry Cologne* (D)
GRET	Grupo de Investigación e Intercambio Tecnológico / Research Group on Technology Exchange* (E)		
		KMK	Ständige Konferenz der Kultusminister der Länder / Standing Conference of the Ministers for Culture of the Länder* (D)
HRDF	Human Resource Development Fund (SI)		
IAB	Institut für Arbeitsmarkt- und Berufsforschung der Bundesanstalt für Arbeit / Institute for Employment Research of the German Federal Employment Services (D)	KWB	Kuratorium der Deutschen Wirtschaft für Berufsbildung / German Employers' Organisation for Vocational Training (D)
ICE-UAB	Instituto de Ciències de l'Educació – Universitat Autònoma de Barcelona /	NCVQ	National Council for Vocational Qualifications (UK)

NIESR	National Institute of Economic and Social Research (UK)		**Terms and other abbreviations**	
NOET-NTF	National Observatory of Employment and Training (CZ)			
NTF	National Observatory of Vocational Training and Labour Market (CZ)		ACP	Production Capacity Assurance
			ADeBar	Arbeitsnahe Dauerbeobachtung der Qualifikationsentwicklung mit dem Ziel der Früherkennung von Veränderungen in der Arbeit und in den Betrieben / Permanent close-to-the-job observation of qualification needs, aiming at an early identification of changes at the workplace and within enterprises
NTO	National Training Organisation (UK)			
OBINCUAL	Observatorio de l'Instituto Nacional de las Cualificaciones / Observatory of the National Institute of Qualifications* (E)			
OECD	Organisation for Economic Cooperation and Development			
OREF	Observatoire Régional Emploi-Formation / Regional Employment and Training Observatory (F)		AHSZ	Accredited Higher Education in Schools (HU)
OSZT	National Council of Vocational Qualifications (HU)		AMS	Arbeitsplatz Master Sample / workplace master sample (D)
QCA	The Qualification and Curriculum Authority (UK)		Ateco'91	Attivita Economica '91 / 1001 Economic Activity Code* (I)
RILSA	Research Institute of Labour and Social Affairs (CZ)		BGR	Bildungsgesamtrechnung / Educational Accounting System (D)
ROA	Researchcentrum voor Onderwijs en Arbeidsmarkt / Research Centre for Education and the Labour Market (NL)		BTS	Brevet de Technicien Supérieur / Higher Technician's Certificate (F)
			CA [...]	Computer Aided [term]
			CAM	Computer Aided Manufacturing
SCOTVEC	Scottish Vocational Education Council		CAP	Certificat d'Aptitude Professionnelle / Certificate of Vocational Aptitude (F)
UNICE	Union of Industrial and Employers' Confederations of Europe		CEDRA	Cedefop Research Arena (EU)
VTF	Vocational Training Fund (HU)		CIRCA	Communication & Information Resource Centre Administration (EU Extranet)
WIFO	Wissenschaftsforum Bildung und Gesellschaft e.V. / Research Forum WIFO Berlin (D)			
			CP	Census of Population
WZB	Wissenschaftszentrum Berlin für Sozialforschung / Social Science Research Center Berlin (D)		DP	Data Processing
			DIF	'Difficult-To-Fill' (vacancies)
			EDP	Electronic Data Processing
			ECTS	European Credit Transfer System
			EMSPS	Employers Manpower and Skills Practices Survey (UK)
			ERO	European Research Overview (Cedefop / WIFO, EU)
			ETED	Emploi Type Étudié dans sa Dynamique / typical job studied in its dynamic* (F)
			ETV	Electronic Training Village (Cedefop/EU)
			GCSE	Secondary Vocational Education level (CZ)
			GDP	Gross Domestic Product

GPS	Global Positioning System	NAP	National Action Plan (for employment) (EU)
GNP	Gross National Product		
HRD	Human Resource Development	NGO	Non-Governmental Organisation
HTML	HyperText Markup Language	NOS	National Occupational Standards (UK)
ICT	Information and Communication Technology	NQF	National Qualifications Framework (UK)
IDQ©	Instrumentarium zur Dauerbeobachtung der Qualifikationsentwicklung© / Method for the regular monitoring and early recognition of qualification trends (D)	NVQ	National Vocational Qualification (UK)
		PC	Personal Computer
		R&D	Research and Development
		SME	Small and Medium sized Enterprise
		SOC	Standard Occupational Classification (UK)
ISCED	International Standard Classification of Education		
		SQL	Structured Query Language
ISCO	International Standard Classification of Occupations	SWOT	Strengths, Weaknesses, Opportunities and Threats analysis
ISDN	Integrated Services Digital Network	TIMSS	Third International Mathematics and Science Study (by IEA)
IT	Information Technology		
LFS	Labour Force Survey	TPM	Total Production Maintenance
MBZ	Maintenance Base Zero	TQM	Total Quality Management
MSMA	Maintenance de Systèmes Mécaniques Automatisés / Maintenance of Mecanical Automate Systems* (F)	TSER	Targeted Socio-Economic Research (programme of the European Commission)
		VET	Vocational Education and Training
MTR	Medium Term Reviews (IRL)		
NACE	Nomenclature of Economic Activities in the European Community		
NAIRU	Non Accelerating-Inflation Rate of Unemployment		

Cedefop (European Centre for the Development of Vocational Training)

Early identification of skill needs in Europe

Luxembourg:
Office for Official Publications of the European Communities

2003 – VI, 334 pp. – 17.5 x 25 cm

(Cedefop Reference series; 40 – ISSN 1608-7089)

ISBN 92-896-0202-3

Cat. No: TI-49-02-353-EN-C

Price (excluding VAT) in Luxembourg: EUR 25

No of publication: 3029 EN